LOUISIANA HAYRIDE

OTHER BOOKS BY HARNETT KANE

Louisiana Hayride

The American Rehearsal for Dictatorship
1928 · 1940

By HARNETT T. KANE

Foreword by
SAM H. JONES

PELICAN PUBLISHING COMPANY
GRETNA 1986

Manufactured in the United States of America
Published by Pelican Publishing Company, Inc.
1101 Monroe Street, Gretna, Louisiana 70053

FOREWORD

LOUISIANA had spawned a weird, governmental monstrosity. Some called it "America's Rehearsal for Dictatorship." Its justifications were the alleged mistakes of the past. It grew, thrived on the most bizarre methods and the wildest propaganda, lived a wild and hectic career, and finally was halted and brought down in its tracks by an aroused and courageous citizenship.

I am writing today to a new generation, most of whom know little or nothing about the actual happenings of that tragic era in the history of Louisiana. So it is proper to remind the reader that during that period Louisiana citizens lost their liberties and their fundamental American rights.

The right of free elections was wiped out, and absolute control was seized by the leader of one political faction. Freedom of the press was attacked by a law that had to be declared unconstitutional by the United States Supreme Court. Freedom of assembly vanished. Laws were passed that were never read by the Legislature; many of them were revised, if not entirely written, after the adjournment of the law-making body.

Public records were closed to the public. The State Police became the law of the land, with authority to supersede any and all local enforcement officers; to arrest citizens on political charges and transport them to distant jails beyond the reach of friends—without benefit of bail by any court, and subject only to release by the head of the State Police. Martial law was imposed on the state capitol for six months at one time, when there was no disaster, no riot, no rebellion and no strife—and hence no justification.

It was a reign of tyranny. Political opponents were forced to meet clandestinely, under the cover of darkness, to exercise their rights as American citizens. Louisianians lived under a government that had the power to make and break banks; or by spite and vengeance, to drive industry out of the state; or catapult it to fabulous wealth as it chose. This was a government which, by whim and caprice, denied men and women the right to practice their trades and professions—or, by favoritism, granted such rights without regard to qualification or ability.

It was a government that held the destinies of private citizens in its hands, with no less power than that exercised by the totalitarian states in the days prior to World War II. When this tragic era began, Louisiana had one of the lowest per capita debts of any American state. When it ended, the debt increase totalled 1600 percent in a period of twelve years.

Factories closed, industry slackened, and businesses moved away, abandoning their Louisiana domiciles. A hundred thousand were jobless; the breadlines lengthened and the welfare rolls mounted. And, finally, so much commerce was driven away that Louisiana's port sank from 2nd to 16th place among the nation's ports. Louisiana had little stamina left with which to resist the general depression.

The state itself fell to the lowest depths in public esteem it has ever experienced. And when the end finally came, it came with defeats and debacles and bankruptcies and indictments and suicides and scandals.

History is not so much what people do; it is much more what historians and others say they do. Or what the dusty archives—good or bad—say they did. Unfortunately, what people say is not always the truth; and what the archives record shows cannot always be depended upon.

More bunkum has been written about Huey Long, and his place in history, than any man in this region I know of. There have been dozens of books and treatises written on the subject of Huey Long and his confederates in the misrule of a state.

I think the time has come to set the record straight. Most of the books about Long are completely undependable. A large majority are dedicated to rank sensationalism and are nothing more than figments of imagination.

Certainly standing high among the authors who have written on this subject is Harnett Kane. He lived with history. He traveled with history. He worked with history. And there is no living man more conversant with "the Huey Long Story" than Kane. During the heyday of Long's career, Kane was there on the spot.

There were pseudo, sham, counterfeit and spurious "historians" who, to make a fast buck, were willing to resort to the worst kind of yellow journalism and sensationalism. But not Harnett Kane. He still stands among the literary giants. And his work, *Louisiana Hayride,* is still the outstanding eyewitness literary accomplishment on the subject of Long and his cohorts.

And why shouldn't it be? He worked a young lifetime on principal newspapers of the state, during the very time when Huey was converting Louisiana from a democracy to "American's Rehearsal for Dictatorship." Kane's *Louisiana Hayride* dramatically, yet truthfully, tells the story of how Huey charted the course for his own dictatorship.

In fact, it can be said that practically every tool and tactic of the dictator was used unabashedly by Huey to destroy a representative form of government and install a totalitarian substitute.

Huey bought every political opponent he could buy. He boasted that he bought the Legislature "like a sack of potatoes." But when I use the word "bought," I do not necessarily mean that Huey always bought with cash. He bought some with patronage—to whom the appointment to public office was the very height of their ambitions. He bought some with state contracts. He bought some with fear and hope of reward.

How did this strange phenomenon happen? This cannot be answered with any one simple explanation. But there can be little doubt that the chief contributing cause was the control of political patronage. It is the extreme example of how the spoils system can contaminate. Literally thousands upon thousands were added to the public payrolls, paid by the taxpayers' money. It was the much publicized political tactic of tax and tax, and spend and spend, and elect and elect.

Added to the state payrolls was another patronage device, under another tyrannical statute, which required that every case of public employment, in every parish, municipality and district in the state, be approved by the ruling powers in Baton Rouge.

The sum total of all this was the spoils system compounded many times over. Without protection, the public employees were herded up and marched to the polls to vote the wishes of the political bosses. With this controlled vote the Legislature was controlled, the laws were passed, and the rights and the liberties of the people were whittled down to the vanishing point. And thus Louisiana became a dictatorship not only in theory but in fact.

Huey never lifted Louisiana out of the poverty class; therefore it was easy to win votes by passing out some of the nearly 45,000 jobs the state government controlled. It was even easier to win other votes by putting people on the welfare rolls, much of the cost of which was paid by the federal government.

And then when one considers that (1) all state and local primary elections were controlled by commissioners appointed by the governor; and (2) that every local job—parish, district and municipal—had to be approved by a state board appointed by the governor, it becomes apparent that Louisiana was in the steel grip of a vise from which it could not escape.

One problem in writing this foreword is that it requires almost a book itself. Nothing like the regime of Huey Long has ever been enacted on American soil before. Only a patriot of the staunchest character could stand up to the power of Huey and the threats and reprisals which he used so freely. Those who were willing to do so paralleled the acts of America's bravest patriots at any stage of American history.

Nearly all the books on this subject end with the death of Huey Long. *Louisiana Hayride* continues through the years of scandals which ended in my election in 1940. Huey's prediction that his successors would never be able to wield his great power without going to jail was borne out by events described in this book.

This is the story of the sowing of the wind, but the major part of the book is devoted to the reaping of the whirlwind. In this telling, *Louisiana Hayride* is unsurpassed.

It is a story for all Americans.

SAM HOUSTON JONES
October 15, 1970

CONTENTS

CONTENTS

ILLUSTRATIONS

ILLUSTRATIONS

LOUISIANA HAYRIDE

The tale is a tall one, a saga of tall ones. . . .

THE MORNING AFTER

LOUISIANA has swept America's first dictatorship into history. Twelve years ago its people went on a spree—a Louisiana hayride for two million men, women and children. They jolted, they jerked, they rolled happily in the straw, over a bumpy but exciting road. They paid their fare; they knew, most of them, what they were getting; they liked it while they were getting it. They had little to say about their destination, but they did not mind that much. They giggled, they gasped, they held their breaths; and the show went on, around them, among them, for them.

And word spread that there was room aboard for others, and these came running. From other states, from other regions, this bayou folks' bacchanale drew new audiences, new participants. There were those, in time, who saw it change its character; saw the hayride emerge as the vehicle of a national juggernaut—its potential victim, America.

A gun spat, and the first driver toppled. But he had hitched his vehicle to a force that took it onward. The self-designated Kingfish, Huey P. Long, was dead. Long live the Kingfish! Other Kingfishes grabbed the reins and held them for the years that followed. The pace slackened. The riders calmed a bit. But the wagon still rolled, and the drivers still collected their tariff at intervals. Then, in 1940, came wreckage.

Soberly, the people of Louisiana are looking backward today, some of them convinced that they were passengers on a test trip, a political tryout in advance of others that might

3

have brought a different manner of life and outlook for all of America. Over, at least for the time, is a thing that most Americans thought impossible: a systematic totalitarianism on North American soil, functioning under the Constitution, under the flag, to the tune of *The Star-Spangled Banner* (with some minor notes of *Dixie*).

The most complete despotism in the nation's history used the institutions of democracy to crush democracy. Through bad years and good years, depression and prosperity, it met the test: it worked. Like most modern dictatorships, it began with revolution, a poor-white rebellion. It went on to shift that rebellion's course, to betray it in a series of deals and understandings with most of the groups it attacked, and in a saturnalia of corruption, from its start to its end.

This full-dress rehearsal of an American tyranny came not through surrender to a power from without, as some fear dictatorship may strike, nor through the appeasement of a force that was feared. It was a conscious acceptance of a régime that applied, slowly at first, then with increasing boldness, the old prescription for power, with new touches: bread and circuses—dispensations from above, free food and free vaudeville—in return for acquiescence.

Its master was the first American demagogue to become a national threat; the first to clutch and use with machine-gun ruthlessness the current tools of mass propaganda and the instruments of violence, including state and national militia. The men who followed him at the reins were simple mediocrities who had learned a lesson and learned it well enough to serve their purposes. The dictator went, but enough of dictatorship remained to keep a state in bondage while a heritage was stolen from it.

Huey the Kingfish loved power too well. His successors loved money too well. Between them, they bribed a people.

4

In Louisiana's shifting background, in the currents that swirl about the South as a whole, it was all too easy for either gold or favor to corrupt. These twelve years have given America a liberal education in the seducing of a populace.

In place of freedom, or the approximation of it which Louisianians had enjoyed, the state took "benefits." For a measure of security it swapped the kind of constitutional protections it had known. It received magnificent roads, tall bridges; eventually it gave its Louisiana Fuehrers a Reichstag that might have pleased a Hitler in its deep-sweeping subservience. The state took free school books for its children, new hospitals, new buildings; and it said little or nothing while its judges were caged. It accepted jobs and retainer fees, while it lost the right to have its vote counted as cast.

Year by year, the pattern developed more clearly: legislators bought, in the dictator's words, "like sacks of potatoes"; a kept judiciary, up to and including the highest court in the state; quick ruin for the enemy, smiling benevolence for the friend.

Some may look on the Louisiana adventure as an isolated phenomenon, a fluke. It was not that, but the outgrowth of a politico-socio-economic problem that cried for solution. Louisiana's dictatorship arose out of the abuses of democracy that preceded it. "His enemies made him" by their puerile tactics; so it has been said of Huey Long, as it was said of Hitler and his Social Democratic opponents. But Louisiana's régime of force, like Germany's, was born of influences that went back for generations, that grew out of a demonstrated condition of inequity. Like other modern dictatorships, it placed its finger on deep-seated wants and needs, and it promised to meet them. Its slogan was "Share the Wealth." Its crusading evangelical creed quoted the

5

Bible and cried Old Testament wrath on a nation that had not heeded its version of the Book's meaning.

Its appeal was national as well as regional. At one point "Share the Wealth" crossed the Mississippi, moved into the industrial East, sent propaganda arms into the Middle West and Far West. The movement claimed 6,000,000 to 7,000,000 members, so threatening the Democratic Party, and potentially the Republican as well, that the professional prognosticator Farley feared that it might bring his party to a crisis. Millions of Americans believed that under the banner, "Every Man a King," they would reach a Utopia in which all American families received a fixed income, land, a home, perhaps an electric refrigerator and other guaranties of security. These millions were ready to back their man to the limit in an effort to achieve these objectives.

The tale is a tall one, a saga of tall ones. Absolutism came to Louisiana with a grin on its lips, a jest on its tongue. The Long men meant business, yes, but they were also Louisianians; and life can be funny at the same time that it is venal. A gallery of engaging rogues, of highly diverting rascals, is the result: Cajuns of a smiling amorality; Italians of underworld background that did not bar them from public honors; Jews who grew wealthier by the process of special favor that speaks all languages; plain Anglo-Saxon thieves, fat men who grew fatter, lean and hungry men as dangerous as they looked. They advanced from rank as barbers and hot-towel men to masters of great estates; from shoe clerks to connoisseurs of expansive living. They invested in gold toilet fixtures. They dug private lakes. They named airports after themselves, to commemorate such arrangements as two-per-cent cuts on the materials used therein. They built steam-heated showerbaths for their cattle and pigs, ordered air-conditioning units for their own bathrooms. "Share the

6

Wealth" was a slogan they understood well. There was so much to share that they stuck together, almost to the end, one for all, all for one thing. They knew exactly what they wanted: everything in sight.

In the process, they took rôles in a melodrama as wild, as picaresque, as fantastic in its drolleries as any in modern American history; an era marked by civil insurrections, riotings and beatings in the legislative halls, by burlesques, bullets and whimsy, mixed in the grand manner. The first dictator was a lusty, gusty fellow. His post-mortem apprentices, carrying on for the Master, were a codfish aristocracy, of gargantuan tastes and humors.

Less than a year before the crash, the Louisiana state machine was ticking along serenely. Opposition had been purchased or crushed, or lay supine in the shade. Over Louisiana shone the sun of a golden Federal favor, showering rays of largesse. Then came one of the most odorous of American state scandals, one of the broadest-gauged Federal inquiries in the history of criminal procedure.

Convicted, or awaiting trial or sentence, are the once political great of Louisiana, the near great and the little great. Two hundred and fifty indictments have broken about their heads, against the machine's governor; the president of one of the South's leading universities; legislative officials, mayors, heads of major departments; millionaire racing and gambling men, allies of Eastern gangsters; the leading contractors, architects and builders; the president of the state medical society, doctor-managers of institutions, tax experts, WPA assistants. Not least, a lady notary described as the Madame Queen (no relation to the Kingfish) of an alleged racket to reduce the taxes of all who would kick back half to the officials and their assistants.

Going, too, perhaps, is a legend of latter-day American

7

tradition, Huey the Martyr. His specter had stalked the South, waiting in the twilight of its swamps for a day in which it might rally the nation to a newer totalitarianism. Now, Louisiana believes, the ghost may have been laid. For the trail of deep-rooted crookeries goes back to this dictator and his doings, and tends to dissipate the illusion of a great man whose only thought was for the economically bereft.

Louisiana knows that it paid a higher price than the "benefits" of the hayride were worth. For every dollar that it gave, the dictatorship took another in the dark. For the security the régime may have offered, it stole the basis of security in the future. Today can be told, and in detail for the first time, the inevitable accompaniments of an authoritarian government, the happenings under the surface of a fully operating American dictatorship. It is an exposition of the meaning for a democratic nation of its loss of a system of checks, balances and public sunlight.

But, you may say, it couldn't happen anywhere but in Louisiana. It could happen in almost any American state. Louisiana was divided. So are many other states—rural against urban elements, sect against sect, south against north. Louisiana had, and has, illiteracy, want, low health standards. So, too, have other states. The process that succeeded in Louisiana has been tested. As in ancient Rome, as in modern Germany, Italy and Russia, the politicians, playing upon the ingrown prejudices, the deepest needs and aspirations of their people, promised everything, gained power—and then used that power to multiply taxes, to dig deep into public funds for their own uses, and meanwhile to give back just enough to keep themselves in power.

Louisiana lost much in those twelve years of serfdom. But the period had some partial compensations—the provision of newer public services, a smoothly functioning administrative

8

system, modernization of facilities. The régime took much, but it also gave something. The democracy that preceded it took less. But it also gave less.

Why did the people of an American state, a member of the Union for a century and a quarter, submit to despotism? Some of the reasons were largely local. Others go deep into the state past, and into the regional past. But, essentially, democracy failed because Louisiana's men and women came to feel that it offered them less than the other form. To too many of Louisiana's citizens, the rights and guaranties of democracy appeared to be academic exercises.

Democracy may fail in America not because dictatorship's guns are stronger, but because the way of dictatorship may seem to hold a promise of greater gifts at home.

At the end, Louisiana changed its mind. But this Southern revolt of 1940 against the system that came with 1928 was one which almost failed. Odds were against its success. Held in the hands of a group that boasted, with show of reason, that its dynasty could not be overthrown, Louisianians made the hard choice, then fought to carry it through. From stream-lined autocracy, Louisiana turned to another testing of the democratic idea. The Louisiana flare-up is more than a nauseous exposé. It is the climax of a significant period in Southern history. Will the new régime succeed? Can such a régime offer to a long-kept populace enough to satisfy it? Or will Louisiana turn again to the easier way?

The problem on which this threat to the nation once arose is still there, still unsolved. Maldistribution of the country's income may be expected to outlast the present war and the defense boom. The fertile ground of discontent is still thickly sown. The seed of poor-white resentment in the country areas, of have-not yearnings in the cities, lies in the topsoil, ready to sprout under the hot rays of demagogy.

9

The South, a Southerner may admit, is more fertile than some other sections for this crop. It is still predominantly rural, largely defeatist in its philosophy, a debtor territory, a region in which wrenching poverty is often too common to excite more than casual pity. Will another Kingfish leap across this state or another state, speed by soundtruck from hill to hollow, roaring joyously to his spellbound listeners?

A superbly effective sample technique of homebred tyranny has been tested out. The resources of a twentieth-century mass-organized American civilization have been tried upon 2,000,000 political guinea pigs, with results satisfactory to the analysts. Available here, as a result of Louisiana's experience, is a blueprint of a broader American dictatorship that yet may come.

H. T. K.

New Orleans,
February 19, 1941.

PART ONE

The Ride Begins

"I came out of that courtroom running for office."—HUEY P. LONG.

I

AND ALWAYS, NEW ORLEANS . . .

From its start, Louisiana has been a land of great wealth, great men and great thieves. About each, conflict has raged through two centuries and more. The bayou territory has been, at the least, seldom tranquil. Sharp contrast developed, in people and in their behavior, from that day in 1699, when Jean Baptiste Le Moyne, Sieur de Bienville, and his brother Pierre Le Moyne, Sieur d'Iberville, established His Majesty's colony on the swampy, inhospitable shores of the Gulf of Mexico.

The first hero came in those first years—the well-loved Bienville, who fought lethargy, time and the Mississippi, as he spotted his settlements up the river in the direction of France's holdings in Canada. The first scoundrel appeared shortly afterward—the hated John Law, whose victims, as he operated in the mother country, were, among others, the men he cheated of their lives in the name of Louisiana.

The territory had its original scandal before its outposts were well established. While the brothers Le Moyne toiled at the scene, Law, the Scotch gambler-adventurer, floated his Mississippi Bubble over Europe. It was a gold-brick scheme that sent thousands of bewitched, bewildered men and women across the sea to a promised land of ready-made well-being. No American high-pressure campaign of the Florida 1920s could have matched this one. The models of the modern tall tales of Louisiana were officially promulgated;

13

the men who first cheated in the name of the state used, like others who came after them, pamphlets and circulars to reach their victims, promising benefits to the extent of their own imagination:

The land is filled with gold, silver, copper and lead mines. If one wishes to hunt for mines, he will need only to go into the country of the Natchitoches. There he will surely draw pieces of silver out of the earth. After these mines, he will hunt for herbs and plants for the apothecaries. The savages will make them known. . . .

Sometimes pearl hatcheries and fur farms were envisioned.

Middle-class Frenchmen sank their earnings into the venture. Debtors, dissenters, earnest young men who saw no chance at home, black sheep of respected families, aristocrats who had fared badly at court—these made up the early human cargoes for the project. These, and others. Jails, hospitals, "the kennels and alleys of Paris," were dredged to fill the inflated quotas. Many died on the long voyage. Others, less lucky, were dumped on the open sands, there to await Bienville's inadequate forces which would try to find a place for them in the settlements, or to die. There was often little or no food or water; there were mosquitoes by the millions, crushing heat for those unused to it, insanity and death. Stinking bodies lay uncovered. Victims of the plague, through cracked lips, cursed the fate and the men that had tricked them. Back in France, the Bubble broke. The French Kingdom faced ruin, and Law fled.

The hardier of the Bubble's victims survived, taking their places with the other colonists. Louisiana's wealth was there, almost as much of it as had been claimed, but in other, less accessible forms. His Majesty's grants of land formed the foundations of early plantations for those who had reserves of

14

cash—or of particular energy. Others, less venturesome, with lesser resources, took up quarters in Nouvelle Orléans, the young capital, in the crook of the river's bend not far above the Gulf. About the Mississippi centered the life of the province. The mother country saw it as a "river of empire," giving access to a vast territory of untold potentialities. The African coasts yielded welcome commodities of import, human black loot, to till the soil, to increase the population, and also to introduce voodoo to America.

Isolated from the mother country, and also from the other colonies—of England along the Atlantic, of Spain in Florida, of France in Canada—Louisiana evolved a life and spirit of her own. It was a Latin settlement that grew up in the lower valley. Its philosophy was "live and understand." Louisianians recognized life's facts, enjoyed its gifts and made the most of them. Tomorrow the Mississippi might flood New Orleans again; who knew? A thoroughgoing Puritan would have been miserable here, particularly in the better populated southern stretches of the province.

An official spoilster was not long in making his début. The Marquis de Vaudreuil, a gaudy, shoddy personage, is the classic example of his Louisiana line. As Governor in the 1740s, "the Great Marquis" introduced bewigged pomp and be-laced corruption. To a capital of mud streets, huts and hovels, he brought a court: a shipload of furnishings, court dress *de rigueur*, "his little Versailles of a hotel." To amazed Louisiana he presented its first theater, its first dancing master. He started also what was eventually to become a settled Louisiana practice of kickbacks. He granted open monopolies in return for premiums and percentages to his personal account; he seized materials sent for the military, exchanged them for sleazy substitutes and dropped the difference into his wide pockets. He inaugurated Louisiana

15

nepotism, a special type which may go as far as the fifth degree of relationship and include pre-adolescents on the payrolls. The intendant-commissary charged that public funds went for supplies of an "official" liquor house. Soldiers and Indians were forbidden to buy drink or drugs at any place except this one. Not to be outdone, the First Lady went into trade: "She forces merchants and other individuals to take charge of her merchandise, and to sell it at prices which she fixes."

Nor was the city long in becoming a good-time town. Taverns sprang up near the waterfront for natives and visitors from upriver. The former flocked daily to the groghouses because they longed for something to remind them of life in Paris, or of the port towns they had known along the Mediterranean, or simply for a place to fill a man's need for companionship. The visitors made trips to New Orleans whenever they could, thus breaking the monotony of their life on the plantations. To the taverns gravitated the vagabonds, the former thieves who waited opportunity to return to their profession, the brawlers, the light-hearted—and light-fingered.

Sometimes, though, the tone of colonial life caused concern among the more stable elements. France sought occasionally to halt the emigration of those considered undesirable. But a vast territory needs a vast population; and still the call went forth regularly for more men—and more women. Bienville had pleaded at an early date: "Send me wives for my Canadians; they are running in the woods after Indian girls." Similar petitions were often repeated, although in language less blunt.

Meanwhile, of course, there were the quiet hard workers, the men and women who came from the mother country with small patrimonies and labored earnestly over their land

and growing properties. Others, of means and of gentility, set up their establishments and lived sober lives that were not much different from those they would have led in the other land. Nuns made the arduous trip; convents were established, and the men who came first sent back for their wives and children. The women brought their furniture with them and set up early replicas of the French drawing rooms and dining halls in the simpler Louisiana.

The territory became a melting pot, more truly than the predominantly Anglo-Saxon East Coast, or the Castilian Florida or the French Canada. From Germany arrived settlers who formed a community and prospered by their thrifty ways. From Italy later came other boatfuls, their passengers to crowd in New Orleans at first, then spread out among the rural areas. Ireland, Holland and Central Europe sent others. Predominantly, however, Louisiana was French.

The home government vacillated. For long periods it paid little attention to the colony, sent little assistance. It had its own troubles. The colony's life became more and more its own, sometimes cruel—but always violent. A story of the 1750s survives. Unpaid soldiers grumbled, sometimes had run away to the English colonies. Swiss mercenaries became the main defense, then, of New Orleans; and they were quartered on a Gulf island, a place of white sand, great trees, soft breezes. The officer in charge was by name Duroux. When supplies arrived, he sold them. His men subsisted on whatever fish they were able to catch and whatever goods they could salvage. Duroux ignored military assignments, put his forces to work for him, burning charcoal and lime. He filled his purse; his soldiers became slaves herded by well-armed favorites of a sadist. Those who did not obey orders suffered prolonged flesh-tearing floggings and mutilation at the hands of a jeering master; burnings with heated irons and torches;

chainings to trees in the sun, some to die under swarms of flies and mosquitoes. "At times, there have been as many as fourteen men, naked and tied to stakes. . . . Duroux walked up and down before them, prodding them in the softer parts of their bodies, enough to draw blood. . . ."

A few, fleeing to Governor Kerlerec, contrived to tell their story. He listened, ruled that an officer could not be wrong, and sent them back. Conditions did not improve. Then one day Duroux returned to the island, to the usual tap of drums and flying of banners. The men stood at attention; and then they blasted him to his death. Captured, the men were tried, and three were sentenced. The jeweled better elements stood with the riffraff in the Place d'Armes, the central square, for the event. For two of the men, spreadeagling to a metal wheel, and the crushing of their bones, one by one, of arms, legs, thigh and back, with a sledgehammer, the victim to face the sun for as long as it might take him to die. For a third, nailing alive in a coffin, which was then sawed in half.

Brutality and imagination married young in Louisiana.

The year 1764 brought a wrench. The mother country and England had ended the Seven Years' War; and France gave to England all of her territory east of the Mississippi—except New Orleans. The rest of Louisiana, with the capital city, went to Spain. Louisianians in the lower valley were enraged at this tossing about of their lives and properties. They had learned to hate the Spaniards east of them. They were Frenchmen; they would not submit. The word "Liberté" was heard on the streets of New Orleans. A delegation went to Paris, but the King would not see it. Spain sent a handful of soldiers to take over. The area which was later to embrace the first American dictatorship saw the first white-man's

18

rebellion in the Americas. Bands of armed men stamped into the city, spiking the guns at one of the gates, so alarming the Spanish representative that he fled to a boat in the river. A group of Orleanians, wine-happy from a wedding party, sliced the moorings. As the vessel sailed downriver, Louisiana cried out that it was free. A separate American republic was proposed in this year of 1768; a union of Louisiana with the British colonies along the Atlantic, with the other territories which France had given to England. Leading aristocrats headed the movement; the lower elements supported it.

Suddenly appeared Don Alejandro O'Reilly, Irish adventurer and a general of Spain, backed by 3000 soldiers, twenty-four warships, fifteen pieces of artillery. The leaders of the conspiracy were shot; the background was again the Place d'Armes. Just before the execution, however, an official burned the memorial of the revolutionaries "for containing the following rebellious and atrocious doctrines: 'Liberty is the mother of commerce and population. Without liberty, there are but few virtues.'"

Spain's rule had its bitter moments and its kindlier ones; clashes, then adjustment. After all, the natives and the new masters were both Latins, both Catholic peoples. Spaniards intermarried with the French. Creole took on an added richness of mixture. Trade was growing, and New Orleans was becoming an important commercial center. Fortunes began to pile up at Baton Rouge among the low hills, about the Natchez bluffs, along the Red and Atchafalaya Rivers. But the Spanish Crown decided that it wanted Louisiana to develop only as a Spanish colony. The British colonies, soon to become the American states, were forbidden the use of the Mississippi. But the expansion from the Atlantic had started; the men of the Allegheny country understood well that the Mississippi must be their outlet. The overland trip for their produce would not do. "Open the River" became the cry.

Again the Louisiana question threatened a revolution. In the Allegheny territory men talked of independence for the frontier areas, an alliance with Louisiana and Spain. But many of the Americans said they cared not a damn about His Hispanic Majesty, and they pushed on down the river. Some got through. Others could only fume, as soldiers took their vessels and cargo. In 1795 Spain and the United States signed a treaty opening the river to American trade. This meant new commerce, new influences, a further cosmopolitanism for the lower valley area, particularly for the metropolitan New Orleans.

For years to come, the Creole society had grace, charm of manner, an appreciation of life's niceties. "The Paris of America" was an appropriate name for the New Orleans of the nineteenth century.

Once more Louisiana became a commodity in international exchange when, in 1800, Napoleon took her back from Spain. Another period of uncertainty; then three years later, shockingly, the Corsican did the incredible, trading Louisiana to the United States for $15,000,000 in one of history's biggest and cheapest real-estate deals. Out of the territory, at a few pennies an acre, came most of the present state of Louisiana, together with Arkansas, Missouri, Iowa, Minnesota, Kansas, Nebraska, North and South Dakota, parts of Montana, Wyoming, Oklahoma and Colorado.

"The day of transfer of Louisiana to the United States," wrote Lyle Saxon, "was a day of mourning in New Orleans." It felt that the barbarians had conquered its civilization. *Ces Américains*, they were crude, uncivilized, brawling. Most of the Americans whom Louisiana had seen, incidentally, were indeed uncivilized and brawling. They were the big-muscled flatboat men, a roaring lot who guffawed at the elegant manner of the Creoles and their civilized pleasures, and fought with the natives whom they found in the groghouses and cafés. These visitors were rarin', after their prolonged trips downstream, for liquor, women, music, lights, in approximately that order. New Orleans was the City of Sin, at practically any price in a man's pocket. As for the Creoles, to hell with you, and a fist in your face; no pistols and coffee for these Kaintucks.

It was America for Louisiana, willing or unwilling. The people took their fate with set teeth and fixed stares at the newcomers, at the flood of arrivals that poured like the Mississippi in spring. And the new arrivals did not hide their feelings toward the settled ways they beheld. These latecomers were not the Kaintucks. They were traders, business men, believers in a hard bargain and a hard life, much work, little play. That was the way this nation must get ahead, sir. They shook their heads at the leisurely manner of things in this strange, foreign-looking, foreign-sounding community; at the peculiar custom of conducting affairs over mid-morning, and then over mid-afternoon, coffee; at the Old World manner, the shrugs and grins of the bankers.

"Slack" was the American word for the morals and behavior of some of these Louisianians, too. The scarlet women and the adventurers on the street, those gambling places; they were abominations. And the quadroon balls, where young Creoles met delicate *café au lait* girls of mixed blood, whom they might set up in little cottages if the matter turned out well—the new Puritans had no words for them. The wives of the Americans looked down their noses at the Creole women. The wives of the natives smiled among themselves, ignored the gauche strangers. The Americans would have none of those odd Spanish-French houses, with their

21

courtyards, iron-lacework balconies and stucco walls flush with the sidewalks, or banquettes, as these natives called them. The older residents remained to themselves in the Vieux Carré, the old section below Canal Street; the Americans moved above Canal, to create their own section; first the commercial streets, then the residential Garden District, a place of cool, stately mansions, white-porticoed in the Greek Revival style.

With the Americans arrived the golden day for Louisiana; and with them, too, a golden day of corruption. The port tonnage at New Orleans increased nearly fifty per cent in the first year of the American régime. The port competed with New York for commercial leadership of the nation. The boast was made that for more than a mile one could walk on board the vessels at dock, without once touching land. These were the first steamboating years, the glory years of the Mississippi. Fortunes were built in trade at New Orleans, or in plantations of sugar, rice and cotton; spreading estates with spreading slave holdings.

After the American business men came the American politicos, who toiled, too, but at the trade of control and intrigue. French and Spanish Louisiana had their public leeches, to be sure, of a venality occasionally in keeping with the semi-tropical lushness of the land. Were the newcomers more unprincipled? Suffice it to say that they were the more enterprising. As the Creoles gave way in business, they were forced to retreat in other respects. By the 1830s New Orleans had a new City Hall in the American section, and a new city charter. "Divide and Rule." The American despoilers did it literally. New Orleans was cut up into three separate municipal corporations; the Creoles were given instruction in political manipulation.

"The period from 1840 to 1860 was an epoch of steady but

unadmitted degeneration," declares John Smith Kendall. New Orleans' masters turned to Tammany Hall for help in bleeding their victim. Thugs were imported to take command on election day. Booths were set up in brothels and the hangouts of felons. Reformers appeared at their own risk. Not too gradually, a complete spoils system was installed; and it included a thorough undermining of the police force. Tax collection and other contracts were awarded under a system of "vile depravity . . . domination of a clique, which has seized upon and maintained power through the hateful employment of means so flagitious and corrupting as to have rendered us a hissing and a scorn in the eyes of the upright, well-organized communities." Purple words, these, of the newspaper *Bee;* but other accounts tell a similar story.

Until the end of the century, New Orleans remained almost a border town as far as public services were concerned. Its bosses received the taxes and gave practically nothing in return. Sewage disposal was a constant hazard: all waste was thrown into open gutters. Politically secure city workers neglected the supposed "daily flushing."

"Islets" was the term originally applied to the city squares that covered the marshy base, and islets they remained, in streams of stinking filth. "Until long after the Civil War, New Orleans was unquestionably the dirtiest and unhealthiest city on the North American continent," said Asbury. The death rate at times was double that of other American cities. Successive scourges of yellow fever, cholera and other plagues took a staggering toll; in a ten-year period that ended in 1905, the epidemic struck thirty-nine times. A combination of cholera and the fever once took a third of the city's population. Through it all the political gentry resisted efforts to improve the situation, to take the simplest

23

precautions normal to the times. Having honeycombed all services with graft, they preferred the status quo.

It has often been declared that New Orleans faced, and eventually surmounted, physical problems unlike those of any other city in North America. These problems could not all be laid at the door of the politico, but the clique could be blamed for failure in many instances to adopt curative measures at earlier periods than they did. Always, until comparatively recent years, the city faced the threat of flood. From time to time, as late as the 1920s, levees were cut in the neighborhood of the city to release swollen waters and save the metropolis. Then too, New Orleans lies in a deep saucer, below the level of the river at many points. A slight rain, and the city might face inundation; often, in the earlier days, it was covered with sheets of surface water. But the "indestructible city" has survived it all.

Intermittent efforts at reform failed conspicuously. The 1850s saw carnivals of rioting, bloodshed and murder at election time. The police chief on one occasion was shot while trying to chase out a group that protested stuffing of ballot boxes. Again, registration records were sequestered by a gang that held them for days while an editing process went on. What was happening was generally known. The police understood that they were not to intervene. The result was an uprising. Orleanians grabbed arms and split their city into warring contingents. One group entrenched itself in the former Place d'Armes (now Jackson Square, in honor of the savior of New Orleans from the British). Canal Street was once more the dividing line of forces. Barricades of cotton bales and paving blocks went up. A war chest of $30,000 was raised by the rebel downtown group against the city government. Ammunition was plentiful; bands of armed men moved threateningly. The mayor hesitated, as ultimatum

24

followed ultimatum. Men were shot down at random; the spark to start the general explosion was expected momentarily. The mayor, however, left office, and the matter was settled. The affair was hushed. More than a score of the vigilantes left town. Bad government went on as usual.

Outside the imperial city, Louisiana was filling up, its character changing. Into the northern and central parts of the present state moved new thousands, on foot or in crude vehicles. They were the men and women who had been squeezed by the life of the cities of the Eastern border or hard pressed on their thin farms along a frontier that had shifted to the West. They came South as far as they could make it, or until they found land that was somewhat more promising than that which they had left; and they became Louisiana's hillbillies, brothers of other millions that scattered about the Southeast and Southwest.

Little was heard in those days of these poor whites. They were not, however, forgotten; a nation simply did not know that they existed. They were the little men who lived off the road, away from the great houses and the bright lights. Their homes were crude log cabins, their illumination the sun and the light of their kitchen fires. Travelers generally saw only the magnolia-and-white-pillar tradition of kindly white master and contented black slave; or, in the abolitionist tradition, only the unfeeling tyrant and his mistreated Negroes. Outside the plantation lived these others, the men between. Their security often was less than that enjoyed by the dark ones. The laws were against them, for the reason that those laws were planned by and for the great. The poor whites could seldom rise. Where would they get the education, the money for education? How could they surmount the property barriers that prevented many of them even from voting?

New Orleans, and the large part of Louisiana that depended upon it, paid little attention to such subjects. They were riding head-high in the 1840s and 1850s. But twin disasters were in the making: first the railroad, then the war. For decades a heavy volume of the national wealth had been moving down the Mississippi, America's major artery of bulk transportation. The city grew richer with every cargo that rolled off the steamboats, to be moved thence to other parts of the nation, or to be hoisted aboard ocean-going vessels at adjacent wharves. But the steam engine challenged the river boats, provided quicker transportation, closer transport to the final destination; and the canals were dug to make further inroads into the Mississippi freight.

A few years before the Civil War, New Orleans realized that change was upon it, that river commerce had seen its best days. Then the conflict with the North ended that other base of prosperity, the commodity of black labor.

A defiant New Orleans fell into Federal hands in 1862. Orleanians sacked their city, went on a spree of destruction, burned every bale of cotton they could lay hands on, poured streams of molasses into the streets. "And that day marked the beginning of years of poverty and misery."

To the city came a plunderer, to make a record to match that of any of the earlier, and most of the later, public ones—Major-General Ben Butler, commander of the Army of the Occupation. He was on duty only about seven months; part of New Orleans still spits at mention of his name, calls him "Spoons Butler." Butler, New Orleans swears, took everything in sight. He closed every gambling house in the city, at the start. Then gamblers learned that they might reopen by paying a fee—and by taking on the general's brother as a half partner. Butler confiscated fifty thousand dollars' worth of horses when he shut down the city's famous race track.

His brother, Colonel A. J., was accused of selling the animals to the Confederacy. The colonel was rated the possessor of two million dollars when he left New Orleans; the general was believed to have taken somewhat more. Even the town's harlots, of which there were many, abominated Butler the Beast; they pasted his picture in the bottom of their bedroom pots.

Worse than the war years, of course, were the years of Reconstruction. Scenes ensued that were more fantastic than those presented by most Southern states during that period. A Negro lieutenant-governor lolled about while drunken delegates cursed and shot dice in the legislative halls. The carpet-baggers united with some of the exultant Negroes in a saturnalia of open robberies, crooked contracts, mounting graft, all contributing to financial ruin for the state. Home rule was destroyed, election laws rigged to keep the 'baggers in power; the state militia was enlarged, and debauchery was flaunted in the name of reform, or protection of reform. The later Long régime, in some of its outer manifestations, paralleled the Reconstruction.

Resentment and guns again. Young men drilled secretly in New Orleans, using rifles, revolvers, guns of the Franco-Prussian War, purchased through Eastern brokers. A White League sprang up to oppose the Federally supported régime in a bloody battle in 1874, at the river landing on Canal Street, around cotton bales and overturned wagons. Forty men were killed, one hundred wounded, and "white supremacy" was restored to Louisiana.

Now emerged the politico-economic pattern of Louisiana of the later nineteenth and earlier twentieth centuries. The Negro was free, after a fashion, but disfranchised. The planters suffered; but many held on, and the labor supply was still large and still cheap for those who could keep their heads above financial water. The poor whites saw new hope for themselves and their children. They might get access to some of the better lands as the plantations fell apart here and there. They might get a better share of the material possessions at which they had gazed hungrily all these years. Their children might become lawyers or doctors, get the schooling to rise higher than their fathers or grandfathers. Slowly, about the South, these hopes were partly realized. But there is still misery, still pain for the rural poor, from Florida to Arkansas and Texas. In Louisiana the process was a particularly halting one; its climax came a generation later than in its neighboring areas; and when that climax arrived, it was accompanied by scenes as different from those of the other poor-white risings as Louisiana is different from its neighbors.

Louisiana, like the rest of the South, opened up to another Northern invasion, a business-industrial-mercantile influx. "Foreigners" moved into a potentially thriving, if at present impoverished, land. Sawmills appeared, to devour the timber horde that covered North and South Louisiana. Rice thrived in the flat well-watered plains of the southwest areas. Cotton spread for miles and miles. The state found itself the nation's sugar bowl. In time, too, it became the country's area of greatest winter strawberry production. Not far from New Orleans, the world's largest sulphur port was created. The tide marshes of the Gulf yielded more pelts annually to the fur trade than are taken in all other states, or in Canada. Railroads spanned the bayous. Oil development began in the early 1900s, though years were to pass before it spurted suddenly upward. Power companies were formed, subsidiaries of financial corporations of the East.

The North sent its men to the South, as it had in those days just after the Purchase. But now there was a difference.

The earlier Yankees had brought their money, their interests, had stayed on to become Louisianians of a newer generation. These latter-day arrivals were hired men, agents for outside capital, for stockholders who remained in Philadelphia or Boston or New York. Louisiana continued, in large degree, what she had been through most of her history—a colony.

These new business men, like the earlier ones, were clear-eyed realists. They knew what they were to take, and what they were to give. They wanted assurances of unimpeded operations, of political "stability"; no hampering laws, no shilly-shallying with such things as public-service regulations later, nor those new socialistic theories of labor's rights. All of this meant understandings with the local politicians, contributions, "insurance." Alliances were formed with those in office; and the alliances helped keep both partners in authority.

In charge of the state government were plantation politicians, some of them aristocrats, others merely rich men newly arrived at their present status, beneficiaries of enterprises which they had started or taken over after the War between the States. In New Orleans, however, professional politicians of the metropolitan variety were at the top, usually in friendly relationship with the group that ran Baton Rouge, now the state capital; sometimes handling Baton Rouge from the city. Both elements, city and country, found no obstacles to quick agreements with the "foreign" elements. The slogan on all sides was: business as usual, everybody satisfied. Everybody, perhaps, but the population beneath. In the late nineteenth and the early twentieth century, that did not matter much. "The people" were words that agitators, revolutionaries and abolitionists used.

In a one-party state like Louisiana, the result was predictable. Most of the elections were mock ones, with home-grown aristocrats or city ward bosses competing only against each other in factional fights. The issues were decided in advance; seldom were fundamental questions of policy brought upon the stump. The conference room before election day—that was the place for determination of such matters. The talking points in the state campaigns were generally Southern womanhood and the Confederacy. A code of gentility, agreeable to all, forbade discussion of fundamentals, of the backgrounds and records of oppositionists. (Such discussion might be fatal to both aspirants, if it became too frank.) In New Orleans debate was on a lower, but not on a more fundamental, basis. Boodle, drainage contracts and street-paving irregularities; such were the questions before the electorate. The victor, in Baton Rouge and in New Orleans, went into office, then did nothing for the lesser ones whom he ruled in his own interest and that of his less-conspicuous associates. Louisiana remained a land of great resources and great poverty—both in the raw state. It ranked forty-eighth in literacy. Even among Southern commonwealths, the levels of public services were low.

Modern Louisiana is divided, as was the mother country, into three parts: the South, the North, and The City—New Orleans. The South is the Louisiana of earlier stories, though altered somewhat by economic trends: the land of the swamps and the bayous, of liquid French and semi-liquid topography, an area of alluvial, enriched soil that "grows where you stick your finger in it." Its people are fishermen, trappers, sugar and rice workers; and plantation owners are still powerful figures.

The North is another land, another people, the red hills and the red necks. The soil is dry, hard, thin, the kind over which a man may break his back and yet not make a living. Its population are small farmers, country storekeepers, small-town clerks. They are so-called Anglo-Saxons, with little mixture of race.

The South is tolerant, easy-going, Catholic. The North is tight-lipped, grim-eyed, Puritan, Protestant. Between the "hard-shelled Baptist country" and the "soft-shelled crab land" are barriers of economics, of race, of creed. In each there is want among the many, but with this difference— that it is differently accepted. In the North it has brought cankering hatred; it has meant lynchings of Negroes, membership in organizations of dissent, anti-Papism, anti-liquor, anti many things. In the South it has meant volatile debate, perhaps; but that has ended in quiet if regretful assumption of the burden, with a shrug and an *"Eh bien!"* South Louisianians have seldom tortured the blacks or one another. They have been inclined to orthodoxy in politics, and have often accepted New Orleans and what it stood for, to them, while the North coldly rejected the scarlet witch.

A rule to herself, then, remains New Orleans. Like the state, she has regained part of her former prosperity. But she is no Atlanta, no city of Southern go-getters. She is still the place of good food, good times, good manner of living; still the place wicked (*méchante* is the proper word) and happy in her wickedness. She draws much of the wealth from the rest of the state and from her trade territory in adjoining states. In her business area center the financial resources of the lower valley of the Father of Waters, and the control of those resources. The South has distrusted the North, the North has hated the South; speaking strictly, of course, of Louisiana. Both, however, have feared New Orleans. Government of the state, within the framework of understanding with the financial interests, has been a succession of shifts and compromises among these three elements: the South, the North—and always, New Orleans.

The story of present-century New Orleans, politically, is synonymous with boss rule. A single powerful organization has controlled it for more than four decades, with the exception of an accidental four-year term. The Ring, the Regular Democratic organization, has been called the Tammany of the South, and with some appropriateness. It has been *the* political party of the city. The same machinery which took the opportunity to vote from the Negro gave an abnormal degree of control to any dominant local group; the Regulars have seen to it that they are that dominant group. They preceded the state's totalitarianism, they adjusted to it, they survived it. The Regulars have been practical. Politics is their business, votes are their ledger records. They have held no burning convictions on social or financial policies of state or nation. They could reach a meeting of minds with any reasonable business man. Through a quarter-century starting (roughly) with the 1900s, Mayor Martin Behrman—"beer barrel statesman," in the words of Hamilton Basso—ran New Orleans, except for that unfortunate lapse when a business-man reformer slipped in. "Let's get togedder" was his slogan.

The local utility, affiliated today with Electric Bond and Share, was kept under city regulation and thus out of the hands of the State Public Service Commission. One never knew what wild men might get themselves elected to the commission up in the red-neck section. The city's electric rate remained among the highest in the country. The Regulars performed other services. As the representatives in the Legislature of the only large municipality in Louisiana, possessing one-fourth of the population, they had the largest single bloc of votes. By fixed rule, they voted always as a unit; and often they had the determining vote. They defeated labor proposals, methodically, without fuss. They opposed minimum hours for women and children, Federal income taxes, child-labor amendments and such schemes. They kept cheap natural gas out of the city, while Orleanians paid steep charges on the artificial product. As to direct taxation on their business friends, they knew their rôle without directions.

The Regulars did not waste time on anything but politics. Hamilton Basso tells of a group of women who called on one of the Regulars' mayors to ask that the Municipal Auditorium be erected in the form of a Greek Theatre. The mayor replied that there were not enough Greeks in New Orleans to support such a venture. By such men was "the most continental city in America" ruled.

Under the Regulars, New Orleans' long-entrenched vice thrived anew. Behrman's remark on the subject is a Louisiana classic: "You can make it illegal, but you can't make it unpopular." The Regulars started nothing new. They continued and improved upon the relationships of officialdom, police, harlots and pimps, and kept a firm hand on the connected trades. New Orleans' fame had spread during the nineteenth century through America, as the widest-open town on the continent. It drew sportsmen, members of the élite set of the East, European visitors, gamblers, the idly curious, the curiously idle. Its restaurants were celebrated, offering a modified French cuisine that is unsurpassed in America. Its racing became a tradition. Its hotels, the St. Louis in the French Quarter, the St. Charles and the Grunewald, had a lustrous reputation. "The promised land of harlotry," Herbert Asbury termed New Orleans. No American city has matched this town's proportion of bawdy houses, established centers of the traffic, over a period of decades. For about twenty years of the Regulars' régime, New Orleans had a thriving restricted district, Storyville, named after an alderman who had made a solemn inquiry of methods of handling prostitution; and who was many times to sigh over the fate that named the place after him.

In Storyville there thrived a panorama of bagnios of every type, from two-bit Negro cribs to brothels of red plush and gilt mirror, which might charge a patron $200 for an evening of champagne, orchestra and the companionship of a devotee chosen from a friendly assortment. One such establishment advertised "European oil paintings" among incidental attractions. A street tour of the red-light district, including a peek through the shutters where the girls awaited their callers, was the final touch to a visit to New Orleans. This was the day of *The Blue Book,* publication unparalleled, an authoritative listing of all the town's brothels, with outlines of merchandise. "Dina and Norma, 213-15 North Basin," read one. "Their names have become known on both continents, because everything goes as it will, and those who cannot be satisfied there, must surely be of a queer nature." "Eunice Deering, corner Basin and Conti Streets," another declared. "Known as the idol of the society and club boys. . . . Aside from the grandeur of her establishment, she has a score of beautiful women."

Circuses, erotic performances among participants of various sexes, were highly patronized. The Regulars regularized the business, fixed charges, guaranteed protection as it was never guaranteed before, exercised intelligence in furthering an enterprise in which they had their own particular concern. When Mardi Gras came around, levies were raised; trade was at a peak, turnover fast. In bad periods, politicians, police captains and ward leaders might reach down to tide the houses over until the next good spell. Harlot Town had "mayors," "overseers," special policemen like those of the city docks and water-purification plant. Accounts are given of "gala openings" of new houses, with city dignitaries and police officials in attendance, champagne, flowers and speeches. Storyville was abolished by Federal orders during the First World War, because of the presence of soldiers from near-by camps. Some of the girls committed suicide. Most of them moved to new houses, many settling in the French Quarter. Vice remained big business in New Orleans. With it thrived gambling and the liquor trade, before, during and after Prohibition; but most of all, affiliated enterprises.

Outside, the rest of Louisiana looked at New Orleans with envy, with detestation, with a discontent over its own lot that broke out only occasionally because it had little outlet. The rural areas saw the rich and the arrogant of New Orleans, as well as the rich and arrogant of the country parishes; and their rage grew. The farmers, the people of the small towns, felt that they received nothing from their state. Roads were jolting hazards, the frenzy of the farmer. Schools were inadequate, and often the family could not afford the basic supplies. Hospital facilities were meager. A bad year, a sick wife or child, and the farm was gone. "Safe" governors, courtly, conservative, who did little, but who always did the "right" thing, moved in and out—high attorneys, representatives of high families, one only slightly different from the next.

In the country sections the little men were stirring restlessly. As yet they were without hope. For better or for worse, a change was indicated. It came with a slow rumble, then a roar that was heard over the nation.

II

A KINGFISH IS SPAWNED

Fᴿᴼᴹ the Parish of Winn, in north-central Louisiana,
arose the force that broke the barriers of Louisiana's
established order.

Winn was poverty-stricken, Protestant and persnickety. It
was ordained to be most of that by the circumstances of its
incorporation in the mid-nineteenth century. When the land
was parceled out, Winn received what nobody else wanted.
Most of its people had come late to Louisiana, members of
the mixed groups that had made their way laboriously south-
ward toward a life they had hoped would be better. The
earth that became theirs was the earth the richer owners
would not touch.

Winn's was the hard-bitten hill country of the less flour-
ishing upper areas. Its harvests were scrawny; what cattle
it had were scrawnier; its people were scrawniest. The parish, as Forrest Davis puts it, "produced only one crop in
abundance: dissent." Others might have slaves. Winn's
people often could not afford the luxury of a mule. They
bit their lips as they saw the planters, with their fine airs
and the cool satisfaction in their eyes. Typical of his con-
temporaries was the father of the dictator, Huey P. Long, Sr.,
at the age of 83, as reported by James Rorty in *The Forum:*

"There wants to be a revolution, I tell you. I seen this
domination of capital, seen it for seventy years. What do
these rich folks care for the poor man? They care nothing—

not for his pain, nor his sickness, nor his death." He recalled his earlier days: "Why, their women didn't even comb their own hair. They'd sooner speak to a nigger than a poor white. They tried to pass a law saying that only them as owned land could vote. And when the war come, the man that owned ten slaves didn't have to fight. . . . Maybe you're surprised to hear talk like that. Well, it was just such talk that my boy was raised under, and that I was raised under." *

The Winn of Father Long was a kind of frontier in a developing state, left in the wake of population's sweep to the West, years behind the growth of other parts of Louisiana. Other underprivileged ones in other parishes (the Louisiana word for counties) might have complained about their fate, muttering over their pone or dry biscuit. The Winn folk talked out loud, tried to do something, dammit. Winn became known as the wildest, orneriest parish of Louisiana, with a mind of its own, a will like a mule's. "The Free State of Winn," it was termed, with scorn. When the Civil War issue broke, Winn sent a delegate to the state convention instructed against secession. Why fight to save another man's slaves? When Louisiana joined the war, many of Winn's sons fled to join the Union Army, while others ran to the woods, there to risk death as traitors to the Confederacy.

After the war Winn Parish led dissatisfaction, embraced Populism, held a People's Party convention, elected three of its men to the Legislature. In words that have a present-day ring, Louisiana's Populists demanded an end to the one-party Solid South, and asked the state's workers to join those of the North to wipe out entrenched wealth and purchased parties. The Populists entered an alliance with the Republicans to support a gubernatorial candidate, and a bloody election day resulted. Negroes, not yet disfranchised, were taken

* *The Forum,* Aug., 1935. Or *cf.* Rorty's *Where Life Is Better* (Day; 1936).

to the polls under guard. After that election, Winn shopped about, supported William Jennings Bryan, and went Socialist when Debs visited it in 1908. One estimate was that half the school trustees and police jurors (members of the parish governing body) called themselves Socialists.

The railroad finally came to Winn by 1900, and the parish moved slowly forth from some of its isolation. Sawmills were set up, the population increased, and the I.W.W.s arrived to organize the lumber workers. They received a sympathetic audience in the older Winn radicals but a less responsive hearing from the younger folk, who were thinking less of the rural life than of ways to get away from it and to the city.

Out of this setting came Huey Pierce Long, the man who was to reshape a state, then threaten to do the same thing for a nation. Like another dictator, Benito Mussolini, he grew from a Socialist or semi-Socialist background but turned from the beliefs of his predecessors.

Appropriately, for a man who sought the White House, the Kingfish was born in a log cabin. Some say that every gubernatorial candidate for the past half-century in Louisiana has been traced to an identical much-photographed cabin. But there is no reason to doubt that this was an authentic one. It had several rooms, ceiled walls, and was comfortable if crowded. One investigator reported: "It had been built by a wealthy slave owner, and among the farmhouses of that period, was counted better than average."

The Longs had not been Southerners for any length of time. The family had moved about; from Pennsylvania to Ohio, to Indiana, to Mississippi, to Louisiana. They were Anglo-Saxons, their genealogy little different from that of their backwoods neighbors. Huey told his audiences: "I'm Welsh, Pennsylvania Dutch, French and a little Cherokee

Indian. My family denies the Cherokee." Some of its members rejected also the French, accused Huey of adding that to appeal to South Louisiana.

Much misinformation has been spread on both sides as to the economic status of the Longs. Huey informed the nation that on one occasion his mother had wept because he had no shoes. His brothers and sisters cried protest at this, called him a vote-hunting liar. Some of his enemies pictured the Longs as upper-middle class, well-to-do. True, an uncle was a banker, and the sisters married merchants and professional men. But the best evidence indicates that the Longs were originally poor whites, whose fortunes shifted up and down. There were nine children, and Huey was the eighth. Huey, Sr., struck his greatest luck when the railroad he hated bought part of his property. He was able to acquire another house and send six of his children to college before a bad stretch came. Huey, born in 1893, saw their town of Winnfield grow into a thriving little community, and the life of the section change gradually during his youth.

The man who was to lead millions of the rural people in protest against their life had little direct contact with the soil. He lived part of his time on a farm, part in town. His father explained: "Huey may have plowed a little, but not much." Huey declared that he "hated the farm work," that his sympathy always went out to those who had to do it. He contrived to be in town as much as possible. He was lively, alert from his early days, a rusty-haired young heller with a large tilted nose. At ten he ran away from home. At thirteen he was handling type in a printer's office. At fourteen he was a practicing auctioneer. A peddler had passed through town and given Huey a supply of books on credit. Huey hired horse and wagon and stormed the countryside, going from farm to farm, then auctioning books on street corners. This was easier than farming. He was a talker for the rest of his life. He told an interviewer: "I can't remember back to a time when my mouth wasn't open whenever there was a chance to make a speech."

The Longs were Baptists; and Huey, by necessity, knew the Bible from cover to cover. The family read a chapter daily, went to church meetings three or four times on Sunday, to regular Wednesday night meetings, revivals, camp meetings, "every funeral within miles." From the gospel-pumping preachers, telling in thundering tones of Old Testament happenings, promising heaven or hell and nothing between, Huey learned a few lessons. He drank in their stories, remembered some of their awesome emotional phrases. There was to be an evangelical note in his appeal that he never lost.

"I was born into politics, a wedded man, with a storm for my bride." So he once declaimed to the Senate. Public affairs, at any rate, came early, before he took to long pants. While still a schoolboy he conducted a campaign for an older friend, and helped him win office as a tick inspector. In high school he formed a political organization among the students, "laid down rules for them to follow; and if they followed the faculty instead of our rules, we kept them off the baseball team or the debating team." Huey's father contributed this comment: "The teachers had it in for him. He dictated to them. . . . They were a sorry bunch, some of them. Huey always had trouble with them." His instructors protested the club. To hell with them. Huey "got up" circulars; he had not worked around a shop for nothing. These were the advance trickles of a stream of denunciatory sheets that was to transform the course of Louisiana politics. He was told to leave school; he was in his last year. He didn't let the matter drop there. He drew up a petition, persuaded a majority of the patrons to sign, and the principal was fired. A tough one, even at fifteen, that Huey.

He dared almost anything. He loved a fight—as long as it did not involve fisticuffs. Throughout his life he was a physical coward, although he repeatedly exhibited political boldness of the first order. His younger brother Earl said that he had to take Huey's side in Huey's battles, or Huey would end up in sad defeat. One day Earl came upon another youngster who was thrashing Huey. Earl pitched in, found he wasn't doing so well himself. He looked for Huey. Huey was dusting up the road, yards away.

From the books that he could not sell, Huey started a period of avid reading. His tastes, Forrest Davis noted, ran to two types: biographies or histories in the classic style, particularly Ridpath's *History of the World,* and novels in the romantic pattern, mainly Victor Hugo and Sir Walter Scott. Ridpath was no modernist, no interpreter of social and economic trends; he stressed the rôles of the kings, the conquerers, the strong will of the strong man. For the rest of his life, Huey quoted Ridpath next to the Bible. In the young man's lighter reading ran a parallel trend, an admiration for brilliant figures who did brilliant deeds to a flashing of velvet coats and a quick oath. Huey chose as his heroes Frederick the Great, the Count of Monte Cristo; Metternich, Bismarck, Robespierre, Napoleon. Repeatedly he was to throw home a taunt: "He took Vienna and let the professors justify it." Huey took many things and looked to his state university to explain. In poetry he knew what he liked, and that appeared to be one thing: Henley's *Invictus.* His head was bloody but unbowed for most of his life.

Like many another rural boy, Huey wanted badly to go to the state university; but the family could not afford a seventh college student. Huey told the public about that for years afterward. He had lost the due of every young American; he was going to force legislation so that that could never happen again. But Huey did not grieve at the time. He chose a calling on which he had already made a start. He became a drummer, one of those lustrous figures of the day, who wore the latest cut of tight trousers, knew the latest jokes, had a way with the ladies. He became an apprentice salesman for Cottolene, which was a vegetable shortening product, his assignment being to give out pie tins and recipe books, and to conduct baking contests. He developed a deadly assault on his subject. "I can sell anything," said the brash upstart, and proved it. He was in the door one minute, in the farm wife's kitchen the next. He put on an apron, baked a cake, or prepared supper for the family. His greatest task, as Hermann B. Deutsch put it, was to convince the ladies that there were other things besides "cow butter and hog lard." If everything else failed, he pulled the Bible, noted how the good Lord told the Jews not to eat anything from the swine. Sometimes, it seemed, it was practically God's command that the housewife use Cottolene.

Dropping the drummer's trail for a time, Huey returned to high school, this time in Shreveport, North Louisiana. On his first day he stepped forward and, as the teacher's pince-nez dropped, waved a hand: "Class, I'm Huey P. Long, and I'm here to stay." The chemistry instructor asked for a sample of a compound. Huey leaped up: "Cottolene is a compound," and zipped through his sales talk.

Back to salesmanship again, he used Cottolene to find a wife. Holding a contest, he awarded the prize for the best "bride loaf cake," and later himself, to Rose McConnell of Shreveport. He took Rose to the theater one evening. The next day he was accused of having shot at a man. Life was turbulent, already. Rose had kept the stubs, helped locate those near him, and won exoneration for him. Huey branched out in his business, turned to flour, chimneys and medicines for "women's sickness," materials which may be said to form some of the foundations of the dictatorship-to-come.

He was turning his salesmanship into discreet preparation for a public life. He would never pull up his buggy in town for an overnight stay; not if he could help it. Instead, he would drop in at a likely farmhouse to ask if he could be put up. He was a farm boy, and he was welcome. He spoke the family's language; he knew what was going on outside. He listened while the farmer spoke, and he and the farmer were always in accord. After breakfast the next morning, the family would not want any money, but Huey would insist that it accept a dollar. ("Which was less than I'd have to pay in town, and made the man my friend.") Huey wrote back regularly, telling about crops, the weather, and city developments that would interest the farmer. He never lost a name and address, and he developed a formidable list of overnight follow-up friends.

His business career was a spotty one. He was fired for his expense accounts and he had to hobo his way around, living for a time on bread and onions. Luck improving, he became a sales-crew manager for nine states. Still hankering after something else, he went to the Oklahoma State University Law School. Here he promoted more trouble and more circulars, according to a story he told Deutsch. Classmates organized a Wilson-for-President club. Perhaps out of sheer cussedness, Huey took up Champ Clark. Officials favored Wilson, and almost suspended Huey. A school "convention" was called for Wilson. Huey raked in all the young fellows that he could find in town to pack it. The other side started a roll call, and Huey withdrew to stage a rump meeting out-

43

side. Unanimously, it came out for Clark. Huey had ordered several members of his crowd to remain inside and prevent a unanimous vote. Thus Clark had the advantage—to the uninitiated. The moral, in Huey's words: "In a political fight, when you've got nothing in favor of your side, start a row in the opposition."

Huey and Rose were married and he borrowed $400, moved to New Orleans and entered Tulane University. Hard as it is to believe, records show that he crammed an exacting three-year law course into eight months. Living with his bride in dusty quarters, he studied night and day. He worked a speed-up system for his instructors, so that they taught him overtime without knowing it. He would watch outside school until he saw a professor leave, would hop on the street car with him, get him talking about law, ask questions and sop up all that came forth. Then he would hurry home and dictate to Rose, at her typewriter, all that he had learned.

His weight dropped to 112 pounds as the year neared its close. Suddenly his money was gone; he had to become a lawyer, fast. Who gave the examinations? The State Supreme Court. To the court he went, and talked the justices into a special one for him. Passing it, he returned to Winnfield, a lawyer on the make, at twenty-one. It was in the Ridpath tradition. "I came out of that courtroom running for office," he said.

He took the kind of cases open to a "new beginner"; workmen's compensation, small claims. A widow sought to sue a bank, but neither she nor Huey had money for a bond. Huey went to one of the bank directors, asked for a loan for the purpose—and got it. The director, State Senator Harper, was a well-to-do semi-radical, one of the Winn believers in the better chance for the common man. To Huey, as to all others who would listen, he argued that America must balance things, get back to the simplicities of the Jeffersonian days. There needed to be a redistribution of wealth. Why, some were practically kings in America now. What Huey heard was to form his springboard, years later, toward a national dictatorship.

Huey became a close friend of Harper, and together they figured in an episode significant for both. The first World War started, and Senator Harper opposed American participation. He issued a pamphlet in which he asserted that two per cent of the American people owned seventy per cent of the wealth; and he called for conscription of money as well as of men. He was indicted by a Federal jury, and Huey defended him. In his autobiography (written when he was thirty-nine) Huey described his own tactics. On the selection of the jury rested the case. He, Harper and the prospective jurors were being closely watched, and Huey decided to make use of that surveillance. One by one, he called aside men whom he was certain he did not want to serve on the jury. He bought drinks, whispered in confidential tones, always on every other subject but the Harper case. When the trial started, each of the men was asked if Huey had talked with him about the matter. He replied, truthfully, that Huey had not. But the prosecution, sure he was lying, excused him. Harper won. But Huey almost had to serve time himself for statements to the press in connection with the case. He published, at that time, his first exposition on wealth sharing, declaring in part:

A conservative estimate is that about 65 or 70 per cent of the entire wealth of the United States is owned by two per cent of the people. From the year 1890 to 1910, the wealth of this nation trebled, yet the masses owned less in 1910 than they did in 1890, and a greater per cent lived in mortgaged or rented homes in 1900 than in 1890, and more lived in rented or mortgaged homes in 1910 than in 1900.

It probably had a subversive sound at the time. But simultaneously Huey was campaigning in the Liberty Loan drive, playing safe, as he did in many things. He did not go to war. He received exemption as a man with a wife and child. He sought to be placed in the last class, as a public official, on the contention that he was a notary.

Huey had been looking around. He was twenty-four now, getting on. The law, for most Louisiana public offices, required that the holders be thirty or thirty-five. But Huey found that for the Railroad Commission someone had forgotten to include any minimum. He announced for the position, as one of four contestants against a highly popular incumbent. Brothers Earl and Julius helped, and Rose, with a one-year-old child to watch, ran the office quarters. Huey went back to the road, in much the same way in which he had taken to it for Cottolene. This time the compound was Long.

North Louisiana saw something new in campaigns. Huey had been advised to wear his oldest clothes, to drive an ancient horse and buggy. He bought a few more city-style linens and an automobile, secondhand but the spiffiest he could afford. The country folk respected him the more for it—he didn't have to convince them that he was one of them, to start with; and they felt right proud that a farm boy was able to slick up with the best of that jelly-puff crowd. On another house-to-house, farm-to-farm canvass, Huey penetrated remote sections about which candidates had never bothered before. He spoke of the condition of the corn, the right way to prepare clabber; about credit, Wall Street and city airs. That Huey, he wasn't none of them stuckup New Orleans or Shreveport fellows, that talked way over your head and

46

then didn't know what end of a cow to milk. Watch 'im. He'll go places. You know, I been a friend of his ever since that night he stopped at our place . . .

He avoided all the courthouse towns, the parish centers to which candidates usually gave their particular attention. He concentrated on the scattered people of the hills and hollows. He was at it eighteen hours, sometimes more, a day. He knew well what the farmers and the small-town people wanted, what they hated. He was with them on better schooling, better roads, better prices. At 10 P.M. he was still at work. Nobody had to tell Huey that rural people went to bed early. "Nothing in my campaigning seemed to please the farmers more, or cause them to recollect me so favorably, as to call them from their beds at night. All over the neighborhoods flew the news of my working through the nights."

Huey poured everything he had, of himself and his money, into this wooing. At one point he needed $500. He remembered an elder Winnfield friend, O. K. Allen, a fuddling fellow of good heart and little brain. Allen gave him the money. Huey rewarded him, eventually, by making "O. K." his personal Governor of Louisiana. Meanwhile, Huey made a deal with another candidate. Huey and the other candidate agreed that if either came second for the commission in a first primary against the incumbent, the other would support him in the runoff. Huey was second on the first count, and first on the second. He had lost practically every courthouse town, but his country folk had streamed out for him, to put him over by a narrow margin. At twenty-five he was panting after his next goal—Louisiana.

He oozed happiness over his first job. He wanted the commissioners to wear a big gold badge, "so that people will know us, and give us the respect we're due." With Huey as a member, the Railroad Commission leaped into sudden new

47

importance in the public eye. People who had barely known it existed now heard of it every day. Huey, it seemed to the public, *was* the commission. He was everywhere. He rained circulars on every subject. He invaded iniquitous New Orleans, even the Cajun country of the South, barnstorming.

His face seemed made for the jokesters. His features were exaggerations, most of them: a comedian's nose, turned up at an impudent angle; wide mouth, heavy lips; roving brown eyes that were deepset and piercing; crinkly red hair that made a natural spitcurl. The jaw was heavy, chin deeply cleft, figure not slow in getting dumpy. Finally, an unwitting habit of scratching himself regularly on the left buttock—and you have the firebrand. He was loudmouthed, he was violent, he was funny. The New Orleans newspapers laughed at him; so did the politicians, and likewise their corporation friends of North and South Louisiana. So, too, did the Germans laugh at the early Hitler. Few called Huey clown who came in close contact with him.

He blasted at the big companies and their big lawyers. He roared insults, issued bulletins that called his corporation "enemies" double-dyed thieves, scalawags and looters. Against one in particular he developed bile: the Standard Oil. Standard is Special Interest in Louisiana, by tradition, by common consent. The largest corporation in the state, it is a colossus over the state capital, where it maintains one of the world's major refineries.

Huey knew the value of a public war on Standard; but he had also a personal reason for stalking it at this time. Though he insisted that he was always for the poor man against the rich, he had managed to accumulate oil stock by representing corporations. (Other "friends of the people" have done it before him.) He believed that he would "some day be mentioned among the millionaires"—even a prospective

48

wealth-sharer, it seemed, would like that—when Standard suddenly ordered a freeze-out of the independents in his field. Huey screamed a warning: "You've done this before, and got by with it. But this time, go do it, and see when you hear the last of it." He maneuvered the Railroad Commission into declaring the oil pipelines common carriers, subject to regulation for the first time. The issue was thrown into the approaching gubernatorial campaign of 1920.

Huey backed John M. Parker, cotton factor, Bull Moose associate of Teddy Roosevelt, reform candidate for Governor. Huey was satisfied that his man was for two programs of Huey's, a common-carrier pipeline law, and a higher severance tax on oil pumped out of the earth. Huey campaigned furiously for Parker for seventy days, helping advertise himself at the same time. "His man" carried North Louisiana by 761 votes, and became Governor. Huey was soon charging Parker with a sell-out. Parker had entered a "gentleman's agreement" with Standard on severance taxes; and on the pipeline question another compromise resulted. Parker called in the company's attorneys to help draft the tax. Huey, apoplectic, turned to the Bible: "Cain has become his own judge." Linking Governor with Standard, he poured out sulphurous pamphlets:

Better to have taken the gold hoarded in the Standard Oil vaults at 26 Broadway and deliberately purchased the votes with which the administration has ruled this state, than to have brow-beaten, bulldozed and intimidated the Legislature for the benefit of the corporate interests through the free use of the people's patronage. . . .

The Governor had him arrested for libel. He was found guilty on two counts and given a 30-day suspended sentence on one, a $1 fine on the other. Always the cockerel, he refused to pay, and the judge asked the counsel to contribute a quarter each, then added fifty cents of his own.

Soon Huey became Public Service Commission chairman and moved on Standard right and proper. He ordered it to produce its books, under the modified pipeline law. The company went to court; a judge enjoined hearings. Huey raged "To hell with the judge," expressing a sentiment which he was to repeat through the years. Ignoring the court, he demanded formation of a separate pipeline corporation and "approximated" the capitalization at one-fifth of what the firm indicated. The matter hung on in the courts, and a later commission tossed out Huey's regulations.

The Commoner invariably put on a show, growled, huffed, and made a number of reductions which meant genuine savings in telephone, electric and other rates. At the same time, in some cases, he quietly permitted the same corporations to make heavy increases in gas and other rates and in assessment bases. Later one of the firms so benefited gave Huey $10,000 for his gubernatorial campaign, according to the sworn testimony of Huey's brother. Other convincing evidence was offered that some of the "interests" were coming to see Huey as a not unreasonable chap, once one got to know him. And Huey was acquiring odd friends for a St. George against the Louisiana dragons: the leading anti-union operator of the Northern section, W. K. Henderson, who carried on a speaking tour against labor organizations in other parts of the country; a group of railroad magnates, a leading Klansman, officials of gas and electric companies.

On his thirtieth birthday, in 1923, Huey P. Long surprised many who did not know him, and few who did, by announcing for Governor. Thirty years was the minimum for qualification. Two days later, and the filing period was over.

Huey came forth at once with a rampaging detailed program: a concrete-and-blacktop system for the farmers, to be built by the state, in place of the present one under which there were practically no hard-surfaced state roads; free textbooks for the children, a college education for the older boys; free bridges where there were only toll bridges or none at all. At the same time he "poured acid," as the Louisiana saying went, in the faces of the many enemies whom he recognized: the City Ring, the Interests, the rotten state administration. He canvassed again, and many laughed; but his crowds grew. However, he received a hard blow. The Klan issue sprang up under circumstances that stirred the state, after the mutilated bodies of two men were found in a small community. Huey was trapped between Klan and anti-Klan sentiment. He needed South Louisiana, but he was a North Louisiana man from hard-shelled Baptist territory. Also, he was said to be more than friendly to Klan officials, was hailed in brotherly fashion in at least one of the Klan publications. He straddled, trying to turn full attention to his own brand of merchandise, but this now proved impossible.

He knew his people; he knew his odds. He predicted that he would win if election day were clear, lose if it rained. His rustics could not get to the polls if the weather was bad. Huey turned his eye to the heavens. He was rewarded with near-cloudbursts. The first box was opened: "Sixty-one—and you got sixty!" The sage sighed: "I'm beat. Should've been one hundred for me, and one against. Forty per cent of my country's vote's gone." As it was, he dumbfounded many critics, coming in a powerful third in one of the closest races of years; 73,000 for him, as against 81,000 and 84,000 for the other two candidates. He had topped them in the country. New Orleans had downed him.

The next four years were preparation, the placing of his

foot in the crack of more political doors, the making of more deals. Some of the "courthouse gangs" in the parishes responded to quiet overtures from him. Canny sheriffs thought they saw a man who would be important as a friend, dangerous as an enemy. The country boy who had cursed the depraved city went to New Orleans again to tempt that lady's favor. He came to an understanding with two of the bigger politicians who had just broken with the Ring: John Sullivan, attorney, National Grand Exalted Ruler of the Elks, a man of racing and related tie-ups, and Robert Ewing, publisher of large newspapers in New Orleans and other parts of the state. Huey had previously used vitriol on both. He had linked Sullivan with Boss Behrman in succinct style: "Wall Street knows how to call them in and make them sleep in the same bed. If Behrman took a dose of laudanum, Sullivan would get sleepy in ten minutes." Sullivan and Ewing brought a new source of strength to the growing Long. Ewing's New Orleans newspaper saw that Huey's face and story were offered to all of the state, and in glowing light. It was the first of many shifts among the state's newspapers, changes of front which speeded the dictatorship and weakened the prestige of the press in Louisiana.

The South Louisiana situation called for attention. Huey scored a tenstrike. A Senatorial race was coming up, and he grasped at his opportunity, displaying a piece of political judgment that advanced him in the eyes of the professionals. J. Y. Sanders, Sr., former governor, an Eastern Louisiana dry, with a strong backing all over the Northern parishes, opposed Edwin Broussard, a South Louisiana wet. North Louisiana was Baptist, anti-tariff, intolerant of the Southern areas. Broussard was Catholic, advocate of a tariff for sugar. Huey's job, as he saw it, was to win North Louisiana for Broussard, the Southern area for himself. He toured both sections. The North was his. With Broussard smiling approval, he told the South that he was part French, tickled the Cajuns with his stories, convinced them that he was one of their kind. They rechristened Huey Polycarp Long. South Louisiana was his from then on; even "Couzain Ed" Broussard, when he broke with Huey later, couldn't take away what he had helped give the Kingfish. Now Broussard had won. North Louisiana had helped elect a Creole.

One or two embarrassing moments followed for Huey. Two hostile members of the Public Service Commission joined to remove him as chairman. He practically retired from that agency, although he still collected his salary. It was disclosed that Huey had become the attorney for a gravel company that profited by current rates which he, as a member of the commission, refused to try to reduce. The other commissioners accused him of making secret deals with corporations; agreements to temper rate reductions which he had promised, and to grant other favors. Huey had taken a new tack, was openly a lawyer for the vested interests. But he had an explanation: "When the millionaires and corporations fell out with each other, I was able to accept highly remunerative employment from one of the powerful to fight several others who were even more powerful. Then I made some big fees with which I built a modern house in the best residential section of Shreveport, at a cost of $40,000." But he insisted that he never took a case against a poor man. All of which, perhaps, was a matter of definition. Throughout his life, he was to receive large fees, while in office, from some of the same firms that he attacked. He had a defense: "Why not? I admit I'm the best lawyer in Louisiana."

The gubernatorial election approached. Luckily for Huey, the opposition could not agree on a candidate, and two opposed him. One was O. H. Simpson, who was completing a term as temporary governor after the death of his predecessor. Simpson was termed by a discerning critic "an opportunist politician whose term of office had been distinguished only by its apathy and several minor scandals." The other candidate was Congressman Riley Wilson, hailed by some of the newspapers as the standard bearer of "the better element." The same observer, Basso, summed him up as "the nominee of the New Orleans Ring, a veteran Democrat who had been embalmed in the House of Representatives for fourteen years."

Huey launched his candidacy with a rally, at which the slogan of his later national forays first appeared on banners: "Every Man a King, but No Man Wears a Crown." It was taken from the *Cross of Gold* speech of William Jennings Bryan. Some called Huey another Bryan. But he was to make Bryan a forgotten man among the underprivileged. Wilson had cited his flood record in Washington, and sought to pitch the campaign on the issue. Another candidate would have lost sleep over that. Huey made a face at the crowd: "Wilson's been in Congress fourteen years, and this year the water went fourteen feet higher than ever before. That gives him a flood record of one foot of high water a year." Then he turned to his own political showcase. He received undivided attention this time, and the voters heard specific promises of a sort never held out to them before—a nightmare to the opposition for years to come. Powerfully, ringing in bitter facts, he pleaded for free books, "to give every child his rightful place in school"; real roads, "so that the farmer can get a decent chance"; free bridges, lower utility rates so that the people and not the high corporation muckety-mucks would get the benefit.

He invaded areas that had never seen a gubernatorial candidate. He was hitting his stride; he had a good war chest

54

from financial friends in North Louisiana and in New Orleans, and he showered the state with mounting piles of circulars. He worked at a personal schedule that would have killed a man with anything short of a mule's constitution. He was everywhere at once, his rivals believed; sometimes they doubted reports that he had been in so many places in so short a time. Louisiana had never beheld a candidate with the ripsnorting energy, the determination of young Huey. He did with four or five hours' sleep nightly for weeks, and, save for bloodshot eyes, showed little effect. He was turning his attention to the towns and cities, and he was spreading himself on the platform. He evolved a windmill, or air-flailing, arm movement. He screwed up his eyes, tossed off his coat, burlesqued the stuffed-shirt behavior of his opponents. He delighted his crowds when he explained that he was wearing new shoes, that his feet hurt like hell, and therefore he "had to take it easy, this way," as he squeaked over the boards.

He took the gloves off Louisiana politics, and they were to stay off for twelve years. He said things that had not been said before, tossed forth charges of specific offenses of the most damaging nature. If he had been a wild man before, he was a one-man riot now. He uttered the once unutterable, then elaborated on it. Laws of slander did not bother him; he imputed Negro blood, safetapping, and backbush immorality to governors and former governors, minor judges and almost anybody else whose names came to mind. (The Supreme Court Justices had to wait their turn, but it was coming.) Gone for years was the Southern-gentleman tradition. "Thieves, bugs and lice" . . . "plundering high-binders . . . blackguards in full dress suits . . . the rattin' old gang, shoving to get back at the trough . . ."

He blasted at the state administration, calling it worse

than the carpetbaggers, charging immunity for irregularities and racketeering. He drew pictures of inhuman treatment of the mentally ill, and pledged himself to "free them of their chains." He cried horrors at the Conservation Commission, "a coon chasin' and possum-watchin' brigade, that does its job cruising around in a fancy boat in the Gulf." "Why, I'll cut off the commission's tail to damn near right behind the ears!" (He was to expand that agency into one of the most malodorous in Louisiana history.) He scored the Highway Commission's custom of giving away free automobiles. (He was to improve on this practice, systematize it as an adjunct to other and larger corruptions.) A special joy to his listeners was one perfervid pledge, a new "occupational" tax of five cents a barrel to be shoved down the throat of Standard Oil. "Pour it on 'em, Huey . . . Rub their noses in it!" His meetings were a cross between a New Orleans Carnival parade, a revival meeting and a Saturday sandlot baseball game.

It was deadly ammunition against the opposition. It was direct, clear, close to home, a revelation to the listeners after years of speeches by candidates who droned on in tremolo voice about the eternal Southern verities, with grandiloquent phrase and little else to offer. Huey called a spade a goddamned spade, and made it clear that he had chosen a place into which he'd like to shove it.

In New Orleans he made distinctions: "We must fight the bears and lions, but the skunks and porcupines we won't bother about." In South Louisiana, in the Cajun country, under one of the South's famous trees, he let out all stops:

And it was here that Evangeline waited for her lover Gabriel, who never came. This oak is an immortal spot, made so by Longfellow's poem, but Evangeline is not the only one who has waited here in disappointment.

Where are the schools that you have waited for your children to have, that have never come? Where are the roads and the highways that you spent your money to build, that are no nearer now than ever before? Where are the institutions to care for the sick and disabled? Evangeline wept bitter tears in her disappointment. But they lasted through only one lifetime. Your tears in this country, around this oak, have lasted for generations. Give me the chance to dry the tears of those who still weep here.

To his country and small-town folk, Huey talked generally of maldistribution of wealth. But he had not yet developed this creed to a point at which he made specific promises of houses, radios and annual income. He was concentrating on concrete state pledges which he knew made quick appeal. The issue of maldistribution was stored in the mothballs, but it was aired out now and then.

For a time it appeared that his two opponents would join against him in the event of a run-off. Already their assistants were friendly. Huey planned strategy to cope with that problem: "We must keep tab on how they are running, one against the other, and direct our fire always against the stronger, until he becomes the weaker, and then switch, and keep those two bullies neck and neck. . . . Fire will break out as sure as lightning." One day word came: "The Wilson papers want our dope on Simpson. They will play up any remark you make on him." The data was provided, but Huey ordered also that "some traitor in our camp" tell the Simpsonites that the Wilsonites were working with him to "ruin their candidate."

Election day was sunny. The hollows poured out "Huey's unwashed." He received a good lead over both oppositionists, but less than a majority. The young heller had topped them in the country; but again New Orleans had rejected

57

him. His splitting tactics worked, however; the opposition could not unite. "Divide and Rule."

Not quite thirty-five, Huey became the youngest Governor in his state's history, and the first poor-white representative in the executive's chair. The tide of hillbilly resentment had come into full effect later in Louisiana than in other Southern states. But it was to have a far different sequel. Conservative Eastern journals were worried about Huey and what he would do to rates, interest and state finances. Liberal magazines wondered if he would be an "Al Smith of the South," a reformer such as Smith was then, who would bring progressivism to a state which had long been in the hold of the ultraconservatives.

Exultant in his New Orleans hotel rooms, sweat rolling down his heavy, now florid face, Huey was telling his boys to "stick by me. We'll show 'em who's boss. I'm gonna be President some day."

The summer of 1928 brought a sight that shocked the capital city of Baton Rouge. Huey's people came in to see him made Governor. Forrest Davis describes the scene. They walked in for miles thereabout. They came by mule wagon, by aged farm Ford, by day coach, by bus. Some had made part of the trip by pirogue, from their swamp houses on stilts. There were 15,000 of them in an unprecedented horde, singly, in couples, in large families. From its neat white-painted cottage porches, middle-class Baton Rouge sniffed at the women in their calico Sunday best, bonnets on their heads; at the men, gallused, tobacco-chewing, felt-hatted in the sun. Upper-class families drew the curtains. Some of the visitors were timid, awed. Others grimaced as they looked at these capital people. These were the privileged ones that Huey was to get even with, for us! We're a-going to get a look-in now. Things will be different, you watch, you young flibberty-gibbert there, with your painted lips. And you watch, too, mister, with your goddamned black chauffeur. . . . The meek knew that they were to come into their inheritance.

The gathering point was Louisiana's old gingerbread-fortress Capitol—the place Mark Twain had once dismissed with the remark: "That comes from too much Sir Walter Scott." The country folk clustered in the halls, on the lawns, in the street outside. Hillbilly bands played. Huey gave orders that there were to be water buckets, with dippers. His people were to feel at home.

The revolution had started. But something else was getting under way, more slowly, more quietly: the diversion of that revolution.

III

"L'ETAT, C'EST MOI"

I F ANYONE in Louisiana had been foolish enough to believe that things were to continue much as before, with
only a few gaudy new flourishes, Huey quickly disillusioned
him. Life was never going to be the same for some of them;
Huey made that clear.

The full-fledged dictator did not appear immediately, but
premonitory signs were apparent within a few days of the
election. Several years were to pass before he could boast
that he had the state in his briefcase. The opposition was to
give him trouble until he had devised his special ways to
club it down. Huey, it is fairly certain, did not plan in advance the full extent of his autocracy. It grew upon him and
upon Louisiana as he realized, first, what his opportunities
were, and second, the way in which he would have to shake
Louisiana, later America, from top to bottom to carry
through those opportunities.

From the beginning, Huey wanted one thing—power. In
this he was perhaps not far different from those other agents
of the have-nots in other Southern offices—Vardamann of
Mississippi, Georgia's Tillman and Talmadge, The Man
Bilbo, Tom Heflin and the rest. But all of these lacked
Huey's daring, Huey's skills in manipulation—and his determination and his ability to grab what he wanted, no matter
what was involved in the grabbing. It took the South some
little time before it realized that Huey meant to get the

things he wanted, no matter what happened to anybody or anything.

He had two objectives at this point. He must take for himself every job that was hanging loose around the state. Then he must launch the biggest public-works program that the South had ever seen. He was going to rivet his own men into every cranny of the state's structure; and he was going out to create new opportunities for employment of worthy individuals who believed in him.

He fired every office holder, every department head, every clerk, lawyer or janitor over whom he had control. He cleaned up office forces by sending in a man to announce: "You're all out—right now." Then Huey moved on those over whom his control was questionable, and on others who, by precedent and by law, were secure from gubernatorial interference. "Secure, hell!" Some gave way. Others resisted, one or two for several years. He shoved out some of the obstinates by cutting the ground from under them, persuading the Legislature to create new agencies, automatically ending the present terms. One board, desiring conciliation, called on him. He did not ask the members to sit down. He yelled: "When do your commissions expire? I've got to pass a law on that," and stamped out.

Some of the state boards were independent, "non-political," supposedly protected by overlapping terms. Huey swung a wide ax on them, too. The members had not taken part in his campaign. "Anybody ain't with us, is against us." Sometimes it was not so easy. The head of the State Board of Health, who had served under five administrations, met his "successor" at the door and announced that he was staying until his term ended. The director had his bed brought in and lived in the department. It took several years but Huey finally got him out.

61

Career workers? Men and women who had proved their worth by serving the state for many years? Huey had an answer: Louisiana had been suffering from Tweedledum-Tweedledee administration. "One of 'em skinned you from the ankles up, the other from the neck down. But you got skinned just the same." And everybody had to go.

He looked for every opportunity to throw out a city man for a country one. He told a rural audience: "I'm tired of taking off my hat when I go to New Orleans. They said I couldn't remove Dr. Leake, whose pappy is the Standard Oil's lawyer, from the superintendent's berth at Charity Hospital down there. Well, I put him out, and I come here and I got Dr. Vidrine of Ville Platte to take it. The country people can hold the big jobs just like the city men." Vidrine was a moderately unprominent rural doctor. Huey placed him in charge of one of the greatest medical centers in the South, a world-famous institution. His was to be a fateful rôle for the dictatorship.

"The Karl Marx of the Hillbillies," someone once called Huey. He was not that, but few revolutionaries understood better the need for a clean-out of all potential fifth columnists left by an old régime. Huey didn't have to read a textbook to know what to do about "them birds." He "stomped 'em." He had a little black book that all Louisiana knew and feared—Huey's "sonofabitch book." Anyone who had ever done him a wrong of any degree was there, marked for vengeance.

He cracked down and broke a rule, even before he took office. The time approached for a state convention to name representatives to the Democratic National Convention. Louisiana traditionally selected its delegates by this method. By common consent, the choice was on the basis of strength of various factions in the Legislature. Huey, unfortunately, lacked a majority there. The Regular Ring of New Orleans had, as usual, a sizable bloc. In the past it would inevitably have dominated under these circumstances. It sent word that it was willing to give the Governor a fair deal, on its terms. Huey didn't reply. He looked into the law, found that the Constitution did not specifically require a convention. Hurriedly he summoned the State Democratic Central Committee. It dispensed with the state convention, named the delegates to the national meeting, and left out completely the City Ring and the country opposition. The Long organization controlled, 101 per cent. The extra per cent was for Huey.

The opposition sputtered, invoked the sacred name of democracy. Huey replied that nothing sounded sweeter to him than the moans of the pie-eaters when shoved away from the pie. The other side was startled into silence when it learned that Huey was getting undated resignations from all of his appointees, and from some of the temporary holdovers as well. This was to be the customary pattern of opposition reaction for the years ahead: shock, disbelief, then sad realization.

Huey's first legislative session had its ups and downs. He traded patronage, made concessions and, although he lacked a majority, managed to put in his leaders in charge of both houses. Huey had the temporary advantage; the gubernatorial-legislative honeymoon always found the chief executive master of the household. He succeeded in carrying through bills, or constitutional amendments to be submitted to the voters, for a $30,000,000 bond issue to give the farmers their roads, for the free school books, for increased appropriations for hospitals and other institutions. He had talked economy and promised to eliminate departments, reduce taxes and remove the "payroll papsuckers" or unnecessary jobholders. But that was forgotten now, as gasoline taxes and the severance taxes on minerals were raised to foot the bill.

He tried a court-packing plan that preceded Roosevelt's by nearly eight years. Appeals judges occupy important positions in the handling of state litigation. Huey proposed to increase their number from nine to fifteen—a baited hook for the legislators or their friends. He failed; but he kept the idea in mind, and used it later on another agency. Emerging inch by inch, the Kingfish-to-be quietly suggested an increase in the National Guard. The opposition objected that this might make it possible for some governor to use the military for political purposes. Here was prophecy without the knowledge of the prophets. Huey tried to supplant the civil sheriff with the criminal sheriff as New Orleans' election supervisor. The statesmanship behind this proposal was clear; the one favored him, the other opposed him. But this time Huey lost.

Scenes ensued which caused national comment. Huey did not sit in his office as did other governors, receiving reports and conferring on the progress of legislation. He believed in direct action. He stepped over to the scene of battle, walked up and down the legislative halls, buttonholed one member, whispered advice to another. Once or twice he walked into legislative committee meetings, took over, and told his men how to vote. On one occasion he announced to his cohorts that he didn't want any meeting of the committee. At his suggestion, they disappeared. This was something new.

An oppositionist tossed a copy of the State Constitution at him. "Maybe you've heard of this book." Huey tossed it back: "I'm the Constitution around here now." In a speech, he bragged that he dealt with the Legislature "like a deck of cards." Of a friendly legislator he snorted: "We bought him like a sack of potatoes." This story came out, and the gentleman was called "Sack of Potatoes" for years afterward. Of another, Huey grinned: "We got that guy so cheap, we thought we stole him."

His Legislature out of the way, Huey settled some old scores. The Public Service Commission was against him, was it? He vetoed its appropriation, and soon the commission was in a sad plight. He had promised much in improved facilities for tuberculars. But the wife of an enemy, a former governor, was a leading advocate of such a program. So he vetoed this appropriation. He had promised to abolish a $15,000-a-year position of inheritance tax collector and use the money for a new tuberculosis hospital on the lake. Instead, he named Brother Earl to the job. One newspaper ran a picture of Earl, with a caption describing him as a hospital on the lake.

Huey had promised New Orleans that he would bring natural gas to its homes. After years of delay, during which the Ring and the Electric Bond and Share subsidiary had worked together to continue artificial gas at a high figure, the natural gas was about to be piped in. However, there was a final dispute on the rate. A measure was pending when Huey intervened. He stormed, he fumed, he cursed the Ring and he cursed the company. But he ended by taking the company's side and fixing a rate far higher than the consumers might otherwise have paid. Another firm was ready to handle the product for 65 cents. Huey said, at first, that 70 cents or less was proper. He ordered a 90-cent rate. He and the corporation were friends from that time forward. The consumers received the gas and thanked Huey for it. He had beaten the Ring at its own game.

The free textbooks met protests. Oil companies fought against taxes upon them for provision of the books. Catholics objected that their taxes would go for purposes in which they could not share. Many of them sent their children to their own church schools instead of the public schools. The Catholics were powerful; sixty-five to seventy per cent of New Orleans belongs to the faith, and South Louisiana is almost as strongly of the same persuasion. Huey announced that the Catholics would get the books, too. He was giving them to the children, not to the schools; thus private schools, Catholic and non-Catholic, would get state books. It was a departure from precedent. Learned constitutionalists declared that it was illegal, and the issue went to the United States Supreme Court. Huey won, in a case of national significance.

At Shreveport haughty complaint was made. Shreveport could take care of its own children; it didn't want them treated as paupers, thank you. Huey waited for a chance. Shreveport was about to receive a large Army air base; it discovered that it needed eighty acres in an adjoining parish, and, because of a technicality, state assistance was required. The project would mean extra payrolls, extra expenditures. All Louisiana was interested in its success. Of course the state would give its assent? Like hell. "Whack up them school books if you want that air field," Huey rasped to a delegation. The sullen hillbilly in him spoke: he wanted a public apology for the way Shreveport treated him; he wanted invitations to public affairs; he wanted folks to "bow to me on the street, and not scowl at me." He won his demand in the matter of the school books, but the scowls continued. Later he told a meeting: "They say I coerced them, oppressed them into taking free books? I *stomped* 'em into it!"

More suits were filed. The opposition was fighting hard to hold up his program. The Governor turned to the banks;

66

his Board of Liquidation, a debt agency made up of state officials, authorized a $500,000 loan. But the banks' attorneys considered it of doubtful legality. Then, replied Huey, he also would be guided by their attorneys. "You know the state owes you fellows $938,000 on liquidation loans now?" Ah, but the Legislature had ordered that paid. "Well, it ordered this paid, too. But that $938,000 ain't been paid yet, and it ain't going to be paid. If it's illegal to make 'em, it's illegal to pay 'em. We'll keep the $938,000 and have $438,000 to spare." Huey walked out of the bank.

He went to a hotel, and glumly he ordered a "thin sandwich." As it came, a banker also arrived: "Governor, we voted to make you the loan." Huey told the waiter: "Take back that sandwich! Fry me a steak."

The country Puritan turned upon immorality in New Orleans and the adjoining parishes. Things were getting out of hand, he told the state; the roulette operators and the harlots were running honest business out of New Orleans. He would stop it if he had to "call out the militia to patrol the city's streets." The shades were pulled down in the city, but operations went on as before. Lying around in his underwear with some friends, shortly afterward, Huey received a call: "They're at it again in St. Bernard Parish. . . . Sure, it's true. My wife's out there." Huey called the National Guard. Sleepy youths jumped into trucks. Machine guns were brought out, while the boys were charged to "shoot without hesitation" if the order came. "We are to deal with most desperate men. You are soldiers, engaged in serious business for state and country. You are to enforce its laws." ("By breaking others," Carleton Beals observed. There had been no call for assistance by the parish. Martial law had not been declared.)

Gambling equipment was burned, while screaming women

67

and white-faced men were lined up. The Guardsmen seized $25,000. Gamblers were sure that it went into "The Bucket," the machine's political fund. Huey made more raids. A furore resulted. Only during carpetbag days had the militia been so abused. The attorney-general declared these forays illegal, charged that Huey in one case had suppressed evidence that might have led to prosecution, by returning confiscated checks to a proprietor in exchange for half the amount. Huey replied: "Nobody asked him for his opinion." Huey pulled still another raid, at which all patrons were searched by the soldiers. A man and his wife objected and were forcibly examined. It was charged that favored friends were permitted to catch a look from vantage points while the lady was stripped by three others. She said a Guardsman took her purse.

Huey's publisher friend, Ewing, and Sullivan, his other city backer, broke with him. The Ewing newspaper called him a Mussolini, a Napoleon. (Hitler was still in his beer cellars.) A front-page picture showed a "naked woman" with whom Huey had "toyed" on the night of his last raid. His Excellency was a creature repulsive to the American family. Huey, in reply, let out that he and Ewing had split over Sullivan and "his business as a gambler." New Orleans snickered and surmised that morality had had little to do with the matter, that political powers and prerogatives had been the explanation. The gambling crusade slowed up, and business went back to normal. The gambling fraternity told its friends that one reason for the raids had been that the pay-offs to Huey's men had not been coming in properly, and that "all this was just to keep things in line."

Huey had more serious troubles. The treasury was dry, while the acts that were to provide the jobs were tied up in court. Suddenly he galvanized the state with a call for a special legislative session, for his often-threatened five-cent "occupational" tax on oil to benefit "the sick, the halt, the blind and the children."

Fury broke over Louisiana. Baton Rouge was filled with anxious legislators, Chamber of Commerce representatives, Huey's country leaders and Standard Oil agents. Standard charged that the Governor was trying to ruin it. Business men generally feared that if the principle of an occupational tax were established, all lines might find it slapped upon them later. (Huey's business-industrial friends were not heard from.) The Governor charged that the "Oil and Gas Trusts" were buying legislators and newspapers—the latter with thumping special advertisements. Newspapers published lists of legislators on the state payroll, and cited the State Constitution as prohibiting this practice. Legislators, frightened, began to back away. Huey slipped into the chambers to give orders as usual. A member demanded his expulsion, and he jumped out of the hall—not a scene that added to gubernatorial prestige.

Next, a hard blow—a stinger. A Baton Rouge paper charged that Huey had ordered it to "lay off" or he would publish the names of persons opposing him who had relatives in the state's mental hospitals. He was aiming at the publisher. Huey's lieutenant-governor, who had broken with him over the disposition of a murder case, now asked forgiveness for having supported Huey at any time, and accused him of signing away millions in mineral rights, "more than in the Teapot Dome scandals." A rabbi declined to "call down the blessings of God on such a Governor." A refrigerator salesman made an affidavit that the Governor had violated the law by buying $20,000 of machinery without bids. The law required contracts on all material over $1000. The state had called for more than twenty broken orders for separate pieces from his anti-union friend W. K. Henderson. Somebody spoke the word "Impeachment." Huey wrote in his autobiography: "My ground began to slip from under me. Rats began to leave the apparently sinking ship."

"Bloody Monday" brought one of the most frenzied scenes in Louisiana legislative records. John B. Fournet, Huey's Speaker of the House, had obviously been forewarned of trouble. As the session started he ignored a request by Representative Cecil Morgan to speak on personal privilege. Angry protest came from all sides. Morgan shouted: "I have in my hand an affidavit that the Governor has tried to procure the assassination of a member of this House!" Speaker Fournet ordered the sergeant to seat Morgan. Twenty-five members formed a human barrier about the representative, amid wild cries and screams. Fournet, over the din, recognized a Long man's motion to adjourn sine die. This might have meant an end to the special session, and to the opportunity for impeachment. Fournet called for a vote—by the balloting machine. A hush, then rage. The count showed the wrong votes opposite the right names. "You damned crook . . ." "The machine's fixed . . ."

Declaring that adjournment had carried, Fournet left. The Louisiana House of Representatives turned into a rioting mob. Men beat each other with ink wells, slugged with both fists. Shirts were torn off, eyes gouged, heads butted on desks. One or two oppositionists sobbed helplessly: "Oh, God, we must do something. . . . Don't let them get away with this." One member, bounding from desk to desk toward the rostrum, was slugged with brass knucks and seriously cut in the head. (A departure, that, for even a Louisiana Legislature.) Men piled on men in the pit at the front. Finally the opposition took over, ending the incident that rivaled a French

Quarter saloon brawl and outdid Reconstruction. The next day Fournet said that everything had been a mistake. The machine had not been cleared from a previous vote, and thus the wrong ballot had been recorded by error.

The crash came, and Huey was impeached. He was the first Louisiana Governor to be so charged in the state's history under four nations. Nineteen formal counts were offered, covering, as was noted, every ground provided by law "except habitual drunkenness." Some wanted to include that. Accusations ranged from grave to capricious, from the criminal to the inane. "Battling" Bozeman, first recognized gubernatorial bodyguard in Louisiana, declared that Huey wanted him to kill J. Y. Sanders, Jr., of the Legislature: "Leave him in a ditch. . . . I'm the Governor, and if you're caught, I'll give you a full pardon."

Other legislators told how Huey tried to bribe them and boasted of bribing others. One said that Huey informed him he would order the bank examiners to keep the banks from foreclosing on any of the legislator's notes. "Misuse, misapplication and misappropriation of state funds" was another count. The Legislature had given Huey $6000 for official expenses at a governors' conference in New Orleans. The committee reported that expenditures were less than $4000. Huey was said to have used the rest to buy a car, on which he painted: *Not* State Property." One of Huey's coming great men, Seymour Weiss of the Roosevelt Hotel in New Orleans, insisted that he had spent all of the $6000 on entertainment. He could tell about all of it except the last $2000 or so. This had gone for "a party of such a nature that I would hesitate to give details until I had the permissino of certain others." Governors of sundry sovereign states wired heatedly that nothing had happened which their wives could not have seen.

"Gross misconduct in public places" was next. The owner of a padlocked cabaret (the Great Experiment was still on) testified that Huey had been a frequent visitor, had danced with the hostesses, become crocked, conducted the orchestra and crooned. Not much of a voice, but the customers gave him a great hand. The Governor had become known at his place as "The Singing Fool."

Helen Clifford, a lady who entertained at parties, told about one of them. It was on the night that Huey ordered a gambling raid. The scene was a Vieux Carré studio apartment. It was *"some* party. . . . Everybody was drunk, and the Governor had *plenty!* . . . I had on a straw skirt, no stockings, and something here—bare between here and there." Huey played with one girl's hair, on a sofa; at another time he pulled Miss Clifford on to his lap. The Legislature demanded that she give her telephone number.

The Governor was charged with illegal destruction of the former executive mansion, a striking example of pre-war plantation home. The Legislature had authorized a new one, but the attorney-general had ruled that this did not mean demolition of the old one. Huey was reported to dislike the place because it reminded him of other governors. He said that it was a rattletrap. Some claimed that Huey had sold or destroyed the state-owned furniture, and had had HPL engraved on the official silver before sending it away. (New Orleans remembered "Spoons" Butler, and snickered.) The new mansion was "a replica of the White House," though one observer called it "a cross between a museum and a post office." "I want to feel at home when I start in at the White House," Huey had told his friends.

A college president testified that Huey called him to inform him that a ballot box near the school "wasn't going right," and that the president had better "get out and get busy." Huey was accused of "habitually carrying concealed weapons." A preacher told how Huey showed him a "blood poisoner" and volunteered the information that Chicago gangsters were after him. There were other charges: that the Governor had made illegal loans, "coerced" parish governments, made appointments to jobs to influence the judiciary; that he had demanded undated resignations; that he habitually cursed like a longshoreman to official callers. As to the last count, when a witness was asked to recall Huey's words, a Long man was shocked: ". . . a disgrace to have it repeated, with women in the gallery. . . . My God, man, where is your Southern chivalry?" Others had a defense. Hadn't everybody, the voters included, known beforehand that Huey cursed all the time?

It was a farrago of accusations, prepared without intelligence or discretion. However, all of it could not be laughed off. Huey was found lying face-down in bed, crying. But such moods never lasted. He stormed at the enemy for the dog-faced sons of wolves that they were, then felt better and got to work. Some suggested a "judicial," dignified defense. That wasn't the way. Huey had two ideas of his own: money, and the people. He needed the first, fast. One of his earliest backers in New Orleans, Robert S. Maestri, a man of real-estate and furniture holdings, proved the friend in need, ready with whatever cash was wanted.

Even while the Legislature was considering charges that Huey had bribed members, he was reaching others. They knew that the stakes were higher; they could pick their reward. Appeals were on other bases: threats against legislators or their relatives, use of the banks or other state agencies. Dazed lawmakers picked up the telephone, each to be told by Huey that one of his cars was waiting, at that moment, outside the house, to take him immediately to Baton

Rouge; Huey wanted to talk to him. This happened to fifteen men at once. Huey pursued one timid fellow from one part of the state to the other. Pretending that he went to bed one evening, the Governor sneaked out of the back entrance, drove until morning and made sure that he caught another man before he arose. He chased evasive senators to their bathtubs, to hotel washrooms. Meanwhile, he sought to trap the opposition into paying one or more of his men, and planned to use this deadly material. And, as was his lifetime custom, he used fifth-column tactics. Secret Long agents were planted in most of the important opposition conferences, and turned in frequent bulletins.

The other part of the task was one that called for a backbreaking job of organization. Huey scribbled his most castigating of circulars while presses waited to turn out hundreds of thousands overnight. State motorcycle policemen, cars of highway workers and trucks stood ready. The messages were poured out to every crossroad, every grocery store, every small-town merchant in North and South Louisiana; delivered to tens of thousands of rural homes, one by one, and dropped over the cities as well. Were the people with Huey, ready to show it when called? Huey was working to get the right answer. The overnight rush-job technique that he evolved here became the basis for a permanent system of propaganda distribution that was unparalleled in America.

Huey meanwhile stormed the state, sweating, waving his hands, quoting the Bible to prove that he was right. He was facing impeachment only because he had dared attack the "Octopus"—i.e., Standard. But he preferred to go to his death a thousand times than to bow before this tyrant. He opened up on the press, cited obvious inaccuracies, charged various behind-the-scenes connections. In this campaign, more than any other, he made the term "lyingnewspaper" a

74

byword. Hereafter, hundreds of thousands of Louisianians ran the words together, like that. "Two cents a lie!" he jibed. A mighty shout went up for Huey.

Brother Earl enlivened proceedings when, seeing Maestri talking to an opposition legislator, he opened his mouth and bit deep into the other man's throat. It took three others to get Earl and his teeth loose. The legislator went to a hospital; Earl went on working for Huey.

The Long men threw up technicalities and delays. The opposition muddled the issues, bickered endlessly, with the assistance of the Longsters. Finally, many of the more ridiculous charges were abandoned and several voted by the House, for trial by the Senate, with a $100,000 appropriation. A wooden platform was built; Huey declared that it reminded him of a "pre-Revolution French hanging." As the crisis approached, he called his commoners to the capital. It was the same procession of trooping thousands that had come before: red necks, small-town merchants, clerks, swamp men, and, in addition, the state jobholders. That night men and women laughed, wept, shouted, clenched their fists as Huey cried scorn, told country jokes, talked of vindication in phrases from his favorite romantic novelists, and ended, as in other exalted moments, with *Invictus*. Meanwhile, the equally important other work was going on in the hotel rooms.

The opposition considered Huey a dying cock. The town seethed, and the newspapers prepared extras. National journals carried thousands of words on the situation. A Southern state was to vindicate itself, remove one who had shown great promise but had gone wrong, who had challenged constitutionalism in the South. And then Huey struck with the knockout blow that he had been preparing. Fifteen members of the Senate declared that they would not vote to convict, regardless of evidence, because they considered the charges invalid. Their number was more than enough to prevent conviction. A dull fizzle was the result. One side had bungled, the other had sidestepped. Huey had not been vindicated, but he had won. He had "thrown back the 'ristercrats," and the folks were with him. Exultant, he signed autographs: "Huey P. Long, Governor of Louisiana, by grace of the people."

Lost to sight in the hubbub was the issue that had caused the whole splashing display, the oil tax. Standard kept on at the same stand as before. But there was a grimmer note, henceforth, in the eye and voice of the Governor when he dealt with the opposition.

A Constitutional League was formed "to keep Long from treating the organic law like a scrap of paper." Huey called it the Constipational League. It published the names of thirty-five Long relatives on the payrolls, at a total of $75,000 a year. Huey chuckled. Why, that wasn't half of them!

The bond issue for public works finally went into effect. The régime had $30,000,000 with which to work; and jobs, contracts, favors spread over Louisiana. But not over all of it; certain sections, New Orleans, Shreveport and others, in which opposition held out, never saw a state concrete mixer. Huey developed a new thought, and used roads as a "come-on." He was thinking ahead. He could never give all of the roads that he promised, all that were needed, with only $30,000,000. What was wanted was at least another $70,000,-000. The way to get it was to give the folks a sample. He slapped down a good stretch here, another one forty miles away, a third one fifty miles off. Between them were the rickety washboard roads of his predecessors. The folks caught the idea.

76

Huey demonstrated, for all who would be interested, what it meant to serve him well. The Famous Fifteen, who had signed the Round Robin document at the impeachment, cashed in. "Theirs is the earth and the fulness thereof," the newspapers declared. They became judges, high-paid attor neys, patriarchs of great payroll tribes. Whatever their constituents wanted—roads, buildings, free ferries, fish hatcheries —the "Robineers" got for them. Some among the fifteen went into new businesses, raked in enormous profits on state contracts which these firms obtained, lived their more abundant lives in childlike happiness.

Some selections had a peculiar odor for a revolutionary. From a firmly anti-union sawmill town, scene of bloody mass murders of organizers, came an open-shop advocate to be Huey's "labor commissioner." O. K. Allen, the white-haired friend of Winnfield, who had lent him $500, became the highway commissioner, in charge of the spending of the new millions. Maestri of New Orleans took over the Conservation Commission, which was to control more wealth than any other state agency. It was to be heard from, under startling circumstances, later on.

The Governor tipped his hand now and then, went too far for this stage, and lost. In a country district, an oppositionist defeated a Long man for Congress in the Democratic Primary. Huey wouldn't take "No" from the voters. He decided to put off the general election until the next year, and to appoint the loser in the meantime. The district rumbled; Huey threatened to use his soldiers. The district declared that the vote would take place as usual, if it had to go to the polls with guns "as we once did." Huey gave way.

On such occasions, the Governor did not conceal his irritation. The dictator was approaching maturity: snapping, resentful of obstacles or delays. One or two mass meetings addressed him as "Your Truculency." He took on more body-guards, six and seven, Jo Messina, "Polo" Voitier and others of a grimfaced gentry. The protection men snarled at luck-less Louisianians who got in Huey's way, and used their fists sometimes if the path was not cleared quickly enough. For a while Louisiana had laughed, as old men, one-legged men and others chased Huey through hotel lobbies or gave him black eyes as he tried to duck. No such stories, though, were heard in these days. The Governor was still allergic to a fist, but the problem was to reach through to him with one.

As to reporters and photographers, Huey told his men to "let go." That order meant sluggings from behind, breaking of cameras, forced ejections of newsmen from the Gover-nor's vicinity. From this time forward, for most of the press, Huey had only a snarl and a swear. Sometimes there was method in his malice. At public gatherings he would shake his head, growl and cry that the cameramen could "go slap damn to hell, and get right along out of here now." But not before a few effective shots had been captured for the nation. Huey had his publicity cake and ate it too.

He came to realize that he could not depend on circulars alone. He set up his own newspaper, the *Progress,* and pub-lished it in Mississippi. He said that he could find no press in Louisiana; the opposition claimed that the location took care of the libel laws. He hired a number of New Orleans newspapermen, doubled their salaries, and told them to go to work on his enemies. The stratosphere was the limit. The *Progress* occupies a unique niche in American journalism. It was probably the most cheerfully venomous regular publica-tion in the nation. It could hold up its head in competition with any anti-Semitic publications that have appeared in New York, with some of the "Rum, Romanism and Rebellion" sheets. Allegations of loathsome diseases, insanity, Negro blood, financial-criminal activities and assorted social indecencies were tossed with gusto at any and all who were on Huey's list. The *Progress* was the journalistic counterpart of the less-elevated aspects of Huey's speeches—undependable, gutter low in its ethics, and howlingly popular. The newspaper needed little more than an editorial staff. State police and highway men and trucks were the circulation department. As for financing, that was simple; everybody in the state employ elected to take the paper, "voluntarily."

Louisiana had a brief peace while the opposition kept quiet and the machine men worked happily at that huge bond issue. Huey was a national figure, an exotic of challenging mien and behavior. Of course, he was only a local phenomenon, and he wouldn't last long, most persons assured themselves. Meanwhile, they read every few days about him and his stunts. About this time he adopted his front-page name, Kingfish. He was conferring one day with Conservation Commissioner Bob Maestri. A group of underlings was whooping it up, in the same office, at a crap game or, perhaps, a discussion of affairs of state. Huey reared up, spat out some mellow oaths, and ended: "Kingfish of the Lodge, speaking." On another occasion, a bondholder at a highway bond sale observed that the commission, not the Governor, was responsible for such matters. Huey replied that he was taking part, in any event. "For the present, just call me Kingfish, gentlemen." Originally, Huey admitted, he adopted the designation when he sat around the radio with the boys, in those early days when nobody in Baton Rouge would have anything to do with him. Kingfish, of course, is the smooth-talking schemer of schemes in the radio script. "Kingfish of

79

the Mystic Knights of the Sea . . ." Huey loved the title, and he rolled the words around.

His assumption of the name was as unorthodox as the man himself. For another politician, it might have meant laughter into oblivion. But there was wisdom in this indiscretion. Daring in minstrel's silk, shufflin', talkin' yo' alls, wasn't quite so daring. Dictatorship with a deprecating smile might be more palatable than the article with a sneer. Huey was grooming himself for a national audience as a kind of Southern Will Rogers, a homely philosopher-guide, who talked of the Bible, country life, the eternal truths. Accordingly he took up a one-man crusade in favor of potlikker, the "heavenly remains" after greens, turnips and salt pork had been boiled together. "The poor folks' staple—food of the gods," he sighed, as he was photographed in kitchens, showing America the way back to the farm for a better cuisine. The natural country humor, to which he had previously given but limited play in his breathless progress, came forward, some of it naturally, some of it by design. Huey the Kingfish was finding that he could hit the newspapers more often with this rôle than with the most earnest of speeches. He was ever one to learn. He hated the newspapers, but he was making them play his game. He started a national controversy between dunkers and crumblers of cornpone, inviting other governors and Emily Post to join the debate. She issued a Solomon-like edict: "When in Rome, do as the Romans do."

Many Americans first heard of him as Huey of the green pajamas. He had a habit of conducting official business in his sleeping garments, rolling back, walking barefoot over his bedroom floor, scratching himself as his callers moved in and out. He was at his hotel in the Carnival season when a German cruiser steamed into New Orleans for the holiday.

The commander arrived at the suite, and Bodyguard Jo Messina grunted as Major-Domo Weiss ushered in the distinguished visitor. Huey looked up as the door opened, inserted toes in blue slippers, tossed on a gay dressing gown, and stumbled forward to shake hands. An international incident was created. The Republic of Germany (dead days, if not dear) had been insulted, and its representative stalked out. Huey called a friend: "There's a hell of a note over here; looks like war between Germany and Louisiana."

The Kingfish agreed to pay a call on the commander as a gesture of apology. He borrowed pin-striped pants from Weiss, boiled shirt from a waiter, coat from a preacher; located, somewhere, a collar "so high I had to stand on a stool to spit over it." No silk hat was available—a gray fedora had to do. Huey, warming up to the situation, typed out his idea of the first page of an adequate news story on the subject for one of his few local reporter friends. There was a hitch. Huey had to apologize to the hill people about them silk pajamas. He usually didn't wear such things, he lied to them. But a political friend had spent a lot of money on them, and he didn't want to hurt nobody's feelings; that was all. Baton Rouge papers recalled that Huey had once received a delegation minus his B.V.D.s. His Excellency was not a man of minor delicacies.

The road program was thinning out, and the time was at hand for his second regular legislative session. Huey threw forth new ideas: a $68,000,000 highway bond issue; $5,000,000 for a skyscraper State Capitol, and money to improve New Orleans' port rating, thus providing additional jobs on the Dock Board, the state agency in New Orleans. All of it would be financed by another three-cent gasoline tax, to be added to the two-cent tax he had already levied.

The opposition termed the plan a $100,000,000 boodle. A long wrangle resulted. The hostile lieutenant-governor, Dr. Cyr, presiding over the Senate, permitted a sit-down strike, and, in spite of all the buying of legislators that Huey could manage, the plan failed. A lot depended on that $100,000,000 issue; Huey's future, among other things. Action was demanded.

He acted by announcing himself for the United States Senate. He would have one platform: the same state improvement program. If he won, he would take it to mean that the voters wanted to "complete the work" and would call a special session to approve the bond issue. If he lost, he would resign as Governor. But, when elected to Congress, he would not begin serving until his gubernatorial term ended a year and a half hence, so that the "tooth doctor" Cyr could not step up. As to the propriety of leaving the seat vacant in Washington, why, it was vacant now, had been ever since the incumbent assumed it.

He took time out to attempt strangulation of New Orleans, for he was really enraged at the old witch this time. The Ring had helped kill his bond issue. He ordered the city's assessment rolls held up in Baton Rouge, delaying all tax collections. He told the banks to hold off loans and call in millions in outstanding ones. They did what they were told; they knew what the bank examiner could do. Huey announced that the examiner had found millions of loans that appeared "illegal and unjustified." The city's breath came fast, but it managed to survive. Wealthy Orleanians underwrote loans from New York banks. The New York *Times* commented that if "anybody of any probity" had made Huey's charges, runs would have started in New Orleans. But everybody knew Huey.

The campaign saw new vote-luring tactics. Huey invested

in soundtrucks at a cost of $60,000. He was described as the first to make full use of this political device. He organized crews of advance men who drummed up crowds with music, had everything ready when he arrived with another machine, and then went on ahead to the next town. He hired personable young men who went about giving water and lollypops to babies who did not appreciate oratory; sometimes the young men took the babies to the side and minded them while mother, and the crowd, listened without interruption. Other new twists appeared. Squads of highway surveyors covered the country landscape with tripods and flags to show where roads were to be cut "any day now." If a native asked that a route be shifted a bit so as to run through his property, that was O.K., mister. After election, the flags fluttered prettily; ornamental little things, anyway. A newspaper discovered that convicts at the state prison were working for Huey, painting his face on tire covers.

His opponent was seventy-year-old Joseph Ransdell, Congressman for thirty-two years, conservative, goateed, with the force of a baby's rattle against Huey's steamroller. The Kingfish called him "Feather Duster" and "Old Trashy Mouth," and cried: "If you've got to have whiskers, we'll raise 'em for you."

Things looked well for the machine. But suddenly Huey was in a tangle, one of the worst of his life. With the vote less than a week away, he faced charges of scandal, kidnaping, perhaps murder. Back of it was his former secretary, Alice Lee Grosjean, whom he had elevated to secretary of state. (She was eventually to become supervisor of accounts, collector of revenue and Governor for a day or two.) Alice was a cuddly brunette in her mid-twenties who "talked freely and said nothing." Her former husband, James Terrell, and her uncle, Sam Irby, chose this time to say embarrassing things. The state's attorney-general called a special grand jury to inquire into charges by Irby against the Highway Commission which echoed other accusations that had been brought to attention at the legislative session. Irby told New Orleans reporters that he was flying to Shreveport to file suit against Huey and O. K. Allen for "slander," for breaking up Irby's home. Terrell chimed in; he was a-suing too, against "the person responsible for breaking up my home."

Arrived in Shreveport, they went to a hotel. That night they were wakened by sounds at their door, and called local police. The locals found that the men were state police, and the locals "got" when told to "get." Irby and Terrell were taken off by a cousin and brother-in-law of Huey's, and others, for "questioning." They disappeared without trace. The most lurid chase in Louisiana's modern history was on. Hundreds of Louisianians turned detective, spread fantastic stories of deaths in a dungeon, tortures to force false statements. Hard-pressed, Huey treated the matter alternately as a joke and a mystery to him. He made conflicting statements, produced an undelivered telegram, assertedly from one of the men to the man's mother. But there was a mistake in her name. As his career hung in the balance, Huey was summoned to Federal court in habeas corpus proceedings.

On the Sunday before the Tuesday election, Huey went on the radio from his hotel room. Without warning, he produced a man—"Sam Irby." A voice declared that its owner, Irby, had asked to be taken into protective custody. He had found $2500 under his pillow in Shreveport, and had been afraid to remain alone with it, not knowing what he was supposed to do for it! Huey permitted reporters a glimpse at a frightened-looking individual, who was then whisked away by bodyguards, one of them waving a gun. Huey had turned near-tragedy for himself into opera bouffe.

Louisiana, laughing, voted Huey in. Irby later declared that he had been kidnaped, chained for a time to a tree on Grand Isle, former pirates' retreat in the Gulf, and covered with a gun that night of the broadcast.

Huey had his wish. He was Senator-elect, but he refused to go to Washington and allow Dr. Cyr to become Governor. He would wait; he was used to waiting. He had been a prisoner in his own state for all of his term, having feared to give Cyr a chance, even for a day. But now Cyr took the matter out of his hands. The dentist went to a clerk and took the oath as Governor, declaring that Huey had vacated the office when he was chosen Senator. Huey zinged to Baton Rouge from New Orleans. Out came the National Guard, the state police, highway police. Motorized troops circled Baton Rouge, the mansion, the Governor's office and Alice Lee Grosjean. Cyr would have to present his papers to Alice as secretary of state. The dentist could get nowhere, and subsided. But Huey at last had a handle on him. So Cyr has taken the oath as Governor? Well, he ain't lieutenant-governor any longer. That leaves that job open. Huey summoned the President pro tempore of the Senate, the next officer in line, made him lieutenant-governor, and prepared to leave Louisiana in his hands as acting governor.

The nation did its part to make Cyr ridiculous. In Louisiana and in other states, clerks, messenger boys and the unemployed swore themselves in before notaries as Governor of Louisiana. In some towns the governor-swearing fee was cut. Governor Long declined an invitation to an out-of-state football game. "The other governors might get miffed," he explained. The courts upheld Huey; and Cyr was left, as the cartoonists drew him, suspended in mid-air, between the two positions and unable to get into either one.

Soon Huey was casually letting the state know who its

next Governor would be. He sent O. K. Allen, his political yard boy, to Texas on an errand, remarking that since he, Huey, couldn't go, he was sending the next best thing, the Governor-to-Be. The occasion was Huey's first overt venture toward a national program, his "Drop a Crop" plan. The year 1931 saw cotton down to five cents a bale. The Hoover Administration had nothing to suggest about the tragic surplus, so Huey volunteered a thought. "Back to the Bible," he told the country. He cited Moses' Sabbatical system, according to which the earth was to lie idle every seven years. If it was good enough for the Lord, it was good enough for America. Huey's plan was on the nation's lips. A widely attended convention in New Orleans approved it. But everything depended on Texas, the major cotton producer.

Texas, despite Allen's visit, didn't move as Huey wished. Governor Sterling drawled that it was a little more democratic than Louisiana. Huey retorted that Sterling was a dirty millionaire who had made secret agreements with the brokers to kill the idea. The Texas Legislature, added the Kingfish, was being "blandished with wine, women and money . . . paid off like a slot machine." Texas paid its compliments to "the arrogant jackass who brays from Louisiana . . . ignoramus, buffoon, meddler and liar, who has the impudence and arrogance to dictate to the people of Texas." The plan died. Had Huey handled himself differently in this controversy, he might have become the savior of the South's cotton industry. His Truculency might have made himself His Excellency, the President of the United States, on this issue alone.

Shortly afterward Huey spoke a new piece: "I'm leaving state politics for good. I've done all I can for Louisiana. Now I want to help the rest of the country." The Calvin Coolidges came to Louisiana, and Huey was photographed

86

with them. He volunteered a caption: "The ex-President of the United States, and the future one." Coolidge managed to ask a question: "What part of Louisiana are you from?" "I'm a hillbilly, like you. Say, are the Hoovers good housekeepers?" The startled Coolidge surmised that they were. Huey explained:

"When I was elected here, I had to tear the mansion down. It started a hell of a row. I don't want to have to tear down the White House."

IV

AMERICA, HERE I COME

THE Kingfish had his sales talk ready by the time he arrived at Washington in January, 1932. It was the part in which the nation was to know him for three and a half years of evangelism, bad-boy shenanigans and cutting attacks on the social evils of the day. He was to be the loud-mouthed advocate of share-the-wealth, beckoning the nation to a patented promised land of guaranteed yearly income, home ownership, radio and refrigerator. What had been a minor note in his appeal to Louisiana now evolved into his refrain to the nation. The principle of his "draw" was the same in both cases: a basket load of benefits held out to the folks, and a political floor show on the side.

At the same time Huey was presenting his own version of dictatorship for Americans to inspect. In Louisiana he was installing a progressively bolder totalitarian state, whose colors grew darker month by month. It is a commentary upon democracy and upon the American people, perhaps, that despite this latter sample, millions turned toward the Kingfish's program for them. What he was saying sounded so loud that they seemed not to heed what he was doing.

He was the economic seer and Bible lover, that first morning in Washington, as shaving lather dropped over his pajama collar and the flashlights popped. "Redistribute your wealth —it's all there in God's book. Follow the Lord . . . but we don't seem to be doing it." Soon afterward he was breaking

Senate customs into bits. He did not present himself with his colleague and former friend, "Couzain Ed" Broussard. He ignored the regulation against smoking, using the clerk's desk as a depository for his cigar while he took the oath, then puffing away again as he finished. He romped over the place, massaged the backs of Norris and Borah with the reassuring explanation that they were his ideals. He gazed over Washington as if he thought it was Louisiana; before long he was behaving as if indeed it were.

He was everything that a freshman Senator was not expected to be. He rampaged, he roared, he expressed views on everything, including subjects about which it was quickly shown that he knew nothing. That didn't faze Huey; he talked on the same subject the next time it came up again, perhaps on the other side. He jumped upon the power trust. He also jumped upon a seamen's aid bill. Before two months were over, he had placed share-the-wealth before the nation in his first concrete proposals on the subject. They changed considerably as time went on, but originally he asked for limitation of individual fortunes to $100,000,000, and a division of the rest among all of the folks.

"Rockefeller and Morgan would sleep much safer tonight if they had $100,000,000 each under their pillow case, instead of a billion or two," he thumped his desk. Share-the-wealth was the answer to Communism, not Communism, as some claimed. And then, to make sure that no one took him for one of those Red fellows, he informed the country: "I would not take a single luxury away—fish ponds for fishing, estates for following the hounds."

His resolution met with little success, but he came back again with his address, *Doom of America's Dream,* hailed by wealth-sharers as their gospel. He lashed out at the "hoarders of wealth" who "have destroyed humanity by millions"; at

89

the advances of science that have meant only "starvation and pestilence" when they should have meant shorter hours, more food, more leisure. What authorities could he cite? Thomas Jefferson, Daniel Webster, Theodore Roosevelt, Andrew Jackson, William Jennings Bryan and God Almighty. He subsided, but he was on the floor once more when the tax bills were under consideration. As amendments he offered a limitation of $1,000,000 a year on earned incomes; a 65-per-cent surtax on incomes over $2,000,000; a 65-per-cent levy on fortunes over $20,000,000, and a 100-per-cent inheritance tax on those over $5,000,000. He had a new modification almost every day.

The Kingfish was learning, picking up thoughts from everywhere. Until this time Huey had been depending on Senator Harper's old figures to convince his listeners. He had not changed them in fifteen years. He knew little or nothing of economics, though he could handle lesser financial problems as well as the next political manipulator. Sociology, economic history . . . he had never had time to bother much about them, or to catch up on his reading. He had received what was approximately the equivalent of two years of college, and he had halted only a little distance past Ridpath. He talked one day with a Washington correspondent who cited a number of recent volumes on America's politico-economic status. The correspondent was amazed when Huey asked "if they got many books on that line." He mentioned some. Huey took down the titles avidly, pulled out a roll of bills, and sent out one of his bodyguards to get a copy of each. Shortly afterward the informed in the press gallery noticed that Huey was embellishing his talks with new statistics, new quotations.

Used to his own way, Huey became more and more enraged when the Democratic leader, Senator Robinson, looked

"JUST SAY I'M *SUI GENERIS*, AND LET IT GO AT THAT"

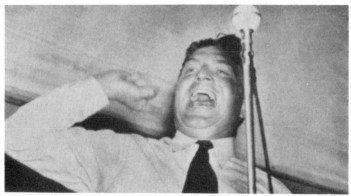

AIR CONDITIONING

TOP: Rev. Gerald L. K. Smith; CENTER: The Kingfish — Earl K. Long;
BASE: James A. Noe.

"A WAND'RING MINSTREL, I ..."

"HAPPY DAYS!"

STANDING, L. TO R., Mayor Maestri, Seymour Weiss, B. J. Crump, Gov. Leche.
(*April 22, 1937.*) SEATED: Mrs. Richard W. Leche, Dr. Stella Leche.

BREAD AND CIRCUSES
Life at L. S. U. before the crash.—Air-conditioned cage with murals for
Mike the Tiger, team mascot; stadium accommodations for the student
overflow.

SHORT ARM OF THE LAW

Attorney-General Frank Murphy, on arrival at Shushan Airport, New Orleans, admires the cut of Gov. Leche's coat. (*May 28, 1939.*)

MAESTRI SAT GLUM . . .

F. D. R., Gov. Leche, Mayor Maestri tour the Crescent City in the gravy days.—Ill at ease, Maestri was reported as addressing only one question (at lunch) to the President: "*How do you like them ersters?*"

RETIRING GOVERNOR

Conference at the sickbed of Richard W. Leche. (*June 23, 1939.*) LEFT, Earl
K. Long, Lieutenant-Governor; CENTER, Mayor Maestri. *"Just to pay respects,"* was their comment.

STRAIN AND STRESS

Allen J. Ellender, U. S. Senator-Elect, at left, and Seymour Weiss get together at a Democratic National Convention.

Wide Wo

"I DREAMT THAT I DWELT..."

ABOVE, George A. Caldwell's home, which had gold toilet fixtures. CENTER, A. L. Shushan's home on the St. Tammany "Gold Coast." BELOW, Unfinished castle of former Conservation Commissioner William Rankin, where the sheriff got ahead of the contractor.

on his proposals without sympathy. He baited Robinson: "What's a man going to do with more than $1,000,000? All I'm advocating is what the Lord gave Moses." Robinson replied stiffly that Huey's ideas were little less than confiscation of wealth. That was all that Huey wanted. Using his windmill gestures, he advanced on Robinson. Why, the Democratic leader was practically in bed with Herbert Hoover. Huey wanted Robinson for Vice-President—on the Republican ticket. The nation was heading toward hell. One party smelled as bad as the other. The Democrats must be rid of men like this Robinson. And then, as the Senators jumped, he let them know that here they had a new phenomenon to deal with. He resorted to a technique which he had perfected in Louisiana. Out came a reference book, a list of the corporations whose business was handled by Robinson.

"The Senator's law firm represents every nefarious interest on the living face of the globe. . . . You don't have to eat a whole beef to know if it's tainted. . . . When a man comes into the Senate without enough clients to make a corporal's guard, and winds up representing every big corporate interest, if that don't mean something, what does?" These were the things that Senators never said about one another. They were like the things that candidates in Louisiana had never said about one another, before Huey. Well, brothers, get ready to hear them from now on. The ring-tailed snorter from Winn was a-changing matters around this place.

Eyes blazing, Huey made the headlines by resigning from all the committees to which he had been appointed by the Democratic leadership. This did not matter much; the assignments had been minor ones, interoceanic canals and such.

Piquing the nation's interest more each week, Huey clowned, arranged for the Senate restaurant to serve potlikker, made his name remembered by little daily deeds of flamboyance. He imported a Roosevelt Hotel bartender to New York as a "guest mixologist," to show how real gin fizzes were made. He entered bars, ordered doors locked, invited everybody there to be his guest, and sang hillbilly songs, then asked them all to visit him at the mansion in Baton Rouge, or at the White House later. If O. K. Allen was in, tell 'm Huey sent you, boys. At the Waldorf-Astoria, as Davis reported it, he demanded a Waldorf sandwich, but decided that Oscar had forgotten the right method of preparation and took him into the kitchen to supervise the project. A bulletin to the world: "From now on, the Waldorf sandwich will figure on the menu as in days of yore."

Louisiana could not get along without him; he had to move back and forth. Allen had gone in as Governor, and with him John Fournet, of the "Bloody Monday" riot, as lieutenant-governor. Huey had made a major shift. All of his political life had been devoted to a cursing scorn of the Regular Ring of New Orleans, "the whore-masters, thieves and tilltappers." Now he made a deal with them and became their bedmate for a period of several years. Brother Earl wanted Huey to back him for lieutenant-governor, and was sorely hurt when Huey refused. Earl joined the opposition, ran against Fournet, and called Huey a yellow-bellied coward, a crook and bribetaker, and threatened to beat hell out of his brother at the first opportunity. The family joined Earl, accusing Huey of ingratitude. Life was never a pacific matter for Huey.

The great bond issue had gone through, but now the treasury was bare again. Government à la Long, though it was giving Louisiana benefits that had never been received in the past, was also costing as government had not cost in the past. In a year Huey spent as much as Parker had used for his full four years. Huey was inclined to blame that on the rest of the country: "Except for being a part of the United States, Louisiana would never know a depression." The solution, at any rate, was more public works and more taxes. Soft drinks, insurance premiums, electricity, corporate capitalization and, as before, gasoline, were chosen for the burden. The opposition called taxpayers' protest meetings, charged that Louisiana had "the worst and most expensive government in the country," and demanded economy. Huey didn't have to go to the hustings this time. He manufactured his citizens' rally overnight—the personnel of the Ring payroll and the state payroll combined. Banners proclaimed the message: "We Cannot Close Our Schools." "Don't Listen to the Mugwumps."

The Legislature knew which set of citizens to heed. Huey had "grown me a new crop" of members. He needed hardly to bend over to harvest it.

He bothered less about appearances than ever. A United States Senator, he had no right to be anywhere on the floor at Baton Rouge; but he was unchallenged as he acted as overseer. When a voice vote was called, he shouted "Aye" or "No" like any legislator, except that he was louder. When a slow-minded fellow did not understand an order and fumbled between green and red buttons, Huey rushed to his desk, pressed for him, and yelled, "This man votes 'Yes.' "

Before a crowd, the Kingfish's brass-knucks domination of his Governor was made clear. Huey was explaining new measures. "Oscar," he called out, "go get me those goddamned bills." Allen, intent or perhaps chagrined, made no answer. Huey blasted: "Goddamn you, Oscar, don't you stall around with me. I made you and I kin break you. You get those goddamned bills, do you hear me, and get 'em quick." Oscar got 'em quick. Usually, when Huey was in town, poor "O.K." couldn't even use his own office. Huey walked in and told Oscar to wait outside. One critic said that Oscar did "just as well as anybody's office boy . . . except that he does it quicker and better." One of Huey's brothers declared that Huey made his Governor sign an undated resignation, like other political retainers. Oscar cried, but he signed. He signed everything. Louisiana's favorite story about Oscar was that a strong wind blew a leaf through a window on to his desk, and that he automatically affixed his signature.

Another National Convention arrived. Huey repeated his act of 1928, had the State Democratic Committee name the delegates. The opposition recalled that at the last National Convention there were indications that the party disapproved this method and might seat other delegates if they were chosen by state convention plan. The antis held their own convention. Huey, taking no chances, formed a rump convention of his own, manipulated a travesty. The payroll paraded with banners, "We Want Our Swag." The platform was a pledge to bring back gin fizzes. The giggling crew called itself "fearless, independent and unterrified voters." It was an unsavory burlesque, coming with particular ill grace from its source.

Huey was foresighted enough to tie in with Roosevelt. The opposition, largely conservative, veered away from the leading candidate. Huey demonstrated his skill in shifting his tactics when he fought for his delegation at the convention. At one point he shouted: "The Democratic Party in Louisiana? *I'm* the Democratic Party in Louisiana!" An enraged partisan gave a piercing cry to the front row: "Bite 'em on the leg!" Then Huey delivered an address which many agreed was a masterly, restrained presentation. Whatever the reasons, he won. When the convention ended, it was agreed that Huey was one of the half-dozen men most important in winning the nomination for Roosevelt.

Farley has declared that Huey itched to "steal the national spotlight" from Roosevelt in the campaign. "There is no doubt on earth that, in the back of his mind, he was already looking forward to the day when he would be a candidate for the Presidency." He wanted a special train, equipped with loud speakers, to cover all forty-eight states, "promising immediate cash payment of the bonus." He didn't ask how Roosevelt felt about that. Huey was curtailed, but Farley admitted that his efforts were astoundingly effective. He did particularly well in the bigger cities. His messages, originally directed at country audiences, had growing appeal for the urban middle and lower-middle classes.

Feeling his strength, Huey invaded Arkansas on a whirlwind soundtruck tour on behalf of Senator Hattie Caraway. Hattie was given a meager chance against six men; nobody bothered much about her until Huey appeared. It was a crusade to "take the feet of six bullies off the neck of one lone, little, defenseless woman," and a "widow woman" at that. In a hellraising, riproaring, steaming campaign that gave the rest of the country a taste of Huey's perfected methods, he won for Hattie, and for himself. He had a new share-the-wealth recruit in the Senate, new prestige for himself, and a warning sign on display for Senators who opposed him. "Watch out; I'll be in your state next; and where will you be when I tell the folks what you stand for?"

Huey put in one of his faithfuls, John Overton, in place of "Couzain Ed" Broussard. But the election had annoying aftermaths. An Honest Election League was formed; and it petitioned Congress for an investigation, charging widespread irregularities. Huey fretted: "Every time I beat them in an election, they get themselves a new league." But some significant facts had come to light. In St. Bernard Parish, outside New Orleans, 3176 persons were recorded as having voted for Overton, 13 for Broussard. The census showed 2500 whites over twenty years of age. Also, state workers generally had been forced to contribute a flat ten per cent of their pay for the campaign.

A Congressional hearing was held. A wild succession of episodes followed, with frenzied testimony, defiance of the Senatorial authority by Huey and his puppets, and blank confessions of fraud. The payroll attended en masse to boo, shout and laugh in a circus atmosphere. Huey ordered witnesses not to answer, jibed at the counsel, jeered at the chairman. Brothers Earl and Julius appeared against Huey. They told of transfers of heavy rolls of bills to Huey from the corporations, in their presence; one roll so large that when he stuck it in a rear pocket it nearly took the pants off. (A possible stretching of the truth, as well.) A procession of "dummies" followed. The machine had turned to "dummy candidates" to make possible some obvious frauds. Under Louisiana law, each local candidate is permitted commissioners to count the votes at the polls. The machine put up men who never intended to run. They submitted their commissioners, withdrew, and those commissioners favored the Long candidates. The Longsters received a preponderance of the poll officials, and benefitted accordingly.

"Dummies" declared that they received their entrance fees from Seymour Weiss, who had been elevated from a mere hotel man to treasurer of the machine; that they had never planned campaigns; in one case, it was noted, a "dummy" appeared at a meeting to speak in behalf of the machine man whom he "opposed." Weiss was asked about the campaign finances. "That's none of your business," he told the committee counsel. He was instructed to reply by the chairman. He was instructed not to reply by Huey. He snapped the same answer, over and over. Once before, during the impeachment, Weiss had given service to Huey by evading questions. Now Weiss went further. He called the committee's attorney a "heel," sneered defiance, told the attorney that he knew better than to "invite me outside." Huey yelled denunciation at witnesses, called the counsel a "second-rate comedian" who should have been in a burlesque house. Both sides lost tempers and judgment, and the hearing went far afield; the record has a strange and violent tone. Months later, even, at a session of the committee in New Orleans, the committee investigator termed Huey "the rat from Louisiana."

In one part of the state, an open-court hearing on the "dummy" question brought admissions by nearly a dozen men that they were "dummies"; that they had had no intention of running. The judge enjoined them from submitting commissioners. But the supreme court reversed him, declaring that the "dummies" fulfilled all of the law's requirements and that the courts therefore had no jurisdiction.

In another section, South Louisiana, Judge B. F. Pavy enjoined the parish committees from accepting commissioners of the "dummies." The machine's attorney-general, Gaston Porterie, ordered that the Judge's injunction be ignored and that the "dummies" be recognized. Judge Pavy ordered the arrest of committeemen for ignoring his injunction. O. K. Allen reprieved the men by telegraphic order. A supreme-court justice, friendly to the machine, issued a writ of review which held up any execution of Judge Pavy's actions. Everybody worked together.

The Senatorial committee was clearly in terror of Huey

and what he might say or do to its members. A Woman's Committee, headed by Hilda Phelps Hammond, worked for years to get action against Overton and Long. It sold heirlooms, dunned business men for contributions, pressed charges of scandals which were later verified in some cases. At last the Senatorial committee reported. The New York *Sun* summed up the matter admirably:

Not since the Emperor of Japan visited the town of Titipu and considered charges against the Lord High Executioner has any public servant been so happily and ingeniously exonerated . . . The committee finds that the election of Senator Overton was accomplished "by the use of fraud, coercion, intimidation and corruption." But it received no probative evidence that Mr. Overton "personally participated in or instigated any fraud." Immortal Pooh-Bah never achieved anything more subtle. The inference is that Mr. Overton has a good title to a seat obtained through fraud, intimidation and corruption.

Huey now showed what a maturing American dictator could do on a regional scale with the banking problem. The years 1932 and 1933 saw financial institutions failing in many sections. Huey kept many from collapsing by forbidding them. The banks were forced to work together; to bail each other out, or face a crackdown by the examiner. In one case Huey heard that a bank faced a run. He appeared as the doors opened, and informed depositors that if they insisted on pulling out their assets, he would do the same thing with the state's money. It had preference, and its claims were more than the bank's full amount of cash on hand. The run stopped. At another point a leading Mississippi bank decided to liquidate, and the state was prepared for a 100-per-cent moratorium. Nervous Mississippians proposed to siphon millions out of the New Orleans banks. This might mean a crash for the whole Mississippi Valley. A delegation of city bankers called on Huey, to propose a Louisiana moratorium. Huey breathed fire. He called a bodyguard: "Jo, keep these bastards here till I come back. Shoot any of them that try to leave. If they get hungry, send for sandwiches." Huey called a Chase Bank official, and a heavy loan staved off disaster in both states.

In February of 1933, Representative Hamilton Fish made charges against a man close to Huey, President Rudolf Hecht of the Hibernia Bank. He cited a recent $1,000,000 RFC loan to shore up the Union Indemnity Company, a politically favored firm which had a state bonding monopoly. The company had failed in any event. Fish asserted that the loan had been used to pay notes held by the Hibernia Bank; that Hecht of the Hibernia had also been a director of the Union Indemnity and chairman of the RFC Advisory Committee; and that Hecht had been in a position to know that the Union Indemnity was in collapsing condition. The charges received national attention, though Fish retracted some of them. This was Friday. Panic in New Orleans, a crash involving all banks, was averted only by the approach of the closing hour. Saturday would bring the blow.

Huey worked through the night, with the RFC and other agencies, and obtained a $20,000,000 loan, due Monday. The imperative need was a Saturday respite. What did that day, February 4, mean in history? Huey called everybody he knew, even those "newspaper skunks." February 4 appeared to have been one of the world's uneventful days. A newspaperman's wife discovered, however, that on February 3, 1917, the United States Government had severed diplomatic relations with Germany. All that couldn't have been accomplished on one day, reasoned Huey; some of it must have hung over. Louisiana woke to a gubernatorial proclamation that Saturday was a legal holiday. Only the German Consul was not in on the secret.

Huey carried his animus toward the press to a new point that night. The newspapers had agreed to print nothing to heighten the situation. But the early editions of the *Times Picayune* carried a few facts that made Huey pound the sofa. He called the adjutant-general of the National Guard: "March down to that goddamn paper with a bunch of your boys. Break every machine they got. Fix 'em so they won't come out again in a hurry." Weiss secretly asked the adjutant to hold up. Huey eventually and grudgingly agreed to "let them fellows alone."

In Washington the Kingfish grew tougher, became a scandal, a terror to his milder and less gifted colleagues. He pulled skeletons out of closets and swung them high in the air for all to see. He mimicked the speech and walk of those he didn't like, goading the hapless ones while the galleries howled. Most of the Senators knew they were no match for Huey. The rules were out the window. One day Huey sent out and bought two shining new Bibles for the guidance of the good brothers. They needed it, he asserted. Again, he so enraged the elderly Carter Glass that Glass charged at him to thrash him. Friends intervened. But Glass caught back. After Huey had filibustered against the Glass Banking Bill, he went to New York on a visit. Glass disclosed that the crusader had called on the chairman of the board of the Chase National Bank. That official, summoned before a committee, said he had known Huey in Louisiana and had performed "some favors" for him. Glass insisted that the Chase Bank was trying to knife his bill, using Huey as a willing agent. Huey tried to laugh it off.

Huey declared war on Franklin Roosevelt. For a time he

had tied close to the New Deal, praising Roosevelt, without marked personal modesty, by declaring: "When I'm satisfied with a man, you know he's got something." But Huey was ambitious, obviously a dangerous man. He was attacking New Deal measures when he wasn't claiming Roosevelt as a share-the-wealth recruit. On the other hand, Huey hadn't received the patronage he asked; and income-tax inquiries, originally brought during the Hoover régime against his men, had not been dropped. There were many reasons for the break, but mutual incompatibility was probably a major one. Farley revealed recently that Huey, at one conference with Roosevelt, kept his hat on as a deliberately insulting gesture.

Huey discovered that the President was worse than Hoover. Hoover was a hoot owl. Roosevelt was a scrooch owl. "A hoot owl bangs into the roost and knocks the hen clean off, and catches her while she's falling. But a scrooch owl slips into the roost and scrooches up to the hen and talks softly to her. And the hen just falls in love with him, and the first thing you know, *there ain't no hen.*" Curling his lip, he called his late friend other names: "Prince Franklin, Knight of the *Nourmahal,* enjoying himself on that $5,-000,000 yacht, with Vincent Astor and royalty, while the farmers starve. Hooray for the President! Let's send him off again."

Striking back, Farley gave the Federal patronage to Sullivan, Huey's one-time ally, now his bitter enemy. The Regular Ring quit Huey, charging that he was trying to grab off all the local offices as well as the state jobs. A city election was approaching, and the Regulars were prepared to fight Huey again. The Regulars tied in with the New Deal; though not, so far as could be discovered, for humanitarian purposes. The Administration in Washington was reportedly anxious to "get Long." Some of Huey's earliest enemies, the most conservative of corporation agents, planters and semifeudal industrialists, became Louisiana New Dealers. Huey charged that the Rooseveltians were "putting their approval on the New Orleans vice ring as safeguards of the people."

The dictatorship tried new strong-arm tactics in Louisiana. The Sixth District, which included Baton Rouge, had been termed "the virgin district, the only one Huey had never been able to rape." Now Huey tried rape. The Congressman, Bolivar Kemp, died. Huey knew that he could not elect a candidate of his own, so he decided to get a Congressman by strategy in spite of the electorate. Under the law, the Governor must call an election in circumstances such as these. Huey would not let "O.K." issue the call. Weeks passed. Thousands of petitions went to Allen, unheeded. A mass meeting was announced, with an ultimatum. Unless the call came by a certain date, a "citizens' election" would be held. On the day before the scheduled meeting, Allen called the general election—one week hence. The Long majority of the district committee, possibly by coincidence, was in New Orleans that day and, learning of Allen's action, possibly by reading a newspaper, it held a meeting then and there, outside the district. It resolved that, since there was so little time before the general election, it would make everything easy for everybody by doing away with the Democratic Primary and declaring the widow of the Congressman to be the nominee.

A district newspaper urged its readers: "If ever there was justification for shot-gun government in Louisiana, *that time is now*." The district fought back. Long men delivered the ballots secretly. Crowds seized the paraphernalia and burned it in public. Shots were fired. "Election day" came. One judge enjoined the poll commissioners in his area, and armed his own deputies—one of them his aged father, a Civil War veteran—to see that no vote was held. Men went to polling places, destroyed the ballots and surrendered themselves to police. In one town a trash can displayed a sign, "Deposit ballots here." About one-eleventh of the voters went to the polls. The "citizens' election" followed. Congress threw out both "Congressmen," and a new election had to be called. This time the opposition won. But the incident, by enraging Huey, helped bring the final excesses of the machine.

In the East, Huey suffered a horrendous mishap. He was mowed down in a latrine, and America laughed—the wrong way this time. He appeared with a party at the Sands Point Bath Club on Long Island. For some reason, no bodyguards were present. Huey's behavior went back to his Singing Fool days. He picked up asparagus tips and other handy edibles from plates of other guests, and made a remark to one of the women at another table which no Southern gentleman, not excluding a Senator, would make. Some thought this latter incident had a connection with what followed, but most indications were that the washroom episode was a separate one. Huey, at any rate, entered the lavatory and found another patron ahead of him. Always the innovator, he stood back, took aim through the legs of the other, but missed his goal. A minute or so later the Kingfish emerged, practically swimming in his own blood from a gash over his eye.

The story could not be suppressed. It was the news of the week in every paper in America, except perhaps the *Progress*. The nation sought to bestow credit. Scores denied having struck the blow, but said that they would not mind having done it. Funds were collected for a medal. Cartoons of the "Louisiana Crawfish" appeared. Huey, enraged, tried to dodge the prying press and public, while bodyguards punched right and left. Huey fled across country, secluding himself en route. Finally he said that it had been Wall Street, four or five of its agents, who had trapped him; one had struck him with "a knife, or something sharp." Addressing a veterans' convention, a group with which he had become a favorite, Huey inflamed such feelings against the newspapers that a body of simple-minded delegates formed a gang that moved on the reporters. Later, rushing back through a train, Huey figured in some more annoying if irrelevant publicity. A conductor said that Huey tossed him into the laps of two nuns.

Huey's sagging prestige dropped lower. In New Orleans, the Regulars outwitted Huey. They charged that the state-appointed registrar of voters was illegally scratching thousands of good Ring men, and a city judge took the books from the registrar. They were put in a safe place—the condemned row of a parish prison. Huey gathered his own city forces and put out a ticket for mayor. Times had changed since New Orleans had last spurned him; he had given her funds and other assistance during his alliance with the Ring; now she had another chance to do the right thing for him. But Huey's man came third, and the Regulars' mayor, T. Semmes Walmsley, went in.

A dictator cannot lose face. Huey barnstormed the state, alarmed and unhappy. Audiences, for once, were cold. Huey told one group that he was "broke." In one town Huey was warned not to talk against Roosevelt. He didn't. In another he was interrupted by cries of "Tell us about Sands Point!" In Alexandria stink bombs and rotten eggs were pelted at him. His name was torn off bridges, his *Progress* burned in bonfires. In one parish a $10,000 reward was offered to anyone who would bring the Kingfish alive into its confines.

But in many other places Huey told his story to men and women who believed it, who are still convinced that "Wall Street mauled Huey."

Mayor Walmsley called him a "yellow coward" and went to Washington to thrash him. The entranced press reported every preliminary move of the two men. Walmsley took up a stand in the lobby of Huey's hotel. Huey ate in his rooms, scurried in and out with bodyguards fore and aft. Walmsley left disappointed. Eddie Dowling announced that he thought Huey just the comedian for a new Broadway extravaganza. He promised to furnish theater guards to protect Huey against Walmsley. The Louisiana opposition was certain that at last Huey was a gone goose. Part of Washington, too, was happy.

Then, as on other occasions, Huey hit back. He gained back all that he had lost. He showed Louisiana and America what one-man rule really could be. He took over Louisiana in an iron fist, extending his control to an extent that the most pessimistic oppositionist had not thought possible under the Constitution.

He crashed down upon the state with a series of special legislative sessions that became a national wonder. In one year his political servants were summoned seven times to Baton Rouge to adopt measures that turned Louisiana into Huey's Reich. He started with more benefits, more show. He tossed forth a "debt moratorium" law, which permitted partial payment of obligations by harassed farmers and others, under agreements supervised by the Banking Department. With it came tax exemption to the individual homeowner on parish and state property taxes, to a promised $2000 a year. (Actually, this was only $1000 until 1939.) Both were powerful assurances to the folks that he was still with them. But this wasn't all that Huey offered. He eliminated the one-dollar poll tax, which had kept tens of thousands from voting. To make up for losses through the property exemption, he sponsored the state's first income tax; he reduced the cost of automobile license plates on less expensive machines; he placed a receipts tax on public utilities; and, crowning touch, he ordered a two-per-cent tax on receipts of newspapers of 20,000 or more circulation—namely, those of New Orleans. "We'll tax 'em for each lie " he said, regarding the last clause.

At the same time he moved to crush all opposition, all opportunity to oppose in future. No more Sixth District "citizens' elections," no more defiance from New Orleans. Each of the special sessions tightened the grip.

Huey's Legislature gave Huey's Governor final unimpeded power to call out the militia at will, without the possibility of court interference, to take over even city governments if so desired. To clamp iron control on the registration records, a law forbade the courts to take any jurisdiction over this office; even an "accidental" hostile judge could do nothing now. Custody over the ballot boxes went from the local sheriffs to state-controlled election supervisors. The next step put Huey or his proxies in full charge of the counting of the ballots. The older system by which the local candidates presented their commissioners was ended. Hereafter the state-ruled election supervisors named every commissioner.

The same election supervisors received the power to appoint an unlimited number of "special deputies" to serve at the polls—and to force the local communities to reimburse them at $5 a day. As the opposition put it, a city or parish would now pay to have an election stolen for it.

The Governor won authority to increase the personnel of

the state police whenever he wanted, to any limit he wanted, out of almost limitless funds. The state police became secret police, Huey's Gestapo. The number of unknown agents increased, and "incidents" not much different from the Irby-Terrell kidnaping became frequent. The machine had its own storm troopers now, with and without uniforms.

The attorney-general received broadened power; authority to supersede any district attorney in the state, and in any case. This had obvious potentialities which were sometimes thoroughly realized. The Governor was given undisputed authority to issue reprieves to convicted men, and this power was extended to contempt cases—assurance to Long men that they could defy judges and get away with it.

And now Huey snapped his fingers, and his legislators stripped New Orleans and placed it on the rack. First, he took away the police department from the Ring, threw out the police commissioners by a legislative act that created a new board composed of representatives of universities, business clubs, the political athletic club and other groups. (Leaving out, some noted, the Red Cross, chess club and Methodist Ladies' Aid Society.) Two of the seven city assessors, locally elected officials by tradition and by law, had died. Huey would not let "O.K." call an election. Instead he had him appoint two of Huey's men to the jobs. The other five, the duly elected assessors, refused to recognize them. Huey stomped *them* down. He named his two men as "deputies" of the State Tax Commission, then created five other posts as deputies for the other five districts. Now, let the taxpayers go to these seven new appointees with their assessments; to hell with the seven city assessors. The State Tax Commission formerly had only the power of review in disputed cases. Huey put it in full control, and the state moved in on another phase of local finances and political power. Property holders, large and small, knew that their favors were to be obtained from a new source.

The Governor now had the power, through his stooges, to raise or to lower the assessment on any piece of property in the state—and to make the change retroactive for three years.

All of the other new measures—election control, registration control, new police powers and the rest—were aimed primarily at New Orleans but would be used against other parts of the state as well. Huey could think of nothing else at the moment in the way of laws, but as his session ended he forged another weapon—a legislative investigation into affairs of the city. Another election, for Congressional offices, was not far off, and Huey had decided not to pass up a chance for an effect. Gathering a group of his country legislators, he descended on the wicked city to inquire into its vice, its pay-offs and corruptions.

Here was a hearing unique, probably the most secret "public investigation" ever held. Nobody could attend it. Nobody could come within yards of it. Troops barred the way. Witnesses were hustled in by freight entrances, and hustled out again. The location was no public building, but the high floor of an office structure. Proceedings were given to the world by radio; but speakers were often not identified, were introduced as prostitutes, pimps, bartenders, "international detectives." The military touch was everywhere. Huey came and went with an awesome set of troops, himself in dead center, surrounded front, rear and sides. Crowds gathered in the lobby daily to await the sight, "the tramp-tramp-tramp of the boys with Huey inside." The witnesses told of regular payments to policemen, of City Hall connections with the underworld, of handsome estates maintained by police officials. O. K. Allen, still a Winn boy, announced that New Orleans must be washed of its sin; and he summoned preachers to "the most important meeting in the city's history." Meanwhile, Huey's agents passed word around to the underworld that "everything will be all right" after election day, but that a good turnout by the gambling element would be taken well by the Boss. He'd be running New Orleans direct, before long, see?

Huey and "O.K." mobilized part of the National Guard, proclaimed "partial martial law" over the city, and took over the registration offices, directly across one of the narrowest of city streets from City Hall. Machine guns were placed in the windows, pointing at the Hall. The Ring swore in 400 extra policemen and bought extra tear-gas supplies. A soldier of fortune, former police superintendent, came home from Central America and took command of a force of "picked men," at a friendly hotel, "to act in any capacity needed." Huey called the rest of the Guard from all over the state, quartered the soldiers, with their grenades, machine guns and gas, on the state docks. National journals talked of civil war. But none ensued; Huey had the upper hand, and the city masters knew it. Neither side fired a shot on election day. Huey won the Congressional elections for that district. New Orleans had gone over to him, against the will of the Ringsters, after all this time. The Ring, however, was still in; and Huey decided that the city would still have to suffer.

Simultaneously, another demonstration of broadening dictatorship. The machine riveted its hold on the State Supreme Court by as flagrant an act as it ever succeeded in effecting. By various methods it had achieved a 4-3 majority not long before this. One of the Long judges was up for re-election, opposed by an "anti," Thomas F. Porter. The judge died on the day before election. Louisiana law was unequivocal on the question; the other candidate must be recognized as the Democratic nominee in the general election. The law did not halt Huey. The "anti" must be kept off the bench; the vote must not become 4-3 for the other side. The district committee met, with Huey on hand. The Kingfish thrust out his jaw at the candidate, Porter: "You'll never get a chance to sit on that court." The committee threw out its chairman, set itself up against the law, and called a new Democratic Primary. Porter went to the district court and was recognized as the nominee. But the Supreme Court was now split 3-3, without a majority. Huey thought a moment. Suddenly, the three Long members suspended the district judge's ruling and set a date for a hearing—twenty days after the general election! Huey, the legal strategist, scored here. A majority, four other members, might have stepped in to halt this trick. But, with one member dead, there was no majority.

Huey chose his candidate for the state's highest court—Fournet of the "Bloody Monday" riot, now his lieutenant-governor. Porter was in a quandary. Should he participate, and recognize the legality of a new primary? Or stay out and see Fournet unopposed, perhaps the winner in a court fight? He ran. The machine pumped every resource into the fight, and Fournet won by a 4000 plurality. He remained thereafter the machine's margin of security on the court.

The state fell silent as Huey crushed one defense after another. The special sessions were now almost reflex actions, sometimes one a month. The Governor (i.e., Senator Huey) received the right to fill any vacancy in any public office, regardless of the length of the unexpired term. A "civil service" board was created to control the appointment of every police and fire chief in the state; one of its first acts was to discharge the Alexandria chief, who had refused to let the bodyguards hunt down men in public buildings on a night when Huey was rotten-egged. The state bank examiner's powers were extended over homesteads—an important advance into a new field. Business men knew that the master had another hold over them. Municipalities lost the power of regulating their public utilities; and the State Public Service Commission, now controlled by Huey, took over that function. The commission was soon hiring Senator Huey as its attorney, with fees in the tens of thousands, to handle investigations in his spare time. The state took over the biggest single employment agency in New Orleans, the Sewerage Board, by creating a new group of directors. It hobbled the city further by forbidding it to levy new taxes of a type not imposed by the state.

Huey showed the world how a "co-ordinated" American Legislature could perform at its best. From now on, all bills went to a single committee, "ways and means," a completely controlled one. Bills were passed at the rate of two minutes each. What's in them? It don't matter. Huey knows all that, boys. Don't bother your heads. Whatcha doin' tonight, babe?

The boys hadn't settled themselves at home before another call came, for another session. A bill was announced, providing a "budget" committee for the schools. Then it was discovered that the committee was to pass on the appointment, past and future, of every teacher, portress, bus driver and other school employee in Louisiana. A new body of 15,000 men and women, hitherto immune, had been brought under the club. Teacher tenure? The security in their posts, won by New Orleans teachers after years of effort, for those who passed a probationary period? What are you talking about, pal? Kingfish says the bill means what it says. You gotta be favorable, no matter who you are. . . . Also, the machine took over the patronage of the sheriff's office above the first five deputies, reaching further into control of local functions.

In another instance, the dictatorship slipped through a "packing" plan. Baton Rouge, ever unfriendly, would never elect men satisfactory to the machine; so Huey assured himself of his kind of officials. The police jury, or governing body, had 13 members—11 antis, 2 pros. The law gave the Governor authority to name 13 additional jurors; and they would run things, 15-11.

But the real shocks were saved for last, with a special new trick. Two harmless little measures were introduced, one a codification of license laws, the other a compilation of city charters. Both passed House committee, then House, then Senate committee, and were advancing to final Senate passage. Then, within minutes of adoption, the machine floor leader tossed up the "amendments," one of them 100 pages long. The secretary, skimming, read two or three words to the page; and, while the opposition cried questions, a vote was taken. Only afterward, hours afterward, did the public, or even most of the legislators, learn what the Legislature had done.

First, the "innocent" city charter measure turned out to be one that threw out the full city officialdom of Alexandria. The Governor would have the right to name a full slate of his own men. Here was vindictiveness of an elemental type. The state didn't like the city administration. Selah, no more city administration except Huey's kind.

The other secret amendment imposed a five-cent-a-barrel occupational tax on the refining of oil. Five years before, Huey had almost lost the office largely because he sought this measure. Now it was a law before Louisiana knew it.

One last stir of mass opposition resulted, temporarily dangerous, then futile and tragi-comic. The Standard threatened, as usual, to pull up stakes; 1000 firings loomed. A chill settled over Baton Rouge; would it really lose its major industry this time? The Standard workers, confused men, formed a Square Deal Association. It took on a martial air, organized companies, held drills, wore blue shirts, talked bravely of "direct action" as a slogan. But it never made clear just what it meant by "action." As members joined from surrounding parishes, the Dealers threatened a "march on Baton Rouge" unless Allen gave way on the tax; and they appealed to Roosevelt to intervene. Huey, however, finally had Standard where he wanted it. After much fulminating, he agreed to rebate four cents out of the five-cent collections, but the tax remained. Standard was satisfied; Huey was satisfied. But the Square Dealers remained organized.

Like wildfire came news: one of the Dealers had been kidnaped by the state police. Men ran from house to house in Baton Rouge, cried the word on the streets: "Mobilize." The Dealers gathered at the courthouse with pistols, hunting rifles, shot guns; they ran out the state workers, then could not make up their minds what to do. A minister prayed, a few members made speeches and the mobilization ended. Allen declared martial law. Baton Rouge became a military reservation, with printed notices appearing on poles overnight: citizens were not to assemble, not to carry weapons, under any circumstances. Machine-gun troops circled the town. On the next day about one hundred Square Dealers gathered for "The Battle of the Airport." The Dealers huddled at one end of the field. Up came the Guardsmen, pointed their guns and called on the Dealers to give up. Some of the Dealers, including the chief Dealer, came forward without their arms; others ran. A shot was fired and a man was injured; by all indications it was an accident.

The Guard used tear gas, throwing it into an open field to disperse the onlookers. The "insurrection" ended. All but a few of the Dealers received their jobs back. The Kingfish stole the show by holding a hearing, with himself as attorney, to investigate charges that the Dealers had planned to assassinate him. And then, crowning irony, the Dealers learned that their "kidnaped" member, who figured in the "plot," had been a Long plant in their organization all along.

Westbrook Pegler, drawn like others to watch the almost unbelievable legislative shows, concluded that the dictatorship was "reducing to the political status of the Negro all of the white people of Louisiana who oppose Der Kingfish." He looked at the legislators, at Baton Rouge, and observed: "They do not permit a house of prostitution to operate within a prescribed distance of the state university, but exempt the state Capitol from the meaning of the act."

It is no wonder that in this atmosphere Huey and his men became more cynical, more careless of appearance with each successive triumph. The Kingfish admitted airily that the crowd attending a hearing was the payroll boys. There wasn't any opposition any more, he said in mock disgust, and he wanted some kind of bunch. On another occasion, a trainload of jobsters were told to descend on Baton Rouge; a citizens' army to let the world know that the people were behind the administration. Huey could have whipped up the folks in the hills with a series of talks. But that would have taken time, and Huey had more important things on his mind. In this case, the demonstration was not a complete success. The payroll citizens took bottles on the train and showed up drunk. It didn't matter. The bills went through. All bills went through, these days.

Huey appeared at the committee hearings, by habit. There

was no more nervous drive, no straining of effort. It was a casual virtuoso performance. Huey tossed forth one bill, found that he had changed his mind when another came along, withdrew it and went on to the next. When he came to one that extended the bludgeon over new thousands of local men and women, he yawned: "This is just good government." When he took away the honesty of the ballot with another, he grinned: "And this is for the purity of elections, and to make sure there'll be no more ballot box stealing."

Glee broke over the crowd—uproarious mirth, uncontrollable guffaws, a cackle of Jovian proportions. Louisiana's leaders were laughing at Louisiana; and the sound was not good.

V

ON TOWARD . . . ?

WASHINGTON and the White House were now the main interests. The Kingfish had outgrown Louisiana; it was a necessary consideration, but not a full-time or even a half-time one.

Huey P. Long was the national question mark, the challenger, the entertainer, the man in whose name millions were praying for salvation, in whose hands were clutched the weapons for enslavement of those millions. He could not be laughed off, sneered off, or ignored.

He changed national policies and threatened to change the game of national politics. He forced the Roosevelt Administration to the left, to the adoption of more and more liberal measures to meet his threat. The National Youth Administration, some observant critics declared at the time, was the result of Huey's pressure, his widely attended radio harangues on the subject, elaborations of his Louisiana sentiments. The Administration's movements toward increased income taxes in the higher brackets were interpreted as answers to Long demands. Once or twice Huey cried joyously that Roosevelt was turning to his program; and a number of commentators believed for a period that the Administration had beaten him at his own game. But Huey reconsidered, and each time he came back a few days later to charge the Rooseveltians with trying to defraud the American people by making meaningless gestures in his direction.

116

Huey told the nation, and the Democrats: "One sure way to avoid Huey P. Long for President, and the only way if I live, is by adopting God's laws. Take them, and I pass into insignificance. Do as God commanded, and I will be as little as one of the sands of the sea." In the next breath: "I'm as big as Roosevelt. Why, he's copying my share-the-wealth speeches now, the ones that I was writing when I was fourteen years old. So he's just now getting as smart as I was when I was in knee breeches." He worked hard to nettle his rival, to pull him off the pedestal that goes with the President's office: "We're just a couple of politicians, him and me," he grinned. "I'm running my job, and Roosevelt ain't got anything to do with me. The difference is, I was elected without his help, and he couldn't have been elected without mine." Always, he accused the President of "ingratitude."

Cheekily he sent an open letter to Roosevelt, asking him to set forth what he would like done in the way of wealth-sharing, if the President meant what he said. Huey promised that he, Huey, would get it passed within seven days.

In raging style he clubbed at the Administration on the McCarran Prevailing Wage Amendment to the $4,800,000,-000 Relief Act. He almost succeeded in passing the amendment, but was forced down by the narrowest of margins. "This Administration wants to make tramps out of the American people!" he stormed. The fact was that in Louisiana, Huey paid state wages far below the prevailing scale; and he was on record as having told a labor delegation: "The prevailing wage is as low as we can get men to take it." Not bothering with minor considerations of consistency, he pressed for a series of measures in behalf of principles which he had fought in Louisiana: liberal labor standards, wage legislation, the programs of the La Follettes, the Norrises and the Wagners.

The Kingfish became more violent with each month. "Frank-Lin De-La-No Roo-Se-Velt!" He rolled each syllable. And then he hurled words not often used publicly of American Presidents: "He's a liar and a faker!" He chose as his main target Jim Farley; and at him he threw charges of implication in a wire service to gambling houses, corruption in awarding of contracts, use of a $52,000,000 RFC loan to force a railroad official to support a Democratic candidate, illegal presentation of $80,000 in new stamps to friends, killing of Department of Justice charges against large party contributors. "Jim can take the corns off your feet without removing your shoes."

The accusations were such that they could not be ignored. After tossing them from hand to hand, the Administration consented to their reference to a committee. Farley returned from a vacation, disturbed. Huey raged with a new claim: important papers bearing on a PWA investigation of Farley had been removed from the files and turned over to Farley. He whirled on Ickes: "It seems like the Valentine season has grown up into the political sphere, and there's a wooin' among the Cabinet members." Farley denied the impeachments, and Huey insisted that a whitewashing was performed.

Huey played no favorites in his compliments among the New Deal officials. Henry Wallace was "Lord Corn Wallace, the Honorable Lord Destroyer, the Ignoramus of Iowa"; Ickes, "the Chinch Bug of Chicago"; Farley, "the Prime Minister, the Nabob of New York"; and he saved his longest words for last: "The Expired and Lamented Royal Block, Hugh Sitting Bull Johnson, the New Oo-La-La of Oklahoma." He was a favorite radio diversion; and he didn't charge for appearances, like Amos 'n' Andy. Chains went to him with offers of free time. He was the most talked-of

member of the House or Senate; more questions were asked
about him by visitors than about any other representative
of the people. Crowds dropped their work and rushed over
at the word that Huey was speaking, to sit spellbound, guf-
fawing, shaking their heads. He took up a staggering portion
of the space in the *Congressional Record*. If Huey did not
appear in the daily digest, that meant that he was absent.

The Government pushed inquiries into the income-tax
returns of Huey and his friends, and brought the first of a
series of indictments in New Orleans. Huey challenged it,
dared it to bring a charge against him. He flung his hands
in the air, shouted at the Democrats in the Senate: "Do
you know where you're headed? Just as straight for hell as
ever martin went to a gourd."

Dr. Hiram W. Evans, Imperial Wizard of the Ku Klux
Klan, added his bit to the flurry against Huey. The Kingfish was "un-American," declared the Wizard. Huey pinned
the Wizard's ears back: "You tell the toothpuller he's a
lying sonofabitch. That ain't secondhand information, and it
ain't confidential."

Gertrude Stein declared that Huey had "a sense of human
beings, and is not boring the way Harding, President Roosevelt and Al Smith have been boring." H. G. Wells called
him "200 per cent American."

In January of 1934, he had turned his Biblical-economic
movement into a formal, national organization. "Share Our
Wealth" was its slogan, patented, and into its operations
Huey poured mounting tens of thousands of dollars provided
by "friends in Louisiana," gallons of sweat, every bit of
energy that he had once used on the Louisiana hill folk. Now
everybody was to get the benefit of his talents. He started
with a staff of twenty girls, retained to handle the mail, and

this force grew steadily, working night and day. Half a million circulars and copies of his speeches went out at one period after another. Soon he was claiming 2,000,000 members; then 3,000,000; eventually 7,000,000; once 9,000,000, when he was in an expansive mood. He took on a preacher of his own, Gerald L. K. Smith of Shreveport, Louisiana, to serve as national organizer, making speeches when Huey didn't have the time. Before long Huey was sending out copies of his Senatorial speeches, government-reprinted, with membership coupons attached—a highly unorthodox practice, and one that drew criticism. "Share Our Wealth" had an unusual rule: no dues. Huey said that this was to keep the movement one for the poor man; but he did not explain just how the financing was managed.

The Administration became much disturbed over Huey. Word leaked out that several Cabinet sessions had considered him and methods to strike back at him. Several means were adopted, one after the other. For a brief time, the membership of the Senate, with a few exceptions, walked out in a body whenever he arose to speak. Huey didn't mind. He spoke to packed galleries, made capital of the absences; and the members read avidly about it the next day. A "Young Turk" movement was started to cuss Huey back. But nobody could ever cuss better than Huey; and Huey won by several full columns of publicity a day.

His skill at garnering copy was amazing. Like it or not, there was nothing that the Administration could do to keep him off the front page. At last Roosevelt gave the word for a full-dress attack by the big guns. Hugh Johnson, retired from the silent NRA battlefields, led the assault. Over a national hook-up Hugh linked Huey and Father Coughlin. "A couple of Catalines . . . enticing bums . . . rash and murderous . . . Pied Pipers." Hugh used Negro dialect to imitate Huey, and reached his height with a choice remark: "These two patriots have been reading last summer's lurid story about an American Hitler riding into Washington at the head of troops. That would be definite enough to Huey, because he knows what part of a horse he can be."

Huey answered Johnson, before what Beals at the time termed "probably the largest radio audience in the history of America." It was one of his great opportunities to date, and he made the most of it. Offering only passing insult to Hugh, he presented an earnest, deeply passionate exposition of his share-the-wealth. To new millions he told everything he wanted to tell about his movement, and told it with consummate artistry. His program, he asserted, had the approval of "the Divine Maker," of Theodore Roosevelt, Leviticus, Jesus Christ, Pope Pius XI and Socrates. He returned to one of his favorite backwoods stories: "What is the trouble with this administration of Mr. Roosevelt, Mr. Johnson, Mr. Farley, Mr. Astor and all their spoilers and spellbinders? They go gunning for me. It reminds me of Old Davy Crockett, that kept firing and firing one night at a 'possum in the tree—but found out that it was no 'possum a-tall, only a louse in his own eyebrow." He cried shame:

While millions have starved and gone naked; while babies have cried and died for milk, while people have begged for meat and bread, Mr. Roosevelt's administration sails merrily along, plowing under and destroying the things to eat and wear, with tear-dimmed eyes and hungry souls made to chant for this New Deal, so that even their starvation dole is not taken away, and meanwhile the food and clothes craved by their bodies and souls goes for destruction and ruin. . . . Is this government? It looks more like St. Vitus dance.

Huey's share-the-wealth scheme, as he was now revealing it, was not essentially new to America. Others had touched often on the need for a more adequate distribution of the products of labor and capital. But none had been able to dramatize it, simplify it and popularize it as did the Kingfish. He thought up a series of concrete proposals to carry out a redistribution, then reduced it to a sales compound. He was selling it to America in the same way that he had sold Cottolene and his medicine for "female illnesses." It was, to the millions who were coming beneath his sway, the Great American Nostrum, ingredients guaranteed by the Bible.

As Huey presented it, it was a highly unworkable scheme. There is need in America for a more equitable spread of the nation's abundance or potential abundance. But it could never be achieved by Huey's methods. Never the economist, Huey had hit early upon a picture of a desired end, and he had plugged that objective and little else. Only toward the close of his career did he seek to explain just how he would accomplish it; and then he ran into difficulties.

At first, the Kingfish proposed to leave the rich with fortunes of $100,000,000 each. He cut this down, and down again, until it reached $5,000,000—a substantial difference. After many alterations, he arrived at these conclusions: a guaranteed homestead allowance or patrimony of $6000 per family; an annual income guaranteed at $2000 or $2500, and a maximum income of $1,800,000. Above this last figure a capital levy would take away the surplus millions. Further offerings were a pension for one's "withered" old age; free education for the children, through college; a radio, an automobile, perhaps an electric refrigerator for every family, the latter utilities not to be sold, but to be replaced if necessary. The Government would purchase agricultural surpluses and store them up until needed by the folks. Hours of labor would go up and down to balance consumption against production of industry; and finally the veterans (Huey's friends in spite of his egregious "war record") would receive immediate payment of their bonuses.

How would he work it all? Holders of various possessions would simply turn them over to the government; not only cash but also houses, automobiles, non-voting stock and so forth, "so the poor devil who needs a house can get one from the rich bird who has too many houses; so the man who needs a bedstead can get one from the man who has more than he will ever need." The beneficiaries would file petitions setting forth their present assets and their wants.

Huey did not go into the question of ownership, of methods of handling such possessions as factories, railroads, ship lines; nor had he a reply for those who declared that chaos would be the inevitable result of such a straightjacket method of dealing with economic problems. Beals, working over data offered by Huey, concluded that his figures sounded like "the weird dream of a plantation darky." The Government, starting out to slice things, would come into possession of about two-fifths of its wealth, "say, $165,000,000,000," said Huey. About $100,000,000,000 of this amount would give every family its homestead, radio and car, end unemployment and child labor. He would use the rest to make sure that the deserving received their college educations, and to provide his other benefits. Beals, however, estimated that there were 30,000,000 instead of 20,000,000 American families with less than $5000 income, as Huey had set down; and confiscation of estates as suggested by Huey would, Beals decided, yield only $50,000,000,000—far less than required. Carrying out his statistics, he concluded that a figure of $1.50 per individual might have been the net result by 1933 standards; the munificent amount of $35 each, by 1929 levels.

Was Huey, too, the victim of his plan; did he delude himself into thinking that it would somehow work? Some indications are that, during his last years at least, he had convinced himself that he had the nation's salvation in his microphone messages. But he would never have allowed his nostrum to interfere with his personal ambitions. Those came first, in Washington, in Louisiana. Whatever would have happened to share-the-wealth once Huey came to the controls, there is no question but that the nation would have had before it what Louisiana experienced: American-style dictatorship.

Huey frankly predicted that his listeners would see an end to both the Democratic and Republican Parties under his régime. He told New York newspapermen that in the place of the parties would arise a new, single organization, his organization. He would not interfere with the press, no, boys. But he would tax it, make it pay its fair share. No great imagination is required to picture what Huey would have done to the American newspapers with a weapon of that kind. The Supreme Court? Huey had ideas in that direction, too.

To Forrest Davis he made the assertion that he would remain as President for four terms. When the people saw how well he was doing, nobody would be able to budge him out in less than that. His "theory of democracy" was this: "A leader gets up a program and then he goes out and explains it, patiently and more patiently, until they get it. He asks for a mandate, and if they give it to him, he goes ahead with the program in spite of hell and high water. He don't tolerate no opposition from the old-gang politicians, the legislatures, the courts, the corporations or anybody." All of which has a strongly totalitarian aspect: reach a position of power, then use that power to destroy all possible opposition. . . .

The 1936 battle lines were forming. Huey put the usual Louisiana fall elections forward to January, so that he could be re-elected Senator and then devote full time to the national campaign. He would run himself, or he might back one of a liberal group including Borah, Norris, Nye, Frazier, Wheeler or McCarran. He was not certain just which course he would follow. He was working hard to develop a coalition against Roosevelt. Although he talked much of 1936, he confided to friends that "1940 will be my real year." For 1936 he might carry through a third party, or go to the Democratic National Convention and steal the show, work for his own candidate or for a riproaring share-the-wealth platform.

Sometimes he said that he might "have to" split the Democratic Party in 1936, with the result that a Republican conservative would be elected. The policy of such a President would bring revulsion that might well sweep him in in 1940, to his way of thinking. He did not need a depression to guarantee him the White House, he was certain. He had come to power in Louisiana before 1929. He appealed to underlying, continuing wants; and he was offering, he could well have added, some concrete objectives that no administration was likely to exceed in the promising.

In mid-1935 he was starting a national share-the-wealth soundtruck tour. He declared that he had four states assured for the 1936 convention—Louisiana, Mississippi, Georgia and Arkansas, "and I'll take Alabama when I get ready." Charles Beard ventured the statement that Huey could take part of the Solid South away from Roosevelt. Huey declared that Beard was wrong; he'd take it all—"you'll see me running Roosevelt ragged." Brightly, Huey talked of an "independent nation of Louisiana"; of reuniting all of the states that had been carved out of the Louisiana Purchase; predicted an alliance, perhaps an invasion of Mexico by Louisiana. "Mississippi has annexed herself to us already, hasn't she?" he chuckled. He had changed the course of elections in Mississippi and Arkansas, and he threatened forays against Bailey (of North Carolina), Robinson, and other enemies.

All of Huey's talk was not idle, or mere guying. Farley, the Administration's political strategist at that time, has written with frankness of the genuine threat that Huey presented. As Farley prepared for 1936, he reveals, the Democratic National Committee conducted a "secret poll on a national scale" on the subject of Huey: *

It indicated that, running on a third party ticket, Long would be able to poll between 3,000,000 and 4,000,000 votes. . . . His probable support was not confined to Louisiana and nearby states. On the contrary, he had about as much following in the North as in the South, and he had as strong an appeal in the industrial centers as he did in the rural areas. Even the rock-ribbed Republican state of Maine, where the voters are steeped in conservatism, was ready to contribute to Long's total vote in about the same percentage as other states. . . . It was easy to conceive a situation whereby Long, by polling more than 3,000,000 votes, might have the balance of power in the 1936 election. For instance, the poll indicated that he would command upward of 100,000 votes in New York state, a pivotal state in any national election; and a vote of that size could easily mean the difference between victory or defeat for the Democratic or Republican candidate. Take that number of votes away from either major candidate, and they would come mostly from our side, and the result might spell disaster.

Raymond Moley, too, has an illuminating passage: †

By late March [of 1935] the Kingfish was threatening to campaign in states other than Louisiana for "Share-the-

* James A. Farley: *Behind the Ballots* (Harcourt, Brace; 1938).
† Raymond Moley: *After Seven Years* (Harper; 1939).

Wealth" candidates. By April the Democratic high command not only expected him to defeat Senator Joseph T. Robinson of Arkansas and Senator Pat Harrison of Mississippi, two of the party's elder statesmen, in 1936, but was chewing its mustaches over statistics purporting to show that he could make himself political master of the whole, vast Lower Mississippi Valley—perhaps even of great hunks of the West. Who knew where Huey . . . would end?

F. D. R. began to doubt whether Huey's followers could be weaned away by logical argument. Perhaps it would be necessary to woo some of Long's support by making a counteroffer. One evening in midspring F. D. R. actually used the phrase "steal Long's thunder" in conversation with me and two other friends of his.

The Washington and Louisiana careers sometimes dovetailed. Huey charged the New Deal with seeking to use Federal patronage to steal the state from him. But it wouldn't get away with that. Speeding back home, he waved a hand, and the Legislature was at it again. At a time when other states were scrambling for Federal funds, Huey took steps to keep them out of Louisiana. A new agency, a "state bond and tax board," was created, its members state officials. No town, city or other subdivision of the state could incur a debt of any kind, unless with the approval of Huey's central government. A companion measure set up state supervision of any and all expenditures of funds or credits obtained from the Federal Government. These measures made sure that Federal moneys would not hurt Long interests in Louisiana; they also saw to it that New Orleans or other hostile communities did not survive by means of Federal money.

An oppositionist waved his hands: "These bills are harmless. All they do is declare war on the United States." The Federal Government was quick in accepting the declaration. Ickes observed that "the emperor of Louisiana" was creating a situation in which funds might be canceled. Huey shot back: "Ickes can go slap damn to hell." To which Ickes made reply: "The emperor of Louisiana has halitosis of the intellect." The upshot was that an estimated $30,000,000 in PWA projects, already earmarked, were kept out. The WPA continued in Louisiana, but under a completely "Federalized" administration.

In the war between the Kingfish and Washington, the little Louisianian was the forgotten man.

A dull silence was upon the state. Huey had foreclosed, taken up his mortgage. As T. O. Harris described it, he had become "owner in fee simple, with all reversionary rights and hereditaments, in full trust and benefit, to have and to hold, in paramount estate and freehold, for the balance of his days." No other man in America has had the powers he held in his hands.

He possessed the state government, the Governor, the university, all commissions and departments; the Legislature, the public schools, the treasury, the buildings, and the Louisianians inside them. The courts were his, except in isolated instances, and he had the highest judges. He had a secret police which did anything he asked: kidnaped men, held them incommunicado, inquired without check into private matters of opponents. He ran the elections. He counted the votes. He disqualified any man or woman whom he wanted disqualified. He could order the addition to the rolls of any number of voters that his judgment dictated. He was becoming local government in Louisiana. The officials of no town or city were secure. Let a brother or an uncle offend, and Huey would have a mayor or an alderman out of a job and his own man appointed in his place. He was reaching into local police affairs; he was controlling municipal finances by new boards. He could ruin a community by cutting off its taxes, preventing it from adopting substitutes, and then forcing new obligations to break its back. He was moving in upon the parish district attorneys, using his attorney-general as a club.

His power was becoming that of life and death over private business. His banking examiner, his homestead agents, his Dock Board, his Public Service Commission and State Tax Commission were instruments of financial salvation, or of ruin. He served as attorney for the state without hindrance, dug back far into the past records of companies on the wrong side, shook heavy payments from them and took a full third as a fee, by law. There was secrecy about most of the state's records. The law forbade officials to give out financial information; they could be put in jail for doing so. Others did not need a law to guide them in closing their records.

And government by thunderbolt had come, apparently, to stay. The Reichstag of the Nazis did what it was told. Huey's Reichstag did not know what it was doing when it did it, and had to ask afterward if it wanted to find out.

Huey's tax against the larger newspapers was under argument in the courts. If some technical flaw were found, he was ready to remedy that; to alter the tax but not the essential principle. Already he had taken over most of the smaller newspapers through the medium of new legislation regarding local public printing contracts, on which such journals depended. A state printing board saw that these newspapers behaved, or died.

A Louisiana man could lose a private position because the dictatorship decided that one of his friends or relatives had aggrieved it. He could be arrested on a faked charge and held as long as the machine wanted, without the knowledge of his friends. He could be tried before a machine judge, receive a sentence, appeal—and in the end find himself turned down by Huey's highest court. If he were on the other side, he could steal, gouge, maim, perhaps kill, and know that he was not in jeopardy; and he could grow rich without capital, without ability, with nothing to his credit except the "right connection."

A few examples of what favor meant: New Orleans bankers were charged with receiving deposits after they knew their institutions were in failing condition. The shifting of one legislator, brother of a banker, to Long, and all won legislative pardon. Again, a friend of Huey's committed an alleged forgery. Huey nodded his head, and a law was passed outlawing criminal prosecutions after a short period; the friend went free. A strong-arm man followed orders by breaking the skull of an enemy at the Capitol. An unreconstructed judge convicted and sentenced him. The judge's words had not died away when the convicted man thrust his hand into a side pocket and drew out a pardon, signed and executed in advance by the dictator's Governor.

As the state lay quiet, Huey's appetite for power remained unappeased. Those last judges were comparatively harmless, encircled as they were; but they were irksome. He turned on Louisiana's Supreme Court: "That crooked legged chief justice" was a politician, said Huey. He and the other two minority members—"those three birds on the Supreme Court have got to be removed"; and with them "three rotten Ring judges down in New Orleans." A loyal attorney arguing a case threatened a judge: "Could you maintain yourself on the bench if the Legislature passed an act that rearranged the court and left you out? They did that very thing in my parish. Where did the judge go? He went to practicing law."

For amusement, Huey had the Regular Ring to toy with. He had reduced the city to abject surrender. Workers went

130

without pay for weeks. Grass began to grow in some of the
streets, as Huey had predicted. Roadwork, most other city
work, halted. Garbage men went on strike. A majority of the
Ring leaders went over to him. He kept them on their knees
for months.

His last attack on the election rules brought a voice out
of the silence, that of Mason Spencer, one of the last, lonely
legislative opponents:

"When this ugly thing is boiled down in its own juices, it
disfranchises the white people of Louisiana. I am not gifted
with second sight. Nor did I see a spot of blood on the moon
last night. But I can see blood on the polished floor of this
Capitol. For if you ride this thing through, you will travel
with the white horse of death. White men have ever made
poor slaves."

As he spoke, the atmosphere was appropriate. The militia
stood on guard over the Legislature. Baton Rouge was under
the military heel. For the first time, the public had been
moved out of the side galleries by armed men. Why? Could
there have been fear of mass uprisings now? The explanation was that Huey Long feared murder at the hands of
one of his subjects, or a cabal of them. For years he had
talked of violent death. "Sure, I carry a gun. Sometimes I
carry four. Can't tell when somebody's going to shoot the
king," he joked. But generally he was solemn about it.

He had seen plots about him in his first days in the mansion at Baton Rouge. A mild-looking young man had walked
past the residence twice a day at the same hour, looking up
each time with marked interest. Huey called police, and they
found that the "conspirator" had only been going to and
from work a few squares away. In another instance Governor
Huey had telephoned officials to arrest a man who was "driv-

ing round and round the place." The suspect had a new car and was accumulating mileage.

Open threats had been made, often, against Huey's safety. There were so many whose lives he had ruined, whose jobs he had taken away, whom he had abused in back-alley language. Such vows of vengeance were made generally in the heat of argument, of resentment against a particular trick. Huey met such talk with more protection, more bodyguards. For months the capital gossiped of hidden emplacements of machine guns that were ready in the state house, in case worst came to worst. To many men the military activities, the overcareful guard which Huey placed about himself, might have encouraged thoughts of gunplay. In his final months, Huey became more and more fearful.

Immediately after the Square Deal debacle, his attorney-general appeared in court to ask for an open hearing. Huey appeared as "special assistant attorney-general" to question witnesses regarding a "plot" against him. The Long man who had been "planted" in the Square Dealers' ranks described a scheme to force Huey's car to halt on the road, and then to shoot him to death. The opposition, declaring that the "plot" existed only in Huey's mind, cited the fact that, despite elaborate testimony, no charges were ever brought, and the matter was dropped. In Washington, Huey charged that the Standard Oil had tried to assassinate him. The Senate was discussing the World Court, and a fellow member suggested that Huey's war with Standard might be called to that organization's attention.

In July of 1935, the Kingfish rose again on the Senate floor, to allege that a plot to assassinate him had been discovered. He called attention to a caucus of oppositionists in a New Orleans hotel, declared that his men had installed a dictagraph and taken records of the conversation. There was talk, he asserted, of "one man, one gun, one bullet," and a question: "Does anyone doubt that President Roosevelt would pardon the man who rid the country of Huey Long?"

Angrily, the participants in the caucus denied a "plot" of any kind. The meeting had been no secret at the time. It was a gathering of the remaining antis to discuss a ticket for 1936. Five Congressmen attended. Some said that in the course of long hours of informal conversation, some one may have talked at random of the benefits to the nation which might follow the death of the dictator. But, they added, it was hardly possible for any sizable group to get together in Louisiana any longer without some discussion of Huey's possible demise—Huey himself talked about it so often.

Back to Louisiana he came for yet additional extensions of power, further exercises of malice, tying up of loose ends. He called another special session for early September. A Congressional subcommittee was planning to go to Louisiana, to investigate charges made in connection with election affairs. Huey prepared a particularly curious law, making it an offense for any person to perform, in the name of the Federal Government, a function which the Federal Constitution did not specifically authorize. He was turning to States' Rights with a vengeance. Then there were two other bills, these against judges. One abolished a position held by a Baton Rouge jurist, W. Carruth Jones, an oppositionist. The other gerrymanded the anti-Long St. Landry-Evangeline district of South Louisiana, to link part of it with a predominantly Long area near by. This would thrust out another hostile judge, Benjamin F. Pavy. Judge Pavy had presided for thirty years in that district. He had enjoined the use of the dummy election commissioners; Huey had marked him down and was now getting around to the matter. It was a minor affair, as such retaliations went.

Sunday, September 8, however, was a Sabbath of travail for Dr. Carl Austin Weiss, a young doctor of Baton Rouge, son of another doctor, son-in-law of Judge Pavy. He was a quiet, gentle scholar, a man who "had nothing to do with politics," but who felt deeply on the subject of dictators and dictatorships. He had done postgraduate work in Vienna when the Social Democratic movement was crumbling, when Dollfuss ordered the destruction of the workers' co-operative apartments. He remembered those days, and he thought bitterly of the days that were now upon Louisiana. Two relatives, one a teacher, and a patient who was a close friend, were victims of Huey's spite. The bill against Judge Pavy was certain to pass. And shocking word came to friends. Long was making unfounded remarks, as he had made them about others, that Judge Pavy had Negro blood. He might go at any time on the radio to vent his utterances. It was a stain that might mark the life of the judge's grandson, Dr. Weiss's young child.

Eight years earlier, Carl Austin Weiss's class book at Tulane University had declared that he would "go out and make the world take notice." On this day he said good-by, quietly, and started on what his family thought was a professional call. In his Capitol, Huey was ending a smoothly functioning night meeting. Walking out, he gave his final order: "Everybody be here in the morning." His black-and-white sports shoes tapped along an ornate corridor, along a marble hallway toward the office of his Governor. Several Long men were there, one of them Supreme Court Justice Fournet. Huey paused to pass a few words. According to Long witnesses, a slight, bespectacled man in white came from behind one of the pillars. From under the bottom of his coat a hand moved, thrust a small gun into Huey's side, and fired one shot.

But others in Louisiana insist that, despite his mental state, Dr. Weiss did not go to Long with the deliberate intent to kill him. Instead, they argue, he sought only to talk with him; and the panicky guards precipitated the shooting, perhaps killed the Kingfish themselves in the scuffle. This is the story that at least one third of Louisiana believes; and it can cite unexplained facts and circumstances to support its contention. In any event, the first bullet hit Huey, and he clutched his side and cried out.

The bodyguards lost no more time. Huey staggered away, hand to his side. One man dived at Weiss, felled him, and they grappled. The guard backed off, firing. Weiss fell forward on his face, the gun slipping along the polished floor, out of his hand. Half a dozen of the guards poured lead into him from all directions. There was no sound from his lips. The body stiffened, but still the guns spat out in vengeance. Sixty-one bullet holes were found by the coroner: thirty in front, twenty-nine in back, two through the head.

Huey was on his way, at once, to a near-by hospital. "I wonder why he shot me?" he asked, as he was driven up. For thirty-one hours he fought for his life, in as determined a manner as he had fought for the gubernatorial chair and for the Presidency. The first person to give him attention was Arthur Vidrine, the country doctor whom he had elevated to the superintendency of Charity Hospital. The bullet had passed through three loops of the intestine and taken part of the kidney before it left the body. The dangers were shock and internal hemorrhage, one almost equal to the other. Should an operation, with the resultant shock, be performed at once, or later? Two outstanding surgeons were called from New Orleans, efforts made to rush them by plane. But no airship was available. They started by automobile; on the way, they met with an accident. Vidrine operated. Huey re-

mained part conscious, part delirious. He talked of his autobiography, which he had decided was to be a best seller, and
he talked of his end: "Oh, Lord, don't let me die. I have a
few more things to do. . . . My work for America is not finished. . . ."

With his family and the leading men of his régime about
him, Huey Pierce Long slipped into death on September 10,
1935.

In the main hallway of his skyscraper Capitol the body lay
on its bier for two days. Eighty thousand persons passed before it and saw the former country boy in his tuxedo. On
the second day the coffin was lowered into a hastily dug
grave in the sunken garden before the Capitol. An estimated
125,000 to 150,000 men, women and children—from the hollows, from the swamps, from New Orleans, from Dry Prong,
from DeQuincy, from Maringouin—packed the area, climbed
trees, stood on roofs to watch. Old women cried. Men wiped
away tears. Their man had died, for them. The Rev. Gerald
L. K. Smith of the share-the-wealth organization pealed to his
listeners: "The blood which dropped upon our soil shall
seal our hearts. . . . His body shall never rest as long as
hungry bodies cry for food, as long as lean human frames
stand naked, as long as homeless wretches haunt this land
of plenty. . . ." And the red-eyed O. K. Allen called upon
Huey's followers to carry on his program by "perpetuating
ourselves in office."

As in its unwinding, so in its final moments, did the story
of Huey Long do violence to American tradition. Assassination has never been a political method that stirred anything
but revulsion in this nation. But Long's death came as a not
illogical sequel to the life he had chosen to lead. The full
account of those last days has never been revealed. Some
believe that if, at a future date, the proper persons may be

persuaded to speak, a sensation may result. This much can be said now: No evidence has yet been offered to connect Carl Austin Weiss with a plot of any kind; and there has been no disclosure of the full circumstances leading up to the moment when the young doctor stepped from behind the pillar, nor of the immediate events that followed. An autopsy was not performed on the body of the dictator.

It was not an uprising of an aggrieved populace that stopped the tyrant's breath. Despite the grim note, the heightened cynicism of the latter excesses, he and his men could still claim that the Louisiana electorate was generally with him and them. He had come close to political disaster on several occasions, but he had always convinced his commoners that he was on their side. He had rigged the election machinery against an unimpeded choice at the polls; he had clearly violated the law, as in the Fournet election and other cases; he had made mock of the democratic process in instance after instance. But he persuaded his followers that only through him could they receive the fulfillment of their needs. He had given sufficient tangible benefits, he had kept enough of his promises, to reassure them that he meant what he said.

"At least we got *something*," a North Louisiana farmer said. "Before him, we got nothing. That's the difference."

Likewise, on the national scene, he could suffer ignominious loss; he could be hooted at and warned against as a hazard to the country. But each week seemed to bring more men and women to his banner. They believed what he told them.

He had aroused in Louisiana an army that might have become a revolutionary one; he was recruiting on the national scene a force that might have turned into a revolutionary

137

one. But he was not a revolutionary leader, despite his spleen and his hill man's resentment toward those who were above him in rank.

He made clear that he had little truck with the ideologies. "I don't know anything about that kind of thing," was his unvarying word. That, to be sure, was smart politics; but Huey had not given much thought to abstract theories of government. He had not evolved, at the time of his death, to the status of the full-fledged Fascist, with a program thoroughly integrated to a central philosophy. One observer called him "pure dictator" only, and hit close to the truth. Ray Daniell, who gained Huey's confidence over a period of years, concluded that the Kingfish favored a capitalism that was drastically controlled. Throughout his life he had shown scant sympathy for schemes that involved hindrance of private ownership and operation. Social control, spreading of ownership, public possession and operation of basic industries—Huey frowned at that. He spoke to some of the technocrats, and talked of remaking cities, of providing a new abundance for the nation. Yet there was no evidence to indicate that he had gone far enough in his visions of a reformed America to determine the rôle that business groups and labor would play, or the forms of ownership, industrial control and labor management that he would impose.

But had he reached the White House, he would have been confronted quickly with a necessary choice. He would have had to admit that his share-the-wealth plan was an impossible one, and face the consequences; or he would have had to attempt its realization, with cataclysmic results. Might he have tried delay, put off the effective date, pleaded years for preparation? This might well have presented an impossibility, even for a Kingfish. Already, at the time of his death, some of his believers in Louisiana were impatiently awaiting their $6000 homesteads. A strawberry operator rejected his usual financial loan, in one case of record, because "Huey will have us all fixed up before the season's started." In some of the rural sections of states outside Louisiana, the pathetically trustful were certain that the mail would soon bring them their checks, whether Huey was in the White House or only in the Senate.

Disregarding surface appearances, America would have been on the brink of a dictatorship on the same day that Huey took the oath on Capitol Hill. He had given clear enough forewarning of his techniques of power manipulation; he had embraced enough of the Fascist thought and method not to hesitate over the final steps toward rigid organization of all groups from above, with special consideration for the favored friend, when the time came.

When his book, *My First Days in the White House,* appeared posthumously, he was presented as favoring for his régime a cabinet coalition of many of the ranking conservative and some of the reactionary public figures of the country (not omitting Herbert Hoover). They were the men who were to put into effect a plan for sharing the nation's tangible property.

Many were certain that, in his final days, the Kingfish was receiving secret assistance from certain Republican ultra-conservatives who saw him as a possible instrument of a future reaction. Toward several financial groups Huey had demonstrated particular friendliness. The "interests" had often found Huey a productive ally. The prospect of a Southern poor white in harness with the representatives of Eastern capital need cause no great amazement. Other less-conspicuous yokels-turned-statesmen have achieved such partnership. There are those in America who would sacrifice democracy for assurance from a domestic strong man that their particular interests would be given iron-ringed protection. Did Carl Austin Weiss visualize another day on which the machine guns would be turned upon the little people, with Huey the Dollfuss of an America of the late 1930s or early forties?

Essentially the same forces that had produced the other Southern hillbilly governors and senators had produced Huey Long. What qualities enabled him to reach a status on the American scene achieved by none before him?

Once, in the middle of a discussion of his attributes, Huey yawned: "Just say I'm *sui generis,* and let it go at that." This flattering description was not far removed from the truth. The Kingfish fitted no mold. He was a mixture of types: the original hill-country rebel, the egotist demanding constant satisfaction, the evangelist who backslid, the overlord of a city gang. He had a single-track mind, if ever man had one. It ran from and then back to one object, Huey. He knew what he wanted, one thing above all, and of that he could never get enough: absolute control.

He had one of the keenest brains in the South; for that matter, in the nation: a hard-driving intelligence and a sharp ingenuity. Two United States Supreme Court justices declared him one of the outstanding attorneys to appear before them. He knew human nature from the bottom; he was an almost intuitive observer. He recognized few rules, even those of cold politics. "Unpredictable" was a weasel word for him; his about-faces were stupendous, his ability to halt himself in mid-action was sometimes incredible. He was ruthless; he was amoral; ethics, to him, was a word that was used in class when he went to Tulane. He was the politician-organizer without peer, a genius in manipulation, in planning and conduct of the drive. "The best campaigner America ever saw," Washington veterans termed him.

Above all, he recognized one principle: that he had to produce something in order to keep in power—jobs and money, money and benefits, benefits and jobs. He must make promises, and keep enough of those promises to maintain his hold; and at all times he must take care that another did not outpromise him.

"He did more good, and more evil, than any man in the history of his state," Dr. H. C. Nixon has declared in evaluation. He left the state with gains that will advantage it for generations to come; and with a heritage from which it will suffer for that same period.

He took Louisiana out of the mud. He threaded her flat lands and her hill country with magnificent, if expensive, roads; crossed her bayous and rivers with towering high-cost bridges. Under his influence the concept of a state's services to its citizens underwent a sharp change for Louisiana and for some of the other Southern commonwealths. He made possible a broad expansion of the schools, of daytime facilities for the children, night classes for the adults. He could claim that he had increased enrollment more than twenty-five per cent by his free textbooks, and had taught 100,000 of the state's 238,000 illiterates to "read, write and cipher." He improved hospitals and set up new ones. He provided employment for tens of thousands on his public works. He granted tax exemption on part of their property to rural and urban small-home owners. He eliminated the poll tax, the device that has disqualified thousands of Southern whites because they can not pay the toll demanded for exercise of the right to vote.

He could point out that he had reduced utility and telephone rates on various occasions; that he had imposed new and more adequate taxes on oil operations, on corporations that had escaped a fair share of the costs of government under preceding régimes. He had introduced the state's first income tax, a step which may be set down as an advance.

Under Long, however, Louisiana demonstrated a general disregard of other aspects of present-day needs among rural and urban populations. Huey consistently rejected efforts to set up welfare and labor standards for the towns and cities or for the parishes. He was charged with further weakening an already weakened workmen's compensation system. Under him, the state lacked legislative and administrative protection that other Southern commonwealths had adopted for women and children in industry, for wage scales and related yardsticks. It was late among the Southern states to form welfare departments, not doing so until after the Kingfish's death. Huey "didn't like to fool with relief." During his lifetime the state did little to share in the support of the unemployed, though others were assuming part of this burden. Louisiana, under Huey, declined to adopt the Federal Child Labor Amendment, while children worked day in and day out in the strawberry fields, in cotton areas, in the factories of New Orleans and the shrimp-packing plants of South Louisiana, sometimes at wages as low as six cents an hour. State payments also went down to ten cents, in line with Huey's declaration that the prevailing wage was a wage as low as a person could be prevailed upon to take. When the NRA set minimum scales of forty cents an hour, the Louisiana Highway Commission by law paid thirty.

And with his unquestioned new services for his commoner, Huey imposed taxes that did not spare him, that often bore heavily upon him, in disguised or undisguised form. He added thirty-five new taxes, increased the state budget seventy-four per cent, from $21,000,000 to $38,000,000, and made the state debt second- or third-highest in the nation. The gasoline levy went up and up; cigarettes, soft drinks and dairy products were some of the poor man's articles of consumption that were directly taxed. Certain it is, too, that although the corporations assumed a greater proportionate share of the costs under Huey, the poor man paid a larger percentage than he realized when the companies passed the burden along.

It may also be noted that Huey's income-tax law had one of the lowest rates on higher incomes imposed by any American state, and one of the smallest spreads between rates on high and low incomes.

Strong questions were raised as to what happened to many of the millions of dollars in this flood of funds on its way to or from the state treasury. Tens of millions of dollars in state projects provided magnificent opportunities for some of the Long men. In Huey's last days, and for a time afterward, some of this picture was brought into the light; but years were to pass before the whole canvas was presented for scrutiny.

Huey's benefits were clearly those closest to the hearts of that class which Huey knew best; his small farmers with their small land parcels, fighting the hard fight to keep what they had and get ahead for the children. On the Louisiana scene, much of these benefits failed to reach down to the lower third of the urban populations, or to the rural tenants. To neither group did homestead exemption or roads or bridges mean much, although the school program was one source of assistance. To these latter elements the consumers' taxes, of course, also applied. Huey's reforms were important ones for a state that was backward in many respects, but they reached less deeply than many believed who looked upon Huey as a major threat to the status quo.

Most important to those who believed in democracy were the underlying changes that occurred in the attitude of Louisiana's men and women, and above all to its youth, during these years of the remaking of Louisiana. For the régime meant at first a slow, then a faster assumption of an attitude of unthinking, unquestioning acceptance of despotism itself in return for the alms of despotism. Democracy was weak when Huey Long came into power in Louisiana. Under his ministrations, it passed into a state of suspended animation.

The personal challenge of a Kingfish to a democratic nation was ended. But the end of the dictator did not mean the end of the dictatorship.

The Gravy Days

"When I took the oath as Governor, I didn't take any vows of poverty."

—RICHARD W. LECHE.

VI

INHERITANCE

BEFORE the flowers had begun to fade on his grave, the Kingfish's kingdom was lashed by storm. The atmosphere was dark as the sleek Cadillacs sped their fretsome owners from New Orleans to Baton Rouge, Baton Rouge to New Orleans. Tempers broke in the soundproofed rooms of Seymour Weiss's Roosevelt Hotel, and jealousies threatened fisticuffs behind the guarded doors in Huey's mansion and Huey's Capitol.

Who would be Kingfish now? Although he had spoken often of death, Huey had never included that possibility in his planning for the future of his organization, national or state. Nobody was Kingfish No. 2; that was not the Kingfish's way. "The only band that Huey will play in is a one-man band," a New Orleans editor put it. Huey had his strong local satraps, but one balanced the other. He had never shared power; he had supervised practically everything, from the location of a new levee down the river to the choice of a new composition for his Louisiana State University band.

Assassination had come at a particularly embarrassing moment for the little Kingfishes. Huey planned, of course, to become Senator again in January of 1936, whether he ran for President later in that year or in 1940. But he had not announced the man whom his people would elect for his main assistant, the Governor, or designated any of the others

147

whom the voters were to put in for him. O. K. Allen was going out; the Louisiana law does not permit a Governor to succeed himself. And now the claimants were coming forward for the crown and the cudgel that went with it.

Millions were in jeopardy; millions in property, cash, staked-out rights. Many in Washington and in Louisiana expected the organization to break apart quickly, like the one-horse shay. Hints of irreconcilable differences, of bitter internal clashes, had come forth from time to time in the past. Huey had always straightened things out. Who could do that now? Huey had agglomerated elements that few men had ever held together. Three main divisions extended through the ranks, with overlappings here and there. The country-politician group was apart from the city money-and-business-men's element. The country men were split in their interests as North Louisianians and South Louisianians. And over and above the others were the professional share-the-wealthers.

In New Orleans presided Robert S. Maestri (of whom much more, later), the richest individual machine man. Maestri had taken a place near but not at the controls in the early days, as a rich backer who grew richer with the years. He still was conservation commissioner and, for a time, had served as titular head of Huey's Louisiana organization. With him were Seymour Weiss, shoe clerk turned innkeeper, turned king-maker, the treasurer who kept no records; Abe L. Shushan, former Levee Board president and partner in a variety of toothsome enterprises; and, as an ally, Senator Jules Fisher of Jefferson Parish, the shrimp king, trapping ruler and Round Robineer. In South Louisiana, inclined to be friendly with the New Orleans crowd in some matters at least, were the French politicos: the wiry, wily Allen Ellender, Speaker of the House; the famous Fournet, sometimes rumored as an aspirant for further political honors, though already a supreme-court member; and Wade Martin, whom Huey had made chief of his Public Service Commission. To the north were O. K. Allen, whose fuddling mentality did not interfere with his popularity among his constituents; Senator James A. Noe, gas and oil man, a smiling entrepreneur whom Huey had drawn into politics and treated as a favorite son, and others.

Between the others, and somewhat apart from most of them, were the wealth-sharers: Gerald L. K. ("Lucifer Kodfish," said some) Smith, Huey's preacher-orator-organizer; Earle Christenberry, secretary to the Kingfish and holder of many of his secrets; and some of the smaller men of North and South, particularly of the Northern hills, who had tied to Huey's evangelical-crusading organization for reasons of their own.

What had a man like Weiss in common with a program that announced it would "cut fortunes down to frying size?" Between Maestri and some of the hardbitten clayhill rednecks there was little except contempt. And the separation between Northern and Southern politico was more than geographical. Huey had sometimes been forced to use stern methods to keep them from each others' throats.

Senator Noe let it be known that he wanted and expected the governorship. Ellender pressed his claim, and his fellow Frenchman Martin pushed a separate demand. Sadly, it appeared that each had been given to understand by the Kingfish, at various times, that he was to be the next executive; and each could cite words to that effect. A fourth candidate unexpectedly came forward to surprise some, send shivers down the backs of others: Earl Long, "long-lost brother" of Huey, who had returned to camp a short time before. Some remembered Earl's charges at his brother, and called him a traitor. But Maestri had always been friendly to Earl, and quietly he backed him. Each aspirant lined up his followers, hurried to make contacts and prepare ammunition.

The Reverend Gerald began to act up. During Huey's lifetime he had been restrained in his dealings with the boys. But events catapulted him into sudden prominence. He had taken the star rôle at the last rites. When the Baton Rouge district attorney held a futile inquest, Gerald stole the headlines by defying him, much as the master might have done. Calling the district attorney "one of the co-plotters of the assassination," Gerald stamped out. The district attorney termed him an unmitigated liar.

Feeling his strength further, the preacher sent word to the organization that "as organizer for share-our-wealth" he intended to "carry on the work of our leader, just as if he were here." He would "support only those I think Huey would support, and that does not include any political line-up."

The boys were alarmed. Gerald, to their way of thinking, had never been more than a hired hand; he had never figured in any of the inner council doings. But he was in a strategic position, momentarily at least. His name was known to millions, was closely identified with Huey's, and many were certain that he had the share-the-wealth movement in his grip. At his word millions might follow; and those millions might include tens of thousands of ballot-holding Louisianians. Many of the machine men had never liked Gerald. He was not a Louisianian but a Mid-Westerner, a fifth-generation minister of the Disciples of Christ. Gerald's activities had always drawn attention. In Indiana and in Wisconsin he had "vitalized" congregations, branched out into related go-getter activities, stirred up the town in various ways. In 1929 he was called to Shreveport. Soon he had broadened the church rolls, taken over the Community Chest Drive with phenomenal results, joined business men's clubs, sponsored athletic teams and inaugurated a radio program of his own over the station of W. K. Henderson, Huey's friend.

Gerald took his microphone audiences in the same way that Coughlin took his. It was not long before Gerald's ideas, as well as his mail, were enlarging. He was jovial, husky, a good looker, a good talker. When he was named a representative to the 1932 Olympic Games, some of his congregation thought this was a bit out of the religious line. Gerald did not help matters by overstaying his leave, or by making a series of trips East after he returned. His answers to the elders' questions did not down the criticism that followed. Rumor spread that Gerald was somehow connecting himself with Huey Long, and was seeing him in Washington. In June of 1933, Gerald's name was linked publicly with Huey's when photographers took their picture together in connection with the threatened pugilistic exchange between Long and Mayor Walmsley of New Orleans. Leaving Huey's hotel with the Kingfish, Gerald was identified by a Washington journal as one of the dictator's bodyguards. He sued. Soon his congregation was split wide open. He was asked to leave, first refused, then agreed to do so. By February of 1934 he had joined Huey.

From then on Gerald was part and parcel of wealth-sharing; a sweating, shouting Bible thumper, second only to Huey himself. He was highly reminiscent of the Kingfish. He could use "ain't" with the best of them, could whip up a fine pity or indignation or sawdust-trail frenzy, as the case demanded. He lacked Huey's racy humor—but then, one can't have everything. He used Huey's thesis, with contributions of his own: "We're getting twenty thousand new members a day. When we have enough millions, we'll make ourselves heard. We'll change things in this country." In Catholic territory he cited Pope Pius' encyclicals; he could

151

quote the Bible almost as well as Huey, no mean accomplishment even for a man of God. In New Orleans, denied a hall, he called the faithful to the levee: "The Lord held so many of His meetings on the banks of rivers, maybe it is better that I should do so, too." He developed a technique that was smashingly effective. "How many of you have five suits? Hold up your hands." No hands. "Four?" None. "How many got three?" One or two hands. "Two suits?" A few more. "One suit?" Still more hands. Finally, "How many got just one pair of pants?" Hundreds up, with a shout.

Gerald's progress was not always peaceful. His violent language sometimes brought catcalls instead of applause. In West Feliciana he was escorted to the parish line and sent "on your way to Baton Rouge, where you belong." At Independence burning statements against two women opposed to the Long régime led a man to shout "You can't talk about ladies like that" and brandish a revolver. He was halted, but shortly afterward a toy torpedo was popped and the crowd jumped. And then Gerald took the martyr's line: "They've tried to kill me before, but if they ever did and I went down in a pool of blood, there would be a thousand to rise in my stead!"

In September of 1935 it looked to Gerald is if he would be using the Long political organization to rise in Huey's stead on the national scene. He talked freely, too freely, of his plans, to Raymond Daniell and others. He was thinking ahead. Nineteen thirty-six was too close for him to do much; but just give Roosevelt another four years . . . His spending millions would be depleted, and Congress would not be so willing to give. Gerald looked to the veterans and the CCC boys. He foresaw the closing of the latter's camps and the turning out of thousands who knew something of group discipline. Those who heard him said that his ideas sounded much like those of a would-be storm-troop leader, and some detected a strong note of anti-Semitism in his remarks about individuals in and out of the Long ranks. Finally, he was mulling over a potent message—repudiation of debts. He was a national figure, these days; a hellbending rallier of the common folk, who gave frequent interviews about his design for America. He was far friendlier with the press than was Huey. Always willing to oblige, the minister once submitted to newspaper questioning as he soaped himself in the bathtub. The reporter said that he took the only other seat available, and there learned of share-the-wealth.

Less than ten days after Huey's death, Gerald joined a powerful cabal that snapped for the prize. At four o'clock one morning, the press was called to the Roosevelt Hotel to receive the announcement of a "Long ticket": Noe for Governor, Martin for Senator, Gerald to go to Washington as secretary to the Senator. Gerald would take on the good work as before, using all those pages of franked matter to carry the gospel. Fournet of the supreme court gave his support. The happy Noe added that O. K. Allen had given his backing by telephone; and as a further inducement to the populace, Noe pledged Louisiana "a businesslike administration and the continuation of the general program of Huey P. Long," whatever that combination might produce.

The forces shifted. The sparring was over. Maestri had himself driven to Baton Rouge. Weiss, paler than usual, followed. Noe and Martin went separately. Allen withdrew his purported blessing via Southern Bell. Maestri and Weiss, the men who handled the money, would have no part of Smith; and they were leery of Noe. Seymour was particularly frightened of Gerald; the preacher was making nightly assaults on the Washington Administration, with thinly veiled accusations regarding Huey's death. Seymour consid-

153

ered the income-tax indictments that were still being returned against him. He was in a sweat that Gerald might
get him behind bars. Gerald, besides, had let his tongue
slip and told what he planned to do with Weiss and "his
kind" when wealth-sharing came into its true estate. The
preacher's wings must be clipped; but first he must be drawn
into a cage for safety during the coming months.

The Maestri-Weiss faction moved fast. Presiding at an assemblage of Long men in and around New Orleans, Maestri
obtained a pledge that all would follow his word. Then he
and Weiss summoned the strongest force at their command:
Huey. The Kingfish was brought back from the grave to
designate his choice. The boys told the world of a statement,
not mentioned until this time, which Huey had made on
his last day—that he had a man he wanted for Governor;
that he wanted Richard W. Leche. There was reason for
the resultant surprise. Young Leche was the darkest of dark
horses. An attorney, a former secretary to Allen, he had been
raised to judge of the appeals court only a short time before.
His only other positions had been of the minor sort. One
of his greatest claims to fame was the fact that the columnist
Pegler had named him as the "finger man" of a plot to get
even with Pegler for his remarks about the régime. Earl
Long, Pegler asserted, was chosen to work upon him. Pegler
"didn't forget to duck," he said.

There were other surprises. For lieutenant-governor the
candidate was Earl Long. His friend Maestri had held to his
demand that "Earl get something good"; and then, couldn't
any galoot see that the name of Long would offer potent
lure to the voters, proving that the organization was carrying on for Huey? Ellender won a prize, the next six-year
Senatorial term. The other claimant, Martin, was consoled

with Huey's unexpired term in Washington. And, final wonder, Gerald Smith came out flatfootedly for Maestri's patchwork line-up, terming it a real share-the-wealth ticket.

Noe, the man who might have become Governor, blazed. He did some appealing of his own to the grave, and told more of Huey's last day. On that afternoon Huey had called him, O. K. Allen and Highway Commissioner A. P. Tugwell to the twenty-fourth floor of the Capitol to talk about the gubernatorial prospects. First Huey offered the place to Tugwell, who replied that he would give up any connection with the state rather than take it. Then Huey put in a call for Leche. Noe realized that Huey was trying to get out of an awkward position by passing over all the leading contenders; and he made it clear that he, Noe, wanted the job. Huey suggested the lieutenant-governor's office. Noe said no. Huey now had Leche on the wire: "Dick, what's your religion?" He was satisfied with the answer, and hung up. The Kingfish had a proposition: he would run Leche in 1936, with Noe for lieutenant-governor. But Leche, who seemed to like sitting on the bench, would run for the supreme court in 1938, while Noe would step up as acting-governor for two years and run in 1940 for the full four-year term. That seemed to settle matters. But after Huey's death, Noe went on, he had talked several times with Leche, and Leche had assured him he did not want to run but would back Noe. Now, Noe asserted, he had been betrayed all around. It was good reading, this account, but a political blunder. Noe had confirmed the story of Leche's claim.*

* Some of Huey's friends insisted that Leche was a Catholic. He was not. Discussing religion years earlier, the sports-loving Leche told Huey that the kind of immortality that appealed to him was that of the American Indian in his happy hunting ground. Just before he telephoned Leche on that last day, Huey pulled this story out of his recollection, and exclaimed: "Hell no. He ain't a Catholic. He's a Indian. He told me himself."

The North Louisianian concluded with a panting blast at Brother Gerald. Smith had told him, he said, that Boss Maestri was threatening to shut off Gerald's share-the-wealth pay checks if Gerald did not stop his foolishness, give up Noe and come home to the family. Gerald, Noe fumed, had then gone to him with a proposition: Gerald was willing to sacrifice those pay checks to the Noe-Smith cause if Jimmy would put up $10,000 as a little consolation fund. "I told him to go to hell," said Noe, "and threatened to beat him to a pulp if he ever showed up in my parish." "Alas," said Daniell, "for pious hopes! Scheming politicians outsmarted Huey's pupil, and the would-be Savonarola, who seemed more like Elmer Gantry, capitulated without a fight . . ."

Noe stormed into the Roosevelt coffee shop that night, jumped when he saw Gerald, and charged at him. An ungodly exchange ensued between minister and Senator, with "doublecross," "chiseler" and "tinhorn" among the mixed tributes that passed before friends separated the pair. Noe swore that he would stay in the race, and left to make a speech. He and Gerald, during their brief but tragically ended honeymoon, had arranged a joint meeting in Jimmy's town. Each started there, each planning to turn the rally into his own. Learning that Gerald was in his bailiwick, supposedly with "twenty bodyguards of Huey Long," Noe sent word that he was giving Gerald five minutes to get out or face the thrashing of his life. Whether for this reason or for another, Smith did not appear at the meeting. Another preacher took his place and enlivened proceedings by charging that another doublecrosser had offered him, the substitute servant of the Lord, a $1000 check if he deserted Noe and went over to see Smith. The meeting closed with a quartet trilling *Can You Count on Me?*

To make things tiring for the Maestri-Weiss-Leche group,

O. K. Allen misbehaved. He had been "tired and ready to drop out of politics" when Huey died. But then he announced himself, without warning, for Senator; and a machine friend put himself up with "O.K." for Governor. The opposition, delighted, prepared its own ticket in the confident belief that the machine was cracking. In New Orleans the Ring was confused. Most of its leaders had gone over to Huey before he died. Should they turn about now? "Strike for liberty; join us and save yourself," the opposition urged. Ever practical, the Ring men hesitated. They proposed a bargain: let the machine perform for the city a bit, call a special session and repeal some of the legislation that had ruined New Orleans. Then the Ring would perform for the state. The state men shook their heads. "First you give us the vote, and then we'll give you what you want." The Ring submitted. Allen was appeased with the short Senatorial term, and, before many weeks had passed, Noe reluctantly agreed to run only for his Senatorial office. Under Maestri's pressure the ranks were apparently closed; but in Noe the organization had made a mortal enemy, who was eventually to help bring its downfall.

Quickly, Huey's men proposed an *anschluss* with Washington. They were ready, from the first moment, to give up the political fight to which he had dedicated the major energies of his last years. But Washington declined. It took the proposals as signs that the Long men were in a state of nervous tension and that they could not carry the approaching election. Washington was right in the first instance, sadly wrong in the second. But the national Administration was then anxious to see the last vestiges of Longism ended.

So it was to be Louisiana against Roosevelt again, was it? The machine was ready for the fight.

The campaign had a ready-made issue—martyrdom. Huey's

casket became the sounding board of the state's politics. In other states men would have gone to prison as a result of their utterances on the subject. In Louisiana, though, the bars were down. The opposition was the Party of Murder. Direct accusations were made that the opposition candidates had taken part in a plot to kill Huey Long. Congressman Cleveland Dear, the standard bearer ("Dodo Dear" to the machine), had attended the hotel conference in New Orleans a month or so before Huey's death; the dictatorship's orators convinced thousands of rural and city men and women that he was a blood-stained conspirator seeking foully to profit by the killing he had planned. Wait until Huey's friends went back into office. Then the folks would see a real investigation. . . .

Dr. Weiss's father gave out a letter charging Allen with "deliberately and wilfully slandering the dead for political gain—a dastardly thing of which no decent man or woman should care to be guilty." Also, "Facts so far as they have been permitted to be disclosed" indicated that Huey was shot because of a personal difficulty "and in all probability by one of his own bodyguards." Candidate Dear announced that he had been informed that one of Huey's bodyguards was in an insane asylum, muttering "I killed my best friend." This was a common belief of the moment, when Louisiana was still filled with stories of the killing, some wild, some not so wild. Leche answered Dear by calling the six guards to the stand. Each said a piece, several called Dear a liar and a "low coward," threatened to smash his face; and Leche brought demonstrations when he declared that "not one of these loyal and good men would be out of a job" when he became Governor.

Mysterious tales spread. One was that within less than ten minutes of the assassination a Washington newspaper had the name of Dr. Weiss, while nearly twenty minutes passed before the body was identified in Baton Rouge. The state administration obtained a court order to check all incoming and outgoing telephone messages of that night. The superintendent of the state police said solemnly that there was "plenty behind this." But no investigation was made, so far as the public knew. Anti-administration rallies adopted resolutions for a Congressional inquiry to clear the names of Dear and the others. Although the machine claimed knowledge of a conspiracy, it had refused to take up the matter with the parish grand jury, the resolutions declared.

Leche, Huey's "post mortem candidate," brought the Kingfish from his grave to speak. Records were played in which Huey called for wealth-sharing. Huey's favorite night-club singer sang Huey's favorite songs. Huey's circulars were reprinted. Huey's face, fringed in red and white lights, looked down from every platform. The machine promised to "perpetuate each and every one of Huey's laws" and to carry on the share-the-wealth movement, although it was not specific as to its plans on that point. Gerald Smith appeared briefly, complained privately that he was being "kept under wraps." Leche termed himself "two hundred fifty pounds of Huey P. Long candidate," and made a novel contribution by challenging Dear to "shoot it out with me, with forty-fours." Clearly and unequivocally, Leche assured the folks that failure to return the organization to Baton Rouge would be "not only a reflection on Huey's memory, but an act of ingratitude."

Dick, as he was known to the Long men, made an inopportune remark at one point: "They're saying Governor Allen and others stole millions. Suppose they did steal a few millions? Look what the people got." Huey had said practically as much, in franker moments. But it sounded odd

159

from a man who wanted to be Governor. It was recalled later.

The opposition hit uncomfortably close to some dangerous scandals of a new nature when it charged that Allen had sold state oil leases for nominal amounts to machine politicians, and that these leases had netted $300,000 within a few days through resale of a half-interest. It also pointed to formation of a "Win or Lose" company by Seymour Weiss, Noe and Earle Christenberry. Dear called it a "legalized steal" that brought in $320,000, "yet not one cent was paid for state leases" on which the money was obtained. Huey's name was brought into the matter of those leases. Had the campaign been conducted in a somewhat different atmosphere, the accusations might have had an earlier repercussion. Circumstances, however, being what they were, Louisiana was to wait four years to hear more of these and related matters.

Washington's New Deal and Louisiana's older one, against Huey—this was still the line of battle. The opposition was sure that the national Administration would pour men and jobs into Louisiana, and it claimed that definite pledges were given to that effect. Two full years before Roosevelt attempted his "purge" campaign in other sections, a start in that direction was made in Louisiana. Here, though, as in some of the later cases, the expectant beneficiaries charged that they did not receive the full assistance that was promised.

The rigid, continuing control of the voting machinery brought occasional trouble. State-designated election supervisors resigned in several instances because they said "mobs" forced them to grant equal representation to both sides. Allen named substitutes who would not be intimidated into giving anybody fair representation. Twenty parish groups appealed to Washington for action to restore "the republican guaranties of the free ballot" to Louisiana. Some urged that a provisional government be established, that Federal marshals man the polls as in the Reconstruction era. The chairman of a House committee appeared in Louisiana, unheralded. A statement assured Louisiana that "we will take a hand if any faction resorts to the practices which have been common in primaries in the past, and which are generally known to the most casual political observer."

Allen replied that the election commissioners would "kick out any Federal men, and even President Roosevelt himself, if they have anything to do with this election." Leche made his contribution: "Not since Reconstruction days in the South has a national Administration, and particularly one Democratic in name, made such attempt through the use of all its resources to dictate the policies of a sovereign state." And he cited the departure from the country of Charles A. Lindbergh, "the foremost citizen of the United States," with the observation that "no one has ever had to leave Louisiana because he could not live here in peace and security." Let Washington look to its own doorstep.

The opposition, which had seldom offered a constructive program of its own during Huey's lifetime, turned more liberal. It held forth a combination of the New Deal and Huey's Louisiana program—social security, old-age pensions, slum clearance on one hand; and continuation of good roads, free books and homestead exemption on the other. Share-the-wealth was not practical, it said; the New Deal enterprises were the only real way to redistribute wealth; and the antis maintained opposition to the dictatorship laws. The machine derided the New Deal's program as mere pap, not the real article that the nation needed. It stood by share-the-wealth as Huey handed it down; and as for the so-called repressive laws, it would back up anything Huey had done.

One other issue was Maestri. The antis called him "the king of the tenderloin," "the master of the red lights." Dear advised "you country folk to find out who Bob Maestri is. He rules the lower part of New Orleans; he's the boss of the professional gamblers of the city, of St. Bernard and Jefferson Parish." Earl Long jumped to his friend's defense: "He's a good, honorable man. He hasn't made a dime out of the state. If you loved Huey, you should love Bob Maestri." Somebody in the crowd yelled: "Did you love Huey?" Earl answered that he and Huey had had a falling out, but what man in the audience hadn't quarreled at some time with his brother, if he had one?

The ticket of Huey's heirs accomplished the greatest victory of any faction in the state's history. Huey, dead, seemed a better vote-getter even than alive. But there was a significant discrepancy between some of the totals. Earl Long received 12,000 less than the ticket's leaders. It was clear that many of Huey's unwashed still resented what Earl had said about his brother and done to him. Had the machine taken the warning to heart, dictatorship might still flourish in Louisiana.

By this time the Kingfish had risen to a kind of sainthood in half of Louisiana. In the name of the Northern hill-country boy, the devout of New Orleans and of the many sections of South Louisiana were inserting paid advertisements in their newspapers, alongside those in praise or petition to St. Rita and St. Joseph:

"Thanks to Huey P. Long for answers to my prayers."

VII

JEFFERSON WAS A SUCKER

WASHINGTON eyed Louisiana, and Louisiana gave back look for look. The New Deal might not be able to keep the Longsters from winning office. It might, however, indict and convict them out.

On the other hand, Louisiana had weapons of its own: twenty electoral votes, firmly in its hand, and an estimated 6,000,000 to 7,000,000 ballots well scattered about the country. The twenty were Louisiana's strength in the approaching Democratic National Convention. The others were those of the share-the-wealthers, many of whom were restive and calling for rededication of the crusade. The Reverend Gerald was waiting on the sidelines, anxious to head the march. Huey, it was recalled, had threatened to take the Solid South and change results in some of the strategic states. Gerald was more than willing to take up in the name of the master, to make a reasonable arrangement with others. Early 1936 saw the forces of dissent, the Coughlinites, the farm-holiday advocates, Townsendites and others, as superactive elements that disturbed the Democratic leadership. The Republicans, too, had hopes. Huey had helped bring the New Deal into office in 1932. Might his successors form a coalition and help break it?

Involved in the income-tax cases against Seymour Weiss and the other machine men were tens of millions of dollars, directly or indirectly. They constituted one of the largest

163

groups of such charges to be brought by the Government. They were based on the same principle used in the Capone case. If a thief cannot be caught in the act, he may be trapped by the proportions of his loot. Also, if state or local government has broken down, if the criminals have become too great or too powerful for local enforcement officials, the Federal Government may step in under its income-tax laws. On the books were nearly twenty-five indictments against some of the greatest of the machine's figures; sufficient, if juries agreed, to place them behind bars for the rest of their political lives.

The investigations dated back to the earliest years of the Long régime. The Hoover Administration had begun them, but had not acted to place them before a grand jury by 1932. With the start of the Roosevelt Administration Huey enjoyed his brief friendship with Farley and other New Deal leaders. He was looking for his place in the sun. It appears that he was also looking for something else. Jim Farley told recently how Huey vented his bitterness against the Treasury Department because Under-Secretary Arthur Ballantine was being continued from the previous régime, if only temporarily. Farley expresses the view that the tax inquiries had much to do with Huey's attitude in that matter.

After diplomatic relations were severed between Baton Rouge and Washington, the Long men noted that the tax matters were being pursued with greater vigor than before. "The man who got Capone," Elmer Irey of the Revenue Intelligence Service, made periodic trips between Washington and points in Louisiana during 1933, 1934 and 1935. Special agents swarmed over the state. Often, principals did not know that they were being investigated until friends telephoned anxiously that persistent young men had just been in to ask about a recent deal. Men whose names appeared in print in casual connection with the activities of the machine; bank officials, heads of supply houses, of companies newly arrived in the state, low bidders on contracts, or losing high bidders—the inquiries that reached them were exhaustive. The staff of Federal men increased, set up two offices in New Orleans. The investigators, who had handled large-scale swindlers, gangsters and Wall Street riggers, told friends that they sometimes could not believe the things they were uncovering.

But the agents found themselves hampered at every turn. Their most promising studies led them up blind alleys. Many who were queried were so frightened that they could give no help. They had been told to say nothing, or to tell fabricated tales which were skillfuly prepared so that they could not be refuted. Advance manipulations succeeded often in covering up trails forever. Louisianians were cagey people, the agents may have decided on the basis of their experiences. Few used checks or kept receipts. They had a uniform slogan: Cash, boys, all the time. Pay it that way. Take it that way. Here's five thousand dollars, count it. Make that twenty-five grand, Phil; two rolls . . .

The search after Huey's income extended beyond Louisiana borders. Agents went into every part of the United States to track down the smallest items. T. O. Harris, who lived in Shreveport, tells of this part of the hunt:

A story got abroad that Huey had paid a small Shreveport bill with a check on a bank in Olean, New York. By the time the investigators reached the party receiving this check, he had cashed and forgotten it. Nevertheless, the clue was too promising to be abandoned. Eventually, the check was traced. It proved to be a cashier's check bought by Long, or for him. This was but one of hundreds of similar experiences. To employ the argot of the street, Huey Long's elusive financing ran the government sleuths ragged.

An exasperated Huey one day told the Senate that "squads, companies and platoons" were after him and his men; but he challenged them to "get anything on me." His annual income for 1934 was $25,000, he asserted—$10,000 for his Senatorial salary, $15,000 from people "that didn't have the sense I have, and hired me as an attorney." He was asked what he did with his money. He retorted: "I spent it on brass bands, football games and drinks for my friends."

Abraham L. Shushan, president of the Levee Board and one of the major beneficiaries of the machine's largesse, was stunned when the Federal jury indicted him for alleged concealment of income totaling about $450,000 for a four-year period beginning in the earliest part of Huey's gubernatorial term. Most of the money, it was charged, came from a rake-off on practically every foot of gravel that filled the spreading lakefront of New Orleans, crowning civic achievement of Mr. Shushan's presidency. In one year, the Government declared, Abe owed it $15,000 and paid $55.94 on an income of $132,000. Abe had no sooner become president of the Levee Board, it was asserted, than he demanded his cut, on the threat of cancellation of the contract with an Eastern concern.

Next came charges against State Senator Jules Fisher, Jules the Robineer, of Jefferson Parish, who, with his fourteen associates, had saved Huey in the impeachment. He was accused of concealing $325,000 for a period beginning with the year after the Robin was circulated. Jules, said the Government, paid only $20.09 tax on his gains. Jules had figured in legislative inquiries into shell reefs which provided materials for the state, and into an automobile firm in which he had an interest, which dealt in highly profitable manner with the state. Jules' nephew Joe had also risen to statesmanship as member of the House; and Joe, too, was charged with concealment of $122,000. For four years, the Government maintained, Joe had not bothered to make a return.

Into the affairs of business-men associates of the machine the agents then turned; and they raised impertinent questions regarding operations of the Highway Commission and its $100,000,000 bond issues. The Nelson Brothers of Louisiana, Texas and Florida, manufacturers' agents and contractors, were indicted for making improper returns involving $232,000. Thereby hung a tale. The agents found that large salaries were supposed, by the books, to have been paid to three company officials and four other minor figures. The seven made returns on these amounts, and paid the taxes according to the brackets in which their incomes fell. But the Government declared that the incomes of the seven men in reality were nothing like the amounts they set down; that five of them received no salary at all during half of the period. Nearly $200,000, it was implied, went to others, whose identities were shielded by this device.

Colonel Harry Nelson was a member of the Governor's staff. He and Brother John first appeared in Baton Rouge in the early days of Huey. Reputedly wealthy contractors, they were not long in becoming wealthier. They chartered a firm with paid-in capital of $40,000. Three months later it was doing boom business with the state. Highway specifications included for the first time a certain type of guard rail and an asphalt which could apparently be supplied only through the brothers. The $40,000 nest egg multiplied prodigiously, by Government calculation. In a seven-month period, $386,000 of materials were reported sold; for the following year, $575,000. The firm did practically all its business with one source, the Highway Commission; when highway work slowed down, so did the firm. The company was only one of the Nelson enterprises. The brothers had a general contracting organization which received what rivals called a lion's share of highway work. And the Nelsons' operations, in toto, covered only a part of the far-spreading road program.

Seymour Weiss's turn was next. The Government linked him with several others in some interesting financing. It charged him, Mike Moss, vice-president of the ill-fated but politically pampered Union Indemnity Insurance Company, and Joseph C. Meyers, bond manager, with conspiracy and evasion of $60,000 in income taxes. Seymour was charged with evading payments on $176,000 of income for himself and his wife, in connection with the same matter.

The Union Indemnity was the firm with which all contractors had to bond themselves if they wished to do business with the state. A scheme was alleged, by which Seymour obtained twenty per cent of all premiums on the performance bonds. An additional favoritism was set forth, by which the Hartwig-Moss company, an affiliate of Union, was to secure the bonds. Seymour, the indictment declared, "used his influence and position" to force contractors with the Highway Commission to furnish bonds secured by Hartwig-Moss from the Union. False entries in the books were claimed to conceal Seymour's twenty per cent, and employees were instructed not to report the payments. And, said the indictment, everything was to be in cash only.

The Government was making it clear to Huey's heirs that it meant business. The grand jury struck again, and deeper. Weiss was accused with three other men of Oklahoma and Arkansas, Louisiana Quarry Company officials, of conspiracy to deprive the Government of taxes due on amounts obtained from quarry operations. The name of a dead man was introduced, a man who was to be drawn posthumously into other highly colored allegations. He was Sam Beasley,

Highway Commission purchasing agent, elevated to tax commissioner before his death. Secret commissions of $275,000 to him, in a single year, were described. The payments, chiefly from road profits, were said to have gone from him to others, again unspecified. The quarry company, it was charged, was organized by Weiss and confederates for the "express purpose of contracting with the commission" and "to facilitate the handling and disposition of certain large sums of money to be paid by the said corporation under a contract with the state." No action was brought against Beasley's estate, indicating the Government's certainty that the money did not stay with him. When his succession was filed, it revealed an estate of $8600.

The same quarry company figured in some strongly spiked Long stories. It had been operated near Winnfield by a firm which lost money steadily. During Huey's reign, engineers surveyed its property for the state, but ruled that the stone was too soft for use in concrete work, and that the quantity was not sufficient for large-scale mining. "Rock's rock, and I see a lot of it there," Huey answered both objections.

The Winnfield rock appeared unexpectedly in highway specifications. The head of the firm was elated. Now the books could show black, at last. His joy was brief; he was called to Baton Rouge. There, according to one version, he was told that a buyer had been found for his firm. "Oh, but we don't want to sell." "Yes, you do," said Huey. "But now we've got a chance to make up our losses; the specifications . . ." "I put it in them specifications, and it'll come right out if I say so." The official was unconvinced. Huey became more specific: "Do you know who runs the Tax Commission? Me. Now, you wouldn't want them taxes run so high that you couldn't pay, and lose the whole thing, would you? You know, we've looked around, and we think that's mighty valuable property . . . mighty valuable." He won.

Huey's brother Julius charged that profits were swelled by the pouring of water into rock shipments for greater weight. He and others declared that a new product was created, which apparently had some special properties. It cost the state $7 a ton, whereas the commission had been paying $3 for similar materials. The new product consisted, it was said, of Winnfield rock, mixed in oil. And, as further assistance, the Highway Commission was charged with paying down $500,000 in advance of operations at the quarry.

Into the rich gambling grounds outside New Orleans, the state territory that Huey had once raided, the agents had meanwhile moved. The careers of these sportsmen had preceded the dictatorship in various instances; but, under friendly protection and loving shakedowns, they reached new heights during the heyday of the Winn crusader. Courtney Kenny, operator of the famous Arabi Club in St. Bernard Parish, was charged with concealment of $90,000. Before appeals boards he admitted payments to officials. Manasse and Marks Karger, who were in the bigger time, were indicted for evasion of about $240,000. Manasse was a beglamored figure of the period, who pioneered in the bringing of "name bands" to the area for the entertainment of customers whose names appeared in the gossip columns; who received other accolades of the local rich or the local sinful. Manasse, originally a tobacco manufacturer, had accumulated a sufficient amount to permit retirement. The night life attracted him, however, and from then on he acquired holdings under the bright lights.

Brother Marks was described as "the proprietor for many years of one of the biggest horse racing handbooks in the

South, operating as a clearing house for smaller operators."
In civil tax hearings, a success story in the American pattern was told; a saga of enterprise and hard work, setback and reward. The brothers' initial venture was on a small scale, little Victory Inn. A murder took place inconveniently within their walls. Resigned to occupational hazards, they moved to a gambling house over a near-by grocery. The trade learned that it had to walk "a few more squares, then up the stairs"; it willingly made the sacrifice. The Kargers' was the better mousetrap. Prospering, the brothers took over a place on the highway, "just two small miles from the city limits," as the taxi-drivers learned to put it. When they gave up this establishment, a religious organization decided it would make an ideal church. The brothers, no hagglers, believers in faith's consolations, made a gift of it; and Mr. Ripley has commented on the building's career. Forging ahead, the Kargers turned to "chicken dinner inns," roadhouses, places along the levee, running $5000 into a half-million-dollar holding.

The Brothers O'Dwyer eclipsed the Kargers in funds and in indictment. The Government accused them of hiding $438,000. Diamond-studded, loquacious, Rudy O'Dwyer told an appeal board part of the epic tale. He and George came of a family that lived by risks. Father operated a lottery, into which Rudy gradually worked. Schoolboy George earned $30 a week for writing tickets after class. Always a good head at figures, George. When Father died, Rudy took over. But the lottery was too slow for him; two years later he was in the big stuff. It was a life of increasing opulence, interrupted occasionally by the workings of the law of averages. A raid forced the brothers to turn temporarily to around-the-corner dice games. Less pretentious, "these paid almost as well as the clubs." Eventually, the O'Dwyers took over

Southport Inn, widest-open, best-established gambling den in the city's modern history. This was in the first year of Huey's régime. Rudy told how a bankroll accumulated, how a cache of $100,000 was always maintained at the club. "I never run out of money," said Rudy, benignly. Once he "put up ten thousand dollars in a minute," when Johnnie Johns' brother "got down on his knees and cried to me." Johnnie had been snatched and was to be rubbed out if the greenbacks didn't come right away. Within a week, Rudy got it back.

He lived high, bought himself a $20,000 yacht and a hunting lodge in Mississippi, added rococo furniture and hired yard boys. He established an aviary, its population 3000-odd, in his back yard; and there he maintained Chinese silver pheasants, doves from India, Philippine bleeding-heart doves, toucans of Brazil. His friends said that he was one of the few persons, if not the only person in America, who had a Government permit to keep migratory birds in such a collection. Through it all, Rudy handled finances informally. "He never could tell," an agent testified, "what his net worth was, within one hundred thousand dollars." He could not understand the Government's tax forms, Rudy declared, "because I only went to the low fifth grade." But he made his money "from smart people, not the poor, dumb ones."

For his part, Brother George told the tax board how patriotism had caught up with him in 1918. He left the lottery business in New Orleans in the hands of two friends, and joined the Navy. He lived in hotels and apartments for ten months in Pensacola, "shot dice with Navy men and did very well." He claimed a take of $8000 on that occasion. The gambling operations, the agents noted, were at least as difficult to follow as Seymour Weiss's and Huey's activities. As in others, no bank accounts, no books, no records. The

Government traced checks from patrons and trailed movements of armored cars between the gambling houses and safety vaults of the banks.

Other aspects of life under the Long men came forth in other civil proceedings. Doctor-Sheriff Meraux of St. Bernard Parish testified to coerced subscriptions to the *Progress,* and to manipulation of poll-tax funds. He explained a $2500 deposit: "Assessments for subscriptions are not levied against individuals, but against the parish as a whole. The leaders receive a quota, and pass that on to the wards and precincts." The $2500 was only one of the periodic assessments. It showed in the sheriff's bank account, yes, but he had not touched it. A deputy picked up the money, deposited it and withdrew it for the *Progress.* Another deposit, $2600, "represented poll-tax money." It did not come from the individual voters. A deputy testified that he had collected funds for the poll-tax payments from "those who could afford them." Did he make a collection from the gambler Kenny? "Three hundred or four hundred dollars." Was it true that there were two other gambling houses in the parish? "No, there are four others."

Another civil hearing disclosed to Louisianians whom they paid, and what, for a "free ferry." The president of a bank testified that the ferry company of which he was a part owner had been losing money. So he went to a proper man to remedy such a situation, the celebrated Jules Fisher. Jules was obliging. It could be arranged; it was arranged. The Highway Commission, with which Jules' automobile company also had dealings, discovered a public necessity for a free ferry at the point, and agreed to pay $80 a day to the firm for operating it. Jules had gone to some trouble in bringing together the divergent viewpoints. So he received a kickback of one-third of the $80—$26.66 a day, for four years. Then the firm gave up operation and sold the equipment; and Jules, who had become a partner *de facto* if not *de jure*, took a third of the proceeds.

In time, the first criminal case, that of Jules' nephew, State Representative Joe Fisher. It was an eyeopener to the public, and perhaps to some of the machine men who were not of the inner circle. It revealed ingenuity, a deft touch and long practice in extracting advantage from state contracts. Joe, it appeared, owned a shell reef. Uncle Jules had admitted that he often urged the Highway Commission to use shells, including Joe's shells, because he was convinced that it was the proper base for a good road. The Highway Commission in time agreed (Uncle Jules denied that he had tried to get the maintenance engineer fired because he did not share Jules' views on engineering) and Joe obtained the contracts he wanted. But Joe did not handle them. Instead, he farmed out the work to others. These firms paid Joe, first, a full 50 per cent of the profits, then 63 per cent, then 75, plus a flat percentage of ten, fifteen or more on each yard of the shell.

Joe had a foster brother, a somewhat mysterious figure, in whose name Joe operated. Testimony indicated that Joe's profits and commissions alone on 50,000 cubic yards of shell in one operation were considerably higher than the value of the shells on the open market. An assistant highway engineer made a statement that in another instance Joe received $22,000 more than the amount to which his contract entitled him. Others testified that Joe placed on the highway payrolls the names of men who did not work for the agency, some of whom declared that they never saw the checks and did not know that they were on the rolls. But Joe had received the checks and endorsed them. One witness admitted getting $60 a month of highway money from

Joe, but not for highway work. He solicited votes, he said. A flat payment to Representative Fisher for obtaining a favorable committee report on a bill was also charged.

Representative Fisher pleaded ignorance. He had not understood that the law required him to report all income. He knew only that he was always in debt and never had any money at the end of the year, said the man whom the Government accused of concealing a $120,000 income. The Government brought out that he had known enough of the law to compromise with the Revenue Bureau on earlier taxes. Joe was found guilty and given eighteen months in prison. He did not appeal. The machine men were shocked. Was this the beginning of the bad news? Encouraged, the Government pressed its inquiries, brought more indictments, prepared for more trials.*

Meanwhile, Huey had died. Through his lifetime and after it, Long partisans gave assurance that "nobody ever found anything on Huey." True, they admitted, some of his men might have been corrupted, but not Huey. No, sir . . .

Late in 1939, Marquis Childs made the flat statement that the Government was ready to indict Huey within the month at the time of his death. It reached this decision twenty-four hours before Huey's assassination, the writer declared. He made his assertion in a *Saturday Evening Post* article about Elmer Irey.† He described a régime in which graft honeycombed the state, with shakedowns in the millions: "The take was enormous. One contracting firm alone, it was discovered, paid graft in excess of $500,000. A state-wide system of collectors passed most of the spoils along to the higher-

* A later supervisor of public funds discovered that Joe continued to collect payments for shell sales to the Highway Commission while serving time in the Federal prison! Uncle-Senator Jules had also continued collecting.
† Marquis W. Childs: "The Nemesis Nobody Knows" (Sept. 16, 1939).

ups. Finally, there were seven collectors. The seven paid over to two, and the two paid over to Long himself. The Kingfish got the big money, and it was big money." The lavish doings of the Kingfish, "tall spending on the $10,000 a year that is the salary of a Senator," started the Government on Huey's trail.

By this account, on September 7, 1935, Irey went to Dallas. There he met former Governor Dan Moody, who handled the Fisher case. "Step by step, they went over their case [against Long]. They could find no flaws in it. They agreed to go before a grand jury on October 3 and seek an indictment of Long. The following day, the Kingfish was shot down. . . ."

The matter of Huey's income is one that still presents elements of mystery. Before he died, and afterward as well, many a Louisianian swore that the Kingfish had garnered millions, or that he could touch such amounts on a day's notice, giving a nod here, opening a box there. Many have been the fantastic stories that the dictator had sizable sums deposited in Canadian banks or in other places outside the country, for future use. One tale told of heavy sums, political contributions and amounts from other sources, which Huey had assertedly placed in the hands of political intimates as a safeguard—to be turned back when Huey gave the sign. But, according to these versions of the Long legend, Huey did not have time to give the sign before the end.

For months after the Kingfish's death, Louisiana waited with particularly keen interest for the financial accounting of his estate. The succession, filed more than a year later, gave a net of $115,000, including insurance policies and oil stock in the politically favored corporation called "Win or Lose." Some insisted that the boys had held back funds somewhere along the line; that "trusted friends" with keys to "secret boxes" known only to themselves turned out to be not altogether trustworthy; that the family received only a small share of the real holdings that were Huey's. But others were satisfied that the size of the estate confirmed repeated statements that Huey had used much of his personal income for political investment purposes, that he poured heavy amounts into his campaigns and other activities. He had demanded that the boys shell out at times, but he himself had also shelled. The Kingfish's god was ever power, not money per se. Still, the stories have not completely downed; cynical (or perhaps only romantic) Louisianians tell one another that "it will come out some day. . . ." At that, a $115,000 estate was not bad for a country boy who had lived to share America's wealth with the poor.

The Long men did not talk much about the indictments, outside of court. But Abe Shushan, as his case approached late in 1935, felt it his duty to issue a statement to America: "It is high time that the taxpayers knew the tremendous waste of their money by the Roosevelt crowd in the politicalization of Louisiana." He attacked "that bunch of Federal spies, eavesdroppers, keyhole-listeners, wiretappers and stool pigeons, sent to harass that great and good man, Senator Long, and his friends and supporters. For about three years, a veritable array of pie-eaters has been quartered in an expensive New Orleans hotel, living on the fat of the land." (Not Seymour's hostelry, by the way.) Abe particularly resented the use of the income cases which, he said, were resorted to "only to insure collection of taxes from racketeers and criminals." The point was that these were the words that many Louisianians were always using for the Longsters themselves.

Abe's case was the most important one to date; conviction of Abe on these charges involving almost a half-million dollars might have sharp repercussions. A bizarre and theatrical entertainment, with mystery, suspense, comedy relief and tears, the latter from Abe, was the result. The elements were a dead man's "little black book," shadowy movements of men and money about the country, disguised packages of currency, secret intermediaries, secret names, "hot bonds" and related manipulations.

The black book had been the diary maintained by the president of the New York firm which had the contract for filling the lakefront. Cryptic little items were read: "Shushan in today. $5000." Abe had pulled down two cents a yard on almost every unit of the filling poured into the area, it was testified. The dead man's successor was not quite settled in his office, he asserted, when Abe asked for an appointment. Abe's visit might best be summed up in the words: "Well, what about it?" He had had a little arrangement with the other president; no contract; nothing formal. Would it be continued? The new official told the court that about $1,000,-000 was owed the firm by the Levee Board. "Our very existence depended on collecting." There appeared strong doubt that the past-due funds would be forthcoming if Abe suddenly became unfriendly. So the plan was continued, he testified.

Abe had a code name, "Ferguson," for his dealings. A subsidiary company official told how funds were telegraphed from New York to New Orleans; how he drew $10,000 in cash and delivered it to Abe. In other cases, checks were interchanged and sent about the country; this method being used, the Government maintained, to hide connections between those giving and those receiving. Vouchers were identified, "for engineering expense in Mexico" or Barcelona, and questions raised as to whether Mexico or Barcelona did not mean Abe of New Orleans. In New York, one Keller, a Shushan representative, was sent to the firm's offices. Forty-eight bonds, valued at $1000 each, were wrapped up for him in advance. He was told by an official that "there was a package there in the drawer for him." The official left the room. "When I got back, the package and Keller were both gone." The package, testimony continued, was handed to Abe. Abe said, "This is not for me." But he took it.

Abe, it was declared from the stand, did not leave a penny untouched. The last interest coupons had been clipped on the bonds. By long distance, "he protested very vigorously that this was not fair, and was not the understanding; and as a result, as soon as we could, we sent him the money for the coupons." A telegram arrived on another occasion: "Ferguson is peeved." Its life at stake, the company unpeeved him. Later Abe telephoned that his income tax was being investigated, and that he was returning the bonds. The company was not to worry. "If any inquiry were made as to whom we had made payment, or delivered bonds, we should say they were made to a Mr. Beasley. I had never heard of him before. I said to Mr. Shushan that I didn't think that was safe. But he said that it was, because Mr. Beasley was dead."

Abe's attorney, Hugh Wilkinson—a former law partner of the Kingfish—offered the view that Abe might not have to pay tax on the income in question, because he might have received it unlawfully. Money obtained by wrongdoing does not belong to the recipient; selah, it is not part of his income. The Government noted that it was not contending larceny. Replied Hugh: "It might be shown that it was secured by extortion." The firm was not sure "whether you could use that term; but we were told that other companies would be glad to get the work on the same basis. . . ." The main defense point was that the payments to Abe were not intended for him personally, but as donations to political campaigns: "The Government calls it graft. It is a contribution to the welfare of a political party in which they are interested. . . . Our whole government is founded on political campaigns. Nearly everyone makes campaign contributions."

The Shushan trial, main event on the New Orleans calendar of the month, kept some from the races, others from their daily radio programs, the payroll brigade from its work. The machine packed the trial as it had packed Congressional hearings. It wanted its side represented. Finally, the case went to the jury, the Government being satisfied that it had scored a second important success. The verdict came in: Not guilty. The payroll whooped, whistled, clambered over the rail to dance around Abe and yell comment at the court. The judge turned white. Order was restored with difficulty. Wilkinson apologized to the court. The judge left. Bodyguards, formerly Huey's, popped up, and the Long men yelled encouragement to them as they felled photographers, broke their cameras. That night the newspapers risked contempt by sending reporters to interview all members of the jury as to what had happened, on what grounds the verdict had been found. The jurors were uniformly non-co-operative. The Government counsel was stunned: "I was more surprised at this verdict than I ever have been before. . . . The fact that one jury acquits should not affect the clear duty of the Government to lay before juries, squarely and fairly, any substantial evidence of violation of the law. . . ." But the case had not come to its end. Years later another Federal jury was to question the men who turned in the verdict, but without result.

The machine leaders were heartened. Still, there were other cases ahead, and some dark ones. The grand jury returned more indictments, one of the heaviest being against Seymour Weiss. Mid-January of 1936 brought the Leche landslide; and Baton Rouge and Washington were silent. Leche halted his attacks on the Roosevelt régime; so did his assistants. Word spread over Louisiana that some interesting conversations were going on, that nobody was to stir up things. But an awkward, raucous interlude ensued. Gerald Smith acted up once more. He conferred in Georgia with Eugene Talmadge, then took a plane East. There he gave out interviews that caused a stir. He and Talmadge had strong plans for downing Roosevelt at the coming National Convention. He and Gene would bring five anti-Roosevelt state delegations and give Roosevelt the fight of his life. Gerald asserted that his followers were strong in Mississippi and Arkansas, and that the share-the-wealth organization would consolidate Georgia for Talmadge, then take the scalp of Huey's old enemy, Joe Robinson of Arkansas, just as Huey had threatened to do. As for Louisiana, the Leche election was "an out and out anti-Roosevelt victory." In a word, share-the-wealth was out after the President's scalp.

Leche, the man who had himself only recently been swearing at Roosevelt, spoke back tartly: "No individual or group of individuals speaks for me or my administration. My chief aim in life during the coming four years will be to promote the best interests of Louisiana." The Governor wanted the skies clear for any stray birds of peace that might be winging their way about.

One day that spring, Seymour Weiss was found in agitated state in his Mayflower suite by Harry Costello, Washington reporter. Seymour was close to tears: "He wants to crucify me . . . He won't listen to reason . . ." It became clear that Seymour was referring to Secretary of the Treasury

Morgenthau. "He's the only one spoiling my deal . . . Yes, I talked to Farley . . . He was noncommital." A few hours later, according to the *Washington Merry-Go-Round,* Costello saw Marvin McIntyre, Presidential secretary (and Costello's former city editor) and said: "Mac, did it ever occur to you that the Administration might arrange a rapprochement with the gang down in Louisiana? . . . I think I could be of some service to you." The answer was: "I think that's already been taken care of." "Then nobody has to worry?" "Nobody."

Before the first legislative session of the Leche administration had begun, United States Attorney René Viosca went into court and moved for dismissal of most of the indictments against the machine men. "The pending cases are weak," ran the argument, "and the changed atmosphere since the death of Long made convictions extremely improbable." The revenue men had done a magnificent piece of work, "but the altered situation made it inadvisable for the Government to spend money and time in trying the remaining cases."

Observers throughout the country thought this a curious statement about a curious happening. Reaction was national in scope. A large proportion of the newspapers, Democratic, Republican, liberal, conservative, scored the Roosevelt Administration, imputing that it had manipulated a sell-out at variance with basic concepts of equity. Angry comment followed in Congress, with charges on the floor that Leche and Farley had arranged the "fix" in a New York hotel room. The Internal Revenue Bureau of the Treasury Department was chagrined, and let it be known that it had no part of the deal. Irey of the Special Intelligence declared: "We made careful investigations and accumulated a mass of evidence which we felt, and which we still feel, provided the basis for successful prosecutions." Complacently, Attorney-General Cummings declared that he agreed with Viosca; that it had been "concluded to leave the decision entirely to the judgment and discretion of United States Attorney Viosca"; that the whole matter was "routine"; that "all this hullabaloo is synthetic."

There was nothing synthetic, however, about the feeling among the men who had served as the grand jurors in the investigations. Nine of the group addressed a bristling letter to Cummings, noted that they had held fifty-one lengthy sessions on the subject, and added: "As to whether the cases were 'weak,' . . . this same United States Attorney, either in person or by his assistants, presented these 'weak' cases to us for investigation. As to there being a 'changed' atmosphere in New Orleans, if by this is meant a change in the wish of the law-loving people of the United States to see that crime is punished, we challenge the statement. It is not true; there is not and cannot be in New Orleans, or elsewhere, among honest and law-abiding people a 'changed atmosphere' with regard to the punishment of crime. If that statement as to the 'changed atmosphere' were limited to official circles, we would readily agree." The group added that during its investigations, it heard that Long men were trying to make their peace in Washington by "pull" or payment of the taxes, and that the Government at that time declared it would not "compromise itself by condoning the commission of crime for a pecuniary consideration." It concluded with a proposal that Joe Fisher be released from prison; "possibly one of the least of the offenders," he was now the victim of "gross and unwarranted official discrimination."

"The Second Louisiana Purchase," Westbrook Pegler and others called it. Jefferson had paid $15,000,000. The United States bought Louisiana back for the sacrifice of some possible prison terms. The Roosevelt Administration made Jefferson look like a sucker.

Some have wondered what might have happened had death not taken the first man chosen for the Roosevelt Attorney-General, crusading Tom Walsh. Cummings, who went on in his place, was a man who knew politics; conservative, easy-going, a stand-patter who was not accused by his closest friends of leanings toward reform. A Purchase under a Tom Walsh seems in the realm of the improbabilities.

Farley, in 1938, wrote * that he had "absolutely nothing to do with the tax cases." As to the propriety of the step that was taken: "Not being a lawyer, I am not competent to pass on the final action of the department. . . . If there was a 'purchase,' it is only fair to ask what was purchased? As soon as Senator Long died, thus ending the threat of him running on a third ticket, it was apparent to everyone in politics that Louisiana would vote Democratic in 1936." It was not all, however, as simple as that. No one was certain just how important were the forces of organized resentment at that period, or to what use share-the-wealth might be put by an alert demagogue in the sacred name of Long. The Louisiana votes in Congress meant much to the Administration on closely controverted issues. The Roosevelt Administration stood to benefit, at the least, by the shutting off of a source of constant criticism and abuse, which had continued to come from Louisiana after the Kingfish's death. Ensuing events made clear the terms of the Purchase.

For some of the cases, a judicial bargain basement was set up; and men, by payment of $1000 fines and penalties, were freed of charges which might have brought years in prison. Civil cases were carried out, however, and the Government succeeded in collecting about $2,000,000.

* James A. Farley: *Behind the Ballots* (Harcourt, Brace; 1938).

June 12, 1936, brought Louisiana in tribute before Roose-velt. The first post-Kingfish legislature dropped all business to call on the President in a body. Most of the members had been elected largely on a basis of violent abuse of him and eulogy of Long; that was not important now. The Chief Executive was on his way to Gulf fishing waters, and passed through the Texas Centennial grounds. Graciously, Governor Leche ordered the legislators to convene on that spot, for the first gathering in history of the Louisiana State Legislature outside the state's borders.

The initial act of the legislators, in setting up shop on alien soil, was to adopt a resolution "praising divine providence for providing a great leader, Franklin D. Roosevelt, who saved the nation from ruin and chaos," and calling upon obstructionist Republicans to "abandon the vain and useless effort to overcome the will of the people of the United States"; to withdraw Alfred M. Landon, in other words. The Louisiana State University band played Huey's *Every Man a King* between speeches.

Seven hundred additional Louisianians accompanied the legislators on the excursion. When the President arrived, the assembled group scrambled for a mass reception. The President, a press association reported, "smiled his appreciation." There was one sour note. At home the unreformed Jimmy Noe snorted: "I see no reason for a junket like that. Why should everybody, including our page boys, go all the way to Texas to see Mr. Roosevelt? We ran on the Long ticket, not the Roosevelt ticket."

June 26 brought the Democratic National Convention. Seymour Weiss was selected national committeeman, though some jaundiced observers thought that the choice of a man who had only recently slipped from beneath a heavy load of criminal indictments was not of the happiest. But Seymour was in gala mood, wearing trick hats, tooting horns, telling all who would listen: "Roosevelt's good enough for me."

Into the Roosevelt bag went the twenty votes. Everybody was happy—too happy for his own good in several cases. Two of the eminent converts, like many newly reborn repentants, overflowed with the message. Out came some startlingly frank admissions. The International News Service reported this interview: "Allen Ellender declared that he did not regard himself as committed to fighting the fiery Huey Long's posthumous battles. Huey Long, he said, was personally ambitious, and saw in his feud with a President a means of advancing his own presidential aspirations." The New York *Times* captured more damaging sentiments: " 'I always thought,' said Mr. Ellender, 'that Huey was subordinating the best interests of the state to his own ambition.' " From Mr. Weiss, via the *Times:* " 'There is no one now in Louisiana with national ambitions. We want to do the best we can for our state, which is, of course, strongly Democratic.' " (But which, he did not add, might have become anything but "strongly Democratic" if Huey had continued to hold it in his pocket.)

Response was furious among the bayou and hill folk, to whom all this was treason. The Legislature dropped everything else to ponder the issue. Earl Long, who had once called Huey liar, coward and bribetaker, stormed out in his brother's behalf: "If Seymour Weiss and Allen Ellender made those statements, then Earl Long is through and done with them both." Jimmy Noe leaped up to tell the people that he felt "mighty bad, mighty bad" about those articles. There was talk that Ellender should be sent back where he came from, "digging potatoes in South Louisiana," if he had made such remarks. One adherent to the old gospel threatened to invade every parish to demand Ellender's impeachment.

186

ON THE SKIDS

Kingfish Huey dedicates the rolling to one side of a state building, which
was rolled right back again. NET RESULTS: The state was relieved of
$500,000, and the building lost one story. LEFT, Leon Weiss, architect of
the maneuver, and RIGHT, foot on skid, President James Monroe Smith of
Louisiana State University.

"YOU CANNOT PRESENT IT IN OPEN COURT"
—Judge George B. Platt.

"THERE IS NO POWER ON EARTH THAT CAN
MAKE ME RESIGN"

—District Attorney Charles A. Byrne.

CONVERSATION PIECE

After a hard day at the office, Mayor Maestri relaxes with an athletic trainer.

PARADE OF MOMUS, 1937

Leche, Maestri and Seymour Weiss enjoying the Mardi Gras.

1 2 3 4

INDICTMENT

Four Newman-Harris defendants line up in court. (1) and (2) are "The Boys," Norvin Harris and Robert Newman; (3) Abraham L. Shushan; (4) Henry Miller, who had the $500,000 idea. Others are attorneys.

LEFT, George A. Caldwell, who went to jail from the house with the golden bathroom.

RIGHT, A. L. Shushan, whose initials covered New Orleans' airport, cost thousands to remove.

STEPS GOING DOWN

THE CARES OF OFFICE

Governor Earl K. Long, at right, with a friend, after conference with Old
Regular committeemen over the future of District Attorney Charles A.
Byrne. (*October 26, 1939.*) Long said he lost years in the campaign.

"THROW THE SCOUNDRELS OUT!"

Another pointed out that Ellender "did go to the President and make some arrangements"; but the speaker was then struck by the thought that the old lyingnewspapers might be at it again. In part retaliation, he proposed that reporters be excluded from public sessions of the Legislature.

In lengthy representations, Weiss and Ellender denied all, or practically all. They were sure that the Long supporters "could not and would not believe that we would be so ungrateful as to make any statement that in any way reflects on the character and work of our great departed leader." If Huey were alive, they would be following him; but they believed it was understood during the recent state election that if Roosevelt received the renomination, the state would be for him. Seymour and Ellender were convinced that Roosevelt would be nominated by acclamation. Thus they were merely looking out for Huey's, and their, Louisiana. Ellender in a separate pronunciamento attacked Wall Street, the newspapers, "the great moneyed interests and the masters of concentrated wealth"; and he praised Huey and Roosevelt in a fine show of impartiality.

The Legislature gave Ellender a rising vote of confidence, then went on to impose a consumers' sales tax, to prove that it still believed in sharing the wealth.

VIII

GOVERNOR DICK AND THE BOYS

THE calmer, lusher era of plenty was at hand for the boys. Washington beamed at Louisiana, a golden beam; and the part of Louisiana that was to benefit in particular beamed back.

Huey had wanted America; his followers were satisfied with Louisiana. The state was soon to be theirs in a way that it had never been Huey's, even in those latter days of the first phase.

Dictatorship remained, but an altered dictatorship. It could afford to be beneficent in most things; as matters were going, there was no need for bad temper. It would be content within its original borders. All that it wanted was title to air, land and sea; a free hand and contributions from Washington; and it came close enough to that goal to give Louisiana a respite from the recent wars.

A few final flurries of preparation, and the boys would be in position to take and to receive. The share-the-wealth movement, pledged to seek Huey's specific national program, was pushed farther and farther into the background, although it was never formally abolished. That would have caused trouble. Instead, everything that Dick and his associates did became share-the-wealth, with approval, by some process of communication that was never made quite clear, from Huey in the beyond.

During the gubernatorial campaign, the Reverend Gerald

and Huey's former secretary, Earle Christenberry, had played a game of wary waiting. Gerald was allowed to take the stump for a few brave (if limited) addresses, in which Leche and Earl Long became the physical embodiments of wealth-sharing itself. Even under these conditions Gerald made remarks that roiled Secretary Earle. New Orleans newspaper readers were enlightened by a little interview in which Earle served notice that Gerald was by no means the head of share-the-wealth, as he was claiming; moreover, that Earle still had the membership lists. Brotherly affection had never been a commodity of exchange between Gerald and Earle.

No new membership cards went out, no new circulars. Complete confusion spread in the share-the-wealth ranks. Some members suggested that since Huey had been so friendly with Eugene Talmadge, it might be a good idea to get the Georgian as leader. Gerald scotched that project. Gene was a fine gentleman; but Gene, so Gerald averred, did not go along with some of the wealth-sharing concepts.

Rebellion was attempted here and there. In Connecticut, Lester Barlow proclaimed that as "New England organizer" he was taking over the "temporary national leadership." "Smith has no right," he told the world and the Associated Press, "to attempt to lift the share-our-wealth banner from the dead hands of Senator Long." For permanent leader he suggested Senator Frazier of North Dakota; for himself, Mr. Barlow promised that he would serve only until he developed "representative leaders of the many districts, to the end that a national convention may be held to establish our legal officials." But nothing came of this either.

Restlessly, Gerald and Earle shopped around. Earle appeared at a Townsend convention, "in a business capacity, returning to my old business as convention manager. No political significance; share-the-wealth is not associating itself with the Townsend movement." Reports would not down, however, that Earle had turned over the invaluable share-the-wealth membership lists to the Townsendites. Gerald himself was dallying with Talmadge and others. Despite the rebuke he received from Governor-Elect Leche after his threat to tear Louisiana with other states from Roosevelt, Gerald went to Georgia for Gene's "States' Rights rally." "Jeffersonian Democrats," these patriots called themselves: Gerald, Gene and the wealthy John Henry Kirby, head of the Southern Committee to Uphold the Constitution. A key-note was Talmadge's appeal: "Let's don't allow a bunch of Communists to have four more years to appoint successors to such stalwart men as Justices Hughes, Butler, McReynolds, Sutherland and Van Devanter."

Earle Christenberry returned to Louisiana with news that was good and also bad for Gerald. Earle was to become "po-litical adviser" to the Townsendites. He did not intend to give the share-our-wealth lists to Townsend, but had already turned them over to Widow Long. Further, he had obtained patents and copyrights in his own name to cover every detail of the movement, and these, too, were in the widow's posses-sion. With a glance in Gerald's direction, Earle explained his actions by declaring that share-the-wealth was Huey's "own idea and his greatest ideal"; that Huey had been "im-placably opposed to collection of dues or assessments"; and Earle wanted, said he, to make sure the organization con-tinued on the same basis. Share-the-wealth's future leader would "have to be someone Mrs. Long can trust, who is hon-est, self-sacrificing and sincere." Earle thought this might be Senator-to-Be Allen or, later, Senator-to-Be Ellender. Gerald said nothing. He still had visions of riding back to power as Senator Allen's secretary. Then they would see what they would see. . . .

But tragedy struck Gerald again. With only four months of his gubernatorial term left, Allen died suddenly. Jimmy Noe, Gerald's mortal enemy, became Governor in Allen's place. Others besides Gerald had cause for alarm. Jimmy was a man with a grievance, and with an opportunity to exercise it. He could bring down the temple about his own head, if he wanted. Maestri, Weiss and Leche maintained pained silence. But Noe was thinking ahead. More than ever, he wanted to be Governor for a full term. He set out to make Louisiana look on him as a model, to give the folks a taste of what they would get if they voted for him four years hence. Comedy took the stage. Noe was a study in linen-and-seersucker joviality, in sweet reasonableness, photographed at veterans' conventions, hailed at state fairs. If there were things he could not do, at least he could always pass the blame to Leche. Mrs. Noe was the gracious hostess to everybody as she and Jimmy opened the mansion wide for receptions, soirées, parties for the country people, while informality reigned. Baton Rouge society chuckled when it appraised the burden that the Noes were passing on to the Leches.

Jimmy tossed about dynamite-packed subjects as he spoke of real share-the-wealth and what it would mean; of guaranteed $6000 homesteads, $2500 incomes and radios. Leche stored up a collection of grudges against Jimmy. But the Governor pro tem caught the other side napping when the question arose of filling the vacancy for the Senatorial short term. Since Ellender was to go in for the full term the next year, it was presumed that he would be obliged with a gift of the preceding period. The State Central Committee was called. Noe beat it by a day or so. Settling a fine point of legal authority in Huey's manner, suddenly, on January 31, 1936, he named Mrs. Huey P. Long. The committee did not dare to contest the action against a widow—and particularly not against this widow. Rose Long was a housewifely soul who had little interest in wealth-sharing or public affairs. But the position paid $10,000 and, as somebody remarked, it would provide her with "a nice change of scenery." Thus culminated a career that had begun when Rose baked her "bride loaf cake," those twenty-three years earlier, for the contest that snagged her the prize and Huey as well. Jimmy's coup sat well with Huey's country followers. It was a right nice thing to do; and it sure showed that Jimmy was a Long man, now didn't it? . . . It was also a neat $10,000 or so of revenge on Ellender.

Surface neutrality was maintained until the last week of Noe's short rule. Unexpectedly, Dick Leche came forth as a man interested in getting the state a better share from its oil lands. Governor-About-to-Be Leche learned that Governor-About-to-Retire Noe was preparing to grant heavy leases on state property. Leche was of the opinion that new legislation was needed, requiring advance geophysical surveys. Therefore he asked Noe to hold up action. Noe granted the leases in silence. He was to be charged with giving away millions of state revenues. But Leche never instituted his "reforms" to give Louisiana its "better share." Louisiana had its own guess as to the reason for Leche's request. The state was to chortle whenever it recalled Dick's oil-stake evangelism.

When Rose Long went to Washington, she needed someone to steer her about the terrifying place. A convenient thought pulled Christenberry from the maw of Townsendism to serve the new Senator as he had her husband. And poor Gerald Smith sickened as he saw a hardy enemy in the place for which he had yearned. . . .

Leche was inaugurated to the accompaniment of high words in praise of Huey, the cheers of Huey's officials and Huey's followers, as great portraits of the master looked down upon the assemblage. Governor Dick received a tent-sized nightshirt bearing the seal of state. (No Kingfish rampant, however.) And a country admirer placed a wreath on the grave near which the ceremonial occurred: "Green be the turf above thee, friend of our better days; none knew thee but to love thee, nor named thee but to praise."

Although a heavy marble slab rather than grass covered Huey's grave, it was not often that he was named except in praise during these next years. The Kingfish, dead, became a different man, much more tolerant, an understanding sponsor of all good things. The Washington-Baton Rouge axis was blessed in his tribute. When new taxes were imposed, they became not only wealth-distributors, but also the kind Huey favored, even though he had specifically opposed them in life.

Leche's task was an easy yet a hard one. He had powers never held by any other American executive. At the start he possessed more dictatorial authority than Huey. The dictator's death had come before he had been able to execute many of his special session laws; in tribute to him, his last session had adopted all of his pending bills, including the punitive one that had apparently been the immediate cause of his death. Members explained that they felt this was the least they could do. "Huey would have wanted it that way." Leche had a legislature that was a rubber stamp such as perhaps no American governor till then had ever possessed. The issue of martyrdom had wiped out even the lingering, locally popular oppositionists. Men who had been returned year after year, sometimes administration after administration, had gone down. Others had elected not to run. "You can't beat a fixed game," one had said. Opposition was to remain in a state of coma for several years.

But Governor Dick had appeasements to make. Some of Huey's more flagrant anti-Federal laws, over which his more practical followers had shaken their heads, were the first to go. In quick time Leche and his Legislature suspended or repealed the measures that had kept Federal millions out of Louisiana. A program of "100 per cent co-operation with the Government" also brought adoption of the old-age pensions, unemployment insurance and other social-security regulations. Only Noe objected: "Hold on. That wasn't what this administration said it was going to give. We promised the poor people Huey Long pensions, not the ones the anti-Long crowd was for. We came here with the biggest majority ever given, and now we're afraid to give what we promised. Who's running Louisiana, the state government or Roosevelt?"

On the state scene, Maestri, Leche and Weiss were agreed on the need for giving in to some of the large voting groups that protested a number of Huey's final excesses. This was political wisdom and political protection; and it did not remove the machine's basic powers. Even Huey would have had trouble with some of these laws. But while doing this, Leche had to satisfy the white-hot Huey adherents, make them believe that he was "following in Huey's footsteps." Leche and his associates kept the larger body of the dictatorship laws, and continued the framework of unprecedented powers within the control of a small group of men. But they gave Louisiana a totalitarianism modified by discretion; joviality rather than the snarl in the exercise of compulsion, favors and inducements; and at the same time they dug in to turn that totalitarianism to a richer personal advantage than had been possible under Huey. In some respects, the Leche-Maestri-Weiss phase was simple bossism; in others, it was

194

kingfishery with the cudgel sheathed in velvet. Dick was no trouble seeker; he didn't like to call for the club. But it's there, boys, and you'll feel it if you insist. . . . Just be reasonable; no funny stuff, and you'll get along. . . .

The state administration had made three specific pledges in the campaign: an immediate investigation into Huey's death, with swift justice no matter how high the hidden culprits' rank; continuation of share-the-wealth; and an eternal ban upon a sales tax. Each was repudiated.

A bill was introduced to provide $100,000 for the inquiry. The plan was much favored in the rural sections, by those who were certain Huey had been the victim of a plot. A committee of one house quickly approved the measure, but it was killed from above. Rumblings brought a statement from Leche that he "personally" was responsible. He did not intend to spend the people's money without good reason. He knew that the man who killed Huey was dead. And Mrs. Long in Washington had never asked for a Senatorial investigation, which would have brought greater powers than the Legislature's into play. If the family wanted one, the widow would have petitioned for it. Many suspected that at least one reason why the state administration wanted no investigation was that it might remove a talking point for future campaigns. The machine men were not ones to sell martyrdom short.

"To finance the welfare program," Leche imposed one of the most unpopular taxes in the state's history, a one-percent sales tax for all of the state, with an extra per cent for New Orleans. But he kept faith with Huey by calling it a "luxury" tax on the wealthy who would thereby lose some of their wealth to the poor. Some few necessities were exempted. Noe declared that it made dying an extravagance, and brought the taking of a laxative and the purchase of toilet paper under the heading of luxuries. "Huey Long always talked against this tax one hundred per cent. It catches a ten-cent can of beans and a five-cent box of crackers. All I'm doing is carrying on what Huey worked for and accomplished, no matter whose administration this is. They say that I've left this administration. It's left me and Huey Long."

Leche assured protesting groups, generally the small merchants, that the tax was "a very fair one, that doesn't favor anybody above anybody else. Everybody pays it." Privately he declared that Huey had taxed so many things that sales were about the only possibility left.

The share-the-wealth pledge was thrown over when Leche let it be known that Gerald Smith was persona non grata in Louisiana; and Dick added emphasis by cutting Gerald finally off the payroll. In the North, lining up with the Lemke third-party movement while he still kept an ear cocked to Louisiana, Gerald spoke back. He charged the Leche administration with "ungodly betrayal" of Huey, attacked the alliance of the machine with Roosevelt, Huey's "worst enemy," and called upon the share-the-wealthers to fight the state administration. He would return to Louisiana to stump against the sales tax.

Replying, Leche did not mention Gerald but spoke of "political agitators"; odd words from a Huey Long man. He added that Huey P. and Franklin D. both believed in wealth-sharing; the fact that "ninety per cent of the newspapers are opposing the President, and that the newspapers of Louisiana were always against Senator Long," convinced him that the policies of the two men were much alike. Earle Christenberry chimed in with a charge that on the morning of Huey's funeral, Gerald had proposed to him that they make a racket out of share-the-wealth, asking Earle to be inside man to

Gerald's front-man act, with a scheme to charge a dime per head a week to an asserted 8,000,000 members. A more obscure Longist tossed off a final accusation that Gerald had "stolen the funeral oration from Robert Ingersoll." At any rate, Gerald was no longer to receive his $650 a month, and warnings were reportedly given that Louisiana's climate would probably be unhealthful for him.

Gerald stayed out of his adopted state for years, a wealth-sharer without portfolio. Emulating Earle, he turned for a time to Townsendism and presided at a mass-scaled semi-revival convention meeting. He was described as whipping the followers "into a fury of enthusiasm and generosity which sent scores of old, young and middle-aged pension seekers prancing down the center aisle, waving bills of many denominations. . . . Flinging sweat from his brow and smashing words into the microphone like blasts, Smith played the organ notes of a shouting crowd as though his fingers caressed and pounded a keyboard controlling their throats and tongues. 'I'm going to show that there is something solid behind your enthusiasm,' whooped the big Louisiana preacher. 'I'm going to show what is behind all this—the hunger of millions of poor people. I am going to ask you to go down in your pockets. . . .'"

Gerald had elbowed in, shoving out jealous Townsend favorites. He had gone with Townsend to Valley Forge and taken an oath with him, hands in air, to stand together until the masses received their due. With Gerald at the convention were Father Coughlin, stripped to his shirt like Gerald, and Lemke, the third-party candidate. As Daniell explains: *

Huey's former henchman told the story of his conversion to Townsendism with considerable candor. It seems that after he was forced to walk the plank in Louisiana, he found

* *We Saw It Happen*, ed. Baldwin and Stone (Simon & Schuster; 1938).

himself in the position of a general with no roster of his army. He had heard in some way that the membership list of the share-our-wealth organization had become the property of the old-age pension organization. Realizing that he could not forever barnstorm the country yelling about his 6,000,000 followers with no membership list to back it up, Gerald hied himself to California, resolved to reunite himself with his mailing list. By the time he had wormed himself into the confidence of Dr. Townsend, however, he found that he had been misinformed, and he said at Cleveland that he was "like a bridegroom still trying to catch up with my bride."

Gerald's candidate, Lemke, who was to have drawn all of the share-the-wealth support and the backing of all of the other dissenters, received less than a half per cent of the national vote for President. Gerald was not to return to Louisiana until another crisis summoned him.

Back in the home state, Dick momentarily grated the nerves of Huey's commoners when the old Standard Oil issue came up. Standard had carried on for about a year with an ax over its head. It had been content for a time when Huey had suspended four cents of the five-cent occupational tax, in the Square Deal days; but the administration still had the power to levy the other four. No crusader, Dick agreed to make the tax a flat one cent. It was a fighting point. Angry cries came from the temporarily aroused Long men in the Legislature. Louisiana was being "surrendered to Standard Oil again, by Huey's own people." History was cited: "Huey was impeached, but he rammed the tax down that dadgummed Standard Oil's throat, didn't he?" Another Round Robin was circulated, this time by a bloc of wealth-sharers who pledged a vote against the proposal. The words were brave, but the machine bore down. Earl Long as Lieutenant-Governor worked for the one-cent levy. Leche hurried to the hall and, in imitation of Huey, fixed his subject legislators with his eye. Revolt was crushed, but not before an uneasy moment when one member charged steamrollering, and another asked: "Weren't you a member of the sessions of 1932 and 1934, when you railroaded measures? And you're complaining?" Standard won again. The Legislature, incidentally, arrested Noe to force him to be present for the vote.

Governor Dick proved that his heart was with the poor when he added free pencils and erasers to Huey's free text books. The older benefits were continued, and so advertised: roads, bridges, homestead exemption; continued, too, were the older taxes with the new ones.

The machine gave way on the law that had placed all local policemen and firemen under the state "civil service." The teachers, who had been brought under the machine and had seen some of their number dismissed for political reasons, wheedled forth a modification of the dictatorship law. Coyly, Governor Dick observed that he "could never say No to the ladies." But state power over local school financing was continued. The secret police were merged with the regular state police, but few, if any, were dropped. Huey's bodyguards became Dock Board or state police employees, and one rose to second-in-command of the latter forces. The sheriffs asked repeal of the bill that gave the state broad control over their offices. The answer was a flat no. Underneath the amiable surface, the outlines of dictatorship remained much the same.

The organization knew where to stop with appeasement. The courts were still in its hands. The election machinery was completely its own. There were no independent state agencies. The Tax Commission retained its power over local assessments, with results that were eventually to be startling. The Banking Department maintained rigid rule over homesteads as well as banks. Records remained as secret as ever. Most business and most industry knew that Dick and his friends still held the power of success or failure over them, and that "co-operation" was an imperative necessity. Essentially, the pattern of co-operation with industry was little different from what it had been in Huey's time, with the exception of relations toward Huey's professional scapegoat, Standard Oil. But Dick's and Bob's appeal was different from Huey's, and "friendship with business," within limitations, became the byword. Leche spoke in new vein: What was good for industry, was good for the masses. What helped business, shared wealth. Dick offered a "tax exemption program for new business," a flat ten-year freedom from taxes. Huey, Dick quietly told his friends, had made so much noise in a few cases that he had scared away a lot of trade. Outsiders who heard mainly of the Standard fights did not realize that plenty of good businesses got along all right with the Kingfish.

Now, within less than a year, a claim of $47,000,000 in new industries, lured by exemption, was put forth by the administration; a total of 15,000 in new jobs was asserted. Some carpers questioned these figures and this picture of rosy economics; others noted that exemption appeared to extend to some curious "new" businesses that were little more than new branches or additions to the plants of friends. One of the questioners was the State University's commerce department, in one indiscreet publication. The result was disconcerting to the department. A new editor was named.

Dick and the boys were cashing in. The more abundant life had come. A flood of jobs, projects and cash poured down from the North like the Mississippi in March; over no dry

lands was the rush of water so quickly sopped up. An estimated $100,000,000 washed down out of Washington in a
little more than three years. Huey had fought demoniacally,
had risked political oblivion in his wars for his $100,000,000
bond issues, at interest. Huey's heirs nodded their heads, and
Washington produced the same amount—most of it free of
charges.

Peace, it was wonderful! Buildings, bridges, hospitals,
grade crossings, zoos, swimming pools, playgrounds . . .
Washington was the father of all good; a kindly, older friend
who cut corners, snipped red tape, looked with a special
altruism on projects marked Louisiana. Evidences of prosperity thrust themselves upward on all sides; parts of Louisiana became gardens of WPA and PWA goodwill. Governor
Dick went early and often to Washington on neighborly,
folksy calls on the President and his assistants. He made
regular rounds of the departments, knew everybody, was
"Dick" to administrators and sub-administrators.

When Senator Rose Long's term ended, Earle Christenberry received another assignment, was officially designated
as Louisiana's ambassador to Washington. He established a
"Louisiana embassy" to "handle" WPA, PWA, regular and
emergency departments, and to prepare case records on all
worthy Louisiana communities. Washington, after delaying
the project for years, approved PWA aid for a $12,500,000
general hospital in New Orleans, to replace the storied but
decrepit Charity. The new structure was the largest of any
kind in the South, one of the most massive of American
medical centers.

Washington carried out another part of its agreement by
granting patronage rights. It dropped conspicuous anti-Long
men who had manned its Louisiana agencies. In here a case
and there a case, where Washington's good will was desired,

Governor Dick was not vindictive. "Neutrals" were retained. In one instance Dick permitted an oppositionist to take a Federal office in Washington. "Gets him out of the state, and out of trouble for us," the Governor explained. "Uncle Sam's money takes care of him, and he won't be wanting to get on our payrolls." Everybody seemed to want a place on the rolls. In this breathing spell, the loudest noises were often the squeals of those pushed aside on their rush to the Louisiana-Washington trough. The machine quietly took in a number of men against whom Huey had made particular cry, but who had friends of friends. Included was one who had been mentioned as a participant in the De Soto "murder conference." An interesting appointment, to which the state did not object, was that of United States Attorney René Viosca, who had acted to end the income-tax cases.

The Legislature was kept as never before, in accordance with the newer affluence. The machine regularized the maintenance of the dual officeholders. Many went on as usual, as special attorneys, inspectors and state agents. But the bulk was nested in one organization, its records specifically withheld by law from public scrutiny. This was the Debt Moratorium Commission, which Huey had established to "help the poor man." Observers declared that its major function was now that of helping the poor legislator, and in a manner which Huey could not have afforded. This private-public employment agency was first created in 1934 to cope with an "emergency." In 1936, despite evidences of improved general conditions, the state administration decided that the emergency was still at hand. In 1938 it still saw emergency around it. Not until 1940 were conditions deemed back to normal, and a reform Legislature had to reach that judgment. One of the machine men charged that the Moratorium

Commission cost the state $1,100,000, and that the bulk of the expenditures went for payments to the legislators.

Huey's old problem of New Orleans was solved. For a full year after Huey's death, the city found itself in an anomalous position, rather like that of occupied France after its surrender in 1940. It was neither Long (or King-) fish, nor Regular Ring fowl. Walmsley, the hangover Regular Mayor, refused to quit, but most of his organization had gone over to the state. Leche, Maestri and the state boys gave the word: they would restore most of the things Huey had taken, for a consideration. The state's man must go in as mayor. This was bitter news to the Ring, particularly to several elder commissioners who had hoped to take the honor. But the Regulars had seen much change, and had survived change by adjusting to it. New Orleans has a saying: "The Regulars, like the Chinese, conquer their conquerors." So the Regulars agreed. But they, and the rest of New Orleans, were taken aback when told who the mayor would be: Conservation Commissioner Robert S. Maestri.

Louisiana had regarded Maestri through the years as the silent, backstage figure, the man against whom much was charged, who seldom denied, seldom asserted anything publicly. A dour, phlegmatic fellow, he was determined and tough, but diffident in his contact with the public. He had never made a speech in his life; he "didn't go in for that stuff." He did his work away from the speakers' table. But then ambition came to Bob Maestri. He would be mayor. He was becoming, more and more clearly as the months passed, the strong man of the organization. Now he would run affairs from a front office. But there must be no campaign; he would make no talks, face no mudslingers.

This was a problem. Huey himself had never been able to eliminate election contests. But such was the state of quietude and flattened opposition that now it was managed. Word filtered about that there was no need for any rival candidate. What chance would you have, bud? What was the percentage? The boys just don't want a fight, see. . . . New Orleans saw. An obscure fellow qualified, and was persuaded to withdraw. Since there was no opponent, the election was called off and Maestri was certified into office. The problem of Walmsley was solved. A bill had been introduced in the Legislature, providing a $5000-a-year pension for all mayors who had served more than a certain span of years; this would have meant Walmsley and one other survivor of the office. The idea fell through. There were reports that a judgeship, or a Federal or state attorneyship, was being held out. Finally Walmsley resigned without taking any other office; for, declared he, since the city was getting back powers which Huey had taken away, he would keep a previous promise in the matter. He received thanks and champagne at City Hall. The man who stepped into his shoes was the ranking commission council member. The New Deal co-operated, and the new acting mayor found a Federal collector's post. He too resigned, and the city had four mayors in less than that number of weeks. This chess-game process ended with Maestri in the king rôle, whither he had been promoted without a brush of any kind with the electorate. A grateful Legislature gave him two extra years, extending the usual four-year period.

Thus New Orleans had no municipal elections for six years. Peace, it was more wonderful than ever! What Huey had never quite accomplished with guns and soldiers, with vice inquiries and blandishments, his successors had managed by simple, or not so simple, maneuvering. His men could say, as did an amused critic, Deutsch—"Lafayette Street, we are here!"

It was a day of all-around vindication. Joe Fisher, sole

victim of the income-tax wars, won a kind of moral victory. His term ended, he came home to a civic demonstration, a welcome such as few receive on their return from the big house: bands, banquets, speeches, the name of "hero." To other Louisiana curiosa may be added a document signed by State Representative Alvin Stumpf:

"Welcome to our friend, Joe Fisher. Joe Fisher will be home shortly; we, his friends, must extend to him a hearty welcome. We all know that Joe was a real friend to the late Senator and Governor. The committee asks of you a contribution to help pay his *enormous cost incurred*. As our time is short, we would appreciate prompt response to Honorable John E. Fleury, District Attorney, Gretna." A list of 780 committee members included the district attorney, three sheriffs and practically every state, town and city official for miles around. Joe "sure felt good." Everybody who counted in Newer Louisiana "sure felt good."

Governor Dick went about things the big way. He obtained a $100,000 appropriation for advertising Louisiana to America. A publicity organization received $60,000 to tell the world about the state and, it appeared, also about Dick. It flooded America with pictures of Creole maidens rising bare-shouldered from hills of rice; equally glamorous Louisiana blondes in brassières and thigh covers of Spanish moss; others in bathing suits, eating Louisiana strawberries; L.S.U. co-eds in rodeo hats, satin shorts and blouses. On the domestic scene, the Governor smiled as the L.S.U. band spelled out the Governor's initials and as his name spread on buildings, banners and other displays, in electricity, copper and granite. From state offices poured hundreds of thousands of bright, expensive, illustrated publications telling of the great new work he was doing for Louisiana. Unvaryingly, they bore the Governor's picture, a personal message from him, or a leading article paying tribute to Dick and written, often, by Dick. A story went that one bold official ran everything but the Governor's likeness one month, and came to grief. The Governor's not hard to please, boys; but he knows what he likes. . . . Over the state, from elaborate new hospital-welfare offices that sprouted in every parish (sometimes without enough cases to keep the staff busy) chugged convertible ambulance-automobiles for social workers, and "dental trailers" to bring oral health to the remote areas. On each trailer the Governor's name was painted.

The payroll hit an all-time high, as did the budget. All of Louisiana's energies were centered on Louisiana. With this heightened emphasis on "services" went an increased efficiency in other things. "Dee ducts are flying" became a sardonic byword among the state's 18,000 or more employees. Like other things, the deductions were regularized, with a vengeance. They flew faster and faster, oftener and oftener. Huey had permitted a let-up in periods of political peace; and always Christmas, Easter and other holidays allowed dee ducts to rest. Now there were no interludes, and they flew higher than ever.

Disquieting reports spread that dee ducts were being trained to wing their way into the personal estates of some of the officials. A rebel later charged that at least $1,000,000 in dee ducts had been collected in less than four years. Nobody knew just what went into the pot, or how it went out. As in other instances, no records, no accounting; always cash.

Though Governor Dick's plans were sometimes less ambitious than Huey's, he outdid the master in several respects. When Huey died, the *Progress* disappeared for a time. Then Dick decided to give his people a "real paper." He saw a bargain plant in the heart of the hostile Sixth District, an anti-administration journal that was winded after a series of losing tilts with Huey. Dick bought it, or the administration did—the distinction might be academic—and the state beheld something new in journalism. The *Progress* had been Huey's vehicle of personal satisfaction, his weapon against the unrepentant. Under Dick it provided satisfaction of another kind. Huey had given away his *Progress,* and he had never had advertisements. Dick saw that he got cash, and that advertising became at least as important in the *Progress* as in the normal journals. Circulation stepped up, almost overnight, to 100,000. Colonel James M. Thompson of the *Item Tribune* called the *Progress* "probably the only weekly in the world which received its full subscription price net." Every man or woman on the state rolls "had to take voluntary subscriptions."

The *Progress* boasted, and could prove, that it stood "second only to the *Saturday Evening Post* in advertising linage among weekly news publications in America." Every firm or interest that did business with the state—dredging companies, stationers, food brokers, lavatory-equipment houses, holding companies and banks—eventually gave, or gave up the business. *Progress* bone-crusher salesmen appeared with the proper contributions figured out. Here's what you ought to take, mister; just sign here. You can't afford it? Out would come a detailed statement of gross and net business, taxes and expenditures for the past five years. The machine knew. So you want to get smart, eh? All right, mister, I'll just turn in the report. . . . The holder of a state contract might find its execution held up for "further study"; or a fault might be noted in the materials, or the construction of a building might be delayed for "correction of defects." The Board of Health inspector might pay his first call in years, to look into a supply shed; or the assessor might send a brief note, disclosing a curious oversight in appraisals. Or a relative might drop in, sweating. What have you been doing? Don't you know five people in the family have jobs and can get fired tomorrow? No, only one of them works for the state, but the heads of their companies are friendly to Leche. You'd better get right, for God's sake. . . . Court records tell of one firm which apparently would not "co-operate." State agents delayed bridge construction work for months, claimed that plans and supplies were defective, changed both, finally broke the contract and passed the work to a more friendly organization.

Salesmen had inducement that could not be denied: letters from department heads with which the contractor or firm had to deal; or from Governor Dick himself. One was from Franklin Delano Roosevelt, a photostat of a glowing recommendation, Franklin to Dick, and citing the advantages of a free press on the occasion of Dick's first journalistic venture.

Some gave their money for the advertisements and asked that the ads be forgotten. "It wouldn't look good." The story of the man who paid to keep his name out of the news was reversed; in Louisiana, he paid and suppressed it from the advertising section. Canny advertisers figured *Progress* costs as part of their regular costs. Others included them in their contract, and the state bore the expense. Sometimes the state did so, more directly than that. Departments that exercised routine functions discovered overnight that they could operate much more effectively if they told the public, through the advertising columns of the *Progress*, that they were in existence. These displays might include only the address of the office, or a brief inspirational message, but somehow a vast improvement resulted in the department's work. State hospitals, even though they sometimes had to place patients on mattresses on the floors, washrooms or halls, decided that they, too, should advertise. One of the mental hospitals offered its wares. Villages off the railroad and bus lines decided to take the citizenry into their confidence as to their attractions. Full pages sometimes bore the seal of the state, inviting new industry to come to Louisiana, although the *Progress* was almost completely a Louisiana-circulated publication.

The tone of the *Progress* changed. From a snarling alley cat, it became a tame, well fed pussy. No more the sarcastic linkings of respectables with crime, lechery and wealth. The *Progress* became the simple man's friend. With its ten- or twenty-times expanded space, it gave him comics, movie reviews and canned Hollywood chat; fashions, jelly recipes for farm or city wives; news of new methods for farming, a column on hunting and fishing, conducted by the Governor himself. There was always something about hunting and fishing. It was not too much to ask, was it, that the publisher be pleased in small things? A pure bred bull went to the farmer who wrote the best letter on the value of livestock, one of Dick's hobbies.

The *Progress* breathed helpfulness; it also breathed Leche: an "exclusive" front page story on state policies, enunciated in vital phrases by the far-seeing young Governor; quoted comment, from Washington, from New Orleans, from Labadieville, regarding this or that Leche undertaking. Jonathan Daniels, as a fellow publicist, called on Dick, and Dick lectured: * the important thing was to develop reader interest, let the farmer and the other subscribers know that one had his interest at heart. As to the business aspect, naturally, with such an editorial policy, circulation climbed; and "naturally, if you have the circulation, you get advertising." "They tell me that the advertising linage is wonderful. I'd like to

* Jonathan Daniels: *A Southerner Discovers the South* (Macmillan; 1938).

know how you do it." "Well," said the Governor, "well, of course, I'm just a small stockholder, but we're building up a great circulation." He tipped Daniels a final word:

Don't believe everything you hear in Louisiana. Lies grow here. Probably no state in the union ever was afflicted with a meaner poison squad. . . . Grimm's Fairy Tales were replaced in Louisiana by grim fairy stories, and unless you listen to some of them, your imagination could not conjure up such concoctions. . . .

The Governor was in an unusually drab mood, though such attitudes did not last long. Stories were beginning to spread about, vague little reports that were hard to track or trace.

Some of the boys had forgotten that in a moment of realism, the Kingfish had mused: "If them fellows ever try to use the powers I've given 'em, without me to hold 'em down, they'll all land in the penitentiary."

IX

EVERY STUDENT A KING

IN THE South of the 1920s and thirties, chemurgists found new uses for sweet potatoes and peanuts. Louisiana found new uses for higher education.

During a recent Mardi Gras in New Orleans, His Majesty Zulu rode a float bearing the motto: "There Never Was, and There Never Will Be a King Like Me." Louisiana State University could not have done better than to adopt that slogan during the early and the late phases of the dictatorship. Among other things L.S.U. was, as a Southern term has it, nigger rich. It seems highly unlikely that there will be another college like it outside Hollywood's sets.

Dictators generally have little truck with academic affairs. Louisiana's totalitarianism took over the state university and made it the shining star of a free, all-year-round Christmas-tree display. Education at the state's largest school became an instrument of the dictatorship, a unique implement whose utilization has no parallel in American university records.

It was an era of learning in swingtime; of hoopla and opportunism for professor and politician; of boodle and ballyhoo, academic-gubernatorial hey-nonny-nonny. Its masters used L.S.U. as a source of propaganda and lush patronage; as a means of political manipulation and official exercises in malice toward other institutions. They offered another kind of education to the state: in time, a school for crime and scandal.

Huey started it all, but his political pupils improved on their teacher. L.S.U. was reorganized, expanded, owned and operated with one point in view: what it could do for the state régime, not what the state could do for it.

Louisiana had a kept college, in the same way that Louisiana had a kept Legislature and a kept judiciary. From a small, moderately impecunious Southern institution, L.S.U. became bigtime, bedecked with everything that one protector, then another, could give. The result was a spree. It began under Huey, but under his successors it became funnier and louder.

By-products resulted: a magnificent plant, magnificently maintained; the presence of some impressive names on the faculty, next to some garden variety mediocrities, or worse; the framework for what may become, years hence, one of the great Southern universities. It will take time. Dictatorship dug deep into the campus near the Mississippi levee at Baton Rouge.

During Huey, after Huey, little of this would have been possible without a man who was totalitarianism's strawboss. He was James Monroe Smith, a small-town, small-bore pedagogue, who was lifted from obscurity to the office of L.S.U.'s president largely because of one consideration—in the words of the Kingfish, "He had a hide as thick as an elephant's." On one occasion James Monroe Smith's employer went further: "There ain't a straight bone in Jim's body. But he does what I want him to, and he's a good president."

Smith received his opportunity when another educator declined to bow to the dictator's demand that he grant a degree to a criminal libeler. Had this incident not occurred, James Monroe Smith might today still be a professional nonentity, but outside prison walls.

Huey had trouble when he first set out to corral L.S.U.

Governor Parker, the reformer, had won wide support for a program that had shifted the university to a new campus and given it increased funds, though still not adequate ones. Parker sought to depoliticalize the board for all time by providing overlapping memberships and near-autonomy. L.S.U. has eighty years of history behind it. Its first president, before the Civil war, was General William Tecumseh Sherman, who went on to Yankee fame. (Sherman gave standing orders during war years that "the academy was to be spared"; and it was, though buildings about it were razed.) The university was well beloved by men and women throughout the state, who had attended it or had sent their children to it, or planned to send them.

The year 1930 gave Huey the opportunity he needed to take over L.S.U. "like any other damned department." With impeachment and other more pressing matters disposed of, Huey seized upon the "*Whangdoodle* episode" as fate's gift. Most colleges have their annual comic issues of the school paper; L.S.U. had its little fun like the others. Not-too-delicate satire, picturing athletes as joining ballet classes, the faculty on a binge . . . such was its usual material. This year, however, brought a secretly issued publication that was gutter-crude, criminally violent, containing jokes of a kind that depend generally on verbal currency; accounts that cited names in telling of a fictitious visit by a town telegrapher to a professor's wife, during the professor's working hours. The author was Kemble K. Kennedy, a protégé of the Kingfish, later a practically permanent payroll member.

Kemble K., sure of his patron, was undisturbed when the university hired a detective, discovered that he was the *Whangdoodle's* sire, and expelled him. He was charged with criminal libel. Graduation was a day or so off. The Governor stormed, demanded that Kennedy be given his final examination and degree. The president and law dean refused. Huey kept the pressure upon them. Kennedy received a year's jail sentence but was reprieved and later pardoned by the Governor. The president resigned because it was found that he had heart trouble. The dean was retired because it was found that he was over age. Huey set out to "get me a new president," and he knew the kind he wanted. He used the same standards that he set up in passing on a supreme-court justice, or a foreman of ratcatchers. He didn't want any of them goddamn highfalutin' suckers. He spoke about it to one who ought to know—a friendly stationery and book salesman. The drummer knew just the man: Jim Smith. He had had some very pleasant relations with him. "Who the hell's Smith?" Huey asked. "Tell him to come see me."

Thus informally, Louisiana's leading educator of the dictatorship was summoned before the man who was to be his czar. James Monroe Smith was a Louisiana farm boy who had put on shoes, gone to town and decided to become a country school teacher. There were probably few in Louisiana who were as surprised as Jim Smith when Huey beckoned. He was 42; he had attended L.S.U., then gone on to a dull career as teacher and principal, then to Southwestern Louisiana Institute, the state college. Taking time out for some advanced work at Columbia, he had earned a degree of doctor of pedagogy and the deanship of education seven years earlier, and had remained quietly at rest at Southwestern since then. His wife, Thelma Ford, was supervisor of the school's cafeteria for a time.

Baton Rouge tradition has it that when Jim Smith first arrived, he shocked the Kingfish. His clothes were country cut, shiny; he carried a telescope hamper, and his car was as drab as its owner. Before he did anything else, according to legend, Huey handed Smith one of his larger bills. "Take that car and dump it in the river. Here's a down payment on a new one. Get yourself another suit. And burn that one, and that damned tie."

Jim obeyed. That is the thread of the next few years' history at L.S.U. He was thoroughly housebroken, ate out of Huey's hand, begged when he had to, and didn't mind a cuffing. He knew his place, and he kept it. He stood public insult, jibing, and silent contempt at the hands of Huey, of many of his colleagues and his students. "Jimmy Moron" was the name by which L.S.U. free souls knew him. Soon Huey had a board to match Jim in independence; a board that could be expected, with some degree of certainty, to behave itself. It was made up almost completely of state officials or political beneficiaries. In 1933, Smith and the board signed a "secret" diploma for Kemble K. Kennedy, in violation of the university regulations, and those of academic organizations generally.

Smith, a poker-faced unassuming gentleman if not a scholar, stood by as Huey ran the place. The Kingfish announced major programs and expansions from his hotel suite, then called in Jimmy and the board weeks later to ratify them, when he thought about it. He honeycombed the administration and part of the faculty with politics and with favorites; imported friends from Winnfield and other places, and put them in charge. L.S.U.'s business affairs were Longized, from letting of insurance to buying of ice cream cones. Huey stepped in and fired an occasional teacher who had chanced to write a book to which a minister objected, or perhaps had offended a parish official. Jim Smith bade such staff members good-by, sometimes persuaded them not to protest to accrediting groups, "because we might lose our rating."

215

PART TWO: THE GRAVY DAYS

In 1928, when dictatorship took a running start, L.S.U. had a scant 1600 students. Under Huey and his heirs, the registration was stepped up to 8500. Probably no other American college ever grew in this manner. It sent out branches about the state, established new schools, took on new functions. In 1928 it was eighty-eighth in size among universities in the country. Today it is thirteenth, "right behind Harvard," and ninth among state universities.

Huey had three main reasons for an interest in L.S.U. which became phenomenal: sentimental, practical, vindictive. He had always wanted to go to the state university, the country boy's dream. Now he was on the campus, enjoying an enormous soul-soothing satisfaction as he whizzed about and ran things. Too, he was using L.S.U. as a showcase for his activities, a sounding board for arguments and demonstrations. Finally, he was getting even with Tulane University in New Orleans, his alma mater for a brief span. Huey, as Governor, wanted an honorary degree, and those highbinders and highhats turned him down. (Loyola, the Jesuit college, had not objected, had given one for his great works and in recognition of a compilation of state constitutions. What Huey did to the state constitutions was something more than compile them.) Then, too, the Tulane board included lawyers and business men on the opposite side from Huey's New Orleans friends, and it overlapped that of his newspaper enemy, the *Times Picayune*. Huey swore that he'd reduce Tulane to a little red schoolhouse.

College for all the boys and girls that want it: Huey adopted this platform early, and used it all his life, eventually as a phase of share-the-wealth. He made good on it at L.S.U. Thousands showed up on the campus—many from outside the state—to take him up. They were given a place.

Work was found for them, or made for them, if they did not have the resources. Louisiana State University was, in the dictatorship's own words, its "baby." It saw that Baby got everything; and by that, it meant every little thing. Buildings sprang up for new classrooms and new laboratories, and were in use before the final equipment arrived. New dormitories appeared, new play facilities. An estimated $9,000,000 was spent on construction; operating expenses went from $1,500,000 to $3,500,000 a year. The school burst its seams. The first thousands found living space; the rest had to stay in town, at boarding houses, anywhere they could find.

Like all self-respecting universities, L.S.U. had a stadium. In a housing emergency, Huey took a good look and noticed all the empty space between the sloping seats and the outer rim. Some universities use it for soft drink concessions, others for effete citizens who wish to get out of the rain. L.S.U. used it for freshmen and sophomores. Concrete, plaster and wood produced narrow cubicles in each of which four men were huddled, with two-decker beds. As Don Wharton phrased it, the stadium "seats 45,000 and sleeps 2500." He noted also that four is the proper number for a game of bridge.

Huey then came upon a country club near the university. L.S.U. bought it, from locker room to golf links. Every student a king, or at least a tennis player, for a dime or so a head. Huey wanted a swimming pool for the kids, and ordered it. Construction was nearing completion when the Kingfish strolled in. "This the longest anybody's got?" No, there was one on the West Coast, about ten feet longer. "Stretch it!" said the Kingfish. It was stretched.

A Huey P. Long Field House popped up, costing about $1,000,000, with drugstore, bookshop, clubrooms, training rooms for athletes. For a time prize players were to be accommodated here, with the best of feeding and care, like blooded cattle. Someone—assuredly not Huey—decided that this might be somewhat conspicuous, and the boys were shifted to a secluded separate establishment, in which they lived in a manner to which they had become accustomed.

Huey walked on the campus, and word spread. Out of dormitories, gymnasium, classrooms came a throng. "Hi ya, boys"; "Hi ya, cutie," the Kingfish threw out homely greetings on the way. He handed a bill to a friend who called him aside. He joshed a professor, while the boys and girls giggled. Into the campus store he led his crowd. "Help yourself—on me." Candy, cigarettes, cold drinks, cigars. Huey flashed a $50 bill, or called on a contractor, or a friendly heeler, or the president, whoever was along, to shell.

Huey wanted a good football team. He had to have it to beat Tulane, and to reach a national spotlight for his L.S.U. and, incidentally, for himself. He gave the order: buy football material wherever the best was available; in the oil fields, in the high schools, in the pirogue country. To make sure it was coached the right way, he decided to do it himself, or at least to add his advice to that of the hired man. Daniell tells how Huey found a sports writer in his hotel room one night in Washington, and sent down for "twenty-two of them little gilt chairs you got in your ballroom." He lined them up like two football teams, told his friend to "show me that Notre Dame shift," and got to work to learn coaching.

He took L.S.U.'s football fortunes with an intensity that alarmed some. He cried happy tears when L.S.U. won. He wept when it lost. He strode the sidelines during the game, shouted encouragement, beat the ground, seized handfuls of grass. Sometimes the crowds forgot the game and watched Huey, a better show. Carleton Beals has set down for posterity a pep talk between halves: "What the hell do you care if they break your legs, while you're breaking their necks?" He promised the team a luxury dormitory atop his skyscraper Capitol—the best thing he could think of—if it won an important game. He offered state jobs to those who made touchdowns. A coach got in Huey's way, and soon left. Tulane protested some of these idiosyncrasies, and Huey sniffed: "That's Tulane sportsmanship!"

Huey loved music, the jews'-harp, hillbilly band, anything except them hightoned symphonies; and he loved his L.S.U. band only slightly less than his team. He went after both in the same way; in music, he was unhampered by conference rules. He increased the band to 175, to 200, to 210. "Music scholarships" were tossed about like football bait. Other university musical groups were scouted, neighborhoods scoured by ward leaders, hunting saxophonists with a high-school education. A good discovery might clear the way for a better job for the talent finder; who knew? "Senator, I got a boy here can toot like Louis Armstrong." "Go right ahead and play, son. Don't mind the lousy politicians. You know the Tiger Rag? I'll sing it for you." Huey was occasionally fretful about his band: "We lost a good piccolo player and a great saxophonist last summer, but we'll come through all right. Anyway, we still got our drum major. He was all through, but I persuaded him to come back for postgraduate work."

Like a freshman with a violent attack of school spirit, Huey frequently dropped everything for L.S.U. He spent hours with the bandmaster, an alumnus of Seymour's Roosevelt Hotel lounge, and worked over arrangements: "Change that eighth to a sixteenth; need some stomp there. . . ." He crooned, he hummed themes, he composed *Every Man a King* with his musicians. The band, preparing to leave for an out-of-town trip, discovered that it had no music for complimentary numbers to its host university. Nobody could remember a single song written about even the state. Huey was called. He cocked his head, while the band held its breath. Then he remembered three, and sang them—"dee-dee, da-da"—while bandmaster and assistants set down the notes.

An important game with Vanderbilt was scheduled. "How many kids going?" Huey asked. "Not many. . . . Can't afford the train fare." "How many like to go?" "Hell, everybody." "Then they'll go." Huey summoned the railroad officials, gave a few orders, emerged with what some termed the scalps of the gentlemen. He talked to them in musing fashion of sending the railroad's property assessments to the skies if they did not show proper friendliness to Louisiana's youth. The phenomenal price of $7 per round trip, to Nashville and back, resulted. "Whoever ain't got seven dollars, lemme know." Huey turned his hotel room into a distribution point, giving out fives and ones to all who filed past him, then sticking out his hands and taking from his friends. In return, he received IOUs, but Huey and his student body never broke over these little debts. In all, 4000 students made the trip.

Huey's football shows could not be kept out of the newspapers, no matter how much the papers hated Huey. They were spectacles in the Billy Rose-Roxy tradition: 2000 cadets, 200 musicians, 50 "purple jackets"—coeds in white pleats, blazers and 50 smiles—octettes of dancing boy and girl cheer-leaders, and 50 sponsors in a row. And the star of the troupe, Huey, swinging, roaring, hightailing it at the head of the march. He led his boys and girls down the main streets of the invaded towns, razzle-dazzled over the field between halves and remained, as usual, perilously close to the players during the game. President Smith went along too, alert persons noted.

Thousands who did not bother about the front page came to know of Louisiana, her Kingfish and her school through the sports columns and the gridiron. As a professional "character," a funny cuss, Huey remained in the not unsympathetic recollections of all who saw him. Anyone who did not see him during these descents upon the outer world of higher education was blind, a homebody or one of the old folks who probably could not vote, anyway.

Rice Institute was preparing for a game in Baton Rouge with L.S.U. Huey received word that Ringling Brothers, Barnum and Bailey circus, coming to town on the same day, had a parade and afternoon performance scheduled. He long-distanced the management, then in Texas. He wanted no foolishness, no performance till Saturday night. The management insisted on being foolish. Huey cut the parleying short: "I don't think you're a-gonna like Baton Rouge anyway." "Why not?" "Did you ever try to dip a tiger? You got vats big enough for your elephants?" "Wh-what do you mean?" "Brother, we got health laws in Louisiana. The way I interpret 'em, every one of your animals will have to get dipped in sheep dip before they cross the line. We can't take no chances." There was no dipping. There was no circus show before night.

Huey gave L.S.U. a music school that was classified as a near wonder for the South: a myriad of studio practice rooms, eighty grand pianos. "Count 'em," begged Huey when he showed guests about.

The board appeared before him one day. A new building was badly needed, but there were no funds. "Go ahead. Put it up. Get your architect started. The appropriation? That's my job." Huey acted. He called the Highway Commission, then bulging with millions voted for roadwork. "We got some nice property on L.S.U.'s books, left over when she moved to the new campus. Now you all need permanent headquarters, don't you? Well, we got buildings for your offices, a big school building for your maintenance crews, and others for garages and testing places. That's worth $1,800,000 to you. What do you say?" Huey's highway comsion told Huey "Yes." Court records indicated a valuation of less than $600,000.

Huey put his other hand to work. The Capitol had not gone up yet. The Legislature had appropriated $5,000,000 for it. L.S.U. had some valuable land along the lake. Wouldn't that be a fine location? It would. Huey suggested that the price be raised from $25,000 to $200,000. That was all right, too. Then somebody looked into the fund and found some additional loose dollars. Huey changed the price to $350,000. Now L.S.U. had its money. The opposition charged illegal diversion of bond funds, called him little more than a thief. "Sure," exulted the Kingfish. "I'm the official thief."

Tulane's ranking department was its medical college, one of the outstanding ones in the South. It owed much to its friendly relationship with Charity Hospital, the state institution; its undergraduates had daily access to the thousands of cases within the hospital walls. Huey hit where it hurt, when he announced a new, rival L.S.U. medical school in New Orleans, and on Charity's grounds. "It ain't fair. . . . Honest boys, bright boys with good records, come out of L.S.U. and can't get into that medical school. You gotta have a lot of money. That medical stuff comes high. And then they only let in a certain number, anyhow. Louisiana needs doctors. We're a-going to fix that—a free medical school, and there won't be a place to equal it."

Within twelve months, with Huey cracking the whip, the building was finished, and the first class was received while rugs and desks were still being placed in the offices. Records were broken in the preparation of drawings, letting of contracts, and construction. Dr. Arthur Vidrine, the Ville Platte boy whom Huey had made head of the hospital, became also medical dean. Huey spent money, snapped up professors from everywhere, including Tulane, and acquired a good faculty. Stories reached the public of clashes between the two medical schools, accusations of favoritism in the assignment of cases. But the matter simmered down; and today both schools continue.

Confidently, Huey was planning to step up L.S.U.'s enrollment even further, to make it the biggest god-damned university in the country, maybe in the world—the crowning triumph of his dictatorship's culture. He boasted:

When you go back to Loozyanna in a few years, you won't see that university the same. Not at all. What would you say if you came back there and saw a row of buildings five hundred feet long, barracks-like buildings; cut up inside with little cubbyholes where a boy could study, with a little space to sleep at night . . . I can't afford to put many more students in the kind of dormitories we got. But what's wrong with putting 'em up in a new kind of dormitory, simple and plain and cheap, with just enough room to sleep and wash and study? I'd feed 'em in buildings like that, too.*

There were grimmer aspects. Huey and his successors turned the student rolls, to a large extent, into another source of patronage, so recognized and so treated—and cheap patronage at that. Huey liked to help all the boys, to be

* Forrest Davis: *Huey Long, A Candid Biography* (Dodge; 1935).

sure. But a lot of those strapping youngsters were getting to voting age and came from large families. It didn't take more than $40 or $50 a month for a job; and if he were a bright boy and could be especially helpful to the organization, a full-time place would be worth the investment. Through the dictatorship's span, hundreds of youths were "cared for" not on the basis of scholarship or need, but of the political faith of their relatives and their ability to convince somebody that they were political "comers."

Huey had an idea which had only started to work out when he died. He gathered a group of smart young fellows who knew their way around. They were the campus politicos, the good talkers, the boys who knew how to maneuver a vote. They became share-the-wealthers, and were forming itinerant units in behalf of the movement. One or two accompanied Huey and Gerald Smith on tours, on several three-week absences from school. From L.S.U., Huey was set to send out share-our-wealth agents to cover universities of every section, to form chapters and weld them into a nation-wide organization. The machine was influencing student elections through Huey's well-designated, and well-heeled, favorites. Cliques of student friends of the political higher-ups were formed, and they kept matters in hand.

One day Abe Mickal, star of the team, learned that Huey had decided to reward him by having him appointed to a senatorial vacancy from Baton Rouge. (Huey was not allowing an election.) Mickal fulfilled none of the requirements; he was under 21, a native of Mississippi, not a resident of the parish. He declined. Huey sent Messina, his heavyweight bodyguard, to conduct a "student mass meeting to draft Mickal." An undergraduate wrote a letter to the *Reveille*, campus weekly, terming Huey's action a mockery of democracy. Huey was shown an advance copy. He cried

"Get me Jim Smith," and had 4000 copies destroyed. He appointed a newspaperwoman as "censor" and announced, regarding the editor, "That little bastard. I'll fire him and all his family. This is my university. Nobody is going to criticize Huey Long on his money. . . ."

Smith and one of the deans joined in advising the student editors to "give way." Smith, the students said, told them he would fire the whole faculty and student body "before I'll offend the Senator." Also: "We're living under a dictatorship now, and the best thing to do is to submit to those in authority." The president of the student body, who had one job and by report was wangling another, declined to call a student meeting; the dean of men broke up a gathering when it was attempted. The payroll undergraduates were docile. Huey's temper grew worse; Smith, acting on orders, suspended 26 journalism students for signing a protest. Five were expelled, among them the editor and a former editor; the latter the highest ranking journalism student, outstanding military student of the university and recipient, ironically, of the President's Medal. Jimmy Smith now called him "just a trouble-maker." A new editor, a girl with relatives in state jobs, took over operations. The incident made national news. The athletic director, the alumni secretary and a dean heard that graduates were planning to protest the matter, and rushed to New Orleans to halt them. The Southern Student Editors' Convention praised the students, attacked Smith for "subservience" and the student body for "apathy."

James Monroe Smith had his mind on other things besides free speech. He and his wife Thelma were going up in the world. Thelma "got ideas," became a great lady, and took or received with happiness a title that no L.S.U. president's wife had previously aspired to: "First Lady of the Campus."

Thelma heard of something called a movable moon, in a Spanish home along Bayou St. John in New Orleans. What was good enough for New Orleans was not too good for Thelma Ford Smith of Lafayette and Baton Rouge. The capital buzzed as Thelma installed hers and swished it back and forth in the sky for her guests. Her boss, Huey, heard about it while telling the country folk how he had cut down extravagance in government. He blasted: "Get rid of that god-damned moon." It was not seen again.

A riding school was the next objective of Thelma's attention. She had become a rider. Wouldn't it be nice if L.S.U. could have an academy? Her wish became law. A former Army man was retained, a handsome fellow who helped Thelma in the project; ten thoroughbreds were purchased, and Thelma had one of her own, Don. Baton Rouge stores advertised riding habits, what the well-dressed young sophomore and matron will wear. A riding student was killed, and newspapers told about the somewhat unplebeian undertaking. Huey sent a telegram from the sticks: "SELL THEM PLUGS." Them plugs was sold.

The Smiths' pretensions were marred, at intervals, when Huey showed up at their parties to find out what was going on. Once he burst in with Bodyguard Messina just as Thelma was being her most impressive self. He took a look at the evening gowns and tuxedos, and burned Jimmy's ears for throwing away the people's money. As he shouted, he grabbed candies from the table, while his bodyguard picked and chose among the other edibles.

As Huey lay dying, his last words were said to have been: "I wonder what's going to happen to my poor boys at L.S.U." But L.S.U. continued, "just as before, but better than before." The university had faced drastic action from accrediting groups, but, with Huey gone, this pressure let up, and L.S.U. remained the darling of the machine. The New Deal's favor toward Louisiana fell most directly upon L.S.U., perhaps because everyone was accustomed to thinking of it as the place for all spare funds. Under Leche more than thirty new buildings went up, most of them with Federal money: an agricultural center which is larger than Madison Square Garden, with the largest copper roof in the world; a baseball stadium which was adequate enough for the New York Giants to use for winter training; Leche Hall, a law building in replica of the United States Supreme Court, a classic structure destroying the Spanish architectural pattern of the rest of the campus; new dormitories, new laboratories, landscaped areas, a WPA-dug lake for canoeing.

Board members, calling on the campus, had to ask what the new places were. L.S.U. found it necessary to hire a full-time construction superintendent to work with the New Deal moneygivers. Not least was a housing achievement unique, the cage of Mike the Tiger. The students bought Mike, a full blooded circus Bengal, to match their stickers. The booming Leche said he would do his part; and he built a $12,000 "personal cage," steamheated, glass enclosed, air conditioned, with an elegant frieze bearing football players' figures, an exterior of rough stone to match the other buildings, a weathervane of a gridiron player kicking a goal. Wealth was shared to maintain Mike at several times the cost of feeding, housing and educating a freshman. Meals for Mike cost $20 to $30 a week. A scholarship student has received $15 a month to look after the 475-pound mascot. Mike has his own trailer for use in football travels.

Two planes were now acquired, one at a cost of $20,000, as part of the athletic equipment. They covered the country, seeking football beef on the hoof and bringing it back alive. When school closed for the year, the plane might take a boy home. Nothing was too good for a good L.S.U. letterman. L.S.U. students went on a trip to Europe, at a cost of thousands of dollars. They made band tours about the country. Everything was in the high manner, higher with each year that passed.

President Jimmy and the First Lady were in new bloom. Huey wouldn't rush in now to spoil things. Thelma was the social arbiter, star of the society that she had created for herself. Faculty wives bowed deep, as did many of the local elegants while Thelma waved a queenly silk handkerchief over the soirées that she gave more and more often. Natives gaped while strange caterers' concoctions were served, specially prepared at her order, sometimes brought from the Roosevelt Hotel in New Orleans by state police car, so that they would be crisp when the evening began. Bartenders were hired. Why not? It might not be *comme il faut* in Lafayette, but this was not Lafayette, *n'est-ce pas?* Thelma was patroness of La Maison Française, L.S.U. home for exchange students, and she managed to get in a lot of French. The movable moon was too much of a gaucherie to revive, but Thelma had something else to show the yokels: a terrace for outdoor entertainments. Thelma liked to walk, in airy draperies, in the moonlight; and she was particularly pleased when the military units once held a starlight parade for her birthday.

Incidentally, Governor Dick loved a parade, and was on hand for most of L.S.U.'s marching displays. He was ready to put his boys up against West Point or any other aggregation. After peace came with Washington, the Administration provided new mechanized artillery. Don Wharton commented: "With this formidable equipment rolling by, the

228

drill field looks like Moscow's Red Square in the newsreels." The boys sometimes muttered that they were no sooner out of full-dress uniform than they had to don it again, the orders for performances came so fast.

Two years after Huey's demise, the Smiths decided to take a fling at high society. New Orleans, not little Baton Rouge and its frumps, was their milieu. Marjorie, the Smiths' daughter, was launched from the Roosevelt Hotel as a full-fledged débutante. This took a little managing. The Smiths, eminently well to do and presumably respectable as they appeared, were not New Orleans élite by any stretch of the imagination. Members of Huey's "spite" medical school staff and others who had social as well as state connections were, however, delighted to invite Marjorie Smith here and there, and perhaps to suggest to their friends that she would be an addition to this or that tea or reception. In return, the Smiths threw affairs which New Orleans party goers will long remember. The co-operative Roosevelt Hotel provided vistas of ballroom space and massive floral decorations. Champagne and highballs flowed like watered county-fair lemonade. It was difficult to walk a step, the more restrained guests declared, without bumping into a lackey overloaded with Seymour Weiss's best appetizers, or into Seymour himself. The taxpayers later discovered that they paid for at least some of these little events. Item: Salted almonds, $20. Item: Punch, $105. Item: Sandwiches, $105. Item: Luxury Token Tax, $9.68.

The Smiths became travelers, fond particularly of Mexico. The First Lady made a collection of Mexican silver and requisitioned faculty members to pick up additional pieces on trips to the South. Mrs. Smith traveled to Europe, had her portrait painted, talked of studying at Grenoble, but didn't.

When Jim Smith first hit the campus, he was a petty investor. He had scraped together small savings and with Thelma's earnings had bought a little property. Visiting New Orleans in earlier days, he had contracted to take $300 of cafeteria stock, but didn't have the $300, so he arranged to pay $10 down, $10 a month. He could not meet even these payments regularly. For years he confined his financial operations to small stuff. About 1937, however, "The Doc" —he preferred this title to "Jimmy Moron"—showed the color of additional money. He gave $10 tips to those who drove him from New Orleans, and he pulled out large bills. Everybody was doing it; perhaps such display was merely a matter of pride. Some wondered where Jim was getting his money, but, in the midst of the general affluence, his did not stand out sufficiently to stir great speculation. Jim, in fact, was not cutting as wide a swath as some of his assistants with whom the Kingfish and Leche had surrounded him.

The new building superintendent, named to help direct the flood of Federal money the right way, was Big George Caldwell, who was not so named for nothing. He was a 300-pounder who lived big, played big, and did Louisiana in the big way. Next to him was E. N. Jackson, a former grocer's clerk from Winnfield, who became business manager and emulated George. They dominated the codfish aristocracy of L.S.U. in these days of 1935-39. Nobody could miss the flush air of the university. L.S.U. was being mined. It was a gold-rush center, with pay dirt on all sides, there for the scraping up by the favored ones. For the lesser aides, the flakes were available.

Big George and his friends basked in their own splendor, as Alva Johnston saw it. Summer camps flourished along streams outside the capital. Horses were kept in mahogany stables, with gold name plates for each stall. In this intellectual atmosphere, crap games were the major diversion, with banquets and beer bats as a secondary pleasure. Thousands were lost nightly. Big George and his retinue took the university plane for football jaunts East or West. At the best hotels—"no preference, driver, just the best one"— they took over suites for days and nights of gala times. The football game? Sometimes the boys saw it; again they didn't. You can always see a game, can't you?

Big George acquired a home to fit him and his mood. In the university outskirts he erected a mansion that put all of its neighbors to shame. Its exterior was only striking; the interior would "knock both your eyes out," George guaranteed. The building was Southern Colonial, with Georgian influence, red brick, cream wooden pillars, a double curving stairway leading to a wide second-story veranda. Mrs. Caldwell was the former Zellie Belle Wahl of Line Creek, near Kentwood. She had seen something like that in France or New Orleans, she thought. Inside was that "golden bathroom" which so stirred Baton Rouge when it heard of it. Everything was not gold, of course; only the toilet fixtures, shower-curtain rings and accessories. The rest was black tile, *à la* Metro-Goldwyn-Mayer. It was an enormous place, lobbylike in effect, the *pièce de résistance* of the establishment. Next door was the master bedroom, with a seven-foot square bed for the master, with all-leather furnishings to carry out the expansive motif. The madame's room was a study in mirrors; mirrored panels in the headboard of the bed, mirrored cornices, mirrored dressing table beneath a huge mirror. Zellie Belle knew just what she had in mind. The playroom was a long one, with a horseshoe bar at the end, and was lighted by chandeliers formed of amber beer mugs on replicas of trays. The room was soundproof and air conditioned, as were other parts of the house.

231

Big George's official earnings were $5000 to $6000 a year. Estimates were that the building cost should have been about $45,000. The assessment rolls showed a complete tax exemption for several years ahead. One of Leche's laws (to increase home ownership) was so written that 100-per-cent exemption applied to all new residences, of whatever type and size.

Across the road was the establishment of Business Manager Jackson. It was quite outshone, because it was in better, simpler taste: a handsomely proportioned, handsomely planned Louisiana Colonial, with deep porch, heavy pillars, beautifully landscaped grounds, lawns sloping to the river at the rear. The cost was estimated at $50,000, but the building was assessed for $8500. Jackson's official salary was $6500.

They were jolly men, Big George and his friends; fat men, lovers of the good life, the good story. They had found their Aladdin's lamp, L.S.U. And if the spirit that came when the lamp was properly rubbed was Uncle Sam and no strange, turbaned Arabian, what did it matter?

As the tree was bent, so were the twigs inclined. Student affairs of these latter days took on extra flamboyance, crudity and post-adolescent venality. With so effective a demonstration about them on all sides, L.S.U. boys turned to tall doings. With so much lying around, they reached out to take theirs.

Russell Long, son of Huey, was on the campus, making his bow as a teen-age boss. "Just like his father," said the sentimentalist who first saw him. She might say the same thing after she saw him in action. In the summer of 1938, Russell was opposed by Blondy Bennett, L.S.U. cheerleader who operated a cleaning and pressing shop monopoly. Russell promised to substitute a student shop, and a variation was provided on the theme of public versus private ownership. Russell, using Father's tactics, averred that Blondy was in the race only "to keep from losing the laundry racket, the juiciest pickings that have come down the pike in many a day." Blondy grabbed hold of young Long in the Huey P. Long Field House and declared for all to hear that Russell had tried to bribe him to get out of the race, promising a state job at $1200 a year. Among other things, Blondy added, Russell mentioned the assistant-secretaryship of Dick Leche's Senate, a post that Russell had held the last time. Further, Blondy declared, another candidate had previously been bought off for $100. Russell reddened and stammered: "It's a damned lie. Bennett will wish he'd paid himself two bits to stay out. It's a frame-up."

The next night brought a rally in L.S.U.'s Greek Theatre. In keeping with the classic atmosphere, tear gas was released, amid hecklings and fistfights. However, a newspaper reported that for L.S.U. student elections, this concluding event was "comparatively calm."

On this occasion, and on others, airplanes were hired by the undergraduates to shower the campus with literature. Russell handed out free ice cream cones and lollypops to all who would promise to vote for him. Especially selected co-eds in bathing suits paraded with "L-O-N-G" painted on their bare backs. One candidate handed out dollar bills at a meeting, to show, perhaps, how wealth would be shared once he went into office.

Candidates promised that they would use their influence with state politicians, friendly utility officials and others to obtain new bus lines about the campus, and other services. Real money, it was obvious, was being spread, and in bigger and bigger lots. Russell started a practice, followed by

233

others, of retaining nationally known "name bands" for one-night stands on the campus to entertain his constituents, as well as anyone else who wanted to listen. The citizens of Baton Rouge knew a good thing when they heard of it; in one case, 6000 persons attended as Russell's guests.

Others, in other elections, hired magicians to entertain the campus voters. (Pulling of rabbits out of hats was omitted.) A cheerleader paid for the services of a corps of Negro bootblacks—the authentic Southern touch—to give free shines to his followers. Acrobats and co-ed tap dancers gave a lift to torchlight parades. An "anonymous" candidate called himself "The Masked Marvel" and rode about the campus on a horse for a week, clad in theatrical black robe and hood. Finally, he revealed his identity in a flash-light explosion in the open-air theater. His name—posterity demands it—was Vernon Woods, one of the older students in the law school.

The student council set a $100 limit, at one point, on campaign expenditures. But it was worth much more than $100 for a man to get the presidency, and many continued to spend more. The office paid $30 a month, with preroga-tives; and any bright boy could start a career and get the promise of a state job before he left the campus.

Crude politics honeycombed the faculty; in appointments, in advancements, operations, policy making. "Fellows" were appointed who, never appearing on the campus, sent "help-ers" to collect their checks. One was a legislator. Friends of state senators were "imposed" on departments without con-sultation with the deans. The director of a school might re-turn from his summer vacation to be confronted with a line-up of new faculty members, appointed without his knowledge. Incompetent hacks were "suggested" by influ-ential outsiders, sometimes for heads of schools, and were

234

given consideration, often favorable; or a "compromise" was reached.

Months later it was revealed that more than fifty per cent of all L.S.U. students were on some kind of payroll—an all-time record for an American college. Nobody could say that the dictatorship didn't take care of its boys and start them on the right track.

X

DICK FOR VICE-PRESIDENT

"WHEN I took the oath as Governor, I didn't take any vows of poverty." So Governor Dick was quoted as declaring, as he reached the midpoint of his term, the halcyon year of 1938, the glad year of overflowing delights, the year that had at least 360 days of Mardi Gras. Dick spoke for the boys.

After two centuries, John Law's vision of Louisiana had come true. It was indeed a land whose soil "had but to be tickled to give up, almost as one wished, either the smiling harvest or the laughing gold." The only difference was that in this later day, no Indians were there to help the ticklers of the state. Dick and the boys did not need Indians; they were doing very well by themselves. They were garnering not only the smiling harvest but also the laughing gold.

In the air was a simple friendliness that warmed the heart. The day was one of loving attention from friend to friend, of stately courtesies and large gestures. The boys were forever doing things that spread employment and happiness for each other: presenting gold-engraved rifles (in this way did Dick most often express his esteem), automobiles, free lumber, free boy agriculturists from L.S.U., or a deadhead job for a friend, who must, however, report or send a proxy to collect his pay in his name every few weeks. (An inconvenience, that, but a minor one.)

Governor Dick had been only middling well off in his

pre-gubernatorial days. Now, Huey's "post office and museum" mansion did not quite satisfy Dick. He moved over
to the St. Tammany Gold Coast, across the lake from New
Orleans, and became one of the landed gentry in the parish
of pines and rippling waters. He invested in a spreading
estate on the banks of the Tchefuncta River, an area to
which retired financiers, presidents and other affluent ones
made idyllic retreat.

Dick's estate had the proportions of its master, expansive
and roomy. The main building was, properly, a glorified
hunting lodge of brick and shingle. A boat landing was
handy, and Dick's friends were not the ones to let Dick
want for a boat or two. Near by were kennels, breeding
stalls, pens, exercise yards. The Governor raised sheep, dogs,
Hereford cattle, Russian caracul sheep and blooded horses.
Accounts of the establishment reached the country folk at
intervals, and they mumbled about it, allowing that the
Governor had "steam heat for his cows" and "hot and cold
running water for his hogs."

The demolition of old Charity Hospital left a large supply
of bricks. Unverified reports, reaching as far as the Northern
hills, told of nightly movements of materials from the site
to points about the state. Unkind stories were circulated
that the brick used on the Governor's estate was remarkably
like that salvaged from the hospital. The Governor denied
that he had received free supplies from anybody. He had
used only bricks dug up on his own estate, after it was discovered that an abandoned Civil War kiln underlay the
grounds, he said. To prove it, he offered to dig at a spot he
indicated. His suggestion accepted, he produced a number
of the bricks.

The Governor had a habit of pulling large bills, sometimes $1000 ones, from his pockets. Narrow-minded persons

looked askance. Dick retorted to destructive criticism, when it came from such sources, by declaring that he would not deny he had made money; but it was largely from oil operations. Any intelligent man with a little capital made such investments. He happened to have been lucky in picking up acreage between lands on which oil was brought in; that was all, he told Daniell. But he had never invested in Louisiana; always out of the state.

Dick liked his new estate and his newer life so well that he spent more and more of his time in St. Tammany, less and less in Baton Rouge. He tended to conduct affairs of state through long-distance wires and through the columns of the *Progress*. Whenever he could, he went hunting. The cares of public life seldom pierced the buoyant mood of the Governor. He remained as friendly as an overgrown Airedale, as jovial as he was burly. The *Washington Merry-Go-Round* described him during this period:

If he comes back from duck shooting with fewer ducks than you, he will be disappointed for days. He has the discretion of a football cheerleader and the judgment of a freshman. Dancing in the Blue Room of the Roosevelt Hotel one night, he held up ten fingers, five times, and shouted to a friend across the room: "Boy, did I knock 'em for a loop today, ten, twenty, thirty, forty, fifty grand!" Where the grands came from, the Governor did not say, but he boasts of new-found wealth without restraint.

Around Governor Dick were the royalty of the newer life, the Weisses, the Shushans, the politicians with strong oil connections, the oil men with strong political connections, contractors, architects, prize-fight figures whose connection with the machine was a strong one, but difficult to define with exactness.

Next to Dick's Tammany place was the estate of Abe

Shushan, now indictment free and fancy free. He was Colonel Abe of the Gold Coast. His mansion, secluded, many roomed, had its swimming pool, its landscaped vistas, its richly maintained groves. Colonel Seymour Weiss had his own estate, but a city one: the Roosevelt Hotel. He had risen from highly paid employee to head of the corporation, and he had financial stakes in other holdings, a second New Orleans hotel and a third in New York.

Seymour and Abe had careers that paralleled. When the grim days of late 1935 had come, each had bid farewell to the world of public affairs. Seymour had made a statement to his political public that, with Huey's death, he became only Seymour the hotel man. Abe had developed several illnesses, and he likewise turned his eyes to a more cloistered life, giving up his Levee Board presidency to prove his intention. But both had come back, happier than ever, to the old pursuits. Seymour also continued on the Police Board and as the machine's head man on the Dock Board. Abe did not take his Levee Board presidency again; that would have been too much, perhaps. But he was taking other things.

Another friend of the Governor was Edward Avery McIlhenny, naturalist, conservationist, owner of Jungle Gardens on Avery Island, a remarkable man, feudal lord of a remarkable stretch of land. Here flourished "Bird City," a celebrated retreat which has saved some rare species from extinction; here grew exotic plants from Africa, from Tibet, from India; here went Leche for sport. McIlhenny sold shrubs and flowers to those who could afford his luxury prices. Dick and the State of Louisiana were included in that category, with later consequences.

It paid to be a Long. Russell, Huey's son, was hanging

239

about the fringes of state politics, eye ready for the first beckoning sign from the electorate or its chosen spokesmen in Baton Rouge; speaking at meetings, shaking hands. Elder politicians gave luncheons at which Russell spoke; and they looked respectfully at the young aspirant, who left no doubt that he would follow Father. Uncle Earl remained in a strategic position. A dynasty seemed in the making.

Rose Long, the Senator's daughter, did a little dabbling in politics. At L.S.U. she was the official darling, president of the women students, vice-president of the student body. Immediately after graduation, Rose was married to Dr. Osymn McFarland, a young Nebraska doctor and former schoolmate. The event was an affair of state. The Roosevelt Hotel chef built "my largest cake"—four-and-a-half-foot base, five feet tall without the towering decorations. It took three weeks to bake, and was transported to Baton Rouge by a truck that was not to go faster than five miles an hour, so that the masterpiece would not break. Swinging wedding bells, confectionary lilies and tall figures of bride and groom topped the cake. At the mansion thousands were disappointed because they could not see what newspapers called "the many hundreds of gifts"; remembrances from the state police, city workers, state workers, state officials, city officials, legislators, parish organizations. Special dee ducts flew for the occasion. The boys in New Orleans contributed to a set of silverware estimated as costing $12,000 to $15,000. There were other presents. Dr. McFarland, described as a "freshman physician" by one Long man, was named medical adviser to the expensive new state-hospital organization; and later he stepped up to the rank of director of the Huey P. Long Memorial Hospital, at $6000 a year, plus a free home, free groceries and supplies. . . .

In New Orleans, however, municipal affairs had taken a turn more surprising to many. Robert S. Maestri was making a name for himself as mayor. He had gone into office with a determination to leave a record behind him. He was achieving that goal.

Maestri had not gone beyond the third grade, but had taken a brief business course in his early teens. At 13 he was earning a living. At 23 he was a thriving business man, at 33 practically a millionaire, at 43 one of the wealthiest men in the city, probably the biggest single property owner. His father was an Italian-American poultry peddler who had set up a furniture store. One of the younger Maestri's first jobs had been to watch about the store along Rampart Street, near the tango belt. Whether or not that location was a coincidence has been a topic of heated argument among men-about-state-politics for a decade. Enemies charged that the Maestri wealth was founded on a combination of store, police friendships and red-light property; that the store sold beds and other furnishings on time, then picked up the goods when an unfortunate raid occurred, and resold them. Stump speakers called the process "the original model of perpetual motion." Maestri denied that the family property was centered in this area, or that sales were managed in this fashion. He did not deny that he kept his ear close to the political ground. His holdings made that a requisite.

He had seen Huey as a comer, and had known that Huey needed him, or someone like him. When the Kingfish-to-be sent a message, according to Don Eddy, Maestri ignored it. As he expected, Huey called on him. Maestri kept him waiting. Once together, the two men lost no time on preliminaries, and talked for the rest of the evening. Maestri placed much of his cash on Huey, to win, place or show—though he had insurance elsewhere, like any investor. He had saved Huey with his money in the impeachment days; he went on to be Conservation Commissioner, though insisting to many that he did not want the job. He did admit that he profited from oil holdings, but asserted: "I never messed with state oil lands. Let the other guys have that stuff."

Now, in his new office, the swarthy heavy-set ruler of the machine worked to make Louisiana forget the things that had been shouted against him. Into the running of the city he put the same drive, the same cold bargaining, the same pursuit of the stray dollar that had netted him his other holdings. He chuckled as he rode roughshod over city ordinances and regulations, sometimes the accepted principles of city management. "Maybe I'm breaking a law. But I want this done. Quickest way, the best way." He ignored divisions between city departments: "Two pockets, same pair of pants." He made brisk deals in the city's name: "We shave 'em with or without soap." His sayings were repeated affectionately by some, derisively by others.

Part of the way was prepared for him in advance. The Legislature, which had twisted New Orleans nearly to her death on the rack, was showering care and gifts on the convalescent: taxing power, assistance in credit, repeal of some, but not all, of the dictatorship laws. The city had been in bad straits when Maestri stepped in. A requisition for a 25-cent brush was refused by a hardware store. Streets were rocky, public buildings deteriorating. Current debts: $15,-000,000; unpaid electric bill, $1,250,000; taxes long overdue, many disgusted Orleanians having stopped paying; city workers sullen as they received twenty per cent of their salaries, if they received anything, three months late.

Maestri asked the banks for a $2,000,000 loan to start his régime. They wanted six per cent, and were not certain that they could provide it all. Maestri asked Baton Rouge:

"What do you pay for your money?" Three per cent. "Get me some." The banks of New York provided $1,900,000. To find the rest would mean argument and time. Maestri made out his own check for $100,000 and loaned it, "without interest." With this he started a rehabilitation program, its subject New Orleans, and poured every spare thousand into public works. In thirty months he and the WPA had built or rebuilt twenty per cent of all roadways, created scores of playgrounds, advanced the city's physical appearance fifteen years. Then he turned to some of those new things called slum clearances. For years welfare workers had called attention to New Orleans' slums, terming Bed Bug Row, the Red Devil and others the equal of the nation's worst. The city discovered these needs; aided, perhaps, by Washington's "change of atmosphere," it obtained a surprising proportion of the Federal housing moneys, $23,000,000, for eight large areas.

WPA projects were planned primarily to give men work, officials declared; heavy, labor-saving machinery "tended to defeat the purpose." Maestri said, "Yes," then took hand shovels from the men, installed cranes, steamshovels and other equipment. The projects must be largely diversified, giving employment to white-collar employees, professionals, the less physically strong, said Washington. Maestri said, "Yes," then sponsored almost entirely the type that call for common and skilled manual labor. However, Harry Hopkins inspected the work and called it one of the best examples in the country of municipal planning for relief projects. By that time, Maestri had diversified the operations, taken on more of the white-collar and other workers; but he was still holding out for mechanical helpers.

Maestri needed another steamshovel. He was anxious not to put up cash at the moment. He telephoned a firm: "I'd like to borrow one of yours that ain't doing anything." The executive hesitated. The firm would like to co-operate, but wouldn't it look odd if people saw its equipment on public projects? "It sure would. We'll see that don't happen." Maestri's men picked up the steamshovel and painted out the firm's name. A salesman was overjoyed to hear that the mayor was thinking of buying, say, eighty tons of material. He hurried to City Hall, left an hour later with his ears burning at some of the plain talk he had heard, and with a verbal contract to provide one hundred and eighty tons, half price. Maestri demanded, and got, as Eddy saw, tires at one-fourth of the retail figure, gasoline ten cents below the market, motorcycles at less than half. He heard of a factory that was piling up carbide refuse and carting it to the dump. He asked for the material, put city employees to work on a formula that turned it into a cheap white paint. With the product, he covered the exterior of practically every public building in the city, private hospitals, churches and private schools. Some protested that city men and materials should not be used on private projects. Maestri went on, building up good will.

The mayor attracted the taxpayers with special sales rates —so much off if they paid their new taxes early and caught up with their back ones. He talked strong language to the bankers, and forced interest rates to two and a half per cent; he cut the city's bonded debt by millions. Orleanians generally began to like Maestri—particularly the business men and the middle class, the small homeowners to whom his policies appealed.

Some saw another side to the picture. In administrative matters, the mayor was an embryo Mussolini, a man who liked authority and more authority. His fellow commissioners were little more than figureheads. He ran all departments; he drew patronage more and more rapidly under his control. At the same time that he centered on public works, he cut other functions and services to the bone—and then he cut into the bone. He was "no reformer," the mayor told callers. By this he meant, among other things, that he was a confirmed non-believer in labor's rights. Civil liberties on one or two occasions during this period suffered as seldom before in open-shop New Orleans. A dock strike was broken in bloody fashion. A cab strike was halted when the city openly took sides and sent policemen as extra passengers in the front seat. The ranking police official announced that he and his men were going to run CIO organizers out of town. The next day CIO men telephoned from near-by towns, charging that they had been beaten, threatened with death and escorted out. Business men sent delegations to the Hall to praise the mayor for his stand in such matters. And there were darker aspects, relating to gambling, favoritism and other aspects of city operations that did not come to full attention until later.

When the mayor had been in office nearly a year, he bought the grounds and property of the Heinemann Baseball Park, and a group of others headed by Colonel Seymour and including Governor Dick purchased the Pelican Baseball Club—all of the enterprise, they said, undertaken as a civic project. The mayor promised that he would see that all attendance records were broken. He kept his word. Attendance at the games became a politically advisable pastime for many. City workers could expect a half-day off from time to time, to permit them to go to the park. And they went to the park.

The community lifted its eyebrows when announcement was made that Seymour and another member of the new aristocracy, Contractor Monte Hart, had bought control of a confection company. "Looks like the gang's in on the candy game now," the word went down the line. Before many weeks passed, drugstores and other establishments appeared to be giving particular attention to this particular candy. Some operators confided to friends that they realized that the assessment rolls were still handy for "non-co-operators." Other machine men bought in on beer companies, dairies and related establishments. There were many who had to be appeased; there were many appeasements.

In Baton Rouge, Governor Leche adopted a new entertainment pet, and a new squeeze was on. Dick was convinced that a good annual frontier show was the thing that would get Louisiana farmers interested in raising cattle, a favorite project with him and the *Progress*. One of the reasons for building the record-sized Coliseum, or agricultural building, had been the presentation of the Governor's rodeos. Dick, wearing a ten-gallon hat, luxuriated in the Wild-West atmosphere, whooped and howled at the broncho busting, and confided that he had always wanted to be a cowboy or a baseball player. State employees, "advised" to attend, sat with their ten-gallon hats on their heads, their smiles sometimes set ones; they had been required not only to buy tickets but also hats, souvenirs and other paraphernalia. From New Orleans other hundreds had to make train trips, buy admission, hats and the rest. The Governor presided over contests to select "the grand championship plantation walking horse of the world," gave a Governor Richard W. Leche Trophy to the winner, and received honorary designation as Chief Short Bull by a group of Sioux Indians. The state paid $60,000 or more a year for the Governor's performances; the amounts contributed by the payroll for the privilege of attendance were not disclosed.

When mid-1938 arrived, Louisianians recalled well-estab-

246

lished earlier reports that Dick would step down about this time to make way for Earl Long. Nothing happened. True, the Governor talked whimsically of his desire to leave the chair at the earliest chance and turn his back on the hurly-burly of partisan politics. But he held on. Several explanations were offered. Dick seemed to be enjoying himself; public life was sometimes irksome, but it had its points. He did not like Earl, and Earl did not like him, and so he was not inclined to hurry on that count. And then, too, the signs indicated that Dick was considering stepping up rather than down. Huey had thought he would promote Dick to the state supreme court. Now Dick's eyes strayed toward something higher, a judgeship, but a Federal one. Two new judicial offices had been created by Congress, one in New Orleans, Dick's district. This was the background for a game of official hide-and-seek that went on for nearly a year and a half; a sport in which the 250-pound Leche alternately chased the office and let it chase him.

Month after month Dick shook his head. No, he didn't want it; where did such stories start? Month after month official Washington let it be known that he was under consideration, eventually that the usual investigation was being made of his record. Once or twice, it was declared in Washington that Dick was "strongly backed" by the Louisiana delegation there and by others, and that he would probably get the office. Allen Ellender, the new Senator, was a hot New Dealer by this time, on close terms with the President, and a frequent visitor to the White House; and he admitted that Dick had a good chance to obtain the office.

The Governor was moving, meanwhile, between Louisiana and Washington more regularly than any other in modern Louisiana history. Between appeals for more projects, he once saw the President and the Attorney-General.

247

But on his return he was "not impressed" with the vacancy. Louisiana decided that this ended the matter; and then the grinning Dick told reporters that he was "never a man to turn down a good job." The question of Dick and the judgeship took on the proportions of a major controversy in Louisiana, ranking with arguments as to whether Hitler would dare go to war in 1939. The Federal Attorney-General's office declared that it would like the matter settled because of the accumulation of cases in Louisiana courts. The Louisiana State Bar Association urged action by the White House. But the principals would not be hurried.

The other new judgeship was filled, and even supine Louisiana received a shock. The appointment was a commentary on the depth of Washington's affection for Louisiana. The new judge was Attorney-General Gaston L. Porterie of the State of Louisiana. He was a member of a distinguished Acadian family, a man of legal ability, a lover of good food, good wine and good French stories; and the possessor of a political background of strong connotations.

He had been selected as the machine's attorney in 1932. Within a few months he was the central figure in several of the Kingfish's most blatant acts. The machine, during one of its periods of alliance with the City Ring, had put across a number of amendments that were anathema to the country parishes. The New Orleans vote had made passage possible; but that vote was akin to miraculous. In one precinct after another, balloting was identical; in others, no single opposing vote was counted. The district attorney, Eugene Stanley, obtained a court order to bring the ballot boxes before the grand jury. Huey and Porterie acted like lightning. Porterie superseded Stanley. For a month he did nothing. Then Porterie called a night session and summoned high banking officials; whispers spread that the machine

248

feared the jury might upset bond issues by exposing thievery.

State and city bar associations, business men's clubs and others condemned the attorney-general and his actions. Weeks later Porterie called the jury. The boxes were brought in, returned unopened, then brought back, opened, resealed. The jury went into court with Porterie, and the attorney-general declared that he had a statement to make for the jurors. The judge told him he could do nothing of the sort; that the law permitted a jury to return a true bill, no-true bill, or pass over the matter. "Is there any other legal information I can give you?" the local judge asked the attorney-general. The jury did nothing more. A month later, a new one came in. The bond issues had been sold; there was now no danger of upsetting the result. Still, no investigation, as Porterie continued to supersede Stanley. The state bar called on Porterie to explain his attitude. Nothing happened. The bar's committee on ethics cited the attorney-general for expulsion; he submitted a resignation at once. The association declared that he could not quit under fire, and expelled him.

Huey was furious. He got back at the lawyers. He had his Legislature "make me a new bar." An integrated organization was formed, to which every practicing attorney must belong and pay dues, with officers chosen by the general electorate. The private bar could continue, but practically all its functions were taken over, particularly those of passing upon disputes over ethics, and the examination of candidates. Huey jeered: "All you boys are now is a god-damned debating club." Then he poured salt on the wound. The first president of the new bar, presiding over those who had voted to expel him, with power to rule on questions of ethics, was Attorney-General Gaston L. Porterie.

The incident brought further resentment toward Porterie

when "partial martial law" was declared in New Orleans to prevent investigation, and when the controlled grand jurors sought to return a blanket vindication of the election commissioners—a step halted by the judge, who "refused without comment" to accept their action. Eventually, an open hearing was held, with Porterie ruled out by the judge. More than 18,000 fraudulent votes were found to have been counted for one amendment. Every polling commissioner in the city was charged. Three went to trial and were found guilty. But Huey "took care of the boys" by adoption of a tricky new election law requiring that wilful fraud must be shown—and omitting the usual saving clause that declares a new law non-applicable to pending cases. Thus, the 500-odd men received legislative pardon in election-tampering matters.

There were some sour reactions about the country when Porterie was confirmed. Pegler asked whether the Roosevelt Administration and Congress could favor "a man who served a ruthless dictatorship which used the courts to whip its political opponents." The nomination, he added, indicated that the new United States Attorney-General, Frank Murphy, was considering politics or that he "approves Porterie's record—which would be even more alarming."

But little overt response developed in Louisiana. "What's the use?" was the byword. Opposition was quiescent, except for that of James A. Noe and a few others. The press was quiescent. The United States Supreme Court had handed down a sweeping decision against Huey's tax on the newspapers. There was no need now to crack down on the newspapers, however. The state supreme court declared unconstitutional the law by which the state took over full control of the primary elections, and the old commission system was restored. This did not disturb the boys. There was no need now to steal elections. But many were doing it to keep in practice, or perhaps because this had become a habit, and habits are hard to break. Unopposed candidates sometimes ended up with more votes than there were voters.

The day had its humors, of course. President Roosevelt paid a visit to New Orleans, and Governor Dick and Mayor Bob rode about in an open car with him while he saw some public works, the results of the Second Purchase. The Governor and the President chatted. Mayor Bob sat silent. At luncheon he asked Roosevelt a question: "How do you like them ersters?" The President was ecstatic, spoke at length of his regret that he could not get such food every day, and so forth. Maestri nodded. As the meal ended, Mayor Bob asked: "So you liked 'em?" The President threw back his head, again waxed laudatory. That ended the exchanges of the two officials. Afterward, a friend asked Maestri what he thought of the President. "Aw, he's full of bull," said the mayor.

Governor Dick was still dallying over the Federal judgeship when the state received another start. Huey had wanted to be President. Dick appeared overnight as a candidate for Vice-President of the United States. A "movement" "swept" the state—"Roosevelt for President in 1940; Leche for Vice-President." A "spontaneous boom," the *Progress* called it. In New York, in the national eye, Governor Dick carefully denied that he was seeking the honor. But his friends would not be downed. Mayor Handley of Lake Charles—later to be named in a gamblers' payoff—saw in Leche "one of the greatest men in the entire nation." Maestri observed that "it would be a fine thing to have a native Louisianian in the official family of the United States," and advanced the further, equally pressing argument that he would "like to see Leche in the Vice-Presidency."

Rushing back from a trip through South and Mid-West, the breathless state welfare commissioner—an indictee-to-be —reported that sentiment was growing in both sections for Leche, that "leading Democrats" wanted him "drafted." Some trusting souls thought the matter settled, concluded that Roosevelt had made up his mind to run with Leche. The president of the Baton Rouge Chamber of Commerce burbled: "I'm for Leche, not only for the Vice-Presidency, but for President."

Soon Dick was finding himself probably the first American governor to call a strike, arbitrate it, "win" it and have it backfire on him. In those trips to Washington, Dick had moved among the professional New Dealers, had heard new words: liberalism, rights of labor, civil liberties. Dick had always been a solid Friend of Business, a man who could damn an agitator as well as the next one. But now . . . so they wanted liberalism? In the strawberry area, a wild-speaking organizer was stirring up the farmers by calling the Governor "Walking Stick Dick, the No. 1 American Playboy," the owner of a "$250,000 home on a $7500 salary" and similar uncomplimentary things. Dick had an opportunity to win the farmers and do himself some good. However it was managed, by whatever encouragement, a strike was proclaimed among workers at a box factory in the area. The Governor drove into the workers' section, visited the homes, and announced that he had seen "poverty pictures worse than those of Tobacco Road." People just could not live on such pay; the country needed a minimum-wage-and-hour law. He wanted Louisianians to write him their views, not to wire, "because the poor workmen have to labor two or three hours to earn the cost of a 25-cent message." General comment was that Dick was taking conversion hard.

The next day, the Governor called at the scene, in limousine, with the First Lady and state police. The latter were strangely friendly to the strikers. A ready-made soup kitchen was set up. State-employed photographers took evidences of the Governor's way with the masses. Venturing farther into strange waters, the Governor invited "hungry farmers" to partake of the soup, attacked sweatshops, agreed that the South was America's Economic Problem No. 1 and, despite his baits for new industry, scored absentee ownership. In due time, the strike was arbitrated and a labor board election held to see whether the workers wanted CIO or AFL, the latter the Governor's union. Alas for new-found liberalism; the workers would have none of either.

Things had been too serene for these past three years. The safety valve had been missing. Steam now leaked through the cracks. A series of annoying little episodes developed. A Highway Commission checker placed a statement on the desks of all legislators, declaring that he had documentary evidence that state workers' pay was being gouged for the dee duct fund and for the *Progress,* and that Federal law was involved in cases in which payrolls were part Federal. The Legislature paused in its task of changing the "luxury tax" to an outright sales tax, and then said nothing. Leche fired the checker; but a controversy had started. A torrent of anonymous protests reached newspapers from the state workers. Among those who objected to the dee ducts and the *Progress* pressure were payroll deadheads and two-check men. Because one was paid by the state for doing nothing, or twice for doing half a normal job, did not mean that one lost one's capacity to suffer indignation at an obvious injustice. Letters that were alternately droll and pathetic poured out. A proprietor wrote that all the bars, liquor stores, groceries, poultry dealers and other small establishments had to buy one to ten subscriptions, or policemen would make them shut off the radio after 8 P.M. or obey non-existent health regulations. One worker said his friends were avoiding him "for fear I'll try to sell them some of the five *Progresses* I have to take." A woman was having trouble preparing a layette for her expected baby, because dee ducts were flying away with all the spare money. The Young Men's Business Club met, and a member urged others to investigate. He made a piquant observation: "All that the older men in business here can do, is sit down and take it. Let the young members, who have no business connections that may suffer, tell the world . . ."

The Governor first treated the matter lightly. The *States* ran a series of stories on dee ducts. Governor Dick sent the editor a string of choice mallards, killed with the gubernatorial guns, and a note attached: "Dese ducks are not flying." Later, he jibed: "I deny the allegation, and defy the alligators." He decided he liked that, and he used it often thereafter. However, becoming aggrieved, he addressed a mass meeting, declared that Huey had started the deductions; that the newspaper wanted only to stop him from becoming a Federal judge, and—again the liberalism motif—that the corporation lawyers were after him because he had been a friend of the poor man while on the state bench of appeals.

The year 1939 began, the year of Dick's torment. The Governor became ill, went to resorts and hospitals; eventually it was declared that he was suffering a complication of difficulties, the most important an arthritic infection. Dick had other trials. He had elevated his secretary to the attorney-general's office, and gave strong indications that he would like to see him as the next governor. Earl Long began to kick up his heels, to show that he was huffed at Dick's actions, at Dick's failure to retire. The sheriffs' organization declared that it would favor no candidate who did not pledge repeal of the state control bill that the machine had previously refused to drop.

A vague uneasiness settled over Louisiana; Dick and others were restive, nervous. Jimmy Noe was more and more irksome. He was now lining up men throughout the state, haranguing at every change, charging betrayal of Huey Long—and worse things, things that were not always printed by the newspapers, because of their dangerous nature. Dick showed his temper when he cracked down on the former *femme fatale* of the régime, Alice Lee Grosjean Tharp, now married again. She had remained on the payroll as collector of revenue. Suddenly she was off, for the first time in many years. Some considered this a departure from Longism greater than the killing of any five laws. With Alice went her husband, who was secretary of the State Tax Commission, and a crew of relatives. The grapevine had an explanation: Alice had gone over to Jimmy Noe. Leche declared that hereafter all workers must be "one hundred per cent loyal to Dick Leche." Stick by Dick, if you know what's good for you. Others claimed that Dick and Alice had differed over other things.

At the Legislature, Governor Dick had put through the repeal of Huey's law allowing suit by the state against corporations for taxes dating far into the past. Huey had reaped rich benefit in such instances; the law set fees of one-third, totaling hundreds of thousands in some instances. The repeal meant, of course, the end of the attorneyship for such collections. It was held by Hugh Wilkinson, Huey's former partner. Hugh had handled a recent Standard Oil case, in which the firm claimed that "probably $4,000,000" was in question, and that Hugh stood to take more than $1,000,000. "Funds will thus be diverted from the treasury, amounting to a King's ransom."

Hugh Wilkinson had been a serviceable ally of the organization. He had been its attorney in the Irby-Terrell kidnaping, and had represented the boys in other scrapes. Hugh was silent for some months. In February of 1939 he offered a series of radio addresses; his theme, the duties of citizenship. At first he said only that times were parlous; that honest and able candidates must be encouraged for the election eleven months hence. The politicians wondered. What was Hugh getting at? Hugh enlightened them; the subject of his next talk would be "The Gravy Train."

A systematic tax-reduction racket, he charged, was "widespread in Louisiana and notorious in New Orleans." Officials and employees of the State Tax Commission worked with outside agents, attorneys and others, to obtain steep tax-assessment reductions for firms or individuals, he declared. For this, the agents received a full fifty per cent split. The plan, he went on, had been expanded into a shakedown. The following year would see the same individuals or organizations approached; the rate would be up again, and once more a reduction could be fixed for half. Wilkinson asserted that at least one high official of the commission in New Orleans had a direct tie to the scheme and a part in the payoff. He told of a "Madame Queen" of the racket; of code names and other dodges for concealment; of a breakup among members of the group, which had led one to come to him and tell of it. The public treasury, Hugh estimated, was being looted of hundreds of thousands of dollars, while tax assessments were reduced illegally by the tens of millions. "That gravy train has been running in this town like

256

the stream-lined Twentieth Century Limited. It has run into the stores, the banks, the theaters, pharmacies, homesteads, pawnshops. . . ." When he went out and talked to one business man after another, he could not find one who had not paid off or had not been propositioned. A bottling company, Hugh added, had its valuation reduced from $113,-000 to $10,000 in one year. A brewing firm arranged a reduction of $500,000 over a two-year period. He reeled off, to officials, a list of firms which he said he had reason to believe knew about the racket. It read like a blue book of New Orleans business.

A quick demonstration of public lethargy followed. District Attorney Charles A. Byrne of New Orleans said that he would go "as far as I can" if Wilkinson presented his data to him. The Tax Commission did nothing. Wilkinson concentrated on the integrated State Bar of Louisiana, of which Leche's favorite, the new Attorney-General David Ellison, was now president. A tiff followed. Wilkinson wanted action taken against the attorneys whom he mentioned. Ellison retorted that procedure adopted when Wilkinson was president of the integrated bar required that action wait on court disposition of such matters. He suggested that Wilkinson call on the district attorney. Wilkinson replied that the district attorney seemed very much disinclined to act; as Ellison was state's attorney-general, he had better information "as to whether or not the criminal authorities are interested in investigating facts and events fairly well known to a large proportion of our general population." The state bar held the matter in abeyance, and eventually did nothing of any consequence.

Within twenty-four hours of the exchange between Wilkinson and Attorney-General Ellison, Governor Dick made it clear that he was fretful. He took a step which might have been an indiscreet one, or a shrewd piece of strategy. He held forth an unmistakable prospect of criminal prosecution against the property owner who might be found involved in the racket. Any investigation, said the Governor, "should begin with the property owner who, by his participation, made any alleged racket possible. And such property owners, if found guilty for their participation, should be prosecuted with the others, for conspiracy and bribery. Any business man who takes part in such a scheme attempts to get an advantage over his competitors—to get a little more than he's willing to pay for." As a parting remark, the Governor held forth the possibility of a "complete revision of all assessments." It was, perhaps, not calculated to make a loose-tongued merchant pause and think; but it had that effect.

Following many delays, the parish grand jury was offered the case by District Attorney Byrne. Finally the jury reported that, after exhaustive inquiry, it had found insufficient evidence on which to indict anybody. Such a report, the jurors conceded, was highly unusual; but they felt that the public was entitled to know what the jury had done in the matter. It noted that it was "an accusatory body, not a censor of public morals" and had no power, in cases of insufficient data against a person, to "denounce or castigate such person." On this inconclusive note, the matter ended, for a time.

May 29, 1939, brought the Federal law to Louisiana, but in happy mood. Attorney-General Murphy and J. Edgar Hoover flew to New Orleans. "Governor Leche, nattily dressed and swinging his cane, was on hand at Shushan Airport when the Attorney-General and the swart FBI director arrived, and he greeted the Attorney-General warmly, throwing his arm around his shoulders, smiling and having his necktie adjusted by Mr. Murphy." Seymour Weiss was another jovial figure. Murphy had come to receive an honorary degree from Louisiana State University, and Hoover to receive an honorary rank of major-general on Leche's staff. The two officials were entertained until considerably past midnight at the Roosevelt Hotel by night club sopranos, dance teams and other acts in Seymour's Blue Room. The Governor, the major-domo, the nemesis of crime and the New Deal's crusader chatted, joked, told stories. Early the next morning reporters woke them all. As they waited for Murphy and Hoover to dress, the news men were entertained by the blue-pajamaed Governor, stretched out on his bed.

"Governor Leche," reported the *Item*, "smilingly revealed a predilection of the Attorney-General's—chocolate ice cream. Mr. Murphy rounded out the night with a call for a big dishful—'double dip,' said the Governor, and he swallowed it happily before retiring." Mr. Leche was soon to wonder about his own use of that term "double dip."

Hoover spoke with warmth of the havoc created by tie-ups of politicians and criminals. Murphy spoke with equal earnestness of his "purge for America," by which he pledged himself to end alliances of public officials and violators of the law. He referred to the sacredness of the ballot, to the need for unquestioned honesty of count in a democracy. Governor Dick sat thoughtful. That night President James Monroe Smith stood solemnly beside United States Attorney-General Murphy and bestowed upon him the honors of Louisiana State University.

Before he left, the Attorney-General was asked if his trip to Louisiana had been purely a personal one, unconnected with his work. To this he replied: "I never go anywhere except on business."

PART THREE

The Wreck

"Major criminals should not commit minor crimes."—O. JOHN ROGGE.

XI

"AND ONE OF 'EM WAS A SONOFAGUN!"

AFTER theater, after the Carnival Ball, on the way to a fishing party below the city or during the mid-afternoon lull, sooner or later, it is said, every Orleanian drops in at the French Market Coffee Shop in the Vieux Carré. It was proper, perhaps, that the forces that toppled the dictatorship should have been given their impetus here, in the original heart of the city, the stronghold that succumbed last to the régime.

It might be proper also that the heirs of the dictator should trace the beginning of their fall to a man whom they had rejected after the sovereign had elevated him.

A chance remark, during a pause in the clatter of dishes in the fragrant room, stirred the suspicions of Dr. Arthur Vidrine, the country-boy doctor who had been Huey's favorite medical man. The speaker who made the comment was one of the few in New Orleans who had the information. Vidrine was now strongly inclined to act upon such information.

One night in May of 1938, Arthur Vidrine stepped into the coffee place on his way home. He was hailed by an old friend, the holder of a minor position in a local business office. They talked casually of the weather and, naturally enough, of the political situation. Then the clerk referred to the treatment that had been accorded Vidrine by Leche and Smith of L.S.U., to the way he had been shunted from the superintendency of Charity Hospital, from the deanship of Huey's medical school, to a subordinate professorship. . . . Ah, things were different these days. And Smith, that sanctimonious hypocrite! Vidrine would be surprised to know what he was up to. Speculating in whiskey-warehouse receipts; speculating in some big amounts, too. Well, the friend had to be going.

Arthur Vidrine agreed that this was an odd thing. He thought about it several times on his drive home. Over in his native French Louisiana, he mentioned the news to a friend who was close to a third man in New Orleans. That friend told the story to the third man, who was Rufus W. Fontenot, Federal Collector of Revenue for Louisiana.

Mr. Fontenot did not have to remind himself to get to work on this tip. It related to a subject that had pricked him sore. He had been in the same office in 1936 when his department, after working for years upon the evidence with which it expected to place the machine's operators behind bars, saw its efforts thrown away overnight. He had been waiting since then, and watching. Mr. Fontenot had a suspicious mind; it was his job to be suspicious. Among the things he watched were the goings-on at Louisiana State University when he went back as an alumnus. He did not like the look, the feel, the smell of things at his alma mater.

Now he had something to go upon. It was not necessarily wrong for a university president to deal in whiskey; less, perhaps, than for a "civic leader" to own slum property or a university to get part of its earnings out of a red-light district. But college presidents usually do not deal in whiskey; for one reason, because they do not have the money to do so.

The revenue collector pursued his inquiries, while months passed. "The Doc" was liquidating his holdings of one thousand or more barrels. One of Mr. Fontenot's deputies, at work on the matter, called his attention to a new name among trading accounts on the New Orleans Stock Exchange: James Monroe. The account was a large one, but the revenue office had no reports of a James Monroe. Fontenot dispatched a letter of inquiry; an intermediate broker responded. James Monroe was James Monroe Smith, who had a trading account for himself and others. For obvious reasons, "The Doc" wanted his connection to remain a quiet one, and the broker would appreciate it if Mr. Fontenot would tell no one else. James Monroe Smith was trading in hundreds of thousands of dollars of wheat. The whiskey had been small stuff.

In January of 1939, Rufus Fontenot went to Washington. One of the first persons he saw there was Elmer Irey of the Special Intelligence unit. Mr. Irey shared Mr. Fontenot's chagrin over the Second Louisiana Purchase; but, unlike Mr. Fontenot, Mr. Irey no longer was so enthusiastic over the prospect of slapping Louisiana crooks. What was the use? But he was won over to the advisability of a check into the Smith situation. That left the higher-ups, whose zeal for Louisiana investigations had undergone a chill. Fontenot talked quickly. He would stake his judgment that heavy irregularities were taking place down there. They were certain to come out, somehow. He felt that they would backfire, reflect on the conduct of his office. In that case he would owe it to himself to let it be known that he had reported the matter to Washington. All he wanted now, he pleaded, was a preliminary study. If that proved him wrong, no harm would have been done. He won his point. Three weeks later, one of the Special Intelligence men informed Fontenot that he had uncovered a case on Smith, with ramifications.

One week after that, in late February of 1939, Fontenot

received a call: "Dick Leche. I'm laid up at the Roosevelt. Could you come over?" Fontenot assumed his overcoat and his caution. Around Governor Dick's bed he found Ellison, the new attorney-general, and W. A. Cooper, who had succeeded Madame Alice Lee Grosjean as state revenue collector. Months earlier, Leche told Fontenot, he had received vague reports that "something was wrong at L.S.U." He had suspicions that "somebody was getting a cut on the buildings." He had asked Cooper to make an audit.

Curious things had happened. Smith offered some of Cooper's best men higher salaries to work for him. Now Cooper had made a report of findings to date. L.S.U., he noted, had grown so fast that it had left its system of financial management far behind. That system was antiquated "to the point where almost anybody handling cash is in a position to help himself," Dick went on. But nothing definite had been turned up. "Although there's strong evidence that something is wrong, our hands are tied." So Dick would like a Federal investigation of Smith's affairs.

To this, Fontenot replied that such an investigation was already under way. "You and Mr. Cooper know that, Governor." "And the Government never stops with one man, but makes a thorough check of everything and everybody connected with a matter." That, Dick nodded, was what he wanted. The Government went on with its inquiries, the state with its own.

It was at about this time that Fontenot received a whispered suggestion from a high state official that "we wouldn't mind if the Government got something on this guy Smith." Somebody, it was obvious, desired for some reason that "The Doc" be removed from circulation. It was equally obvious that this was a delicate situation. Fontenot said nothing.

Senator Jimmy Noe, the original man with a grievance, was meanwhile losing no time, playing detective on his separate hook. He had spread the word that he was looking for information in anyone's possession about the organization. State employees and others were turning in affidavits, lists, rumors and tips. The effervescent Noe had a loosely integrated investigative agency, a "fact-finding crew" of men who knew their way around. Occasionally he offered some of his material to the newspapers. But they were afraid of it; it was dangerous stuff, much of it unverified. Unless, and perhaps even if a case were waterproof, who would believe the lyingnewspapers? He was advised to continue work. Why not try for a few pictures? "They can say that a man heard something wrong, or saw it wrong; but they can't lie out of the camera's testimony."

Jimmy had never been able to capture the specifically incriminating scenes he needed. He had photographed stolen state hogs which, for all the picture denoted, might be Uncle Hiram's down the road. He had pictures of "hot" gravel in transportation; but all that they showed was a truck along a highway. On one occasion his men were planted for several days in front of a Dock Board warehouse to catch a shipment of "hot" state-owned grain. But the boys had been tipped in turn, and the shipment did not take place. Still, Jimmy Noe went on, accumulating what became an awesome collection of affidavits—"Noe's 980." There were really 980 of them. Sometimes the pile lacked quality; it had quantity. Jimmy was writing Roosevelt about it, calling to see Frank Murphy and others in Washington, although he did not always get into the inner offices.

Early in June of 1939, Jimmy made another Washington visit. He called at the Department of Justice. He saw Congressmen, Republicans and Democrats, and he called on

Pearson and Allen of *Washington Merry-Go-Round* fame. The columnists took what he offered, checked it and consulted attorneys.

Returning to his home in North Louisiana, Jimmy received a call at 6:30 one morning. From L.S.U. one Hicks Batts of the building department reached him, not without difficulty. Batts was excited. A truckload of L.S.U. window frames was starting to New Orleans, its destination a home under construction for a colonel on Leche's staff. Batts lowered his voice and gave the license number. Noe hung up, clicked the operator, reached the New Orleans *States* and then one of his New Orleans dependables, a former football player. At the *States*, the Noe telephone call received prompt response from Major James E. Crown, managing editor, and F. Edward Hébert, city editor. What followed was eventually to be hailed as one of the major factors in the development of the scandals. A reporter, a photographer and a Noe man drove slowly along the highway to Baton Rouge. They met the truck, followed it at a discreet distance, and parked when it parked. Workmen started operations.

The Noe man stayed at the wheel of the car, motor running. Meigs O. Frost, the reporter, and Wilfred D'Aquin, the photographer, squirmed through a weed-grown lot, and the latter shot everything in sight—truck, frames, men putting them in place. The pictures would be clear, effective; they showed the license number of the truck and the men at work. The task now was that of getting the films to the office; in Louisiana of recent years, it has often been more difficult to transport photographs past those who do not want them printed than it has been to take them. With a flourish, D'Aquin handed a film roll to Frost, who tapped off briskly in one direction while D'Aquin ambled to the car. If the reporter were tackled, nothing would be lost. The roll was blank. The photographer would be off with the real article. In this case, they were not intercepted.

The newspaper had shown other uses of public property for private purposes: the paving of a yard beside one of the gambling palaces, the cutting of a road through a private tract. Slight indignation had resulted; Louisianians were not in indignant mood in those days. The window-frame episode involved only a few hundred dollars of materials. But it came at an inopportune time, and proved the copy-book maxim that little things count.

When the pictures and the story appeared, they drew attention; but their real effect was not felt for a day or so. Then Leche, obviously nervous, acted in a way to exploit the incident to his own disadvantage. He elected to do a Huey, to play prankster. An open hearing, the kind that all great crimes call for; that was the thing. As Huey had done at his "secret public" vice investigation, Dick planned a radio broadcast, so that the people would know all about these things. Dick would be special assistant to the attorney-general, Huey's rôle in such inquiries, "death plots" and others. Dick would be there also as personal counsel for "my good friend," the staff colonel whose wife was putting up the house to which the window frames had been trucked, and for the truck driver, and for "the fellow who told the truck driver to drive the truck." He would be "counsel for the downtrodden. . . . And there'll be plenty of others who need defense before I get through." He called *States* officials and the president of Tulane University. This was a plan to show that the newspaper was a pot calling a kettle black. The newspaper's board included Tulane board members; and Mayor Maestri had paved roadways and created parking lots around the Tulane stadium.

But just before the date of the scheduled hearing, Leche

and Ellison called it off. Governor Dick's tone was different. The investigation was being "extended to include other and more serious matters." Ellison was to hire extra investigators. Meanwhile, a whitewash: Dick and Ellison declared that no law had been violated in the window-frame episode. The builder had availed herself properly of university facilities, in the same way that private individuals bought pottery from Newcomb College, Tulane's women's department, and dairy products from L.S.U. The staff colonel's lady had paid for the millwork; the men had been L.S.U. workers, but were unemployed at the time, and she compensated them; L.S.U.'s truck was used, yes, but she paid for it.

It may or may not have been significant that Fontenot went to Washington again at this time.

Public interest was piqued by the Governor's backing and filling, and by this new turn. Newspapers wanted more information. Were such services for private individuals offered generally by Louisiana State University? Who set the rates? Dr. James Monroe Smith was not available; and here was a puzzle. Prexy did not appear at his office for several days. He could not be found at home. In his absence, Big George Caldwell, from whose construction department the truck and frames had come, said that there had been nothing unprecedented in the episode. Would he show the records? He was miffed at the lyingnewspapers: "My records were open once. They're closed now." The next day, "The Doc" was back, to contradict Governor Dick and Big George. Sales to private individuals were not L.S.U.'s policy. They had never occurred before. They would never occur again. Big George must have been "befuddled." Big George had no records; the auditor's office had them all. Jim Smith was agitated, more agitated than he had been since he fired those students on Huey's orders, some thought.

The same day, June 19, brought something that made the boys' breaths come faster. The *Merry-Go-Round* column appeared. It presented affidavits of workmen that WPA men, using WPA materials under Big George's direction, had built a barn and log house for Richard W. Leche at his St. Tammany estate; that two tenant houses had been built inside Dick's Coliseum at L.S.U. and taken to the estate; that WPA carpenters and others had been employed on Business Manager Jackson's mansion; and that sand, gravel, cement, lumber and pipe belonging to the WPA had likewise been diverted to Big George's and Jackson's establishments. A further charge was that twenty WPA workers had moved a WPA-built playhouse to the property of Attorney-General Ellison. Finally came statements that WPA and other workers who were paid in part or fully with Federal funds were victims of dee ducts and were used to foster the operations of the state machine.

The story was of national interest; it could not be ignored. The WPA declared that most or all of the men were not WPA workers, and that it would look into the matter. Dr. Smith would not check into the *Merry-Go-Round* material, but would wait until the WPA finished. Meanwhile, he said, Jackson and Caldwell would "co-operate" with the WPA in its inquiries. From Governor Dick came silence. In New Orleans, Fontenot's income-tax inquiries sped up. The state's political atmosphere was sullen, sticky. Too many things were happening at the same time. The steam was pouring out of too many holes.

On June 21, late in the evening, Richard Webster Leche summoned reporters to the mansion. He was in bed, wan and tired. His visitors had to promise that they would "not excite him by asking questions." They were merely to take his written statement. He was resigning as Governor, on advice of his doctors. His withdrawal would leave Earl Long in the chair. "Mr. Long has tremendous backing in the country, and is the announced choice of Mayor Maestri"; and so the organization's interests were in "safe and sound hands." Looking on were Seymour Weiss and Attorney-General Ellison, the man who might have became Governor if Dick had had his way.

The next day, a Thursday, found the Governor back in blithe mood. No Louisiana chief executive had resigned before this, and there was doubt as to procedure. "I don't care which way is followed," Dick chuckled. "I'll try anything short of dying. If they don't find me a way out by eleven o'clock Monday, I'll walk out." Growing more expansive, Dick waved aside those curious reports that the WPA matter had anything to do with his action. He had hired Caldwell as a private contractor, and had paid the men by check; whether they were WPAs or any other kind of men he did not know, because he had not asked. He recalled an appearance before a House committee just a month before this in Washington, in which he had declared that Louisiana was a "model" on WPA matters; that there was no politics in its operations; that he "didn't know how we could get along without the WPA." Now he renewed a free-handed offer of expenses up to $10,000 for any Congressional committee that wanted to investigate. The state WPA administrator was at the bedside; and he termed Dick's resignation a "great disappointment," because Dick had co-operated "in every conceivable way, showing deep interest in the needy and underprivileged."

In Washington, Attorney-General Murphy commented somewhat irrelevantly that there was no connection between Dick's resignation and Dick's consideration for the Federal judgeship. Dick's name was still being strongly pressed by "certain elements in Louisiana," but Leche himself had told Murphy "it would be best for him not to have the appointment." And the Attorney-General was not investigating the Louisiana situation. From what he read, it appeared to be "a local matter." If WPA materials had been used, that "might give it a Federal character," but this had not yet been demonstrated.

Less than twelve hours before Dick's scheduled retirement, political frenzy broke over Louisiana. It was June 25, 1939— a Sunday.

The day began as a gay one, with newsreel cameramen at the mansion, and Maestri arriving in company with his protégé Earl. It was clear now that Maestri had reached the high point of his power in the organization, that he was more than ever the strong man. All bows for Bob, the biggest lines at Bob's door; only slightly smaller ones for Earl, less for Dick. The day was one of handshaking, of flowers, and of nervousness. Earl, about to become chief executive, was alternately meek and touchy. Someone addressed him as "Governor," and he snapped: "Don't call me that. That man may change his mind tomorrow. He gave me absolute assurance that he would resign, in the presence of twenty-five people. But I'm like the crapshooter that refused to pick up the money until he won it." These remarks had a peculiar ring. Wasn't Dick anxious to get away, as he assured the good people?

Late that night a grim and harried Leche called the press again. It arrived to find all lights on at the mansion, extra police on guard, tension in the air. Dick gave his statement quickly. He had ordered the arrest of Jim Smith for questioning about "financial irregularities that may total several hundred thousand dollars." Jim Smith had been asked about the matter, and had disappeared. State police were hunting him. Would Dick resign as planned? He would not say. Shortly afterward a brief bulletin was issued, signed by Dick and Earl. Dick would stay in office until the investigation of the L.S.U. shortage was completed. As to what had happened at the mansion in the past few hours, no one was saying much. At hand were Maestri, Ellison, the superintendent of the state police, and Supreme Court Justice John B. Fournet, a leading member of the L.S.U. board. This much came out: the matter had been under discussion since early afternoon, but nothing of a final nature had been done until after dark.

The lid had blown off. In the hills and the swamps, the politicos threw on their coats and started to Baton Rouge. Before they left, or at stops en route, they called the capital. Wires were clogged; they would not stop talking to each other; telephone girls fainted in Baton Rouge. Hotel lobbies were packed with mumbling men, each with questions in voice and eye: Where to jump next? Who was involved? What could be proved? That night the parish bosses and the state bosses met, and the boys acted. It was not known until later, but Dick received an ultimatum: investigation or no investigation, cloud or no cloud—get out. Or else—impeachment. With Dick in, the boys were afraid. They liked Dick, but he had to take his chances now.

Dick was stubborn; he would not resign. The next day, he did.

The revised news went out suddenly, and hundreds of the faithful milled about, apprehensive, smiling brightly. The Kingfish's successor was dead; long live the Kingfish's brother. Sworn in, Earl announced that his administration would have a motto: "Better a little with righteousness, than a great revenue without right." The Bible was in the man-

274

sion again, the official word went, under the arm of another Winn boy. The investigations would be pursued, "let the chips fall where they may." The guilty would be hunted out, "even though this should involve my best and closest friends." Dick kissed Earl's wife, and Earl kissed Dick's. The new day of "a little with righteousness" was started.

Outside the mansion, the newsboys were yelling "De Eminent Dr. Smit' Takes a Powder." The First Lady of the Campus was a fugitive with "The Doc." They had packed up and driven off, with the First Lady's nephew, J. Emory Adams, at the wheel, shortly after dusk the previous night. They had left Thelma's mansion in disarray, in a quick take-off. J. Emory until recently had been a campus official, operator of the profitable bookstore, but had gone on with new capital to operate a chain of stores at Baton Rouge. This kept the affair more or less within the college family. There was particular amazement for Baton Rouge; the First Lady had started to pack her famous Mexican flat silver, but had had to abandon it. "Thelma must have been in a *real* hurry. . . ."

In New Orleans, the financiers shared a shattering discovery with the politicians. "The Doc" had got away with $500,000 in the past few weeks. The "hard-boiled bankers" had turned over an even half-million dollars of their depositors' money to Jim Smith for university purposes, and he had gambled it into nothing on the stock market. Jim, the man whom Huey had picked because he always obeyed, had branched out for himself. He had profited by example, and had improved on some of his mentors. He was a bigtime swindler, Grade A classification. The country hailed him— "America's Scholastic Lamster No. 1," "Jim Smith, the Absconding Academician."

A tale of horror was told by New Orleans' leading broker-age house. The *Item* dug up the sequence of events, and sadly the company confirmed it. Sixteen months after Huey's death, "The Doc" had moved into the market. Through an intermediate broker, J. M. Brown, he had declared that he represented a group of individual investors, men of means. No other names were given, but it was emphasized that trading would be on a large scale, collateral available at all times. One of the brokers was almost overcome by the glad tidings. As he told Johnson, Smith's friends had all the funds these days. The original families, unfortunately, seemed no longer in the money. Jim had appeared, and he talked importantly. War was certain, and soon, and with it inflation. Commodities were the surest investment. "The Doc" had his private maps and graphs; and his knowledge of world trends so impressed one member of the firm that he almost asked to be given a part with the others.

"The Doc" had an idea that has wrecked smaller frauds before him: he might corner the wheat market, if all turned out well. The account started big, continued big. In time, it reached a figure of 2,000,000 bushels, the maximum al-lowed by Federal authorities. Broker Brown took 1,500,000 in his own name. Smith gave L.S.U. and other bonds as his collateral. The grain market was on the rise. Europe's pre-war agonies were proceeding as "The Doc" had predicted. The dictators were practically working for his account.

But, at Munich, Chamberlain and Hitler scuttled the professor. No war for a time, no upward spurt in grain. More collateral was needed. It came promptly, $375,000 of L.S.U. bonds. The brokers noted, however, that the bonds were not accompanied by a legal opinion as to their valid-ity; and they asked for "compliance with the usual routine." The routine was not complied with. But the brokers thought they had no reason for continued complaint. In place of the bonds arrived a $300,000 cashier's check on a New Orleans bank. This was in April of 1939. In May, Broker Brown unexpectedly delivered another $375,000 of L.S.U. bonds, with word that instructions would follow. Again, there was no legal opinion; again the brokers asked for one, and suggested the leading bond attorneys of the country. The other side disagreed, and a compromise was reached on a New Orleans attorney. His opinion was that the bonds were a legal and valid obligation—provided they had received approval of Huey's State Bond and Tax Board, and had, further, actually been sold and paid for. An awkward wait followed. The approval did not come, and Brown was asked to take up the bonds.

The brokers suffered new pangs of doubt. What about the obligations that Smith had first given them, for $214,000? They asked "The Doc." No approval came on them. "The Doc" was asked to take them back and provide more acceptable collateral. Broker Brown delivered his personal check for $100,000 on one bank in New Orleans, and a $100,000 cashier's check on a Baton Rouge bank. The account was closed on June 15, during the agitation over the window frames, and ten days before Jim disappeared. Jim's temporary absence at the time, and his mental disturbances, had an explanation.

Jim's account was paid up. He did not owe the brokers a dollar. But somebody, it was clear, owed somebody something. Attorney-General Ellison issued a statement that he was happy to inform the people that the state would suffer no loss. The half-million dollars that had gone down the drain-pipe belonged to the banks; they had, in effect, thrown it away. The authorization of Huey's Bond and Tax Board was needed for such loans, but it had not been provided.

The banks screeched; they had never been required to get such approval of the Bond and Tax Board; they had followed the same procedure here as in the case of all other L.S.U. loans. And also, Smith had presented a resolution from the L.S.U. board, specifically authorizing such borrowings! The state was sorry. But such a resolution must be a forgery. The L.S.U. board had never taken such action. Earl Long, the new Governor, turned to his dice-game simile: "The banks were just plain lucky, before this. No L.S.U. notes are legal without the Tax Board's O.K. If the banks took any of them, it was at their own responsibility. It's like this: a man may make good a debt from a crap game. But that ain't a legal debt."

One banker, it transpired, had begged to be robbed of $100,000. The financier, who was also Baton Rouge's mayor, heard in the trade about those other loans from New Orleans banks, and he called on Jim as a friend. Now Jim hadn't shown proper local spirit, had he? Jim agreed. "You're right. I wasn't fair. I'll make it up. You give me $100,000." The friend was grateful.

Every few hours brought another disclosure of Jim's prowess. Practically all the bonds he had offered as collateral had been "hot," of varying degrees of heat. He had juggled a full $1,300,000 in bonds, or reasonable facsimiles thereof. Some were parts of issues that had not yet been sold, but might be disposed of eventually; they had been entrusted to "The Doc" for safekeeping. Others had been printed, but decision reached not to issue them, and Jim had been told to burn them. In other instances Jim merely thought up an issue and ordered it printed. He had walked into a printing house with a sample of a $1000 bond, and said: "I want three hundred of these, as fast as you can turn them out." He had forged the names of O. K. Allen and another dead official to some of the bonds. Growing careless, perhaps because things had appeared so easy, he had once switched the signatures. That, said the brokers by way of understatement, was one of the reasons why they became suspicious.

For the next week or so, it was feared that Smith might have cost investors a full $1,300,000 additional, by use of the hot bonds. Bankers, brokers and others, throughout the country, went hurriedly through their Louisiana obligations. Urgent wires were passed between New Orleans, Baton Rouge, Boston, New York and other points. It turned out, however, that "The Doc" had used his bonds only as the fake collateral and not for any other purposes.

Broker Brown added to the state's hilarity by disclosing that he had received some "highly valuable" "bond collateral" from Jim one night, and had employed a private detective to guard it until morning. He learned later that these, too, were Smith bonds. But Brown did not answer the question that most literate Louisianians were asking: Who were "The Doc's" market associates? Smith had listed twelve partners: J. Monroe 1, J. Monroe, 2, and down the line. Would other high names come crashing down, as colleagues in this and other thefts? And could this have had anything to do with the clean getaway?

For a clean getaway it was. No trace of Jim or the First Lady could be or had been found. Full descriptions and photographs had been spread about the country. The Federal Bureau of Identification was assigned by Murphy to hunt for the man who had given Murphy his degree a month earlier; here, at least, was a Federal angle to the matter. Suspicious Louisianians, recalling the kidnaping of Alice Lee Grosjean's uncle and former husband when their talk had become embarrassing, assured each other that Jim would never be seen again. Some thought that there was unusual delay in starting the hunt; "The Doc" might be well out of the country by this time. Others hinted that he would not be seen again for another reason; that he would be disposed of, or given opportunity to do the disposing himself. "That would be nice for everybody; kind of final." Earl Long, talking in unorthodox fashion, surmised that Smith was "somewhere near the capital, trying to make good his losses, in return for dropping any charges." Smith, he let out, had been trying to raise the money among his friends before he disappeared. But the new Governor insisted that he knew nothing definite of the matter.

"The Doc," it was learned, had tried to get the L.S.U. football plane in which to make an escape—a new use for a vehicle that had seen many unusual ones. But it was on a scouting trip. Smith had tried to call it back, but arrangements could not be made in time.

J. Emory Adams, the First Lady's nephew, drove quietly back to Baton Rouge, alone; he surrendered to police and refused to talk. In the state capital, WPA agents were at work on the L.S.U. records, questioning workmen and officials. Some of the men mentioned in the Jimmy Noe-*Merry-Go-Round* affidavits declined to confer with them, declaring that they "wouldn't give away our information to an organization that's investigating itself." In New Orleans the Federal Grand Jury began what was planned as a WPA inquiry only. In Washington, Attorney-General Murphy disclosed that the revenue men were checking into Smith's income, and that he already had a report on the matter. Yes, investigations were going on in Louisiana, he admitted, but were "limited entirely to matters touching on Federal laws." It was a cautious statement, but Mr. Murphy was a degree or two less cool than the last time.

Congress was in the process of approving a $50,000 appropriation to investigate WPA and related political matters, and it was certain that Louisiana would be a major point of interest. The situation was a continued, continuous national sensation. Cartoonists portrayed America holding its nose near a swamp labeled with the state's name; one showed a hand tossing dice between classic pillars: "Craps in the Louisiana Cloisters."

The search for the Smiths warmed. Nephew Adams admitted that he had driven them to Memphis. "The Doc's" handwriting was identified; he had signed the register of a Memphis hotel, at which they had stayed briefly, in the names of "Mr. and Mrs. J. M. Southern." His script was shaky. A porter was sure he had spoken to them on a fast train to Chicago. A Detroit automobile agent sold a car to a couple who gave the name of Southern; the woman peeled off cash from a heavy roll, and they drove off with expensive luggage, bearing foreign labels. In the interim, the Smiths were seen everywhere: in Texas near the Mexican border, in Canada, in California, by garage keepers who suspected a woman who was hunched down in a car seat, or a driver who kept his head turned. Another Louisiana official, motoring in a car with an aristocratic low number, was temporarily detained in California, as Smith.

At home, the Baton Rouge Parish grand jury received a charge from the judge that it should "spare no one if the evidence points to his guilt." Earl Long disclosed that Building Superintendent Caldwell had been drawing a regular two-per-cent rake-off on all L.S.U. construction, and that the board had not known about it. "The Doc" had put across another of his fake resolutions, and Big George had gone merrily along, collecting it every month! Governor Earl assigned a special aide to the parish grand jury, Attorney-General David M. Ellison, Leche's pupil and friend, the man who had been mentioned in the affidavits on L.S.U.-WPA diversions. He remained with the jury thereafter in most of its deliberations. A North Louisiana attorney was also retained, to demonstrate the state's zeal.

The Public Works Administration announced that it would check "in a routine way" into all its $51,000,000 worth of Louisiana projects, including the Charity Hospital that appeared to be sinking into the ground before it was well finished. Calling its state and district officials to Washington, the WPA insisted that it would carry out its inquiries "without fear or favor." The Securities and Exchange Commission and the Commodity Exchange Administration confirmed reports that they were looking into phases of the situation. The Treasury Department acknowledged that it was finding interesting data on other figures besides Smith. The Federal Bureau of Identification was checking several matters, including passport applications of certain Louisianians. It was a small taste of what was to come.

Smith made an abrupt surrender in Canada. He had been staying with his wife in a cottage beside a lake, "enjoying a quiet vacation," until he saw in a newspaper that he was wanted. This was the first inkling he had had that he was being sought. Jim had in his possession $315, a passport, a quantity of papers on which he had been working—a "history of L.S.U." during his régime. Mrs. Smith had $9400. She wept to another woman as she stood in the middle of the floor of the town post office: "We're decent people. But my husband's in an awful lot of trouble." She pleaded: "Oh, don't put us in jail." She and "The Doc" went, instead, to a guarded hotel room. Smith announced: "I'll waive extradition. I'm ready to go back and fight. I haven't stolen as much as five cents in my life. I won't be made a goat." In Baton Rouge, a Keystone comedy chase was threatened

CARRY ON THE WORK

Posters exhorting the faithful to "carry on the work" of Huey Long and O. K. Allen flooded the state shortly after the death of the Kingfish.

"HELLO FOLKS—I'M BACK"

James Monroe Smith pauses at the door of the airplane to survey the crowd as he returns to Louisiana from Canada in the custody of law enforcement officials. The president of LSU,

IN CUSTODY

Law enforcement officers hustle James Monroe Smith into a waiting automobile at Shushan Airport after his Fourth of July return to Louisiana to face charges of using university funds for personal gain.

MONUMENT TO HUEY

An imposing bronze statue of Huey Long marks his grave and towers over the picturesque gardens on the lawn of the state capitol in Baton Rouge.

over the honor of bringing the Smiths back home. Parish
and state police clashed, with Earl Long forcing a compromise. The football plane in which Jim had hoped to make
his getaway would be used, with both sides represented. In
Canada, another contretemps. The plane was a four-seater.
Jim would not waive extradition unless Thelma went back
with him. The two Smiths could not be accommodated unless either state or parish police gave way. Neither would.
Then, too, Jim indicated that he would not feel safe alone
with Louisiana police. So the return was begun by airliner,
with the Smiths receiving howling receptions at airports en
route.

While the Smiths were on their way, Former Governor
Dick came into the spotlight once more as he rested on his
Gold Coast estate. The Baton Rouge jury summoned him to
"tell what he knows, like anybody else." On the next day,
before he was due in the capital, Dick gave the newspapers
his version of the hysterical Sunday of "The Doc's" disap-
pearance. It was at 11 A.M. that "The Doc" telephoned him
from New Orleans for an appointment, without saying what
he wanted. About 1:30 P.M. Smith arrived at the mansion,
wrought up. "He began the conversation by saying that he
had done a very foolish thing, borrowed $200,000 without
authorization of the board." Dick paused: "I was flabber-
gasted. I didn't then realize the full import of his remark,
that he had diverted funds to his own use. He wanted to
know what I thought about it, and if I could get the board
to approve it. I told him I'd see what could be done, and to
get in touch with me later. There was a lot doing around
the mansion that day." Dick had, however, found time to
call Attorney-General Ellison and Cooper, the state revenue

man; and he referred to their earlier investigations. But the newsreel men and others had interrupted. Dick continued:

Somewhere between six and seven P.M., I guess, Mr. Ellison called Smith and asked him to come over. Supreme Court Justice Fournet came in. Because he's one of the board members, I asked him to sit in with us. Ellison is, too; I appointed him. When Smith arrived he mentioned his speculations, for the first time, and mentioned a figure larger than his previous $200,000; I think about $400,000. He said that he had opened a little trading account on behalf of the university, and owed on it. I told him I was certain that the board would not approve any such transaction. Judge Fournet said, "I for one will not approve it." Then I asked him:

"Well, Doc, do you want it the hard way, or the easy way? I think you ought to resign and let the board look into it." He said, "If you'll write my resignation, I'll sign it." A stenographer made it out, and he said he wouldn't put his signature on it if it contained anything else. It didn't. He signed and left.

Asked why no action was taken then, Former Governor Dick was emphatic:

I didn't order his arrest. I certainly didn't expect him to run away. A Dillinger, a Capone—they might have had some chance. But an amateur like the Doc—he was known from one end of the state to the next. You know what has happened since. And remember, he has said he didn't flee . . . Smith told us he felt sure everything could be straightened out, and that he probably could raise money to make good. At no time, did he ever admit any wrongdoing. I never did know where he borrowed the money. I never asked him. I didn't suspect any act requiring arrest. I was in a tough spot. Here was a friendly, kindly fellow, head of the university. The attorney-general and the district attorney were there. It was their duty to determine if any law violation had been committed, not mine.

Indicating that he might not have ordered Smith's arrest if he had to do the matter over again, the Former Governor observed: "You know, the Attorney-General has said that the loans the bank made were invalid, and that L.S.U. won't lose, whatever happens. I don't see where the state or L.S.U. can claim they lost anything."

When Smith left, Ellison and Cooper "worked like beavers." Cooper went to his office, pulled out Smith's state income returns and found that the trading account had been set down as Smith's personal property. Other board members were at the mansion when Cooper and Ellison returned, added Dick. "As soon as they felt they had concrete evidence —I don't know what that was—they ordered Smith's arrest, about an hour and a half after he left."

The state police superintendent, giving his part of the events, declared that he was not called to the mansion until 6:15 P.M., then went to the campus, lost nearly an hour hunting keys to Smith's office, and finally found mutilated L.S.U. bonds in Smith's desk, the false signatures ripped off. By 8:30 P.M. he was back at the mansion, and a few minutes later the arrest order came. But search warrants were needed to enter Smith's house and those of his relatives, and they were not obtained until 10:30 P.M. Meanwhile, the Smiths had a start of hours. In the Smiths' kitchen, police found gallons of bonded whiskies and wines of good vintage years, ready for Thelma's next soirée. The rural folk were shocked. That went to show you, didn't it? In a closet, Dr. Smith's black academic robe was hanging from a hook. Over it was a striped convict's cap. "The Doc" had worn the headgear to one of his last presidential functions, a masquerade.

Dick had a few more remarks for the world. He called attention to the fact that it was he who had asked Fontenot of the Revenue Department to investigate Smith; but he did not add that Fontenot informed him that such an investigation was already under way. Dick contended that he had known nothing of Big George's two-per-cent rake-off; he knew only that George was a good contractor and that he would hire him again if he had work to be done on his estate. As to that little WPA matter: "If I wanted to rob Uncle Sam, I wouldn't do it through a couple of WPA workers. I'd hire a steamshovel, and move in on Fort Knox, where they store the gold." In retirement, he was reading Emerson's *Compensation*. Impressed with its stress upon self-reliance, he talked dreamily of his growing conviction that the rewards of public office were not worth the sacrifice. (One of Dick's more raucous campaign critics insisted that three men, of whom he had knowledge, suffered apoplectic strokes on reading that passage of the interview.) In any event, Dick would devote any future public activities toward the support of Roosevelt and the New Deal. Roosevelt had done so much for Louisiana. The problem before the country in 1940 would be the same as that before Louisiana in 1936; "Then it was between those that loved Huey and those that hated him. Now it will be between those who love Roosevelt, and those that hate him."

On July Fourth, the Smiths came home to receptions that Lindbergh's and Corrigan's had not matched. The thousands who packed Shushan Airport and the streets of Baton Rouge were a cross between a French Revolutionary mob and a family-picnic gathering. They applauded, shouted, laughed and booed: "Give 'em hell, Doc!" "Tell everything about them sonsobitches!" "You rat!" "Ain't she mighty!" Grandmothers pressed against fences with their sons and daughters, who held up five- and six-year-olds, ice cream cones in hand. Amateur photographers formed a circle about the Smiths, snapping, snapping, getting in the way of the

battalion of professionals. A 12-year-old girl, with a minia-
ture, kicked her way forward, crawled on hands and knees
and got her shots. A radio station offered the Smith arrival
as a "community special event."

Smith was subdued, pink-faced, confused. A microphone
was thrust at him. "Hello, folks. I'm back. I'm glad to be
back. I was ill advised." The former First Lady was a chic
figure in blue print, with turned-up felt hat—an attractive
matron who might indeed be returning from a vacation. She
walked forward quickly, leading policemen in her haste.
She replied coolly: "Of course I'll stick by my husband, to
the last notch. . . . Our plans? I don't know what you're
talking about." Thelma still had her manner. Among the
reporters who spoke with them was one of the students
whom Smith had expelled in the free-speech case, on Huey's
orders.

Then, the automobile trip from New Orleans to Baton
Rouge, and there the greater ordeal, the sight of the boule-
vards over which they had shown Latin-American presidents,
diplomats and others of their former peers. As the car approached the packed entrance to the jail, the sirens whined.
"Couldn't we do without that?" Thelma asked, trembling.
The answer was drowned in shouts, jeers, some applause.
Haggard now, the sting of humiliation in her face, she
stepped out. She put up her handkerchief. "Look, she's crying!" shrieked another woman. Thelma Smith took the handkerchief away to show them that she was dry-eyed, and went
upstairs with "The Doc" to be fingerprinted. There she regained composure and chatted that she had always wanted
to have this done.

Some of the faculty members waited to offer bond.
Thelma, charged with aiding Jim in his embezzlement, was
allowed to leave; but Jim had to stay. One of the professors

who went to the Smiths' assistance was an English teacher whom Huey and Jim had fired, years ago, for writing a campus novel on sugar and sex, *Cane Juice*. Smith had taken him back, with Huey's tacit approval. Tonight the professor philosophized. . . . "There, but for the grace of God . . ."

That evening there were many Louisianians whose apprehension was sharper than ever. What would "The Doc" tell? He was "ill advised"; he "wouldn't be made a goat." How far would he go?

That same day, before a holiday crowd, Earl Long made his first address as Governor, and cried out in defense of the state administration:

"Smith is only one man. Don't blame everybody. Look at Jesus Christ. He picked twelve. And one of 'em was a sonofagun!"

XII

KINGFISH'S APPRENTICE

EARL KEMP LONG, the man who had yearned to be Governor, now had what he wanted, but not in the way he wanted it.

It was the worst time that he could have chosen for his accession, or the best. He had before him the most difficult barrier of his lifetime, or the most magnificent opportunity. What he did in these next brief months would cinch a kingship for him, or lose it.

On his course depended his own personal fortunes and the future of the strongest political machine in the South; a machine which was still the nation's nearest approach to a European-style dictatorship. On his course was contingent, too, the freedom—in some cases the lives—of many men, and the ownership of millions of dollars. He had the power to save or to wreck what his brother had built and left behind.

But Earl K. Long had to choose his rôle, strike right or left: a reformer, removing the money changers from the temple, as so many were urging; or a canny politician, shifting, dodging, countercharging. He could be a Dewey, or a Huey. An active political virtue might well bring its own reward in the America of 1939 and 1940. The District Attorney of New York was headed with self-confidence toward a Presidential nomination on that appeal. Frank Murphy had achieved high place under the same banner. But if this

Governor of Louisiana took such a line, he might bring the structure crashing about him. For the elements of evil, sad to say, provided many of the foundations of that edifice.

On the other hand, Earl Long had before him his brother's example, the guidance of a master in the art of maneuvering the difficult. Huey the Kingfish would never have given in to the clamor of others. He made his own demands, his own terms: "Tell 'em to go slap damn to hell. You say worse against them. You make 'em forget what they're allowing, they're so busy listening to you. And when you've got nothing on your side, stir up trouble in the opposition."

But Long the Second was not the Kingfish, and he knew it. The man who was to "carry on for Huey," to take up the Long torch where it had been dropped, had come to the Governor's chair only by a series of accidents. Earl was the traditional younger son, the frustrate lesser brother to a hero. He shared the family's predilection for politics. But he lacked Huey's swashbuckling qualities, his political genius, his devastating appeal to the populace. He had moved along in the Kingfish's shadow. Huey had beaten him to the gate, latched it and pocketed the key. As he took office, Earl compared himself with his brother:

"I ain't like Huey. He could go a-champing around and get away with it. I've gotta go slower—I might get my head knocked off." But, with a glint: "Maybe I ain't as much a genius. But I got more horse sense."

In earlier years he had been less philosophic. He had sulked and he had muttered against Huey: "He wants to hog everything; can't see his own kin get ahead." This was partly true. Huey would give Earl jobs, but not the ranking ones; and he told friends: "One politician in the family is enough." He could see trouble from several points of view with two Longs prominently in the public eye. But Earl claimed high rewards, and for other things besides blood relationship. "I went broke trying to keep him out of trouble when the Legislature was full of men trying to impeach him," Earl told a Senatorial committee.

Brotherly love had gone sour as Long faced Long at the Overton election-fraud hearing. Earl stared at Huey: "I do not know how they hold elections in Mexico or Russia, but I do not think they could surpass what has been going on in Louisiana since Huey P. Long was elected to the United States Senate." Huey asked if Earl had not put out a fake ticket when he ran for lieutenant-governor to make it appear that Huey was supporting him. Earl replied: "I never tried to make people believe you were supporting me. I knew you would not, and I knew why. I knew you knew you could not control me." Huey asked if he had not denounced Earl's "fake ticket" and if Earl had not followed him on the air, to dare him to a fist fight. Earl curled his lip: "I may have. But I knew you weren't going to meet me. I never heard of you meeting anybody."

Huey shook his head, quoted the Bible to Earl at another point: "Lying is a sin." Earl retorted: "You must have committed a million sins in your life."

In his person, Earl bore a resemblance to Huey: the same cleft chin, the same look that Louisiana called "imp." But he had less forceful features, as he had less force of character. Where Huey bellowed and cracked the whip, Earl grimaced and gave a pettish order. Both had violent tempers but expressed them in opposite ways. Physical action was no light matter to either. Huey ran from it. Earl, when his rage was aroused, knew no rules. He met one enemy on narrow Royal Street in New Orleans, and the battle was an all-out one. The victim claimed later that Earl scratched and clawed, and almost bit one of his fingers off. Another opponent declared on another occasion: "He not only punched me, but he stuck half his hand in my mouth and tried to tear my cheek in two." Dangerous men, these Longs, though not in the same manner.

Like Huey, Earl made politics his career. Like Huey, he started as a traveling salesman and took law courses on the side. The Kingfish, when he became Governor, gave him a well-paid attorneyship; Allen fired him, on Huey's orders, when Earl bucked the organization. As his brother's enemy, Earl snagged a Federal job with the Home Owners' Loan Corporation. But toward the end of Huey's life, Earl had been reconciled with his brother—through the influence of Maestri, some claimed. Before his death, Huey said he had Earl "on probation." As Lieutenant-Governor, Earl had received repeated advice from Maestri and others to watch his course, to play the game more carefully than he had done in the past. He had nevertheless managed to lose sectional prestige by mixing on the losing side in several factional fights, usually on the basis of personal likes and dislikes. Earl, said those inside the machine who did not like him, had a single attribute of strength: Bob Maestri.

Such was the puzzled man who faced two roads these July and August days. Watching him were, among others, the country folk, the original believers in his brother. It was too early to gauge full reaction, but there were indications that the rural stretches were genuinely stirred at the excesses that "their" régime seemed to have produced. Toward Earl, the feeling was mixed. Many had not voted for him when they voted for Leche. They remembered well those things he had said about Huey. Others thought that a Long was a Long; and Huey had taken him back, hadn't he? The upland farmer assured his wife that none of this devil's business had happened in Huey's lifetime. It was

"Leche and his crowd" that were responsible. And now Huey's brother had come in. Wouldn't it be a fine thing, and a right thing before God, if Earl settled these things for Huey? Also looking on were many who were less interested in Huey than in an answer to the question: what would the new Governor do to clean up the mess left by his predecessor, and how far would he go? Inside the machine, still others focused their attention on Earl with hate and fear in their eyes. He was a man who harbored grudges. Would he take revenge for past insults, real or imagined? Earl inspired none of that automatic loyalty that had been one of Huey's assets. A final group were Earl's friends who gave quiet advice: Go slow, boy. Who knows what will come up. . . ? The cart's tilted now . . .

The Federal Government appeared to be feeling its way: for the time being, at least. Just what it would do was a matter that remained in the balance during these weeks. There were reasons for the machine men and others to question Washington's intentions. The Second Louisiana Purchase, in the absence of official abrogation, was still in effect. It had been signed in the last presidential election year. Now another approached, when those twenty votes in convention might again be on the auction block. Leche was still national committeeman. Nothing had yet been proved against him. He might still "deny the allegations and defy the alligators." Once again, the Roosevelt Administration was finding itself at a point at which every assured vote in the "Solid" South was important. The Garner forces were in the ascendancy in Congress and out of it, and others were aligning with them in these days before the Second World War.

A bitter nomination fight seemed certain between Old and New Dealers. Then, too, the Louisiana delegation was voting down the line with the White House, although members admitted that their orders sometimes went against the grain. Roosevelt needed every Congressional supporter whom he could marshal on many issues. Allen Ellender, always welcome at the White House, was known to be making calls at this time. Some were unimpressed with the status of Federal justice in Louisiana to date. The scandals that had thus far come to light were the result of efforts by the newspapers and by Jimmy Noe. Would justice, without a prod from the rear, have waked at all? Considering her record for somnolence in Louisiana, would she doze again? There was always the matter of "lack of jurisdiction" (States' Rights); and there was "atmosphere." If Washington did nothing, it might be easy for the machine to center on Smith and one or two minor victims and see that parish grand juries behaved.

Earl Long hesitated, then made his choice. He decided to assume both rôles, to clean up with one hand and to cover up with the other. It was the choice of a weak man, or of a skilled tactician. Earl was never a strategist.

Citizens' protests over the scandals sprang up overnight about the state. A group of one hundred Orleanians—business men, lawyers, clergymen and others—formed a Citizens' Voluntary Committee and demanded a "Louisiana Seabury Investigation." It urged Long to appoint a new special assistant to the attorney-general with full authority to make a "complete, impartial and independent" inquiry into all city, parish and state agencies. It urged that all state records be opened to the public, and at once. Disclosures thus far "had startled even those who for a long time have suspected extensive wrongdoing in public places." But to date the investigations involved chiefly L.S.U., whereas general be-

294

lief was that the violations there comprised "only a part, perhaps a small part, of the abuses throughout Louisiana."

As subjects of examination, the committee cited the presence of legislators on state payrolls; the "practical monopoly" of one firm of architects on state buildings; a similar near-monopoly by an insurance firm; a disproportionate share of public work which went to one contractor; the fact that a former active political figure, who had retired, enjoyed "exclusive control" over sales of materials to state institutions, including the new Charity Hospital; that in one instance alone, a brokerage house was paid upward of a half-million dollars for financial advice in bond refunding. "No investigation that is being made, or will be made by any person now occupying a political position, or by any friend, ally or appointee of such person can be expected to satisfy the public demand," it was declared. A state-wide meeting of citizens' groups resulted in the submission to Earl of a list of three attorneys from which he was asked to choose a Louisiana Seabury, and thus convince the state that he was honest in his declarations.

For days the new Governor dodged the committee; but finally he replied that he had "no right to shirk or in anywise delegate to other persons the fulfillment of my duties." The *Progress* had clearer comment: "Citizens' Gang Kicked in the Pants." Speaking his mind with greater frankness, Earl declared eventually that he would not be "entrapped, hobbled, stampeded or frightened into a condition of self-abdication." One of the men whom he declined to appoint as suggested was a South Louisiana attorney, Sam Jones. Earl and his men were to have reason to remember the name.

For the rest of his term, Huey's brother was to be fretted by such citizens' organizations. Some of the members were old anti-Huey conservatives; others were new self-seekers, some who had been with the Long crowd or on its fringes; others were men who had taken little part in politics before, the independents, among them young ones who were liberal in their viewpoint, in contrast with a large part of the old oppositionists. New alignments were in the making.

The state wondered what would happen to Dick's *Progress*, his wonderful circulation and advertising organization. Grand juries were showing signs of interest here and there in the *Progress*, in the way it functioned and made its money. The word came down that Dick had sold the paper to the machine, with Maestri or the dee duct fund, or both, figuring in the purchase. On the witness stand, Former Governor Dick at one time admitted that he had earned $225,000 in less than three years from his venture in journalism. He sold his stock at the end for $187,500, and he received about $36,000 in dividends. The original purchase price, he said, was $38,000. It was little wonder that he had "coached" fellow newspapermen, upon occasion, on the technique of success.

Earl now announced that the *Progress* would go back to its former status as "a political paper only, just like under Huey." It would be smaller. It would carry no advertisements after the present contracts were fulfilled. "There'll be no shakedowns or rake-ins or anything else," he told an applauding crowd. No state employee or anybody else would have to subscribe, and the paper would be given away in lots of places, "just like under Huey," to make sure that people received it who would be benefited by the message. "And anybody that don't advertise will get as square a deal as if they did. If I have anything to do with it, there'll be no advertising from state boards or offices." All of this contained damaging admissions regarding operations under Leche. But it had its advantages for Earl.

Other things were more difficult. A. P. Tugwell, a man whom Huey had once proposed for Governor, announced his candidacy against Earl, and, together with Jimmy Noe, began a process of nettling that sorely tried the tyro executive. Tugwell declared that if Earl wanted to "do right" as he assured the state so often, he could halt the greatest source of corruption readily at hand: dee ducts. Would Boss Maestri let him? Tugwell charged that Earl had previously told him that he, Earl, was getting $400 a month from the dee ducts; and Tugwell asked if other members of the Long family were also beneficiaries. Earl replied that he had once received that amount and more, but only for campaigning. Tugwell, he asserted, had received $2500 a year from the same fund during the whole time he was highway commissioner. Tugwell snapped back with a statement that his $2500 had come from Governor O. K. Allen's personal fund, to make up for Tugwell's loss in giving up a good private job to work for the state. Earl snickered: "Everybody that believes that, go stand on his head." Tugwell pulled the record on the question of the dee ducts' masters, quoted Governor Dick's statement to a mass meeting that Maestri was dee duct custodian and that therefore the state knew that the system was honestly handled. Maestri declared that he was no dee-duct man. Disgruntled state employees here and there came forward with statements, admitting that they had been compelled to contribute. The Federal Grand Jury at New Orleans began an inquiry into the matter, to see if beneficiaries of dee ducts had paid their income taxes on them, and also if the Federal "kickback" law had been violated.

Pressed, the new Governor announced that he would soon

have a "statement" settling the dee-duct matter. The *Progress* ran a coy paragraph declaring that it had learned "from a reliable source" that dee ducts were going off. But it was soon evident that Earl had spoken too soon. The dee-duct fund was then nearly empty, whether for purchase of the *Progress* or for other reasons. Some of Earl's backstage helpers pointed out that the dee ducts' line of travel might be termed the life-line of the organization. New word was passed around. Dee ducts were to be continued, but "voluntarily." Those who received less than $100 a month would not contribute unless they "insisted"; those who took in more than $100 would give ten per cent, instead of five.

A muddled situation followed, with some paying one rate, others another, and some paying none. This was no time for a show of force. Tugwell declared that the dee ducts were still flying, but at a slower rate, and he had the last laugh: "The Governor said 'Better a little with righteousness than great revenue without right.' What he meant in this case was 'Better a little graft with reasonable safety, than great revenue without Federal immunity.'" A minister chimed in with a question. Were Earl's remarks on righteousness "prophecy or mockery"; was this a Governor "quoting scripture for his own purpose"?

Earl made another concession. Attorney-General Ellison handed down a ruling that dual job holding was dual job holding—that a man could not be a legislator and receive employment with a public agency, a point which the opposition had long maintained. The "nesting place of the doubledippers," Huey's secret Debt Moratorium Commission, now lost its population, though it was many months before the state knew just who had been employed on the rolls. Ellison's ruling did not apply to machine legislators who were also college presidents or teachers. In New Orleans, the city attorney ruled that municipal-payroll members could still serve as state legislators. The grapevine carried a message to the boys to "hold tight till after election."

Annoyingly, "Doc" Smith was crowding the new Governor for attention. Slowly, he was emerging in his full stature as one of the merriest, most ingenious members of the Long rogues' gallery. From grand juries, from L.S.U. records, from associates who "suddenly remembered something," came fragments that provided an enlightening mosaic portrait of James Monroe Smith, or James "Jingle Money" Smith, or simply "Old Jingle Money," as the state designated him in admiration.

Jim, it appeared at last, had gone on a spree of falsification of the university's books and records. No one knew what to trust in the minutes. They were, said one official, "mixed up, crooked up and a complete mess." Jim had been collecting thousands of additional dollars of salary without the board's knowledge. He had raised his pay by proposing, seconding and adopting a resolution of his own, then secretly inserted into the minutes. He took $18,000 a year instead of the $15,000 plus food, lodging, free gas and other gratuities which the board thought he was receiving, and became the highest paid official in the state.

He had forged minutes to give a "supplemental" salary of $4000 a year to Business Manager Jackson, advancing him from $5000 to $9000. Big George Caldwell's two-percent rake-off had been achieved by degrees. "The Doc" had first inserted a resolution declaring that the board had elected to give George one per cent. Then, since nobody said anything, "The Doc" decided that the board would not be averse to doubling George's "cut" in recognition of George's good work. Since there were still no objections,

"The Doc" had stepped out farther and "adopted" a resolution giving himself blanket authority to raise the pay of any official or staff member; and he played Good Samaritan to many a professorial sufferer who may or may not have known that the board was unaware of these benefits.

Old Jingle Money had taken out a life-insurance policy in his name, with the family as beneficiaries, and had billed L.S.U. regularly for the premiums. He had developed a habit of pocketing university group-insurance rebates. A $1000 check was found issued in the name of his daughter, Marjorie, for "a portion of expenses" for a "study tour" of Southern states and Mexico. It was a tour about which no one had any recollection. "The Doc" was sly about such little things. Also, there had been an L.S.U. student organization called "The Louisiana Kings" (Every Player a King, perhaps) which had made a tour and run up a $4171 bill. For some reason, "The Doc" thought the board might object. So he had paid this, too, by another of his Smith resolutions.

Sometimes "The Doc" showed a particularly deft touch. One of his "resolutions" authorized him to enter a trading account for an L.S.U. endowment fund—a fund that was as real as the resolution. "Doc" told an investigator: "All I did, I did for L.S.U. I wanted to help by earning some money." These and other resolutions had a verisimilitude that was impressive. This or that board member was amazed to learn that he had made a motion, that another had seconded it, and that he had spoken with some warmth for a change in procedure of which he had never heard. Sometimes, to give an air of extra reality, Old Jingle Money had set down some dissenting votes; but never enough to defeat his own resolution. The doctoring took place sometimes more than a year after the original meeting. "The

Doc" simply called in a stenographer and dictated the resolution.

At the same time that these oddities were coming to light,
investigators were finding a hodgepodge of frauds, rackets,
shiftings of L.S.U. funds and accounts, "flagrant dishonesty,"
and simple cavalier carelessness in financial matters. The
way to receive many a contract appeared to have been to
submit the high bid. Despite the legal provision that purchases over a certain minimum, or construction over that
figure, had to be by bid, ten and twelve times these amounts
were given out without contract or competition. A prejudice
against keeping of records had developed. Payrolls, cancelled
checks and ledgers were burned. Over everything, though,
had reposed the happy confusion of a day-in, day-out holiday.

Tens of thousands of dollars' worth of materials were
bought retail, although the university could have obtained
considerably lower wholesale prices. And these retail purchases, by coincidence perhaps, had been made from the
same firm, over and over again. Everybody was taking a
cut, as high as he could manage it. The state university
lost tens of other thousands because for months it did not
bother to pay its bills. Cash discounts for prompt payment
were something of which the boys had not heard, or which
they had not bothered to learn about. They might have
saved a few thousands in that way; but there were more
important things at hand. Firms that owed L.S.U. had waited
for bills for years. Sometimes they inquired about payment
and received no answer. What was the percentage for the
boys in bothering about a $4000 or $5000 matter, when it
would probably go into the university treasury without a
kickback to anybody? The university was nominally operating former student barracks on its old campus as high-priced

apartments, which were among the most popular properties in the capital. Waiting lists of applicants grew by the month. Inquiry showed that the boys had not bothered to check up on the tenants; some were in arrears as long as twenty-two months. And heads of departments had fallen into the pleasant habit of merging their personal bank accounts with those of their division, and thereafter withdrawing at will.

All in all, $385,000 had "accumulated" in uncollected debts. A total of $210,000 was due from students and former students, for tuition, board and loans dating back to 1934. This included amounts advanced to Huey's favorites, the prospective share-the-wealth organizers. Auditors were informed that a large part of the total consisted of "notes" that were not notes. Staff members explained that nobody, really, had expected payments for a lot of these $75 and $100 advances. They were mere formalities, exercises in penmanship, perhaps a buoying-up of the morale of students forced to take funds in this fashion from their superiors. The auditors had checked, nevertheless, sending out inquiries; and they received some strange answers, even for a régime such as that of Jingle Money Smith's. Many denied that they had ever received the amounts; others declared that they had repaid the institution; still others that they had been there on "special scholarships" out of "The Doc's" fund which was set up especially for the purpose, and had understood they did not have to pay. Had their elders snagged this money, on its way from the treasury or back to it, from the students? The records of Louisiana State University will never provide the answer.

Athletic affairs were in a particular maze. In one year, sports activities were leaving the university $113,462 in debt. But "The Doc" had informed the board that affairs

were going so well that L.S.U. could afford to send the full
student cadet corps to a Tennessee game—at $27,000 for the
junket. Records of ticket sales and other operations had
been destroyed by the time auditors reached the department.
An estimated $100,000 was given out in some years to main-
tain the athletes in the newer style. An interesting compilation showed $43,000 for "board of athletes," charged to
"contingent fund" or "cafeteria"; $10,455 for "wages of ath-
letes," charged to the summer session; $3217 for rooms;
$8805 for "spending money furnished to athletes"; and $2298
for their books. Other universities did the same thing, of
course. Most of them, however, were not so frank, nor, by
comparative standards, was the scale usually so lavish.

Some of the records had engaging candor. A voucher under
"operation and maintenance" read: "One copper pan, $3.75,
Governor Leche, Covington"; another, "traveling expenses
in connection with the Covington job." Auditors expressed
the view that the university would be justified in demanding
return of the $3.75, on the ground that it was an expendi-
ture for purposes not wholly educational.

Suddenly, it was discovered that L.S.U. faced a financial
crisis. The boys had quietly ignored rigid requirements for
sinking funds of the university bonds, totaling $430,000.
The Board of Liquidation was called into emergency session, to make a special half-million-dollar appropriation to
save the university's credit. That was another half-million
for which "The Doc" could claim full credit.

Old Jingle Money maintained a becoming modesty in
this flurry. Arch Burford, ace Revenue Intelligence agent,
interviewed him in his cell. Earl Long called him a "Ponzi."
Smith found himself more often, not less, in the headlines.
He was indicted on the average of once every two days for

more than a month: for forging of public records, embezzlements, operation of a confidence game in the banking loans, and other offenses. For a time he was practically the only person indicted, wherefor reaction developed. "The Public Wants to Know That Smith Is Not Taking the Rap," a newspaper editorial declared; and it expressed the general opinion.

The Federal Government decided that it wanted "The Doc." New Orleans wanted him. Baton Rouge maintained its claim. Charges mounted to thirty-seven separate indictments, and his bond to $219,000. "The Doc" retained two of the best criminal lawyers in New Orleans. One of them fumed: "We don't want to hurt anybody unless we have to. But we're not going to let the state jim-jam him in front of a jury." A threat followed: unless Smith's "persecution" by "harassments," over-large bonds and such methods was stopped, he would "tell exactly who advised him to leave Baton Rouge after his resignation—and who told him there would be no criminal prosecution, but at most a civil suit." A petition for his release, offered in Federal court, insisted that Smith had been so advised, but omitted names. Dick and the boys who had been in the mansion that night made denial. Judges refused to let Smith go free, maintaining that there was strong likelihood of still additional charges against him and that, considering circumstances, the bond was not too heavy. Federal prison officials, gaining custody for a time, used Jim as a night-school instructor. Some citizens wrote furious objections, fearful of what Old Jingle Money might teach impressionable youths.

Broker Brown, under questioning, ended his silence regarding Smith's "partners" or "associates" in the stock-market plunges. He gave the names of Monte Hart, favorite contractor of the machine; Summa and Verne Caldwell, affiliates of Monte's and relatives of Big George; Coach "Red" Heard of L.S.U., Big George Caldwell, Business Manager Jackson, and Leon Weiss, the favored architect. But he said that none were actual participants with "The Doc." Smith had merely borrowed funds or bonds from them. Some of them did not get their money back. Monte Hart contributed an explanatory statement which became a minor Louisiana classic: "Dr. Smith borrowed the bonds from us to be used as collateral in purchasing warehouse receipts for whiskey. After looking into the speculative side, I felt sure President Smith could not lose any money, on account of whiskey becoming more valuable as it aged."

Brown offered a crowning detail: he had lost $20,000 of his own when Smith borrowed that amount and gave him $25,000 of bonds in return. These, of course, were "Smith" (or hot) bonds. Broker Brown himself was eventually charged by Baton Rouge and New Orleans juries in connection with "The Doc's" operations. New Orleans police discovered that his name was not Brown, but Murphy. He had been in a minor brush with the law in another state. Murphy-Brown said that he had been framed for political reasons, and had adopted a pen name. The incident provided variety in the scandal diet.

Attention here shifted back to Governor Earl. He made a "discovery" which surprised few but himself. He had learned that officials of state departments had formed their own supply houses and were getting rich through favored dealings with state agencies. He had given orders. "It's one thing or the other; they can't be in private business and the state, too."

Who were the men and their firms? Earl was not saying. "You probably know them anyway." Didn't such practices violate state law, and would he take action against those involved? "My main object is to stop it. I'm only responsible for what goes on under my administration." A. P. Tugwell asked if the new rule applied to the Governor, too. Earl, he declared, had been supplying state institutions with "a large part of their beef and pork requirements." Did he mean that everybody except Governor and Lieutenant-Governor must stop? The Governor, flushing, admitted that while second man he had made such sales, "but only in small quantities, at market price or lower." Now, as chief executive, he was halting all of it. But he added a side statement that concerns in which employees were financially "interested" might yet get state business if they submitted low bids. He could see nothing wrong in that. It was evident that in these instances, when he talked of "a little with righteousness," he meant a little at a time.

The newspapers now disclosed that L. P. Abernathy, the head of the Highway Commission and member of Smith's L.S.U. board, had a financial interest in a firm which did business with L.S.U., the commission and other state divisions. Abernathy admitted ownership of 25 to 30 per cent of an office-supply company. He used Earl's words—he saw nothing wrong. The Baton Rouge grand jury, turning for a time to others besides Smith, did. It indicted Abernathy and a partner for benefitting illegally from state purchases. The indictment was a highly disturbing one all over the state. Who did not know of transactions in which officials or subofficials had, as the charge read, "direct and indirect pecuniary interest, knowingly, wilfully and feloniously" in private dealings with their agencies? Who did not know about the mushroom growths of supply houses that dealt in supplies ranging from paint brushes to mules? If the Baton Rouge jury carried through here, it might purge the state of a staggering proportion of its higher-ups. But the jury did not carry through; and a judge later dismissed the charge, on the grounds that it had not been shown that Abernathy voted on the project in question, although his fellow L.S.U. board members did.

A little note that elicited comment crept into the papers. In a line-up of the Baton Rouge jurors appeared the name of one of the contracting Nelson brothers, who had been indicted in one of the earlier income-tax cases in connection with alleged cover-up payments. A plea of nolo contendere had been entered in the matter about the time of the Second Purchase, and small fines had been assessed. Now Nelson was not only a juror but acting foreman in that official's absence, which included a summer vacation.

Big George Caldwell went down to New Orleans on the call of the Federal jurors. He refused to talk, and, as he stepped outside, deputies arrested him for violation of the Federal Relief Act. With him were charged his assistant, who had taken over the L.S.U. superintendency when Big George quit by request, and a WPA foreman. Shortly afterward Federal and Baton Rouge juries handed down a series of charges against Business Manager Jackson, Caldwell, his assistants, and several other L.S.U. figures, business houses, and others. A range of lush schemes was outlined for use of the WPA and L.S.U. as free employment agencies and private warehouses for the privileged. Big George, Business Manager Jackson and some of their aides were found to have been getting their carpenters, yard boys, plumbers and other workers from the WPA for the construction of their estates with the gold bathroom equipment, stately pillars, badminton courts and the rest. For their mansions, and for hide-away camps along rivers near Baton Rouge, the relief agency also had provided the boys with garden stepping stones, paving materials, wood, fences, barns and other supplies. Sometimes the boys dispatched the WPA men to their homes and stationed an overseer to watch for any snooping individuals; or sometimes, they simply had the WPA men fabricate the WPA materials on L.S.U.'s campus and then use the WPA trucks to transport the blocks or the building sections out to their homes. Governor Dick's big Coliseum (with the largest copper roof in the world) was the ideal place for this private-public construction; it was closed in, and yet it was commodious.

One of Big George's second men had apparently used the WPA men to help build an apartment house and his private camp, and also to attend to the garden of his town house. The workers would check in on the project at the campus, then catch a bus and report to whichever of the other places their master had designated for the day. Later, catching the bus again, they would check off at the campus.

Big George branched out from there. He worked out-and-out rackets on L.S.U. with supply houses, which disclose discernment and noteworthy perception in taking advantage of a good thing. Big George went to these firms, persuaded them to hike their bids and then made them kick back all or most of the hiked amount. He received his share; they were guaranteed the contract. Presently, the United States Attorney-General's office estimated that George received about $120,000 from a score of firms in these little deals. He pleaded guilty to "sample cases," and a number of the firms were fined by the court. In some cases, the raises in costs which resulted to L.S.U. were nearly as high as the original contract. In such instances, L.S.U. was paying twice for its work; once to the contractor, again to Big George. He worked a triple play here and there. He would tell the supply companies that he would provide part of the materials from his own stores. They would pay him for the amounts he asked. Then he would steal the goods from L.S.U. and WPA supplies, bilking the university. Finally, however, he would not steal as much as he told the firms he would. Thus he would be overpaid for the theft, and would have that much additional in supplies on which to work his arts with the next contractor. And meanwhile he would have the hiked bid. Big George cheated everybody— L.S.U., WPA and the supply houses. Some of his associates were bitter when they learned of George's refinements of the subject. He had not told them half of what he was do- ing. Had they known, they could have done the same thing, or perhaps claimed a cut. That showed you how unethical the fellow was . . .

George had yet additional tricks up his ample sleeves. Several times he arranged with contractors to obtain a mo- nopoly on L.S.U. work. Under Jim Smith, he had carte blanche on such matters. Then he would provide WPA labor and materials, and in consideration of this little serv- ice, the firms would kick back the amounts they would have spent for such costs had the WPA not been available. This was direct governmental aid to industry in a way that Con- gress had never envisioned. Interestingly, these activities took place in the construction of the Huey P. Long Field House, the stadium-dormitory facilities, the Coliseum itself and other famous structures of scandal. They went back, too, to the lifetime of the Kingfish.

George's final example of finesse was found by auditors a year later. George put in his bill for his two-per-cent rake- off on an $89,000 construction job; and on this basis he was paid. But the work had cost only $84,000. George, or a friend, had simply lifted the figure. Here was a racket within a racket.

Mrs. Rose Long figured indirectly in a related charge. The widow lived in these days in a mansion which was superior to most of the homes Huey had provided for the family in his lifetime. She, Russell and her daughter Rose had set up quarters in a new and strikingly attractive residence, white-columned and impressive, by the lakeside in the university suburbs. Caldwell handled the construction and Jackson the business details, arranging matters while the widow was away. An indictment for use of WPA men and materials on that operation was returned against Big George, Business Manager Jackson and an assistant; but Mrs. Long was cleared of any blame. On the Leche matter, similarly, a later indictment mentioned the same men for construction of two tenant houses, a barn, stock sheds, bull pen, fencing and concrete stepping stones on the estate itself. Leche, like Mrs. Long, was not indicted. But the Government was not overlooking him in other matters.

Into the net, the Federal jurors next drew one of the more dazzling parish bosses of the Long-Leche period, Dr. Clarence Lorio of Baton Rouge, president of the Louisiana State Medical Society and a beneficiary extraordinary of the régime. Thereby hung a story of politics and doctoring. Lorio had struck up a friendship with Huey Long, on the basis of a mutual interest in golf. The game paid Lorio rich returns. He was one of the first professional men to go over to Huey in a parish that prided itself on its hostility. He became L.S.U.'s medical director at $6000 a year, a job that was not a full time one; the state penitentiary's physician and surgeon, $2400; medical director for the tuberculosis sanitarium near Baton Rouge, $2000; state senator and official patronage distributor. His sanitarium job he "farmed out" to a younger friend.

Lorio was charged with a scheme to use the mails to defraud under which he, an L.S.U. officer, entered a formal agreement with an electrical contractor to get L.S.U. business for him and split the profits, fifty-fifty.

The two men, it was alleged, would get together and decide how much a legitimate bid would be hiked to give them a higher return. In one instance, it was declared, a bid of $29,000 was raised $20,000 as "illegal profit." Contracts went to the partner without competitive bidding, through what might be termed "dummy bidding." The contractor later testified at Lorio's trial that he obtained three sets of bid blanks and asked for "complementary" bids against his own from two friends. The friends signed the blank forms, and he then filled them in so that they would be higher than his own. He entered his agreement with Lorio because "Monte Hart had been receiving all of the business." After that, matters were different. Lorio's part of the project was to "get business for me and keep Hart from getting it." Although the contractor had told the Federal Grand Jury that he and Lorio conferred to raise the figures in the bids, he repudiated his statement and claimed that the bids were always "legitimate."

The case had a curious result. The jury found Lorio guilty, but on the smallest count, involving a few hundred dollars. The judge gave Lorio a novel sentence: a $1000 Federal fine; a two-year prison sentence, to be suspended during a five-year probation period. Then, adding what attorneys called one of the most unusual provisions in their recollection, the Federal judge ordered Lorio to repay the state $12,500—the full amount which he had been charged with taking from the state under the complete indictment; and made suspension of sentence contingent on payment.

Thus far, however, the Federal Government had confined its indictments to L.S.U.; but its preliminary investigations indicated that it might be interested in other matters. Governor Earl set in motion machinery for "co-ordination" of efforts between state and Federal agencies. With a flourish, he and Ellison announced that they were working in complete teamwork with the Government, providing it with all information that came to the state. In return, of course, they anticipated similar co-operation from the Federal sources. Earl telegraphed Attorney-General Murphy, and Murphy replied. He would be "happy to comply with your request, and will keep it under consideration. At present, however, and pending further inquiry, it is deemed inadvisable to divulge any information in our possession. Thanks for your message." It was a new note, coming from the Administration that had made the deal with Leche. Washington, obviously, was not convinced of the use to which the Long men might put the material it had gathered on other Long men.

Ominously, the Federal Government was getting more and more interested in the scandals. An Assistant Attorney-General was dispatched to New Orleans to take charge of income-tax matters. The Department of the Interior assigned an oil expert and a staff of assistants to look into reports regarding oil irregularities. Then Attorney-General Murphy himself announced that he was sending O. John Rogge, his newly appointed chief of the Department of Justice's criminal division, to assist in the general situation. The informed were disturbed, for this was unusual procedure. The head of such a division had never been ordered to the state before, in all of the zeal against Huey. But the boys were not much impressed when a thirty-five-year-old, open-faced fellow, who looked like the former farm boy that he was, stepped diffidently off a plane at Shushan Airport and declared: "I will be here as long as I can be of service, but I hope not longer than a week."

Before very long, Washington had answered the question that Earl, Dick, Bob, Seymour and the rest of the boys had been asking: How's about the Purchase? Rogge's one-week stay was to lengthen into eight months. One of the broadest and most thorough-going criminal inquiries in Federal history was on. The Washington-Baton Rouge alliance was a scrap of paper.

Under Rogge's guidance, the Federal jurors made most of the figures previously indicted in 1939 look like ward heelers. He and the Government were after the big game, and there was no limit on the season or the bag, they made it obvious. The jury quickly smashed down with charges into one of the most bare-faced lootings of the Long régime, early or later, then moved on to others of equal import. First it indicted Seymour Weiss, the man who had once been burned, but was not twice shy; the wealthy Monte Hart, the most favored contractor in the state; Louie Le-Sage, Standard Oil Company vice-president and lobbyist; J. Emory Adams, the Smith nephew; and finally, of course, James Monroe Smith. For variety, it was a hotel furniture racket.

From now on, it was to be Washington against the machine. The New Deal had cast an appraising eye about Louisiana. Reports from its agents had made clear that under the surface there was new dynamite which might make the earlier matters seem petty. Who knew who would explode it? The New Deal, it was pointed out by observers, was known to be looking about for its own crusaders and crusades to match the Republican Dewey and his activities. Purity had become popular. Murphy, it was now apparent, would welcome an opportunity for an onslaught. He had the signal; and, it appeared, he had the man for the assignment. The events that ensued were the result, in large measure, of the prosecutor and investigator chosen as the spearhead of the movement.

O. John Rogge was a man such as the Longsters had never encountered. He was forthright, frequently naïve, in grim earnest, and the possessor of a deadly legal intelligence. He had a capacity for indignation that amazed most Louisianians on both sides. He made announcements that caused the machine, and sometimes the more urbane opponents, to grin, until both sides realized that he meant what he said and intended to carry out what he had threatened. He did what he did, said he, because "it makes my blood boil to see people behave the way this bunch behaved." A set of thousand-dollar bills in the hands of Richard W. Leche, for instance, brought the Rogge blood to the bubbling point. He had called on Dick for questioning, and Dick pulled those bills out casually, then stuffed them back, to demonstrate how little the big money signified for him. "It was the first time I had even seen a one thousand dollar bill," Rogge, his eyes wider than usual, told his friends. From then on, he itched for a kill.

He was six-foot two and a half, with a physical stature to match Leche's. Rogge had been a chore boy and farm hand in his youth, a native of Illinois, son of a German Friesian. Until he went to school, he had spoken nothing but Low German. At eighteen, he was the youngest graduate in the history of the University of Illinois, the proud twirler of a Phi Beta Kappa key. At 21 he left Harvard as the youngest to receive a law degree since that institution had required modern standards for admission. He went into private practice in Chicago, and was retained by the Reconstruction

Finance Corporation for its "Dawes Bank" suit against the institution that had crashed after the Government loaned it $90,000,000. Rogge was hired to sue for $14,000,000 from the stockholders. He fought some 325 opposing attorneys in actions that covered twenty-six states and 2000 cases. "It will take you ten years to get ten per cent," the older heads told him. In about four years, he had won $10,000,000; the stockholders of the other $4,000,000 were themselves bankrupt.

It was Tommy Corcoran of the "brain trust" who drew Rogge into the Federal service, first with the Securities and Exchange Commission in the Transamerica Corporation investigation, and then with the Treasury Department in holding-company cases. When Murphy took over the Department of Justice, he had a free hand in cleaning out lame ducks, political hangers-on and other non-Murphy types of the Cummings and preceding régimes. Rogge, whose contact with criminal law had been brief, was appointed to head a criminal division with a new emphasis. Rogge was in his office less than a full month before he was assigned to Louisiana, with results that may have important influence in several directions in determining trends of Federal jurisprudence.

O. John Rogge struck heavier blows at the dictatorship than any member of the Louisiana opposition, during Huey or after Huey. He became a Paul Bunyan of the grand-jury system and the courtrooms of Louisiana; to some a titan, a hero; a French Revolutionary murderer to others. He ruined more reputations and more businesses, cracked apart more fortunes than the genius Huey himself; and he caused, perhaps, almost as many suicides. He received laudatory poems, marriage proposals and a bullet in the mail. For a time, even, Louisiana's delegation to the Democratic National Convention of 1940 planned to offer him in nomination for President, by way of recognition for what he had done.

As the *Item-Tribune* told it: "O. John Rogge came to town, and from then on, it was Oh, Johnny, Oh!"

XIII

THE ART OF CONSERVATION

EARL LONG talked rectitude, country style: "I am determined to remove from the seat of authority every man who in any degree worships Mammon rather than God."

To this the annoying A. P. Tugwell retorted that Mammon was worshiped nowhere in Louisiana more avidly than in and about the Conservation Department. He pointed to some of the worshipers, who were, said he, close to Earl and Dick and Bob Maestri, the former commissioner.

Wasn't it true, Tugwell asked, that the only way gas concerns could obtain enforcement of production control to protect certain fields was by signing a contract with a former state representative and friend of Earl's? Specifically, didn't this friend get a rake-off of four cents a thousand cubic feet?

Also, Tugwell inquired, hadn't the present conservation commissioner—William Rankin—permitted friends in North Louisiana to make heavy extractions of oil and gas in excess of published limitations, under "special permits"? And had not at least one of these permits been issued only as a post-legalization after other operators, becoming suspicious, protested? And wasn't one of the members of the firm a member of the State Mineral Board?

The Conservation Department now became L.S.U.'s rival for public interest. It was the agency that handled more assets than any other, its province being oil, gas, sulphur, and other natural resources. And it was the agency about which the régime of wealth-sharers suddenly became most skittish.

Tugwell called attention to a "mystery building," involving not only the Conservation Department but also L.S.U., and an arithmetical *cause célèbre* was created. The Public Works Administration was completing a geology hall on the campus, for joint use by the two agencies. The Conservation Department was to handle the funds. Glancing through official reports from the two sources, Treasurer Tugwell thrust daggers into his former friends. He noticed a $75,000 difference between the amount received by L.S.U. from the commission for the work, and the amount shown by the commission on its account. Had this little item been lost in the shuffle? Commissioner Rankin had brief comment: "The hell with Mr. Tugwell. I have nothing to say."

Mr. Tugwell pressed on his knives. The machine's favorite architects had run up the cost of the building beyond a half-million by "extra" items, he asserted, so that L.S.U. had to spend $55,000 of its own money to finish the project. Also, without letting L.S.U. know of its arrangements, the Conservation Department had ordered $50,000 of the furniture for L.S.U.'s part of the building—from the firm of Abernathy, former highway commissioner and L.S.U. board member, and a current indictee. Dr. Paul Hébert, acting president of L.S.U., declared that L.S.U. was being shunted around, that Rankin's figures made no sense to a man seeking to understand them by normal addition and subtraction. Disturbed, Earl Long called Hébert, Rankin and others together, and a lengthy statement was issued, which jumbled the finances still further. There had been a "little transfer of funds" from one account of the Conservation

Department to another, "to tide them over." Rankin volunteered the information that he had spent another $15,000 on furniture for L.S.U. through another favored firm, that of Monte Hart and the Caldwell Brothers, without telling anyone about it. Now he asked the firm to give the money back to L.S.U. Everything was honest, he concluded. But not clear, outsiders thought.

The Young Men's Business Club of New Orleans played a game of tag with Rankin. A committee decided that the best way to find out the truth would be to examine the conservation books themselves. The members called on Rankin. "You have no appointment," Rankin, a former Irish Channel boy, informed them. "Come back tomorrow." Would he then allow the club's auditor to see the books? the committee asked. "I told you fellows I'd talk over those things with you tomorrow." The committee left. That night Mr. Rankin sent the members a "statement," which was "all that is needed for the proper understanding by the public." He did this to save the men the trouble of a walk through the hot sun. But the members walked through the sun anyway and still wanted to see the books. Rankin said that they could not do that, at least until the Governor or his Attorney-General said they could.

Other unexpected situations were arising. Governor Earl announced that he was firing Dr. J. A. Shaw, a former dentist and the director of the oil proration or "hot oil" division, who had served under both Maestri and Rankin. The Governor would not explain why, but his intimates confided that Shaw was one of those Mammon-worshipers, connected—whisper it—with an oil supply company. In Dr. Shaw's place, Earl appointed his brother-in-law, brother of Widow Rose.

But Dr. Shaw was a man who would not be fired. He appeared daily at his office, and still received his checks. "The Governor and I aren't getting along so well now," he explained, "but it will be all right." Dr. Shaw went to Baton Rouge, saw Earl, and Earl declared that Dr. Shaw had been misrepresented to him. Dr. Shaw had no side line. He would continue his work practically as before, but would "share the job" with Brother-in-Law McConnell. The state shared the extra salary.

The public grew more and more intrigued with this odd department. Earl acquired curiosity of his own. Federal "hot oil" men were making intensive inquiries; Earl announced that he was launching an investigation for the state. "Between us, we ought to find something if there's anything to find." But as before, the Federal Government did not appear anxious for co-ordination of activity with the state. Rogge called Dr. Shaw before the grand jury, and told him to bring a heavy volume of files. On the same day Rogge summoned Richard W. Leche, and through Louisiana the story spread: "The heat's on Dick, and Rankin, too."

Maestri, Rankin's predecessor and a patron of Rankin as well as of Earl, came forward in the unsettled situation. Governor Earl hurried to New Orleans, reportedly on summons of "the boss." After a conference with Maestri, the word was announced: "Rankin's out." The commissioner declared that he had resigned because he had been asked to do so. In his place, Earl installed a country-boy friend, Senator Ernest Clements. He was "a better man," but "he didn't have much experience with oil and gas"; and so Dr. Shaw would help him run things. This was an impressive change in position for the man who had been dismissed a few days ago.

The next day, Rogge had Rankin squirming. Rankin appeared at length before the grand jury, fainted, was revived, wrung his hands and wept as he was questioned. He was located afterward at a hospital, with two Federal guards outside. The Government was taking no chances. At the same time, the Conservation Department's books had become more rather than less interesting to citizens' groups which were having trouble in seeing them; the organizations pressed harder for the privilege. Attorney-General Ellison issued a ruling: the public had an unquestioned right and must be permitted to look at the books. However . . . the Supervisor of Public Funds had been requested by the Governor and the new commissioner to make a thorough audit, and for the time being the books would be unavailable. The Young Men's Business Club had a word for it: "An old American custom, the runaround."

Less than six weeks after his off-again on-again departure from the state mansion, Dick Leche once more made history. He had been Louisiana's first Governor to resign. He became also its first Governor or Former Governor to be indicted by the Federal Government. At the same time, Seymour Weiss was snagged again.

The grand jury and Rogge charged that Dick and Seymour had split $134,000 equally between them as loot after fixing matters so that some of their business friends could run a half-million barrels of "hot oil" out of Louisiana. Dick, it was charged, had not waited until he became Governor to start operating, but had reached out several months in advance of inauguration day.

The $1000-bill motif entered. Still marveling at the sight, Rogge declared that a sizable part of the pay-off was in that denomination; crisp new bills which Seymour split into separate piles at the Roosevelt Hotel. Violation of the Federal "hot oil" or Connally Act was alleged. That act declares that oil which is shipped in interstate commerce after having been produced in excess of state oil quotas is contraband, or "hot." State conservation departments set quotas for maximum production, field by field, well by well. If producers disregard these state limitations and run excess oil, the Federal act is violated. This is a roundabout way of coping with the subject; but it was devised in an effort to avoid conflict with States' Rights.

Louisiana's Conservation Department had been giving "special allowables" or special orders in certain cases to permit production over the regular limits. Under the law this might be done, but only after investigation into the current market demand, and upon compliance with other requirements. In this case, the Government charged, a "special allowable" had been secured, but only through corrupt connivance and manipulation on the part of Dick and Seymour; by misrepresentation and without an inquiry into the market.

Dick and Seymour were accused of taking a neat rake-off of ten cents a barrel on practically all of 480,000 barrels of oil. But the Government had stepped in, inconveniently, to stop the flow when the boys had produced only a half of what they had planned. A pipeline had been constructed from Louisiana into Texas especially for the flow; and this was then sold, with Dick and Seymour getting $100,000 for their kind efforts, according to the indictment.

Bob Maestri had been conservation commissioner at the time (in 1936), and he too was questioned by the Federal grand jury. But the indictment implied, and Rogge declared, that Maestri had no guilty part in the operation. Instead, Seymour and Dick had practiced deception to "cause and induce him and others" to approve a special order. Indicted with Dick and Seymour was Freeman Burford, self-made Texas oil millionaire, an important figure in his state, who transported the oil and who was charged with making the payments. Named but not indicted were the Texan's attorney, Martin Winfrey, who received $14,000 out of the operation; A. C. Glassell, North Louisiana oil man who produced the oil which was run through the pipeline; another attorney for Burford, and various oil companies and subsidiaries. The oil had been moved across the Texas border to Longview, then returned to Louisiana by rail and tank car, and thence sent by vessel to Europe. Critics claimed that it supplied Nazi Germany and Fascist Italy. Stump orators assured their listeners that Hitler and Mussolini had won their early battles on the strength of the flow.

The case had a furious course, with the two states storming at each other, with Federal justice in Louisiana lined up against Federal justice in Texas—the issue being, to all intents and purposes, which state produced the more despicable type of citizen.

Burford charged that the matter was a trumped-up piece of nonsense. He was only a legitimate business man; everything had been legal. His attorneys filed a writ of habeas corpus, and a Federal judge of Texas ordered a hearing. Burford admitted sending $48,000 in $1000 bills to Weiss, wrapped up and by express. ("Just like he was sending a pair of socks," Rogge fumed.) But this wasn't Burford's money, Your Honor. It was, said Burford, actually the money of Glassell, the Louisiana man from whom Burford bought the oil he shipped. Out of Burford's payments to Glassell, Glassell had ordered him to take the money and send it to Weiss. Why the Express Company method? That was at Seymour's request, the Texan insisted.

Burford admitted that he paid the $100,000, but only to Weiss, not to Leche. It was a proper commission on the sale

323

of the pipeline, ten per cent of $1,000,000. "I never paid Leche one penny. Leche never served me. He may have served Weiss, but not me." Burford's lawyer, Winfrey, who received $14,000, added that Weiss received the $100,000 "for getting Burford in touch with the buyer." Burford explained: "Weiss was powerful in Louisiana affairs. I was a Texan and going into a foreign state with the reputation Lousiana had, I wanted to know whether we would be harassed by changing proration laws and taxation." But Seymour told Burford that it would be a "good thing" for a buyer to enter the field in question, and assured him of "his support." The attorney chimed in: "I doubt seriously if we could have continued to build our pipeline if Weiss had been unfriendly or belligerent."

Despite Burford's statements that Governor-Elect Leche had no part in the deal, Burford's attorney declared that Dick was "in and out during the day" when the order to run the excess oil was obtained at the hotel. Also present were Dr. Shaw, the oil-proration director, and Glassell, the Louisianian. Glassell testified that he previously had trouble finding a buyer for his oil. So he called on somebody who might do him some good, Weiss. Weiss suggested that Glassell see Burford. Glassell promised to pay Seymour a "reasonable commission," but no amount was discussed. Glassell signed a contract with Burford, and then Seymour made his demand of ten cents a barrel. "I had a lot of oil on hand and I had to get rid of it," explained Glassell. "I told Burford I was being gypped by Weiss, and Burford agreed." What did he think would have been a fair commission? Two cents.

And there was Burford's defense: Burford sought out Weiss. Glassell sought out Weiss. Seymour brought them together. Dick Leche was hanging around. But no, Dick had no part in the business. The "special allowable" was obtained, Seymour received a ten-cent rake-off on the oil flow, and this he split with Dick—but the money came as a payment from Glassell, although through Burford. And when the pipeline was sold, $100,000 went from Burford to Seymour and was split with Dick—but without Burford's knowledge. And Burford's attorney received $14,000.

Rogge shouted that Leche and Weiss "took graft in one of the most venal single transactions I ever came across. . . . The central fact is that the company did pay $148,000 to Weiss. Of that, Leche and Weiss each took $67,000. The Governor-Elect of Louisiana took $67,000 from Seymour Weiss."

Rogge turned to the order itself, and summoned Shaw and Maestri to the Texas court. Odds in New Orleans were that Bob the Silent would never appear. Bob balked. It happened that the day for his court appearance was one of the annual occasions on which all the boys, business men and others, dropped work for a day-long party to Bob at City Hall, with gallons of champagne, yards of floral pieces and compliments. Would Rogge be so heartless as to take Bob away, especially when Bob was upset about all the criticisms? For four hours Maestri sat with Rogge in the United State's Attorney's office, and an affidavit resulted. Bob had his party. Rogge had his statement.

Stories that differed in important respects were told about the "special allowable" order. James O'Connor, the First-Assistant Attorney-General of Louisiana, declared that Seymour had called him to the Roosevelt and told him that Commissioner Maestri had investigated the Glassell holdings and the market demand, and that he wanted O'Connor to declare whether he could approve an increase in the allowable. O'Connor wrote an opinion that this could be done if investigation were made and an actual demand found. O'Connor was asked if he would have given this ruling if he had known that ten cents a barrel was to be paid in connection with the operation? "No. Had I known it, I would have told Maestri and warned him of what was going on."

Maestri's affidavit declared that early in 1936, Glassell had asked him to issue an order for the extra production. He told him he could not do that unless the Attorney-General's office so advised. Weiss asked him for the same thing; he gave the same answer. Meanwhile, Maestri went to a health resort outside the state. He handled the matter by telephone from then on. He told Shaw, when he was telephoned from the Roosevelt, that the order could be signed if there were a market demand; he was told that the Attorney-General's office had declared the order legal. And he had no knowledge of a ten-cent payment; he would have issued no order had he known of it.

Then Shaw offered barbed testimony, the surprise of the hearing. Weiss had called him, told him that he had an order for him to sign. Leche was at the hotel, and mixed in the matter. Leche was in his own rooms, and Shaw saw him there. "I told them I couldn't sign without instructions from Maestri. I told them the order was going to raise hell, that the offset producers would kick about it." They told him to telephone Maestri. Maestri asked what Shaw thought of the matter, and Shaw repeated what he had told Leche and Weiss. "Maestri asked me if the order could be legally signed, and I told him I did not know. Maestri said that he had read the order, or that it had been read to him over the telephone, and he was familiar with its contents.

"He told me to sign the order, so I signed it and turned it over to them." He had put nothing in the order about market demand; he had made no investigation. "The order was brought to me already made up." Did he know about the ten cents to Weiss and Leche? "I didn't know they were going to get a thing. But I had an idea. Because they don't do things for nothing."

Judge Davidson took over the questioning: "You signed an order without investigation?"

"Yes."

"Do you still hold your position?"

"That's the only way I hold my position. I do what they tell me to."

"You mean you would sign such orders without investigation?"

"I would sign anything they stuck in front of me, except an order to hang me."

Rogge asked what the public thought of the order.

"The public," replied Shaw, "didn't think anything of it, for the very good reason that they never knew anything about it."

Rogge introduced another matter as the hearing reached a climax. Burford had not told the whole story as to why he paid the $100,000, he said. Rogge had information that, in another transaction, Burford sold gas to another Louisianian for two cents a thousand cubic feet. This new man sold the same gas to another company for four cents; and Governor Leche had an interest in the contract with the new man, which netted him more than $125,000. "I know this from Leche's income tax returns, and from what Leche told me."

A Federal agent offered a statement by Leche which presented a somewhat different picture from that of Burford's account. "Leche said that he had discussed the deal with Weiss *and Burford* several times," and had also talked it over with a representative of the firm that bought the pipeline. And somewhat later, in slightly different circumstances, when

Rogge asked Leche who employed him in the $67,000 payment, the answer was: "Freeman W. Burford and Seymour Weiss."

What did Leche do to earn $67,000? He rode up to the field, looked the property over and held several conferences with the principals. "And you didn't invest in it at all?"

"No, sir. Not a penny." Leche then added that he knew nothing, "of my own knowledge," of a payment for the flow of 480,000 barrels of oil; "I was paid $67,000 on the sale of a pipeline, and I know nothing about the oil business at all."

Leche, on this subsequent but related occasion, admitted that in the gas deal which Rogge cited, he had earned about $189,000.

"You didn't put up a penny, but you collected more than $189,000?"

"That is correct." He had a third interest in a contract with the man who, Rogge said, had bought the gas from Burford and resold it at double the price; and with two others. One was Tom Hill. Here Louisiana pricked up its ears. Hill was a man of gambling and related connections in New Orleans, political adviser to the Regular Ring. Rogge asked if Tom Hill had given him his interest, just like that?

"Absolutely not," said Leche. It had happened in this way. Hill approached Dick and asked if he would take part of Hill's contract, with the understanding that if there were to be expenses in connection with drilling and leasing, Dick would share them. Later it was found that gas could be purchased without the necessity of drilling. And Dick insisted that he be given the share he had been promised. His contract with Hill was not recorded. His interest was in Hill's name; he was paid by Hill. No, sir, Dick's name was not on Hill's contract with the gas company, and not on the records of the gas company. But he received his $189,000.

Meanwhile, however, Judge Davidson was turning Rogge down on the Burford matter. The Federal judge of North Texas refused to allow the Federal justice of East Louisiana to have Burford for arraignment. He attacked the Federal jury at New Orleans for "indicting one criminal and not indicting another who is equally guilty under the same act. It has been an elementary principle or practice of law and justice that if A hires B to go out and shoot a man or burn a house, then B is the representative of A, but both are criminals.

"Governor Leche of Louisiana and Seymour Weiss, his political boss, could not have pulled down this money and put it in their pocket but for Dr. Shaw and Commissioner Maestri. They (Maestri and Shaw) are just as guilty, from the face of the record, as are any other men indicted in this case." But Burford, the judge ruled, did not know the payments were to go to an officer of the state. The conferences of Burford, Weiss and Burford's attorneys at the Roosevelt were legitimate, and did not indicate a conspiracy but the act of a "cautious business man." The judge barked: "It is a matter of general and common knowledge that the State of Louisiana was more or less under a dictatorship and had been for ten years. . . ."

Therefore, the court saw no criminality in investigating not only the physical facts but also the political environment of a place in which one was about to put one's money. Weiss was a "friend of the dictatorial government." It would have been foolish for Burford to have gone to an enemy of the dictatorial government. (The judge was clearly a practical man.)

The case had reverberations. It did not raise Maestri's prestige in Louisiana, though Rogge declared that he was convinced Maestri had not known of the payoff. It did not help diplomatic relations between Texas and Louisiana. Rogge declared Burford "a fugitive from justice in every part of the nation except the Northern District of Texas." His description was broadcast, with fugitive warrants. "We'll get Burford if he's any kind of traveling man," Rogge warned. Federal agents watched oil conventions, offices of Burford in other states, offices of friends in other states. Texas journals roared at Rogge: "A bad loser," who subjected "a court to criticism that borders on abuse . . . resumes trial of his lost cause in the newspapers and hounds a man already ruled innocent . . . as if this business man were another Al Capone. . . . Rogge has plenty to do in Louisiana without orating over a last year's bird's nest."

New Orleans newspapers retorted that Judge Davidson was a "good Texan"; a man who found all the principal figures in the case to be villains except one, and that one a Texan, while the others were wicked Louisianians. "And this one Texan, according to the evidence, is rich and stands well with the Church and the Dallas bankers." The judge had declared that he did not believe Burford knew the money was "being used for corrupt purposes to buy the officers of Louisiana." "Yet before the judge rejected all unfavorable inferences against Burford, the court had been informed that it was Burford who hunted up the 'powerful' Weiss, and also Burford who sent $48,000 for hot oil . . . and that instead of mailing the money by check in the normal way, Burford bundled up forty-eight thousand-dollar banknotes and sent them to Weiss like a package of socks by express. This, however, was one of the easiest and safest ways that Burford could have transferred the boodle from Dallas to New Orleans if—perish the thought—he had wished to escape the penalty that the postal law imposes on use of the mails to promote crime." A cartoonist showed two men across a

330

table. A finger, "Guilty," pointed to the Seller. Another finger, "Not Guilty," pointed to the Buyer. The caption was: "The Cockeyes of Texas are Upon You."

The day after Dr. Shaw returned to Louisiana, as he was driving alone, his car hurtled full-tilt into a railroad overpass. It was badly smashed, he only slightly hurt. Officials termed the incident an accident, denying rumors that the tires had been cut. Reports were general that Shaw was about to be fired from the Conservation Commission, and that this time the firing would stick. The new commissioner, Clements, promised the public a statement on Shaw's status, then held it up. The next night Shaw paced the floor for hours, went into the bathroom of his home and fired a bullet into his brain.

His wife said that he had never owned a gun. There were sordid rumors, stories of "tips" to Shaw that it would be advisable to close his mouth; of threats and "advice" from anonymous callers. He was given no "protective custody" as had been accorded Rankin. On the other hand it was generally known that, on the night of Shaw's death, the United States Attorney's office was preparing new indictments for return the next day. He had reason to know about them. He had been grilled by the jury before and after his return from Texas. Shaw's death hurt the Government's case against Leche and Weiss, and limited other indictments that were in prospect. Had he lived, more men might be behind bars in Louisiana today, or dead or disgraced. So ended the story of another of "Huey's men." He had gone to dental school with Huey's brother, Julius, had practiced for twenty years, then entered the oil business, before Huey picked him up in 1929 and placed him in charge of all oil proration in Louisiana. While Louisiana was emerging as the fifth largest oil producer among the states, Dr. Shaw had prospered by "signing anything they put in front of me."

Earl Long's new conservation commissioner was soon in difficulties, and the fault could again be laid to Mammon. In early September, Richard W. Leche drove in from the Gold Coast, left an envelope in Clements' hand, and walked out. Statements flew like dee ducts.

Clements' was first. One of the state agents, still looking into the books (still closed to the public) had found four checks that had been issued during 1938 by the agency, signed by Former Commissioner Rankin. Traced, they were found payable to a Michigan construction company, and "while apparently given in payment of a Diesel engine, in reality it appears that they were given in settlement of a boat presented to Former Governor Richard W. Leche." A demand had been made on Dick, and he had come quickly with an $11,000 check. From the hard-pressed Rankin came an explanation. Late in 1938, a number of the Governor's friends had "suggested that a boat be presented him in appreciation of his services for bringing new industries to the state." Such a boat would cost about $13,000. But the Governor's friends knew that it could be obtained for much less through the commission; for $11,000, in fact. This plan of purchase was followed. Later Rankin took up the matter of reimbursement with "several of the gentlemen expected largely to subscribe, but without much success." That seemed to have ended Rankin's interest in the matter. It was not his boat; it had not been his idea; and "Governor Leche did not know of the method in which the matter was handled."

Part of New Orleans snickered, part groaned. The city well remembered the "gift yacht." While the gratified Governor had looked on, an imposing collection of business, industrial and luncheon-club luminaries had gathered to tender the boat "on behalf of your hundreds of friends." Dick replied that he did not deserve all this; that he felt as if he were "acting under false pretenses." He explained that remark by declaring that "no one man is responsible for bringing industry into this great, rich state"; and he praised the co-operation of his business helpers. Then he laughed loudly, waved his hand—"Come at your own risk, gentlemen." The next day, a group of hotel men, New York financiers and Assistant Attorney-General Joseph Keenan, who was one of Louisiana's good friends in that also co-operative agency before Murphy, were guests aboard the yacht. Now, to their horror, all the Governor's business-man friends and co-operators were called before the parish jury.

The story came out gradually. Seymour Weiss, it developed, had been chosen to handle the presentation; and he it was who enlisted the front men, the business men, to attend. Each of the "donors" now insisted that he had been led to believe that all the others had contributed; that he alone had not done so. Naturally, none of the "co-operators" advertised this fact to others. The first time they knew that their friends had not paid was when they read the papers at this late date. The politicos who had originated the plan had remained in the background, then evaporated. Parish charges of embezzlement of $10,700 resulted against Rankin. A number of inquisitive organizations asked District Attorney Byrne if he had finished investigating, or whether he planned to go deeper. "The grand jury's action speaks for itself," he replied.

But Rogge and the Federal jurors worked more slowly, and in a somewhat different manner. A month later they acted, and named Leche and Rankin. The amount was larger, $12,000; and the charges covered a wider span. The

333

jury declared that Leche and Rankin had entered a scheme, ten months in advance of the "gift," to buy the yacht with conservation funds; that they selected the boat together and told the manufacturer that the Conservation Commission was purchasing it. Further, it was charged that the commission had gone beyond the purchase of the boat, having acquired fishing tackle, awnings, plumbing and boiler equipment, pillows, drapes and bedspreads, and having paid for repairs, painted part of the boat and provided employees who operated and maintained the vessel for a time.

Rankin walked into Federal court, pleaded guilty to the charge, and also entered a guilty plea in a North Louisiana "hot oil" violation. He received a year's sentence. His departure from the free Louisiana life was a particularly touching one. He had emulated his superiors and had chosen a domicile in the Gold Coast area. He had planned an establishment that would outshine Abe's, Dick's or Caldwell's, had chosen a vista on the banks of a stream which, coincidentally, the Conservation Commission was deepening and improving. It was to be a castlelike all-brick-and-glass mansion, planned for a large-scaled way of life; two-story gaming hall, partly roofed sun porch which gave commanding view of the countryside, wide passageways, new glass materials which had never before been used in the Deep South, specially colored semi-transparent walls—all for the former Irish Channel boy, who rose from waterfront to St. Tammany stream bank. The walls had been finished, the interior construction begun, when Rogge and his jurors became interested in the master.

Through it all, the conservation records remained closed. A cartoonist started a new joke. A woman tourist asked an Orleanian: "What does your Conservation Department conserve?" His answer was: "Books."

XIV

DIPS AND DOUBLE DIPS

IN HUEY's day, the Federal Government's weapon against the Long men had been the income-tax blank. Now it became the stamped envelope. In the first instance, Washington had reached for the boys because they failed to pay its claim to a share of their plunder. This time it trapped them because they could not avoid using its mail boxes.

After the Purchase, Seymour, Abe, Monte and the rest of the crew had mended their ways. They could learn from experience. They followed not new rules of conduct but new rules of the game—their game. No longer would they run risks because they had not taken Washington into their confidence. Honesty in reporting, if not in daily operations—that was the best policy. The rule, "Thou shalt not steal," had a proviso—"unless you inform Washington about it."

So they set down everything; grafts, gouges, two per cents, ten per cents, rake-offs, frauds. Suppose it did tell what was happening? That did not matter. Uncle Sam, boys, was getting his cut. That ended his part of it. . . . These were state violations, see? . . . The state, it went without saying, was not an agency to inquire too deeply into the irregularities of those who were themselves the state.

When Rogge the serpent first invaded the Louisiana paradise, the major amoralists were not at once made more apprehensive. Seymour and Dick reported their $67,000 oil money in large black letters. Abe had no compunction over enumeration of the results of an artful piece of fraud which has won him a place unchallenged in Louisiana. Rogge worked closely with Elmer Irey of the Special Intelligence Service and with Revenue Collector Fontenot. The Fontenot and Irey operatives uncovered some of the best of the scandal information at an early date. But the boys had paid the Government the proper percentage on nearly everything. Every theft seemed to point to ripe cases—for state action only.

The Longsters were not disturbed, either, when the first postal agents appeared in Baton Rouge. Just another squad to watch for, boys; not as dangerous as some. The Longsters were no fools. They had propositioned no one by letter. They had dealt directly with the state; no intermediate suckers, no guaranties of your money back. They had operated no fake marriage bureaus; they had sold no cancer cures or trick gushers. Everything that they had done was between them and the state treasury.

But Huey's successors had forgotten a few little things. The income-tax returns were "confidential"; their neighbors could not peer into them. But that did not mean that one branch of the Government could not tell another what it knew.

Rogge had, besides his suspicious nature, a healthy imagination, and both attributes were linked to a fixed idea. Justice need not be blind, or stupid, or both. Methods of crime change; use of the law to catch the criminal should change accordingly. The mail-fraud statutes were elastic, he recalled from past, not-too-close acquaintance with them. He looked into the subject, and he stretched their elasticity to an extent that made contemporary criminal precedent. He clamped the fraud upon the boys, and on top of that he clamped a charge of using the mails in connection with it. The boys cheated the state, true; but they themselves hooked the Federal Government into the act.

"We didn't even send a postal card," cried the Long men. They did more than that, Rogge blandly assured them. They had not sent letters; they had sent checks. No, said the boys. We had had nothing to do with those checks. Others, L.S.U. or those bank clerks, had sent them forth—and they weren't cashed until we had finished our stealing, if you can prove it was stealing. But Rogge shook his head. The checks with which they were paid had to go through the mails, from one bank to another and to the clearing house, or they would have done the boys no good. Under the stringent mail laws, they were a part of the act of fraud. And he cited decisions that the Government need produce evidence only that the defendants put in motion a series of circumstances that resulted in the use of the mails. Ah, but, the boys said, in one case only one check was used by one man. How did that incriminate them all? To which O. John Rogge cited simple law to support his view that the act of one conspirator binds all of the others.

Hotly the machine men and others have maintained that these tactics were not cricket. It was, somehow, beneath the dignity of the Government to trip smoothly functioning wrongdoers on lesser statutes in their paths. This treatment, the Long boys contended in shocked tones, was not only vicious but also a reflection on their rank and methods. To which Rogge, addressing a meeting, made succinct retort:

"Major criminals should not commit minor crimes."

He added that the Federal aspects of the cases permitted the Department of Justice to exercise an "educational function," to demonstrate to Louisiana how its public affairs were being managed. He went to work, then, to teach everything that he knew on the subject.

In early September, 1939, in the Federal Building across from Maestri's City Hall, the first criminal trial of the scandals was at hand. It was the Bienville Hotel swindle sale, in which Seymour, "The Doc," Monte Hart the contractor, J. Emory Adams, nephew of Mrs. Smith, and Louie LeSage, self-styled "contact man" for Standard Oil, were charged with calling upon the postal facilities to relieve L.S.U. of $75,000.

The Government had connected Huey's favorites with the agent of Standard Oil, Huey's professional enemy. It was a tie which could not but impress the country folks and cause them to wonder further about "their" régime.

Monte and Seymour, associated in their hotel enterprises, had had a white elephant on their hands in the Bienville. It had never made a satisfactory return. They had tried, with the help of Huey and others, to get rid of it in a variety of ways: to palm it off on New Orleans for a skyscraper City Hall; to get the state to take it over for a "spite" dental or pharmacy school at a time when Huey was peeved at Loyola University; or to persuade the Federal Government to take it for an office center. But always something happened, and Seymour and Monte had to wait.

In fraud as in other matters, persistence brings its reward. Late in 1936, maneuverings had taken place to assure the boys of what they wanted. The old Charity Hospital was being torn down to make way for the new one. Ears pricked up. Surely, there would be need of a place for patients during the period of demolition and construction. Why not this nice hotel? After that, why not keep the place in the family, and use it for dormitory space for the L.S.U. medical students in New Orleans? The project went through. Then somebody's mind was changed, but the purchase was not. The building was utilized as a nurses' temporary home rather than as a hospital-hotel. Louisiana State University bought the building, rented it for a year to Charity Hospital, then took it back. Seymour, Monte and their company took cash. They received a higher price for a third-hand hostelry than it had cost them, $575,000 rather than $541,000.

But the boys were not satisfied. Somebody apparently noted that L.S.U. had some extra money in the bank. The tribe had been taught to reach for everything in view. Almost automatically, they reached again. The hotel had been sold in its entirety, furnishings and all. The furnishings were sold all over again to L.S.U. for $75,000.

Could Rogge prove it? A showdown was at hand. On this case depended most of the hopes for a new régime in Louisiana. If for any reason the Government failed, the psychological effect might well save the machine. Who knew what might happen if this case were lost like the original Shushan trial? But if the Government won, dictatorship might be on the way out. . . . In a Southwest Louisiana city, Attorney Sam Jones was considering running for Governor. He told his advocates that if the jury convicted, he would be a candidate. He was enough of a realist to know what the case portended.

At the center of the subject was a shadowy little corporation, the National Equipment Company. It had acquired the hotel furniture in some fashion, had sold it to L.S.U., and had split the payment three ways; $25,000 to Monte Hart, its president, $25,000 to LeSage of Standard, and $25,000 to Nephew Adams of the Smith family. But most of Louie LeSage's part and most of Adams's part had gone, respectively, to Seymour Weiss and James Monroe Smith as "loans" or "payments." The National Equipment Company appeared to be Monte Hart, Incorporated. One Jules Szodomka declared that he "believed he was president" when the firm had

339

been organized by Hart in 1930. He held the connection for about two months. Projects for selling a cleaning device and a type of rudder equipment quickly failed. Szodomka thought the firm had been disbanded. Frank E. Ames, the next witness, said that he continued as vice-president, while Monte became president. The firm earned a gross of $6500 in six years. But suddenly, in 1936, prosperity had arrived.

Vice-President Ames identified "rush order" billheads of the company. He had not seen them until Government agents investigated, these years later. The billheads left off the name of President Hart, but listed that of Vice-President Ames. "Is there anything unusual in the name of the vice-president being placed on a billhead?" demanded the defense. "Nothing more unusual than omitting the name of the president," replied Ames. The billheads described the firm as "specializing in hotel equipment." Mr. Ames had never heard of such specialization. He was shown the $75,000 furniture check, bearing his endorsement as vice-president. But he said he had never seen the front of it. Monte had placed it before him, its face down, as Monte often did.

A procession of L.S.U. board members filed in. Uniformly, they understood that the purchase of the hotel would cover everything, "lock, stock and barrel" . . . "a going concern" . . . "ready for immediate occupancy." The secretary and a director of the hotel company declared that there had been no discussion of a separate furniture sale, no indications of a separate sale in their records. The company's auditor noted that he included furnishings in the original hotel sale. Another example of profit-taking appeared in the books. The company figured a difference of $37,000 between evaluation and sale price; of this, Seymour received $27,500 as commission. Thus Seymour had benefited in three ways: by dis-

340

position of an unprofitable holding, by the furniture rake-off and by direct commission.

Into the record went a letter from "The Doc" to the hospital board, offering to lease the building, "fully equipped and furnished." It was received at a hospital meeting attended by Governor Dick, who used his good offices in behalf of the project. Next came testimony that the $75,000 payment to the Hart Company had been made on Smith's order, before the final payment on the hotel itself. The boys were taking no chances. And L.S.U. had paid the equipment company $14,000 for taxes on the hotel for all of 1936. But the general bill of sale showed that all property taxes had been paid by the hotel company to December 3, and the university had agreed to pay only for the remaining twenty-eight days. In any event L.S.U. could not have owed Monte's equipment firm anything in taxes. Monte's firm had never owned the hotel.

National bond attorneys had ruled against issuance of bonds to purchase the hotel, on the grounds that L.S.U. had no legal right to acquire the hotel and then lease it to Charity Hospital. But the board and the boys had gone ahead. Now, it was brought out, the unfavorable attorneys' opinion was missing from L.S.U.'s files. "The Doc" had guarded against awkward accidents. It was this proposed, but never consummated, bond issue that Smith had used as some of his fraudulent collateral in his wheat operations.

A statement by LeSage the lobbyist was offered. How had he entered the deal? Louie wasn't sure. Hart had asked him to help out with sale of the furnishings. Louie had asked: "What could I do?" "That's all right, just use your influence." He had no further meetings with Hart until Hart handed him his $25,000 check with a comment that Louie had "earned it." Louie was "flabbergasted"; he had "contacted not a soul," could remember no single service. But he cashed his check, put the $1000 bills in the safety deposit vault at the Roosevelt. (He was a permanent guest; Standard knew where its men belonged.) A bit later, he had lent $16,-500 of his $25,000 to Seymour. Seymour needed money; Louie volunteered to let him have what he could. Seymour signed a note, without interest, but Louie lost it. Louie guessed that he had gambled the rest away at the famous 118½ Baronne establishment, across from the hotel.

The manager of the loan department of a bank noted, however, that while Louie was presumably $25,000 to the good and lending to Seymour, he was renewing a $2800 loan and running it up to $4300.

Young Adams was the Government's witness. He had made two statements to Federal men. The first declared that Hart had paid him the $25,000 as a commission for services in arranging the sale, and that he had given most of it to Smith to meet an earlier obligation. The second, repudiating the first, declared that Adams had never seen the $25,000, and had known nothing of the matter. Smith, his patron, had asked him to report that he received it, to save Smith embarrassing questions. And Rogge closed the Government's side with the statement of a representative of the "official" candy company into which the machine men had bought. A month or so after the deal, Monte and Seymour each purchased $37,500 of stock, and Smith $10,000.

From Former Governor Dick, jaunty and assured, came testimony for the defense. He it was who had conceived the thought for the sale of the hotel, to help along the hospital project. Dick spoke to Seymour. Seymour thought it could be arranged. Dick asked Leon Weiss, the machine's architect-designate, to consult with hospital authorities and to look over the hotel, to see if it could be used for patients. Sure enough, the answer came back; the proposal was timely, constructive. But Dick knew nothing about the furniture sale. No, there was no necessity for L.S.U. to give the furniture or anything else to anybody as a commission. The Governor had taken no part in the matter after bringing together the "proper parties," Smith and Hart. How and why the project was changed to a nurses' temporary home, he did not know. No, he was not offered money to approve the project. He did not recall discussing the matter with Hart, LeSage or Adams. He had never talked with Adams in his life.

Hart, gum-chewing, natty, easy-talking, was the main hope of the defense. For five hours he grinned, shrugged and perspired as he gave much detail, much explanation. For several years he had had an understanding with Seymour, his associate at the hotel, that he was to get the furniture. This was to be his "fee" for his past efforts to work out a sale, and for his other help about the Roosevelt and Bienville Hotels. It was never contemplated that hotel and furnishings would be sold in one lot. "Dr. Smith and myself had been discussing the use of the furniture for some time." When it was first planned to use the building as a temporary hospital, Monte proposed to sell the furniture to L.S.U. for campus dormitories which Monte's firm was erecting. Then Monte came to the heart of his part of the defense. The furniture had already been sold to L.S.U. when it was decided to change plans and use the building for a nurses' home rather than a temporary hospital. And so the furniture could remain, and be used as before; and Monte would get his $75,-000 just as if he had sold the furniture for use on the campus.

As to the pay-offs of $25,000 each to Louie LeSage and J. Emory Adams, Monte could clear that up. He had never seen Adams before, but he understood Adams had "a lot of influence in Baton Rouge." With Smith? he was asked. Was

Adams needed to make sure that the deal would go through with Louisiana State University? Oh, no. Hart had not known of Adams's relationship to "The Doc" at the time. Was Adams, then, to work on Leche? No, Seymour had seen Dick. Was Adams to work on the L.S.U. board? No; Hart felt that the L.S.U. board had no interest in the arrangements. (An interesting commentary on Smith's board, this.) Who, then, was Adams to influence? "Anybody; the police jury or anyone who might be interested. You never can tell who will help."

Monte paid Louie LeSage his $25,000 because he knew that Louie attended every session of the Legislature, and because Monte knew also of Louie's "connection" with Mayor Maestri. Monte wanted Louie to help "in case somebody in the city was interested." Further, Monte was looking ahead; he had not been receiving any city business, and he wanted some. . . . Louie had not looked so surprised when Monte paid off. "Didn't you hear his statement that he was flabbergasted?" Monte chewed the harder: "I don't know what you mean by flabbergasted, unless you mean knocked down. He certainly wasn't that."

"Did you yourself do anything for your $25,000?"

"I did plenty."

"Yet you were satisfied with the small share you took?"

"No, but I took it. If I knew then what I know now, I wouldn't have needed LeSage and Adams." He had had no idea that his associate, Seymour, or his close friend, "The Doc," would get money off the deal from Louie and J. Emory. And Adams had not told the truth; he, Monte, had paid him $25,000 in person, in cash, in an automobile outside a New Orleans bank when Monte turned in the $75,-000 check. (Later, though, Monte was not sure whether the payment had taken place there or somewhere else.)

344

Adams took the stand, and the split among the defendants grew wider. He did not know even the location of the bank of which Monte had spoken. He had never heard of the hotel deal until Smith asked him to report the $25,000 falsely as his income.

The defense decided not to put the suspect Smith or the inept and shaking Louie on the stand. But Seymour, assured, reasonable, appeared in their stead. Yes, he had agreed to let Monte have the furniture. Monte had asked for it, during one of the many abortive deals to dispose of the hotel. He gave it to Monte for Monte's general labors as unpaid vice-president of the hotel organization. No, he had not consulted the hotel board. There was no need for that. Seymour had "carte blanche" at the two hotels, did not consult anyone when he decided to spend $950,000 on hotel improvements, or $10,000 of hotel money to buy Metropolitan Opera tickets to encourage the organization's visits to the city.

Seymour's money from Louie was a personal matter, had no connection with the furniture deal. On that day he had persuaded Mayor Bob Maestri and others to buy the New Orleans Baseball Club, as a civic enterprise. All had subscribed to stock. He, the president of the new organization, was the last to do so. He had been quite embarrassed at the moment. He needed money; he had borrowed $50,000 from Mayor Bob and other amounts from other sources. Louie came forward with the money; "I would have done the same for him." No, no interest was mentioned. Seymour paid no interest, either, to Mayor Bob. It was a story of large dealings for a large man, who had once received $25 a week as a shoe clerk. The implication was clear. Seymour occasionally needed cash, but he had resources. He would not have stooped to steal $25,000.

The use of the mails was a crucial issue. Rogge insisted

that the $75,000 check could not have been handled in normal modern banking routine had it not passed through the mails. It was turned in by Hart in New Orleans, sent to the Federal Reserve Bank in New Orleans, then to the bank in Baton Rouge which had issued it for L.S.U. But, said the defense, the $75,000 in cash was already in the hands of Hart before the check went into the mail pouch; the fraud, if any, was over before the postal facilities were brought into play. To this, Rogge replied that the aim of the operation had been to cheat L.S.U., and that L.S.U. could not have been cheated until the $75,000 was taken from its treasury—after the check went to Baton Rouge through the mails.

Rogge's argument, raging, burning, touched off an almost continuous series of explosions from the defense. "These men were plain, simple looters. Hart, Smith and Weiss robbed the university of $75,000—and the money ends up in a candy shop! LeSage and Adams were little cover-up men, that's all. Hart, Smith and Weiss did the lion's share of the looting, and they took the lion's share. The two little fellows got the drippings. Hart is a liar, unworthy of belief. He had his eyes on this secondhand furniture, just waiting for a chance to buy it up, he says. And then what does he do? He gives $50,-000 of his $75,000 to two little fellows who could do nothing to bring about the sale. It doesn't make sense."

Smith's lawyers contributed an unusual note when they bore down on the university board, for "laxity, for having no interest in the university, leaving everything to Dr. Smith to do." Adams, a "self-confessed perjurer," was the only link to Smith. Seymour's counsel talked of the love of man for man, Louie for Seymour, Seymour for Louie. Rogge was seeking to distort motives of friendship into something wicked. . . . "Oh, justice, what crime has been committed in thy name! . . . The only thing I can conclude is that

MEMORIAL EDITION

The American Progress

5 CENTS PER COPY

FIFTY CENTS PER YEAR   VOL. 2, No. 10   SEPTEMBER 1935 ISSUE   PUBLISHED EVERY MONTH

The NEWS Digest
★ ★ ★

REQUIESCAT

THE MURDER OF HUEY P. LONG

★ ★ ★ ★ ★ ★ ★ ★ ★ ★ ★ ★ ★ ★ ★ ★ ★

Followers Of Senator Name Allen Leader Then Select The Real Huey Long Ticket

Huey Long's Wishes Carried Out In Selecting Leche For Governor

Leaders From Each of the Sixty-Four Parishes Meet and Unanimously Put Forth Ticket That Had Been Agreed Upon Before Assassination of the Senator, a 100 Per Cent Huey Long Ticket

BATON ROUGE.—The murder of Huey P. Long which for several years had been incited by his political enemies in this State and elsewhere has brought the people of Louisiana to realize two facts:

FIRST, that the only salvation for continued progress in the State lies in the hands of those people who are definitely pledged to carry on Huey Long's work and who can be attained only in supporting politically the ones that Senator Long had chosen as candidates.

SECOND, that the opposition to Senator Long has now for once and for all been clearly characterized by the manner in which he was eliminated from State politics—with the belief of an assassin.

Even while Huey Long's body was lying in state in Baton Rouge his enemies were already beginning to lay their plans and attempt to profit politically through his murder.

The members of the loyal Huey Long organization, stunned by the tragic and cowardly act that took the life of a great man, waited a short time before embarking upon any politics.

Then Governor Allen, the new leader of the Louisiana Democratic Association, began to summon his leaders from the parishes and held conferences in Baton Rouge.

Leaves Grief-Stricken People To Mourn Death

Nation Is Stunned 'As Assassin, Incited By Steady Campaign of Slander and Lies, Fires Fatal Bullet In the Capitol Building At Baton Rouge

By now the whole world knows of the murder of Senator Huey P. Long a fortnight ago in the State Capitol in Baton Rouge, and by now a whole nation mourns the passing of the man who will be known in the histories of tomorrow as "the President who was assassinated before he was elected."

As the shock of the tragedy of Senator Long's death becomes felt and more understood by the people of Louisiana for whom he labored so long, it is only natural that they should feel that they have suffered an irreparable loss.

HUEY P. LONG
1893 - 1935

The Funeral Oration by Rev. Smith

TICKET PICKED BY SENATOR LONG

Register Now

So You Can Vote Against Murder In January

BATON ROUGE.—The election of January 21, 1936 will mark the first time in history that citizens of Louisiana may go to the polls and vote without having to pay $1 per year for the right to have a voice in government.

HOUSE ORGAN OF THE LONG MACHINE

Created by Huey, *The American Progress* developed into the Long machine's house organ and relentlessly attacked all opposition through ruthless news stories and vicious cartoons.

The Goldurndest Gang Ever Seen Anywhere!

(from *The American Progress, Sept. 22 1939*)

The Great Sideshow of Freaks, Fakes and Frauds

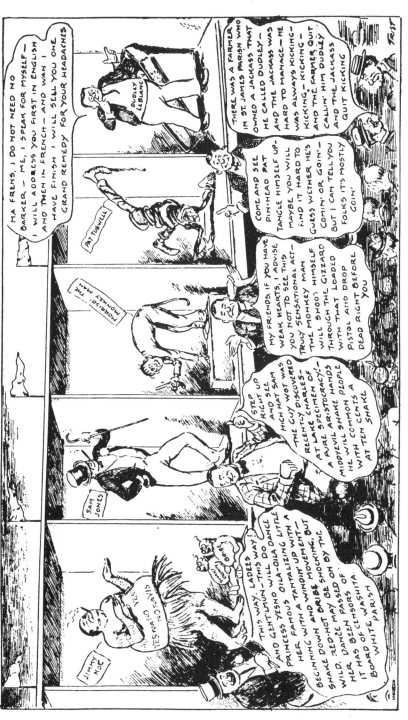

(from *The American Progress*, Sept. 29, 1939)

The Great Fit Throwing Contest of 1939

(From The Atlanta Press, Oct. 13, 1939)

At Sea.

(from *The American Progress*, Oct. 20, 1939)

This Beats Mardi Gras

(from *The American Progress*, Dec. 1, 1939)

The Progress All-Star Team 1940

there must have been some message from Garcia in Washington, to declare Seymour Weiss in on this case, evidence or no evidence." Louie's attorney saw Rogge as a man "seeking to have his name in headlines in the nation's press, for political purposes." Hart's attorney cast shame on the Louisiana political situation. Wasn't it a known fact that in Louisiana a man had to have influence to get a state contract? This, the jury may have decided, was a somewhat questionable defense for Monte, who was one of the major beneficiaries, early, late and always, of just that situation.

All five were found guilty. Seymour, one of the Big Three (with Leche and Maestri), the man they said could never be caught, was headed for Atlanta and a term of two years and a half. "The Doc" and Monte received the same sentence, the "two little cover-up men" a year each. As they left court, it was clear that the political "atmosphere," which had provided Washington with an excuse for freeing the boys in the earlier cases, had changed. A crowd gathered to boo, yell and curse. A woman thrust her head into their taxicab and let them know what she thought of their kind—a loud "razzberry."

Louisiana had a new scandal term—"double dip." The boys had sunk their scoops twice into the pap. Like the Roosevelt Hotel employee who had filled Attorney-General Murphy's order for chocolate ice cream on that faraway day in May, they had reached back for a second dig. The case started the parade of the Long men to Atlanta and Leavenworth. But would enough of the general electorate—including Huey's hill folk and swamp followers—change their minds after giving this same régime its record majority four years earlier? In South Louisiana, Attorney Sam Jones thought that the opposition had a chance again. He gave the word that he would run for Governor against Earl K. Long.

Double was the word for it in more matters than furniture.

A Charity Hospital building, it now appeared, had been "double moved," as the newspapers put it, from one spot to another and then back to the original location—at a cost to the taxpayers of almost $500,000; the net result, loss of the basement in transit.

The L.S.U. architect took a check for $24,000 for his fees on Huey's dormitory-stadium in 1932. Four years later, according to the grand jury, he took another check for $24,000 for his fees on the dormitory-stadium.

The cost of a building was set by a winning bid at $101,-000. When work was finished, the state had paid $202,000. The State University's physics department was gratified when it received a new electric switchboard. Later it found that it had paid for it once on December 13 of 1937 and again on January 10 of 1938. And Monte, in the "double moving" episode, acquired further stature. The man who had sold furniture that was not his own was paid by the state for not doing work.

The "double move" came about as the product of Huey Long's spite toward a university and his heirs' friendship toward the New Deal. Huey moved the building as part of a plan to get even with Loyola, then on his blacklist. Dick and the boys moved it back to get cash from Washington. Loyola had awarded Huey his honorary degree when Tulane would not; but Loyola would not award him unlimited radio time, and now he was going to show it a thing or two. He would strike at its pharmacy and dental divisions, two of its best, in the same way that he had struck at Tulane's medical department. He would put up a pharmacy-dental building for L.S.U., and operate it in connection with his "spite" medical school on the hospital grounds.

348

But the hospital's white female building was in the way. It was a sturdy one, about twelve years old, erected with funds raised by popular subscription. There was talk of tearing it down. Instead, an engineering feat was achieved. While Huey presided and spoke of "economy" and first consideration for the suffering poor, the high building was started on a sliding process along a series of rails to a point 162 feet away. The operation took two hours. Less than two years later, it was moved back with the same equipment to a point within a few inches of the original location. It had been found in the way of the new hospital. Plans for the pharmacy-dental building had been forgotten, and the place from which the building was moved had never been used. The original building had cost $335,000. *Sic semper* economy. . . .

The Orleans grand jury saw more than waste in the situation. It indicted Monte Hart the contractor, Architect Leon Weiss and James Monroe Smith for embezzlement of money paid for "restoration work" following the re-moving. But, said the jury, the work was never done. The District Attorney's office added that it was prepared to show that Monte had previously withdrawn $40,000 from his firm's funds, and had told others that the money was for "campaign contributions." Then, it was said, $62,000 was paid him by the state for "restoration work"; and Monte informed his associates that this was a "refund" of the contributions. Architect Weiss's part in the alleged operation was to issue a certificate approving the "repairs"; Smith's, to approve payment with L.S.U. funds. Finally Monte and his firm received about $65,000 for cancellation of the contract for the dental-pharmacy structure.

A rich new field of inquiry now was opened, that of "extras" added to construction costs during the gaudy Leche

349

period. The Public Works Administration, which had previously managed to keep off the official list of victimized agencies, joined the others. The Federal jury acted in the matter of a "mystery" geology building about which Tugwell had raised questions. The jury saw nothing mysterious. It charged that the resourceful Monte Hart and Summa Caldwell—one of his partners and an uncle of Big George of L.S.U.—had hiked building costs about $10,000, by a little plan that involved double sets of plans at the time the contract was let. One set, said the jury, went to the Public Works Administration; the other was used for the real work. Subcontractors, it was added, were required to provide two sets of invoices, one real and one inflated for the Federal Government. A rollicking little item of indictment was this: the firm in one case had calmly added enough to reimburse it for the work it had done on the Louisiana Colonial home of Business Manager E. N. Jackson of Louisiana State University. Thus, the Government was paying for its own work and for a piece of private construction at the same time.

The State Board of Education announced that it had found $150,000 in "extras" in construction work at two other state colleges. The money had not passed through the board's hands, but had been managed in a special fund under the control of Governor Dick. The board's building superintendent in due time estimated that it had been overcautious in its figures, and placed the "extras" at $275,000, after making "generous" allowances for expenses and profits. In one instance a 221-per-cent profit was estimated. The contractors, again, were Caldwell Brothers and Hart; the architects, the firm of Leon Weiss.

Grand juries, state and Federal, acted. Monte Hart and Leon Weiss were indicted by a Federal jury in North Louisiana for obtaining $56,000 fraudulently on one building at one of the colleges, Louisiana Polytech at Ruston—about half by the "extra" route, the other half by the device of running up the contract figure between the time the board accepted the bid and signed the papers. With Leche handling the fund, the State Board of Education was allegedly deceived and bilked, and did not note the latter difference. A parish jury made similar charges, and added Leche's name and those of two other members of the architect's firm.

The building was the second Leche Hall to be built at a state institution during Leche's term. (This one, it was brought out when Dick went to trial separately, had almost escaped the honor.) Dick was charged with obtaining $27,000 under false pretenses and operating a confidence game in the hiking of the construction figure during the interval between acceptance of bid and drawing up of contract.

Monte Hart, Leon Weiss and others among the boys turned at last on Former Governor Dick. Times were changing. Hart took the stand. The $27,000 had been added on Dick's orders, and because of a delay demanded by Dick, he said. Construction was about to start at an awkward time— before Dick took office. After Hart's firm received the contract, Dick told him that he had promised the people of the parish that he would give them the new school building. Unexpectedly, however, the college had suffered the loss by fire of its administration center. A new structure was needed quickly. But Dick was only Governor-Elect. The enemy Noe was temporarily chief executive, and, as has been noted earlier, he was hurrying things to get the building started during the Noe, not the Leche administration. Dick, Monte now explained, told him frankly that he did not want Noe to receive the honor. The college treasurer described a hurriedly called meeting at which efforts were made to hasten operations. The treasurer at that time informed Dick that

Governor Noe "had agreed to get the money." To which Dick commented that "Noe would like the credit, but wouldn't get it." Dick was adamant. Polytech went without its building until he became Governor.

When Dick finally called him to start construction, said Monte, material costs had increased, and he could no longer build at the original prices. The extra cost was the $27,000. Dick told him, said Monte, that "it would be O.K." to add the $27,000; and this was done. However, state agents testified that an audit of the books of Monte's firm indicated that Governor Dick had not received any of the $27,000. Dick was acquitted. But in time Leon Weiss went on trial separately in Federal Court in the same matter, on charges of use of the mails for a larger amount, $56,000. He was found guilty and sentenced to five years. Several bits of testimony then made it clear that the boys had not been missing much. The moving of a tool house was set down as having cost $3600. The State Board of Education's building superintendent said the figure should have been $300. In another instance, a portion of the plans was abandoned. The boys, it was testified, added that to the total as though they had followed the original thought and the new plan as well.

In another parish, a jury indicted the same pair, Monte and Leon, for fraud in the amount of $145,000. Profits in one instance were estimated at 106 per cent. In other cases, work costing more than $275,000 was granted, according to the jury and the State Board of Education, without advertising, bidding or letting of contract. "Preliminary estimates" thus resulted in heavy "extras."

Soon L.S.U. was bringing civil suits against Monte Hart and his contracting affiliates for $411,000 in overcharges on its campus. The university claimed that the men made exorbitant charges for work performed, for work specified but not performed, and for work neither specified nor performed. The largest "extra" alleged for any of the buildings was a $225,000 one for Leche Hall, the Supreme Court replica. The original figure, it was estimated, had been jumped from about $675,000 to $905,000. Tens of thousands of dollars now poured in to the state in voluntary reimbursements by the Hart, Caldwell and other firms. Sometimes they returned more than the university or the Board of Education thought they owed; but, believing that the boys knew far more about the subject than they did, both agencies took all that was turned in.

Eventually, providing more than a suggestion of floral tribute, came the "bush and shrub case," about which tall tales had been woven. It involved Dick and Edward Avery McIlhenny, his wealthy naturalist friend. Dick and his assistants had developed lavish tastes in trees, hedges and camellias, as in other things. Landscaped vistas, stylized groupings, magnificent formal patterns appeared at state colleges, about private residences and in other places previously notable only for front or back yards and common rose bushes. But even the best-pedigreed hedges might not have cost as much as the state was charged, said some who had looked into the prices. For months, the Baton Rouge grand jury had investigated, without result. It took the Federal jury to turn to its favorites, the stamps and envelopes, and charge Dick and McIlhenny. According to the Government, Dick instructed "Doc" Smith that McIlhenny would be the university's landscape artist, and that there would be no contract. Beautification work then in progress at L.S.U. was to be abandoned, and the regular horticulturist was to be assigned to other duties. McIlhenny would have a free hand, with no supervision of any kind from above.

Dick and McIlhenny, the jury charged, prepared an estimate of $45,000 for the work. Dick made one of his infrequent appearances before the board to urge the great need of McIlhenny bushes at the university. "The Doc" also let it be known that what L.S.U. needed were grounds in the McIlhenny manner. Once the proposal was approved, Dick and McIlhenny allegedly told "The Doc" to cancel it, and a substitute was drawn up, increasing the work by about $70,000, bringing the figure to $115,000. "The Doc," it was said, approved the expenditures as they occurred but kept the increases from the attention of the university board. The prices, the jury asserted, were not those that would be expected for quantity work, but were above retail; the stock was "inferior"; the participants in the scheme refused to use any of the stock on hand, at the same time that they charged "exorbitant, excessive and unconscionable prices" for what was brought in by McIlhenny. Further, McIlhenny assertedly did not provide some of the items; never intended to do so; billed L.S.U. for transportation expenses although the original plan had provided for all costs, including freight delivery. As a final touch, the jurors accused McIlhenny of taking several large azalea plants from the campus.

McIlhenny was charged with giving a $9000 bribe to Jim Smith; a $2500 bribe and an elaborate free landscaping job over the wide acreage of his Gold Coast estate to Former Governor Dick; and a $1000 bribe to Dick's favorite, the then Attorney-General of Louisiana, David Ellison. The grand jurors did not appear to believe Dick's story of his own surprise when L.S.U. irregularities were first suspected. And "The Doc," who had not concealed his feeling toward Dick after his return from Canada, might have the last laugh here. He was mentioned as the Government's star witness against Dick.

354

Earl Long told his country audiences that the bush business was a scandal to the heavens. He could have got a few farm women who were handy with their little gardens to do it for a few thousands, he said.

The Governor of Louisiana then permitted the release without comment of a series of previously secret audit reports to Leche regarding L.S.U. matters, made by the Supervisor of Public Funds as early as September, October and December of the preceding year, 1938. These made it clear that Dick Leche had known considerably more than he had ever disclosed; had known it, moreover, as long as nine months before the scandals broke. By the end of 1938 he had been informed of Big George Caldwell's secret rake-offs on L.S.U. construction; of President Smith's surreptitious addition of $3000 to his own salary; of the purchase of large supplies at retail prices; the letting of contracts as high as $175,000 without competitive bids as required by law; of the "extras" on the buildings, and the inability to reconcile receipts and other items in various university divisions.

Dick had said, while Smith was on his way back to Louisiana in July of 1939, that he had received reports which showed only broad suspicions of irregularities pointing to no individuals. This statement was contained in the first of the reports to him. But the later ones, received before 1939 started, gave names, amounts, dates. At his fallen predecessor, Earl Long released one of the most painful of the blows that were raining upon him. For Dick had declared specifically at the time that he had known nothing of Caldwell's rake-offs and of other matters which Earl now revealed. These were subjects that had resulted in general resentment, discharges and indictments when brought forth months afterward. But Governor Dick had known.

XV

THE JURORS' REBELLION

THE Federal investigations could not be halted. The machine, however, decided that it could quiet the inquisitive impulses of justice within the state's confines. Suddenly all was not well in the parish law-enforcement offices. The lid was on; officialdom was sitting atop it; beneath, sometimes stewing, were the grand juries.

During the months that followed the crisis of June, the Federal jury at New Orleans and, to a lesser extent, the Baton Rouge parish jury did all of the investigating and the indicting. In New Orleans and in other parts of the state, the parish jurors began to stir, to look about themselves and wonder at what they saw. July and August were the months of mumblings and grumblings. October and November brought rebellion, and reaction.

In the delivery of Louisiana, these jurors played the rôles of quiet martyrs. They did not look the part. They were clerks, salesmen, young business men. They regarded their conduct as having little to do with sacrifice or renunciation. But a martyr need not be an ascetic; nor need he die for his cause. If he suffers only abuse and humiliation by a judge or a district attorney, he has his value. The jurors of Louisiana stood up and called the men in power over them the things they considered them: violators of their oaths; men who placed themselves in the way of the law they were chosen to uphold; partners, by extension, in the matters they worked to hide.

Some of the jurors were mauled by the agents of the judges and parish officials. Some went to jail. Others lost their private jobs. Against them were exerted all the pressures that the machine could marshal. A number of the juries lost, were stamped down in one locality, then another. But they had started something that did not end with their part in it. Their protests called attention to conditions beneath the surface; they provided further education to Louisiana, enlightenment as to another of the prices that the state was paying for "the benefits of the machine."

During the past twelve years, grand juries had been quiescent bodies, another arm of the central government, like the Legislature, like the courts. If they or the district attorney fell out of line, Baton Rouge could take over matters through the act of supersession by the attorney-general. The handling of the election theft cases under Former Attorney-General Porterie was the best example of what the machine could do as a last resort. Understandably, it was a shock to officialdom when the docile jurors lost their docility and wanted to "go too far." Too far meant a foray across the borderline into the forbidden land of graft, corruption and related topics.

In New Orleans, the district attorney's office was taking scandals in its stride, and the stride was not a brisk one. District Attorney Charles A. Byrne was a Long man, formerly one of Huey's legislators, who had taken over in place of the man who had exposed the election frauds in the Porterie affair. Huey had conducted a raid on the office, removing from the district attorney's power the hiring of assistants, telephone operators and clerks. He had also held over Eugene Stanley's head the prospect of supersession by Porterie whenever the machine found it necessary. Stanley quit; and although the term had barely started, no new election was held. When Maestri became mayor, the term was extended as were those of all city officials; so, for nearly eight years, New Orleans had no opportunity to vote on its district attorney.

The first eight months of 1939 saw a mixed situation in the parish grand jury. It had acted inconclusively on the city "tax racket," and had met infrequently afterward. Attorneys attacked its right to serve in an unrelated case, charging that it was "handpicked to whitewash the racket." An open hearing followed, with no resultant action. Further claims were made, as the scandals broke, that the parish was without a jury; that members would not attend meetings, one having suffered a breakdown because of "the notoriety created by the uncovering of the whitewash," while another threatened to leave town if summoned.

September brought a new jury term. The citizens' groups, considering the city-state political combination, demanded that the selection of the members be made as public as possible. The judge was George Platt, another Long man before he stepped upon the bench in 1936.

The People's League, an organization of young attorneys, persuaded Judge Platt to permit it to discuss qualifications of veniremen with him. Newspapers published the lists and asked the public to provide information about any persons who should not be chosen. Meeting with Platt, the league protested 34 out of 75 names, informing him that some of the veniremen had relatives on city and state payrolls, or were so employed themselves; that others were connected with firms that did large business with the city, or had political connections of their own. The judge was not over impressed: "I guarantee if I left everybody off the grand jury that you say, I'd end up with about three Negroes." As to those who were "interested in politics," Platt parried: "Shouldn't every man be interested in politics?" He was the jurist whose relations to the subject were to be among the most angrily debated of the period.

The judge selected the jury. Its foreman was an executive of a power and light company, an organization with interests that were clear. To the jurors, the People's League dispatched messages urging "independence and vigor, so that confidence may be restored in democratic government in Louisiana."

The league meanwhile devoted its attention to District Attorney Byrne. It accused him of do-nothingness, cited a series of specific cases. He replied that he had received "only rumors" about a certain flagrant piece of thieving, that the persons concerned had refused to talk about it; and he concluded in somewhat confused fashion: "I will not pillory anybody on the cross of suspicion." Also, said he, he was uncertain which statutes covered some of the alleged offenses. The league prepared a list of laws for his edification, and suggested that impeachment might be one way to budge him. He replied that he would not be intimidated. The league came back: "Perhaps you have forgotten that public officials in Louisiana are still responsible for the discharge of their official duties to the people, and if the promise of exercise of the constitutionally granted right of impeachment constitutes in your mind intimidation, then you can make the most of it, with the assurance that intimidation of that character is always present."

Under strained circumstances, the new jury was sworn in. For a few weeks there was quiet, but then rumors spread of differences of opinion. Byrne once or twice declared that the jurors were finished for the day; but they went back into session alone. The jurors called on the judge; he would say to reporters only that they had wanted "instruction in the law."

On October 9, the jurors arrived early at court and called a mechanic to fix their door so that they could lock themselves in. The district attorney's staff reported in advance of the usual hour, grim, untalkative. Something was in the wind. Six of the jurors walked into court. Platt was waiting. The foreman, one of the six, remained seated as Juror H. H. Powell rose, nervously: "I have a request to present . . ." Platt cut him short: "You cannot present it in open court. Anything pertaining to the business of the grand jury should be secret." "But it's just a request . . ." and Powell began to read from a petition.

Platt rasped out: "I'm ordering you not to read it! Is that clear?" But Powell continued. Platt turned: "Mr. Sheriff, take this man and lock him up." Deputies closed around Powell, a slight, bespectacled man. He scuffled, managed to toss copies of the petition in several directions. A reporter grabbed one and scurried out with it. Another juror, young Sidney DeArmas, caught another as he might a forward pass. He took it, as if to read it. Platt snapped another order. For a moment it appeared that there might be a free-for-all. The other jurors hesitated, trembling, hot words on their lips. Deputies half dragged, half shoved Powell and DeArmas outside. Platt left the bench, sent for the other judges and conferred for nearly an hour while deputies stood guard outside and the two jurors remained prisoners.

The petition, signed by a majority of seven members but not the foreman, was public property by this time, Platt or no Platt. The district attorney and his staff were charged with doing all in their power to prevent honest investigations, "stalling," "delaying," refusing to produce records, withholding answers to legal and other questions, "insulating" some witnesses to keep them from the jury, giving others opportunity to escape jurisdiction by forewarning them. The jurors had become victims of "simultaneous and concerted efforts from without," designed to demoralize them, with anonymous callers demanding that they "go along" with Byrne, and with others who were in politics bringing pressure upon the jurors' employers. Then a particular surprise: the jury's majority felt that it could not adequately inquire into numerous violations "without investigating the affairs of a number of associates of the district attorney and his staff." Therefore, they asked that Byrne and staff be recused and that the court approve appointment of other attorneys for a thorough-going investigation into numerous parish scandals.

Byrne was near-apoplectic as he read it. "They're goddamned liars," declared the district attorney.

The judge, after his session with his colleagues, had made up his mind. Returning to the bench, he declared the two jurors guilty of contempt, and sentenced them to the hour's imprisonment which they had already spent under guard. A pause: "And I hereby dismiss you from the jury. You cannot do your duty." By this method, the judge deprived New Orleans of a grand jury for months ahead, until the election that was to decide the machine's future had come and gone. An incomplete jury could not meet.

At Byrne's request, an open hearing was called for the next day to inquire into the jurors' charges. The People's League summoned a mass meeting for the same time, on the broad steps of the courthouse, "so that all citizens who want to save democracy may give a demonstration of the united support of the city behind its grand jury."

Thousands of men and women, housewives, college professors, clerks, attorneys and shirtsleeved laborers, met that next morning. An engraved inscription across the building read: "THE IMPARTIAL ADMINISTRATION OF JUSTICE IS THE FOUNDATION OF LIBERTY." The speakers used it as a text: "The people of New Orleans have found their district attorney acting in defense of the lawbreakers he was sworn to prosecute." "New York grand jurors wanted to do the same thing as ours. They got Tom Dewey. What did ours get? The bum's rush!"

A petition was started for the recall of Byrne. It began: "Honorable Earl K. Long, Governor." The booing crowd forced a change: "Earl K. Long, Unelected Governor." Simultaneously, to make certain that Mr. Byrne would receive his due, the meeting began the circulation of an impeachment petition, addressed to civil court. The people of New Orleans were stirring again. This was the first such meeting to be held in years in the bought and beaten city. As it ended, thousands rushed to the hearing upstairs, threatened to "break the door down" when policemen sought to keep their chairman out. He was admitted.

Attorney-General Ellison, who had originally insisted that Byrne was doing "a good job," and that he saw no reason to supersede him, now ordered a temporary supersession. First Assistant Attorney-General O'Connor, who had figured in the Leche-Weiss-Burford "hot oil" controversy, was designated to take over in place of Byrne. Byrne would defend himself at the hearing.

The jurors and their attorneys took advantage of the opportunity that Mr. Byrne had provided them. They could tell their story now, and reveal what they had been permitted to do during these recent weeks, what they had been prevented from doing. Juror DeArmas was asked why the jury majority felt that Byrne or his staff would be embarrassed if they investigated some matters. "We had heard rumors . . . We meant the District Attorney's office as a whole. . . ." The jury wanted particularly to inquire into two subjects, "the tax racket and the gambling racket." The latter might bring in the name of "Fabacher." Fabacher was one of the leading handbook operators of the city, who was later indicted.

Repeatedly, DeArmas went on, the jurors had sought to study payrolls of city and state to find out about "double-dippers" and "deadheads." But Byrne and his staff would never produce the records, declared the work "too burdensome," assured the jurors that they would start no "fishing expeditions"; that the jurors themselves "wouldn't know what you're looking for." But meanwhile the citizens' groups had been publishing lists of legislators on public payrolls, and of men and women who were paid for doing nothing. "Once, out of sheer desperation," another juror declared, "I went to the office of the *Times Picayune* to hunt up those lists." Finally, the majority put in writing a demand for affidavits from employers of six suspected men and women. But the results were not satisfactory; Byrne and his staff had never produced clear, unequivocal answers.

Did the jurors try to investigate gambling? they were asked. Yes, they had talked to Byrne about it, especially about the establishment at 1181½ Baronne. But the District Attorney had declared it the duty of the police department to bring in evidence. Nothing was ever offered regarding gambling. A case was cited at the hearing in which an Orleanian was charged with an $86,000 embezzlement, most of it lost at 1181½. But the legality of operations at the establishment was not discussed by Byrne, the jurors asserted.

The jury, they went on, had been able to act on only two

scandal matters, the Leche "gift yacht," which broke after the public was told about it from other sources, and a case which the Baton Rouge jury had developed fully, but had passed on because of a question of jurisdiction. "The District Attorney's office brought in the yacht case complete—a nice case against Rankin, and Rankin alone." The jury was cautioned not to question Rankin too closely; "Byrne told us he had a weak heart and had fainted before the Federal grand jury. He did seem nervous and drank a lot of water. Some of us felt sorry for him. Others thought he was acting." A majority of the witnesses presented by Byrne had said that Leche was not involved, but some members of the jury thought he was. (The Federal Government agreed with them.)

In the same case, the jurors had wanted to question Seymour Weiss and William Rankin, Jr. They asked that Weiss be summoned on a day they knew he was in town, in connection with the Bienville double dip. A summons was issued, but the jurors were told that Weiss had left New Orleans for ten days. Two weeks passed before the subpoena was served. As to young Rankin, Byrne had questioned him and decided for himself that the fellow was not "mentally fit." Byrne had given the grand jury a graphic demonstration, with vacant stare and finger twiddling, and had quoted Rankin, Jr., as discussing a firm called "Boats, Inc." "Papa mightn't like me to say it, but he owns it, and I am only president." The jurors wanted to talk with Rankin, Jr., more than ever. But Byrne declared that he was "in Mississippi."

The firm of Boats, Inc., was a particularly petted organization that had grown up suddenly, with elegant glass and chromium offices and a thriving trade. An auditor, the jurors added, had told them that he did not see how the firm

could have remained in existence without the trade provided
by the Conservation Department under Rankin, Sr. But the
jurors had difficulty in getting at this subject, too.

Unable to keep track of involved figures and other information, the jurors told how they proposed stenographic help.
But they were dissuaded from this course; "The records
might get into the hands of the wrong people." Individual
jurors wanted to question witnesses, but they declared now
that Byrne and Platt advised them that it was best that one
person, the foreman, do this, putting queries which other
jurors might submit to him. However, if the foreman (who
was not one of the "rebel" majority) did not wish to ask
any of these questions, he need not do so. Some of the majority members called this gag rule.

The majority had held a number of meetings at the homes
of members, to discuss what to do. Somehow, word of these
meetings, open only to the jurors, had spread. Jurors were
"tipped" by telephone callers not to attend such sessions.
One such caller advised a juror to "follow Charlie Byrne"
and gave the name of a member of the City Commission
Council. That member denied having made the call. At one
of the jurors' meetings, a city inspector called in person,
ostensibly to talk about a business matter with the host. But
he had opportunity to observe all who were there, and he
warned the host that the jurors certainly should not be getting together in this fashion. One of Byrne's assistants at the
hearing asked if the jurors had not suspected that a dicta-
phone was secreted at one of the meetings and had not scurried about, prying into bushes. Apparently, the sessions had
been much less confidential than the jurors believed.

Discouraged, the jurors had appealed to Platt. He told
them that they could meet outside, but by no means could
they talk over jury affairs with others. And they could not

obtain other counsel in place of Byrne. He urged them to work in "harmony" among themselves and with Byrne. Matters had not improved, and the jurors had decided to make a formal appeal to the court. A Tulane law professor had given advice in the preparation of the document.

The hearing took a new turn as Hugh Wilkinson was summoned to tell of the tax racket. Byrne protested vehemently. The whole matter had been presented to another grand jury, he said. The rebel jurors interposed through their attorneys: "The only way to prove a crime is to go into the details." Then followed one of the upsets. Assistant Attorney-General O'Connor, as acting District Attorney in Byrne's place, agreed with the jurors' attorneys; let the matter be heard. Thus, after months of silence, the cases upon which the previous jury had refused to indict were brought up for their first full public scrutiny. Wilkinson told more of the matter than had been known before, cited names of additional alleged victims, participants, pay-offs.

Essentially, the tax-racket material was the same as had been presented to the earlier grand jury with no result. Now came action. While Byrne sat silent, the presiding judge announced that he had heard enough to justify him in approving the filing of charges. Four persons were cited—two men and two women—among them Esther Stein, notary, the "Madame Queen" of Wilkinson's evidence; James Stewart, chief clerk in charge of the State Tax Commission at New Orleans; Arthur Steiner and Mrs. Mary Connolly, attorneys.

New Orleans was learning more of the things that had been kept from it. The hearing took on new life. Subpoenas went out for the mysterious conservation records, still unavailable to the public; for records of "Boats, Inc."; for payrolls of deadheads and doubledippers, for voluminous records of other firms in the tax racket. It was clear that only the top crust of New Orleans' scandals had been scraped.

The city's safety commissioner testified that his son, a doctor, was assistant bacteriologist for the City Board of Health, held the same position with the state and had until recently been bacteriologist for the State Welfare Department. A state legislator conceded that he was an "inspector of inspectors" for the state Dock Board; but he declined to say whether he also held a full-time position as secretary-manager of a homestead, or to divulge where he was when summoned.

The court by this time had a high pile of data at hand on the tax racket, the Conservation Department activities, and a variety of other matters. The jurors' attorneys put in late hours on Saturday and Sunday, for what was obviously to be an eventful week. Monday came. An hour or so before the scheduled resumption, Earl Long acted, in several ways. He called out state police in Baton Rouge and ousted Attorney-General Ellison by force. In New Orleans, police converged on the district attorney's office, declared it in a "state of siege" and took it over. O'Connor, who had made possible the lifting of the lid in the tax racket, was removed from his capacity as assistant attorney-general and also as the superseding district attorney; and Byrne was back, smiling, in his office. The National Guard was called out "for a drill," and there were reports that Earl would use it, if necessary, to make sure that neither Ellison nor anybody else went to court to get around him. Once martial law was invoked, no court, under Huey's laws, could intervene.

For once, the Kingfish's apprentice had acted in a manner reminiscent of the mentor. He used force; he used surprise; and he poured salt on the wound. Why had he removed Ellison and O'Connor? He grinned. Why, he just happened to read an opinion by his arch enemy, Former District Attorney Stanley, that Ellison's appointment as attorney-general was illegal. Earl looked up the law, and by gum, Stanley was correct for once in his life. That was what them reformers wanted, now wasn't it? And if Ellison were in illegally, so, too, was his first assistant, O'Connor.

Earl neglected to mention that on the previous day Ellison had qualified unexpectedly as attorney-general to succeed himself. The machine had its own man as its nominee for the job. Chilling reports spread that Ellison was to launch an unlimited investigation into all state affairs during the rest of his current term, using his own intimate knowledge against the machine that had not rewarded him as he expected. Some were sure that he would name Eugene Stanley as a special aide to sink shovels into the muck.

Earl seemed to have the law on his side, thanks to jurisprudence developed under Huey. The Louisiana law does not give a Governor power to appoint an attorney-general, but he may name an acting one. Ellison, as Dick Leche's secretary, had been elevated to the first-assistant's office, to permit Dick to name him attorney-general. He had taken the oath as highest legal officer of the state. Now, Earl pointed out, he had vacated one post without validating his claim to the other, just as Dr. Cyr had done in Huey's day; and Ellison was out in mid-air. Those who thought that Dick's protégé would act up in this crisis were disappointed. After spending an evening in consultation with politicos, he called on Earl and assured him he planned no court action and harbored no ill feelings.

The jurors' hearing hung in the balance. The grapevine carried a message: It had to be stopped, once and for all, and Byrne had to go. Its disclosures had become dangerous, he a liability. Earl Long hurried to New Orleans. Byrne declared: "There is no power on earth that can make me re-

368

sign. Of course, if I am dispossessed of my office by force, that is a different matter." Then Byrne called on Earl and announced that he was quitting because his doctor had told him he "could no longer stand this constant turmoil." One of his Old Regular assistants took his place.

The lid snapped shut. The new district attorney, Niels Hertz, made a motion to end the hearing, since complaints against Byrne had "ended with his resignation." The jurors' attorneys protested that Hertz' own claim to the office was defective, that an election should have been called, since the term had years to go. "This hearing is a matter of public interest and necessity; it must go on to its conclusion. . . . The whole staff was charged, not Byrne alone. . . . Certain people are using this hearing as a political football. They want it on when it seems to their advantage, off when it doesn't." Another voice, another note: "We are in possession of new information, involving a high officer, and we have seen that law enforcement authorities are not willing to bring it out. . . ."

The new matter touched on Robert S. Maestri. The judges cut it off. If the attorneys had material of criminal interest, it was their duty to take it to the grand jury. "But there is no grand jury now." Nevertheless, the hearing ended. The case of the jurors against Platt was in the appelate courts, and no meetings were possible. The seven rebels received a statuette at a public ceremonial. An inscription declared that "their act of heroism and courage in one of the darkest moments in the state's history is paralleled only by that of the White League of 1874, in defending the rights and liberties of a stifled and oppressed citizenry." Cried one speaker: "If the time should come again when we should take up arms, we are ready to do it!"

The new district attorney had his troubles even if the

jury was at pasture. A group of Noe supporters, bearing more of Jimmy's "famous 840 affidavits," presented the new material against Bob Maestri. Statements declared that while mayor, Maestri had used a Conservation Department yacht for his own profit and pleasure. Always ones for photographs, the Noe men offered studies of the vessel, photostats of bills, log records and other data. The boat, the *Ruth*, had assertedly been used for gala week-end trips for Maestri and his "kitchen cabinet," including James Moran, former convict due shortly to figure in a highly significant slot-machine case. The *Ruth* had been stocked with imported wine and fine foods charged to the state, and Maestri was said to have signed the log as "owner and master."

District Attorney Hertz, after some hesitation, announced that he would not receive these or similar charges until after the election, three months hence, because they were "political." This seemed to put a strain on the concept of justice above partisanship; but Mr. Hertz saw no inconsistency. Subsequently the Citizens' Voluntary Committee enlivened a dull day for the community by reporting that under "fish, game and oyster" accounts of the Conservation Department, it found bills for "White Rock, lime rickey, Vichy water, etc.," for use on the yacht, which "may or may not be proper purchases for the department." But a further check-up, the committee said, showed that the purchases were in reality "perfumes and other personal toilet articles."

Next, the jurors' attorneys offered the district attorney fifty-two pages of material charging specific violations of the law: $1,000,000 a year in bribes; dual jobholding; open handbook operations; Conservation Department irregularities, and corruptions in the School Board, Charity Hospital and State Employment Service affairs. Since there was no grand jury, the attorneys called for an open hearing. Hertz turned them down. He hoped for a Supreme Court ruling on the matter of the jurors in the near future. In the meantime, he disapproved of open hearings, because they "obstruct justice," frighten witnesses, allow tampering, give opportunity for bribery, intimidation and perjury, "subject innocent persons to undeserved humiliation and public scandal" and "afford publicity mongers the opportunity to engage in pernicious self-exhibitionism and partisan purveyors of publicity to emphasize parts of testimony favorable to their temporary policy and minimize or suppress those opposed to it." Finally, he would not file bills of information on his own initiative, because the charges were "vague."

It was a formidable array of arguments, but the attorneys were not satisfied. The Supreme Court was delaying the jurors' case. The last public hearing, the attorneys commented, had shown how the jury itself was subjected to "intimidation, interference and tampering," and might be so subjected in future. Also, an open hearing had been required to produce action on the tax racket. As to "vagueness," they called attention to sworn testimony at the last hearing, in which doubledippers admitted their status, and in which others had declared that Former Conservation Commissioner Rankin owned the boat firm which did hundreds of thousands of dollars in business with his department. "What more information could you want?" Some of these charges became the subjects of indictments in 1940. But, for months ahead, New Orleans had no state or parish investigations into its public affairs.

In other parts of the state, other juries fought to clear their way. In North Louisiana, at Alexandria, all members of the jury appealed to the court for a new adviser, declaring that the district attorney had promised dual office holders that he would kill any indictments returned against them. The jurors' request was rejected, but they went ahead and charged twenty-five political figures, among them the treasurer of the state dee-duct system. One of the indicted group, a legislator who was also an official of a state institution, filed charges that the jury had "illegally performed its duties" by ignoring the advice of the district attorney and citing him for cases of doubledipping, taking of dee ducts and violation of state income-tax laws. All of the jurors were arrested. When they tried to function further, the judge dismissed them, and the district attorney quashed all indictments.

After a long interval, when the charges against the jurors went to trial, the jurors' attorney declared: "This is the first time I can find in the history of any state that a man indicted succeeded in throwing out a grand jury without trial of himself. It is also the first time I ever heard of an accused wanting the grand jury to work with the district attorney. Most of the time they wish there were no district attorney." The trial judge reprimanded the legislator: "The grand jury cannot be attacked from behind. Those charged by it should defend themselves in court. Certainly he put a cog in the proceedings of the court. . . ."

In Southwest Louisiana, a district attorney charged that the jury clerk had punched him during a session. The other jurors denied it. But as in other cases, all jury proceedings were held up pending determination of the new issue. The juror was acquitted. But the district attorney struck again. He called upon the police jury to withhold further funds for investigators, declaring that $1700 had been spent by agents, on liquor for stool pigeons, on women and on meals, and that the money could otherwise have gone for the "poor children of the parish." He explained the grand jurors' offenses: "They indicted four officials against my advice that the law was close, and everybody in the parish knew these men held these positions. . . ." This district attorney was no loose gossiper; the jurors had gathered nothing but "rumors, and there are rumors against every man who succeeds." He was alarmed, too, that the jurors had declared they would investigate for months into the future, and he urged the police jury to "call upon the grand jury to adjourn and go home." The police jury complied.

Elsewhere, a juror declared that state income-tax agents had threatened him with criminal prosecution if he did not deliberate "satisfactorily" on a state senator who was under investigation. In Baton Rouge, the department declared that the juror's returns were under scrutiny, but in a "routine way"; it had "complete confidence" in the agents.

At Lafayette, eight jurors sought to resign because "we can get indictments only against small offenders for trivial charges, while serious matters are blocked to us regardless of evidence." But the judge told them they must function regardless of "personal feelings." In another case, the judge advised that the jurors hold up all action until after election, still several months off.

But in Natchitoches Parish, adjoining the Long territory of Winn, one of the most whimsical judges since the First Louisiana Purchase came forward in one of his most whimsical lights. He was James W. Jones, Jr., a man of frequent fame in the state. A series of scandal matters had accumulated in the parish. The State Board of Education had called attention to several hundred thousand dollars of "extras" on buildings at Natchitoches State College, and had urged action. Judge Jones, according to a later attorney-general, threw out a full jury panel in this manner: Five commissioners prepared to select a group of twenty men for the panel. The judge went to each man and gave him four names, with instructions to place them on the list; this would make certain that it would be the judge's personal panel. The commissioners disregarded his order, and selected others. Jones then cancelled the selections and called off the jury term, giving out an explanation that all of the group chosen were over age or "otherwise disqualified."

Resentment spread over the state. The Citizens' Voluntary Committee investigated and announced that not one of the twenty was over the legal age, and that all were of "character and standing in the community." The attorney-general's office in a later petition to court declared that all of the group were thoroughly qualified, and that Judge Jones acted "solely for the reason that he feared the said grand jury would function as an impartial body and might indict the said James W. Jones, Jr., or some of his political and personal associates." The citizens' committee noted that the judge was an active Long partisan and declared that he was Earl's parish campaign manager. The judge admitted his ties with the Long organization, but said that he was only one of a committee handling Earl's candidacy; that his court was "not in politics" and could manage its affairs without the help of citizens' committees. Earl called the judge "my friend," attacked the judge's attackers, but denied that he influenced the judge's actions.

In 1940, when the Attorney-General's office caught up with this matter, it asked Judge Jones' removal for "high crimes and misdemeanors in office, incompetency, corruption, favoritism, extortion, oppression in office and gross misconduct." It charged him with soliciting and taking a $300 bribe to dismiss three suits against a country bank, after having delayed decisions for a year to extort money; with obtaining a $1000 bribe for influencing a grand jury to return a no-true bill in a manslaughter case; with forcing the parents of a man convicted in an assault case to give him a mortgage on their property in return for amelioration of sentence.

The judge was simple and direct in these instances, it was said. In one case, his intimate friend made the original suggestion to the litigant; but the judge himself called the litigant by telephone for an interview, at which the bribe was allegedly accepted. In another instance, the same intermediary was said to have cleared the way; but the litigant was doubtful that he represented the judge. So, declared the Attorney-General, the judge himself called at the agent's house to advise the hesitant one that it would be "safe" to deal with the agent, as the judge would "back him up."

The Attorney-General went into some of the circumstances surrounding the election for the Natchitoches judgeship in 1936. Seeking re-election, Jones ran 165 votes behind at the count, and the judicial committee was preparing to meet for the promulgation of returns. If these followed the original tabulation, Jones' services on the bench would have been ended. On the day before the committee's meeting, the judge "induced several of his friends," according to the Attorney-General, to file an injunction restraining the committee from acting. Then, though he was the principal party at interest, the judge declined to recuse himself and signed an order preventing the promulgation. He also ordered all election records seized and sequestered. The opponent filed suit but for some reason withdrew from the contest, and Jones remained.

Judge Jones was often in public wrangles with others over money. The Attorney-General noted that a $194.18 judgment was rendered against him on a car for which he failed to pay. The machine was seized. But the judge "used his official position and official prestige" to compel the sheriff to turn the car back to him "as custodian for said sheriff." This itself was illegal, the Attorney-General contended. The judge also filed an injunction against the creditor and sheriff. Then, although he was the plaintiff, he, as judge, signed the petition granting himself a restraining order that prevented them from taking the car. Finally, he put the machine beyond execution of judgment by selling it; and he never paid the bill.

A series of "hot" or "rubber check" cases was cited, in which the judge refused to meet obligations ranging from $2.15 to $743 over a period of years. The judge made "open and public boasts that his office put him in such a position that he could not be forced to pay any obligation that he might incur; and that because of such position, no judgment against him could be enforced." Involved were promissory notes on law books, part of the purchase price of a piano, accounts for lumber, gasoline and lubricating oil. The record showed, finally, that out of 158 cases which had gone from his court to the higher ones, His Honor had been overruled in one hundred and twenty. And all of North Louisiana recalled the case in which the judge figured in a shooting. The grand jury of his court, however, returned a no-true bill. The dispute took place over a rent bill which the other man said he was trying to collect. Such was the Law West of the Natchitoches.

Thus, in New Orleans, in Alexandria, in Lake Charles, in Natchitoches, and at other points about the state, the jurors waited. Evidence disappeared. Cases were prescribed. The machine went ahead in its management of parish affairs and its electioneering, assured for the most part that there would be no awkward moments for it and its men, at least on the state front.

376

The independence of the Louisiana jury system rested on the case of Judge Platt and the rebel jurors of New Orleans. The Louisiana Supreme Court, after a protracted wait, ruled at last—for Platt. The jurors had gone beyond their powers. If they had believed the district attorney or his staff guilty of criminal actions, they should have indicted them; if they believed them guilty of malfeasance, they should have called the matter to the attention of the "proper authorities." Juries, the court decided, had no right in Louisiana to seek outside counsel. The decision meant that hereafter the juries of the state were to be gagged when a district attorney or a judge wanted them gagged.

The chief justice, dissenting, declared that the jurors had been, at most, overzealous. "We must remember that Louisiana is in a new era, to which no one is accustomed. It is an era in which there have been so many accusations of crimes of dishonesty in public office that it taxes the understanding and the patience, as well as the courage, of the grand juries—both state and Federal—to investigate all of the charges. . . . We cannot avoid the knowledge of this state of affairs, for it is commonly known and commented upon with the utmost publicity throughout the United States. The average citizen in Louisiana has heard more and has read more about grand juries in the last few months than he has ever before heard or read in his life." Another justice observed: "This ruling will fetter criminal procedure and hamper the administration of justice in Louisiana."

He was right, for the time being. The parish grand juries would be hobbled. But the fetters would not remain permanently upon them. The jurors' flare-ups had taught Louisiana, if the state had not known it previously, the kept status of another aspect of its government.

Governor Earl Long, in the interim, was going about the

state and asking caution and freedom from hysteria: "I haven't tried to scandalize a man, or make anybody a goat by singling him out. We're going about this quietly, decently, in an orderly, legal way—through the constituted legal authorities." Parish jury investigation, it appeared, was neither constituted nor legal for the duration of the war.

XVI

SOUR GRAPES OF WRATH

THESE were the days when the remaining great of the
Louisiana earth walked in apprehension; when to be an
official was to know that the shine of one's car or the new-
ness of one's suit was the subject of debate among the neighbors as indication of a possible indictment; when to erect a
new home was to lay oneself open to a suspicion of having
stolen the bricks, filched state lumber or requisitioned WPA
workmen and foremen. These were the days, too, when the
Mayor of Baton Rouge ordered newsboys not to hawk their
extras through residential areas at night. Too many persons
were receiving bad starts and frights.

A candidate for Governor told his audience: "Things
have gotten so bad that when you drive your car out of
Louisiana to the West, people spy your license and cry 'Fugitive!' When you drive East, they yell 'Lock the doors!' "

To make matters worse for the state administration, the
auditor of the Louisiana Prison Farm confessed one night
that he had embezzled $53,000 of penitentiary funds over
two and a half years of the Leche régime. A state employee
for ten years, he had gone straight until that time, he said.
"It's contagious," declared the opposition. Outside the state,
a critic asked the nation: "If we forgave France her war
debt, would she take Louisiana back?"

Federal grand juries were in operation in North Louisiana
and in West Louisiana, finding subjects for indictment al-

most as wide-ranged as those uncovered by the jury that functioned in New Orleans. In the history of the Federal Government, no investigation or group of investigations had had so many aspects, or had required the services of so many agents of separate departments. With Rogge, the Department of Justice had three to five assistant or special-assistant attorney-generals on the job. The Post Office Department shifted teams of experts from other states to concentrate Southern efforts on Louisiana. Leading agents of the Internal Revenue staff moved in and out of the state. The WPA investigative agency continued about a score of men between New Orleans and Baton Rouge, and the national director visited the state. The Securities and Exchange Commission and the Commodity Exchange officials conducted inquiries. The Public Works Administration had separate offices and separate agents fanning out from New Orleans. The United States Attorney-General's office at New Orleans assigned an assistant with a group of aides to make a special inquiry into the Charity Hospital mysteries. Ickes' hot-oil men worked for eight months in and about the oil fields and in and out of state offices. Oil operators from practically every field came forward to lay bitter charges before the Ickes men and the Federal attorneys.

The special Congressional committee inquiring into relief matters arrived and launched its own study. The anti-trust division of the Department of Justice was considering action of its own. The Baton Rouge grand jury studied athletics, dairy operations, poultry sales and drug purchases. Another group of inquisitors found graft in purchases of fishhooks and hogs at a state college. To make sure that no agency and no charge would be omitted, Avoyelles Parish citizens made accusations of "immorality in the National Youth Administration."

Earl Long, in a lighter moment, declared that he heard somebody had tossed a five-dollar bill on the L.S.U. campus the previous week, had gone back that day and found it still there. Everybody was watching his step.

If life in Louisiana had been unsettled on that day after "Doc" Smith disappeared, it was now in turmoil. Not the least affected was Society, in particular Official Society in New Orleans and Baton Rouge. The First Lady of the Capital was doing no entertaining whatever, except for farmers on Four-H days, and then—the rustic Winn touch—these guests received buttermilk; no highballs, not even beer. The First Lady of the Campus, only recently out of jail, had announced not even a tea. Other hostesses had their difficulties. One never knew when a party might not be wrecked by the day's indictment; when a state's witness might show up, to glower across the table at a man on whom he had turned informer. And everybody had one subject on his mind, but was afraid to voice his thoughts in public for fear he might say the wrong thing.

A wag put out an advertisement for his clothing store: "Leavenworth gray suits, Atlanta striped ties, Angola khaki flannels." The display was not repeated. Protests made it clear that the prank had hit too close to home. Youths about town went to the printer and ordered cards bearing "L.S.U. Football Schedules: L.S.U.-Angola State Prison, Thanksgiving; L.S.U.-Sing-Sing, New Year's Day; L.S.U.-Atlanta— Homecoming Game, Any Day Now."

But there was no mirth in the situation for many who had gone to the state university, for the parents of students, for the farmers who looked on L.S.U. as their school. Smith and Leche were not the only men responsible; what about the board? they asked. What was it doing when all of this was happening? What kind of men were they that such a

381

parade of rackets had passed before them without their understanding? The answers were not hard to find. The majority were jobholders, controlled, placed on the board for that reason; others included some in private capacities who were usually equally manageable. The list took in heads of the Highway Department, the State Penitentiary and other agencies; one of the Round Robineers whom Huey had made a judge; until recently, the attorney-general, Ellison; legislators on the machine's reservation, including one with a well-paid additional state job; the celebrated Justice John B. Fournet, and, not least, an enthusiastic South Louisianian who once made an illuminating assertion: "Water's wet; heat's hot; two and two make four; and Huey Long is right."

Over the state, alumni and other groups charged the board with "gross, wanton and perpetual negligence," with efforts to whitewash when the debacle broke and with failure to take decisive steps at any time. A complete clean-out of the administrators was demanded, with sweeping changes in staff and management. Again and again, the board was asked why it had not taken the simple precaution of requiring effective audits, or of reading the minutes of preceding meetings, or of keeping a watch upon the whereabouts of its bonds. Others accused it of acts of commission as well as omission. It was noted that the board had voted the purchase and renting of the Bienville Hotel to Charity Hospital in the face of rulings by bond attorneys that such a project appeared illegal. "They did this," exclaimed Tom Dutton, president of the alumni, "knowing full well that the men involved in the deal were mixed up in graft and corruption and had been for years." The alumni council, declaring that any member who had served with Smith should welcome a chance to get off the board, called for voluntary retirements. The board met, and gave out a crisp statement that the "best interests of L.S.U." would be served if it remained. The opposition called this attitude arrogance. The Baton Rouge jury, in a special report, joined others calling for wholesale resignations; its inquiries had shown that the board "failed and neglected to attend to the affairs of L.S.U. to an amazing degree. . . . This neglect and astounding indifference have contributed to the crimes and misconduct of the president and staff."

In reply, one of the board members asserted that he felt the university "needs me more than ever. I shall, more than ever, be careful to see that my confidence is not misplaced. Of all the public and civic services which I have rendered, I can truthfully say I am proudest of my years on the board. . . . We built and we built like Romans, and we are proud of it." To which the alumni president retorted by quoting Scripture: "Everyone dealeth falsely . . . sayeth peace, peace when there is no peace. Were they ashamed that they had committed abominations? Nay, they were not ashamed, neither could they blush. . . ." Gradually, however, board members dropped off; but late in 1940 some of the Smith men still remained. The undergraduates took the scandal with a grin, shaving George Caldwell's symbol—"2%"—into the heads of freshmen in hazing.

The board ordered the name and face of Former Governor Dick removed from more than thirty buildings on the campus on which they were displayed, and those of James Monroe Smith from whatever places Old Jingle Money had seen fit to imprint tokens of himself. This was no light assignment. From the marble face of the replica of the United States Supreme Court, the name of Leche had to be chiseled out; and from another section a heavy bronze plaque bearing the likeness of the former executive had to be broken out. From nearly every pillar of the football stadium and the baseball stadium, from three girls' dormitories and from the cage of Mike the Tiger, other gubernatorial mementos were ripped. An inquiry disclosed that $9000 had been spent for plaques to memorialize the Governor. The source was the "extra" items account on Leche Hall.

Earl Long announced that the state would not carry through its original plans for installing 145 additional Leche faces on bridges and along highways throughout the state. These objects had been gathering dust for several months in a basement. They had been ordered by the Highway Commission and had arrived shortly after Governor Dick's retirement. They had cost $4645; now they were sold for junk, at $211. Original cost, $32 each; sale price, $1.47. Some were used for ashtrays, others for university forging operations. (In the metal department, officials hastened to explain.) A side note was the discovery that the manufacturer of the plaques was the company of L. P. Abernathy, former highway commissioner and prominent indictee.

In one instance, a Louisiana family did not wait for Earl to expunge evidences of Leche. Newspapers reported the incident. In a little town, one of the dental trailers which bore the name in imposing letters was parked before an office building. A man and his wife drove up, took out a rag and a bottle of chemical paint remover, rubbed away the offending letters, and then drove off without identifying themselves to an applauding crowd.

The university's National Youth Administration executive killed himself, and this New Deal organization ordered still another L.S.U. investigation. In New Orleans, a former Federal revenue collector, who was Dr. Smith's adviser and who assisted a number of other scandal figures in these matters, also ended his life. In his cell at the Baton Rouge jail, awaiting further trials in the dozens before him, James Monroe Smith sent out for sherbet and bichloride of mercury, the latter to "cure some foot trouble." At the last minute, the warden decided not to give him the bottle. A few days later Smith was found in his cell, one foot in a tub of warm water, an artery severed with a razor blade. Very weak, he had almost succeeded in his attempt. He was taken by ambulance to the same hospital in which his patron, Huey, had died. Smith recovered.

In late November of 1939, the former president settled matters with the state. He pleaded guilty to four "typical" charges out of the twenty-seven against him in Baton Rouge Parish, and received a term of eight to twenty-four years. His Federal double-dip sentence of two and a half years was to be served later. In New Orleans, sixteen other charges were still pending. Now James Monroe Smith went to the State Prison Farm. He was well known to the officials. He had visited there as a special guest from time to time. Now he donned the costume he had once worn to a masquerade, and cut cane on at least one occasion, when a photographer took his picture with the administration's approval.

The shifting scandal limelight moved to another part of the state, the largest hospital for the mentally ill, and to another member of the official family—Cousin Wade Long, the general manager. This was the institution about which Huey in 1928 had drawn such pictures of callous neglect and suffering of patients that his listeners cried. A series of charges broke out in late 1939 against the management. Months of delay followed; finally the Attorney-General's office turned over a report of an investigation to the parish grand jury; and then came more delay. At last, in 1940, shortly before the gubernatorial election, the jury issued a report but did not take positive action. The report declared that a transaction in which the institution had participated—the sale of a plantation property to the wife of one of the board members —bore "the earmarks of a conspiracy to defraud." The property had originally been purchased for $25,000, but was sold for $5000. Almost immediately, the purchaser disposed of the timber alone for $5000, and retained possession of 1700 well-drained acres and a 25-room house. The sale, the jury commented, justified a "charge that the manager, the board and all parties connected with the sale utterly disregarded the principles of good management and failed to regard the trust imposed upon them, by law and the decency of good conscience, to guard carefully and promote the welfare of the institution."

Records showed that shortly after the $5000 sale, the board members had distributed about $5000 in extra salaries and bonuses. Board members had also increased considerably their own reimbursement for attendance at meetings. The jury questioned the large salary of $10,000 a year to Cousin Wade; the sale of cattle, mules and farm equipment of the institution at non-public sales; and it called for "further inquiry." Earl said he would call together everybody, grand jury, board and others, to "thresh out" the matter—after election.

The institution clearly was not one of the "benefits" or services to which the state administration often referred. Despite Huey's promise that the forgotten insane would be remembered, their plight had gone from bad to considerably worse. No little stir resulted when it was disclosed that food expenditures went as low as nine cents per capita per day. Forty-one hundred patients were packed tightly into aged, dangerous, poorly protected buildings planned for 2500. Not a single new building had gone up in the dictatorship's twelve years. While the pay of the general manager was lifted into the higher state brackets, the hospital dropped occupational therapy, an essential for a modern institution of this type. About 3000 acres of farm properties and orchards had been permitted to deteriorate. Medical and nursing care were tragically inadequate; a country doctor, without particular training in mental ailments, was made superintendent. Nearly three years passed without the serving of fresh fruit to the patients. Ancient refrigerators would not preserve food for more than two days; dangers of spoilage were high. A twenty-year-old power plant had not been repaired in twelve years.

The management was not fanatical about the needs of its wards. It recognized that there were more important matters. Over a period of a few years, it obligingly turned back to the state treasury $215,000 of funds appropriated for it, and, in effect, urged the Legislature not to embarrass it by uncalled-for riches. In 1937 Governor Dick told the State Board of Liquidation of a tragic situation at a new L.S.U. junior college. It lacked a football stadium. The mental hospital had $90,000 which it did not want; and so funds intended for the patients, meager as the hospital budget was, went for that purpose. In the following year, another state college found it needed a new gymnasium; and although the hospital had not even an old one, although doctors had appealed for such a facility for years, another $100,000 was taken from the convenient fund. Governor Earl himself took a final dip by removing $25,000 for extra pay for his friends, the judges and district attorneys. No matter what the *Progress* said about all of this, these findings did not increase public confidence in the machine. . . .

A $315,000 golf course was disclosed one day as having dwindled into $315,000 of practically nothing. Here was a venture projected in coincidences, executed in the majestic manner. Governor Dick, Abe Shushan and other eminentoes were ensconced along the Gold Coast when someone noted with regret that there was nary a green for miles around. Accordingly, the Conservation Department branched out as sponsor of a golf course. Just what this had to do with conservation was not clear; but the agency was developing a general park in the area, and it was argued that the links would work in admirably. The WPA approved an undertaking to produce "the sportiest links in the South," with twenty-seven holes, caddy house and club house and other facilities. The new conservation commissioner, succeeding Rankin, abandoned the sponsorship and the WPA threatened to sue, but eventually did not. Newly sodded, destumped and graded grounds deteriorated. Uncompleted buildings weathered in the rain. Discrepancies of at least $85,000 appeared in the conservation accounts; the Citizens' Voluntary Committee subsequently noted peculiar incidents in handling of funds and payrolls, disappearance of invoices and canceled checks, monopolies to various individuals. This situation, like the preceding one, did not increase the general respect.

Worse, a North Louisiana Federal grand jury indicted the Speaker of the House of Representatives, his father, a judge; his brother, a state highway inspector; the secretary of the parish police jury; a state senator and a North Louisiana mayor, for using the mails to defraud in an alleged racket which left the parish $40,000 in the red and themselves $20,000 or so richer.

A highly ingenious little operation was set forth. Some of the group, it appeared, had purchased farm equipment from an Indianapolis concern for $38,500, as a private venture. They planned to rent it to farmers, but the farmers did not take to the idea. Then, the Government asserted, the group went to the police jury, persuaded it to assume the debt, and obtained approval from Huey's State Bond and Tax Board. Next, it was said, the men went to the Indianapolis concern with the word that their good offices would be necessary to make any collections; and they persuaded it to employ one of the group to make collections—at fifty per cent. For a $38,500 debt, the firm would accept half its bill. In the name of the company, suit was filed against the police jury, asking that a new tax be levied to pay the judgment. The defendants "corruptly, improperly and illegally" influenced the jury not to file an answer, the grand jury charged, and the judgment was won. Next, said the indictment, the police jury authorized issuance of bonds for $40,000; the firm received $20,000 and the defendants about the same amount, and the parish had equipment that was a burden on its hands.

The indictment had repercussions in the rural sections. Speaker Lorris Wimberly was a staunch Huey man, from Huey's earliest days; a voter against the impeachment on every count. He had gone on to the secretaryship of Huey's "civil service commission," which controlled all patronage. He had missed nomination as lieutenant-governor on the 1940 ticket by a narrow margin. Here, in any event, luck was with the machine.

When the farm equipment case went to court, a mistrial resulted, though one of the men had entered a plea of nolo contendere. Immediately afterward, charges of jury tampering were filed by the United States attorney's office against a close friend of Judge Wimberly.* All of the defendants ex-

---

* As another aftermath to the case, Judge Wimberly himself and one of the jurors were charged with contempt of court in connection with the alleged jury tampering. The juror pleaded guilty. As to the judge, a verdict of guilty was rendered; but the case is still pending.

cept the one who pleaded nolo contendere were named in the tampering charge, but not indicted.

Alice Lee Grosjean now suddenly returned to Louisiana, after months of absence, and made a series of request appearances before Federal juries and state groups. Alice had been in California, where she saw her brother-in-law, E. L. Cord, the automobile manufacturer. From him she was reported to have sought advice. She was known to be bitter toward some Louisianians. A Washington column declared her ready to tell "everything she knew"; a chill ran down the spines of a number of the boys. Some said that Alice had taken other things besides luggage with her when she left the state: a collection of public or not-so-public documents, photostatic copies of records which had passed through her hands as revenue collector, supervisor of accounts, secretary of state, Governor for a few days and, not least, private secretary to Huey. What she told or did not tell the jurors was not disclosed. But Alice was seen about the executive mansion one day, engaged in "campaign work" for the Kingfish's brother.

Oil, "hot" or cold, was causing increasing concern. The machine's candidate for lieutenant-governor figured in some questionings not long after he was chosen. He was Harvey Peltier of South Louisiana, floor leader of the Senate, a young man whose fortune had grown with his fame in the decade that began in 1929. His money did not come through drillings, but largely through the holding of state leases on which oil was found.

By the record, Harvey was at least one of the luckiest of Louisiana men. He was almost always, it seemed, stumbling on ventures that thrived in tropical luxuriance. The lands in which he obtained interest from the state practically invariably turned out to be money makers. Estimates were made that he had acquired a half-million dollars in about five years, with the prospect of a large increase in this total through continuing royalties.

B. L. Krebs of the *Times Picayune* noted that in one instance Harvey put out $1000 for his lease and stood to receive $150,000 in royalty payments. Here, as in other instances, he purchased the original lease from the state or from a man who had just acquired it from the state; and then Harvey turned it over to another to drill. In a second instance, Harvey spent $500 and received $30,000, with indications that the amount would increase over a period of years into the future.

Harvey, O. K. Allen and S. A. Guidry, a mutual friend, had begun joint mineral dealings in 1931, the year before "O.K." became Governor. The undertaking was an immediately lucrative one, and the continuation of the royalty payments may have induced a jovial relationship among the three men. Whether it was in token of this joviality or by simple exercise of public duty, Governor "O.K." in 1932 gave Mr. Guidry a lease for which the state received a payment of $500. Shortly afterward, Mr. Guidry transferred a three-fourths interest to Harvey Peltier and another friend for $1500. Out of this came several hundred thousand dollars of royalty returns. The transfer to Peltier was not disclosed until four years later, when a document showing the sale of interest was filed.

Harvey defended himself against all questionings. He had succeeded only through "hard work, honest effort and diligent application." Many of his friends had been "alarmed that I had lost my mind in speculating so heavily." The opposition retorted that Harvey's oil dealings did not sound like speculation, but a sure thing, to them. Campaigners declared that Harvey was a "fellow that has a wonderful nose; he can sit on his front porch and smell oil all over Louisiana." The publication of photographs of Harvey's front porch did not make the organization happier. Harvey's home was the showplace of his town, a structure that might have shamed in grandeur and in proportions some of the plantation houses of an earlier day. Its great interior stairway was a triumph of design; its gallery large enough for the community meetings. Newspapers pictured it in its shimmering beauty and contrasted it with a quiet little cottage in which Harvey had lived before he struck royalties.

Oil was bringing trouble for Maestri as well. He was called before several grand juries, Federal and state, and asked about the excess shipments during his term as commissioner, and about his own dealings in oil during that time and later. Particularly were the juries interested in his operations with William Helis, Greek-American multimillionaire, who had discovered several fields in Louisiana and had become one of the richest men in the South as a consequence.

Helis was Maestri's partner in a company that had been a major independent in South Louisiana. He went to Louisiana after a career of ups and downs in California, in Tennessee, and in other states. He was a former dishwasher, an immigrant boy who had knocked about the country, following a trail of oil. His Louisiana operations had made him rich almost immediately. He became an owner of mansions, of yachts, of great estates. He went to Hollywood; he went to Greece as a guest of rulers and churchmen. He became his country's consul-general for the South; he bought an El Greco for $25,000 after hearing of it through his friend, the Greek Ambassador, Dimitrios Sicilianos; he endowed churches and orphanages; a fossil was named after him by geologists in Greece; King George II made him a Commander of the Ancient Order of the Phoenix; he figured in some highly charged lawsuits by former partners. Then in mid-July of 1939 he left Louisiana for the native country, and apparently had no intention of returning in the near future. It had been announced previously that the Greek government had granted him an "exclusive oil concession" for drilling in all parts of the country.

His attorney denied that Helis was "hiding out." "Mr. Helis will return when his business affairs require his presence. It might be tomorrow, or it might be a year from now. But at present, his interests require him to be in Greece."

The criticisms and questionings which Maestri had been spared by the elimination of the mayoralty campaign were upon him now in a form worse than he had ever expected. Reports spread that he was planning to resign as a consequence. He remained, but said little. The Citizens' Voluntary Committee asked him to what extent he may have profited by hot oil run through his and Helis' company; pointed out that the Conservation Commission records were still closed, and told him he owed it to the public to clarify the situation as to his own oil interests. "During all of these months, you have not given the facts in answer to repeated rumors that have been brought to your attention that you personally profited by your position as conservation commissioner." Maestri, pressed for a reply, made laconic reference to Joseph Airey, chairman of the citizens' group: "Mr. Airey isn't there."

In New Orleans came a series of other disturbing incidents, one a hard blow. The election campaign brought the sporting world of the wicked metropolis to attention, in sometimes depressing fashion for the boys. With Mayor Bob

Maestri, the man who was no reformer, had come a new golden age for more than one element of the population. Handbooks flourished as seldom before. New bowers of gaming thrived for the poor, the rich, the middle class. Lottery prospered with the rest. National authorities have estimated that the city's proportion of gambling devices in the present day exceeds that of any other American metropolis, North or South. A new semi-restricted district spread itself about the Vieux Carré, with the girls behind the iron lacework instead of the older crib shutters. During this period, the newspapers reported the growth of the handbooks in particular. On one occasion, it was noted that Mayor .Bob could see a handbook in operation if he went to his window at City Hall and looked across the street; again, that the district attorney need not go to that effort, had only to lift his head from his pillow at home to see another.

Affairs had become better organized down the line. That organization was nowhere more clearly demonstrated than in the relationship of the race track and the handbooks. The books were O.K., boys—when racing wasn't on. And then the books became suddenly illegal, and the police developed eyes. The bookie business was probably the biggest in the city to take so long an annual lay-off, three to four months a year. In the earlier days, police enforcement of the vacation had been somewhat less than markedly zealous; a raid here, a warning there, while occasional operators managed to make a little profit by exercise of discretion and an extra pay-off. A few days in the business and a raid . . . no harm done, Joe. I'll watch it next time. . . . During the second part of the dictatorship, however, matters changed. The bookies received firm warning: stay open at your own risk. It was a real risk. Police did not content themselves with an arrest or a padlocking. They "fixed it so

394

you won't operate again for a while." They brought along axes, hatchets, sticks; they chopped up chairs, benches, tables, broke windows, ripped rugs. In one or two instances in the poorer city sections, in which living quarters adjoined the handbook place, the officers "fixed that up real nice, too," tearing down furnishings, breaking up beds, cutting clothing to shreds. . . . A month hence, it would be all right for you to operate, if you could fix up the place again.

Mayor Maestri's intimate friend, Placide Frigerio, had the largest bloc of stock in the Fair Grounds Race Track. The mayor's name had figured years earlier in the original negotiations. The Long organization had squeezed out a previous owner by raising his assessments to a prohibitive level. He gave up, and soon the valuation was lower than before. In 1938, some widely publicized charges were made in connection with the track operations. At the trial of the New York Tammany leader, Jimmy Hines, lieutenant of Arthur (Dutch Schultz) Flegenheimer, testimony was offered regarding a "fix" at the New Orleans track and a selected group of others. It was a scheme that was worked by the Dutch Schultz organization as a part of the Dutchman's numbers racket in New York.

The Schultz organization stood to lose millions if the "bad figures," the often-played ones, came up. The pay-off was based on the last numerals of the pari-mutuel figures at certain tracks about the country. One of the Dutchman's men declared that a lightning calculator, self-named "Abadabba," was introduced into the mutuel office at the New Orleans track and at the others, under a deal made with the managements. "Abadabba" would receive telephone calls from New York, learn the "bad numbers" and slip in split-second final bids to change the odds and the numerals, so that the worst figures did not appear. This story was told also by Dixie Davis, former "Kid Mouthpiece" of the Schultz gang, and by Craig Thompson and Allen Raymond in their *Gang Rule in New York*. The latter authorities commented that, as a result of the operations at New Orleans and at the other tracks, "The whole policy lottery became a gigantic swindle in which hundreds of thousands of trusting bettors were robbed."

Jimmy Noe, campaigning in 1939 for Governor, stirred the boys when he charged collusion among the city, the handbook operators and the Louisiana State Employment Service, an affiliate of the United States Employment Service. He produced records showing that employees of the handbooks were carried regularly on the unemployment insurance rolls during the period when the track operated and the bookies had to shut down. As soon as the track closed, the bookies took on their workers again. Noe argued that "the mayor of the great city of New Orleans permits city and state agencies to be abused and compels them to support people engaging in illegal activities." A photostatic copy of an employers' request for workers from the service described one organization as "pool hall, gambling." Under the space for observation, the Employment Service representative had noted: "Dump, but has other places O.K." The employment official of one of the handbook syndicates was identified as a well-known Orleanian, a former tax expert for the Special Intelligence unit of the Department of Internal Revenue.

Eventually, the Long-appointed manager of the Employment Service at New Orleans was indicted, with A. J. Fabacher, the handbook operator who had been mentioned in the rebel grand jurors' hearing. The handbook man was charged under the state gambling laws, the employment officer with aiding in the operation of the handbooks. An additional count against the state official was one of "falsifying public records with intent to defraud." This was done, it was said, by sending representatives to private firms and private employment agencies on the pretext of checking names to eliminate duplications. Instead, the indictment declared, complete employment records would be obtained, and the state agency would list thousands of additional workers as having obtained employment through its facilities. Thus, great cases were presented of the expanding work of the Employment Service, its efficient assistance to the working man, and also of improving conditions in this state of happy dictatorship.

Returning from one of his frequent trips to Washington, Rogge admitted that Louisiana was to get its "first big gambling case" of the scandals. The grand jury took him at his word. Against four Orleanians and two New Yorkers it brought the second-largest income-tax-evasion case in history, the largest ever to go to trial. It dug into the mysteries of the slot machines and their sponsors. During two years of operation in the city, the jury charged, the machines had grossed $2,592,000, on which a tax of $529,000 was claimed. Only the Moe Annenberg case involved larger sums. The indictment revealed that Frankie Costello, one-time "slot machine king" of New York City, had assumed the same rôle in New Orleans as an absentee monarch operating through a connection man, Philip (Dandy Phil) Kastel. But the name on the indictment that meant most to Louisiana was that of Jimmy Moran, friend and drinking companion of Huey Long, latterly an associate of Mayor Maestri. Jimmy Moran was tied directly with the others in a variety of alleged dodges to defraud the Government by false reports, dummy partnerships and other devices.

The slots had disappeared a short time previously, after an unprecedentedly flush era. New Orleans, for a combination of reasons, previously had seldom had the slots. They had thrived in the free-and-easy parishes on the outskirts, but not in the city proper. Then, in 1936 they had poured in, obviously well backed and well protected. They invaded restaurants, cafés, groceries, cigar stores, establishments that had never had the devices or any related to them in the past. For a time, in those days of peace after Huey, nothing had happened. But then the women's clubs and the ministers had started after Mayor Bob and the police superintendent, and had threatened ouster action. Finally, reluctantly, the slot men were ordered to move out.

But almost immediately their place was taken by other instruments, pinballs, expensive and handsome, equipped with electric lights and trick gadgets. These games, too, clearly had official as well as popular support. The year 1939 saw the pinballs at their peak. Who were behind them? The Government now answered that one, too. The new boys were, in large part at least, the old boys. Deputies of the Internal Revenue Office descended one day on barrooms, drugstores and other establishments, sealed the pinball coin boxes and marked the machines: "Seized for the account of the United States." This action was taken, it was explained, because "Dandy Phil" Kastel owed personal income taxes. Kastel, it was declared, owned forty per cent of one of the two major pinball agencies of the city. Others named as engaged in the pinball business were Jimmy Moran of New Orleans and most of those included in the slot indictment. For one day the Government was in the pinball business with the boys. At the end of that time, it unsealed the boxes, took out Phil's forty per cent, and found it had most of the $3500 which it claimed.

While the machine men squirmed, notice was called to the figure of Jimmy Moran. New Orleans knew Jimmy well.

Like his pal Huey, he could be called *sui generis,* a man
without counterpart in New Orleans, in New York, in Zan-
zibar. He was a city pagan, a happy little primitive, who
had survived circumstance and miscalculation through the
years, to remain always clinging to the coat-tails of his chosen
great.

Once a barber, then a minor prize fighter and referee,
he had been Huey's confidant of the Singing Fool days. He
was born James Brocato, a product of downtown New
Orleans. A devoted follower of Pal and Vic Moran, ring
men of another day, he had chosen their name for his; and
when others referred to him by his earlier designation, he
lost his temper: "It's Moran—Moran—Moran!" Jimmy had
been Huey's guide of an evening, at Jimmy's club during
the Prohibition period and at other brassy establishments in
which the Kingfish took his first plunge into the inviting
waters of the city's night life. Jimmy spent week ends at
the mansion, was seen often around the Governor's office.
In 1930, however, Jimmy met misfortune, and was sent to
Federal prison for a year as a second offender for violation
of the Prohibition law. Huey assured Jimmy that he and
the boys would take care of him on his return. They did.
Jimmy's connections had never been clearly defined, but
they were connections, and good ones.

Jimmy was now a salesman, by official explanation. He
became closer to Maestri. Jimmy rode about the city with
the mayor, went to prize fights with him, smiled when he
was introduced as Colonel Moran, a title bestowed upon
him by the amiable Dick Leche. Jimmy had always been a
clothes horse, astounding judges and others with exotic combinations of light-blue suits, pink shirts and spats. With
more cash on hand, he achieved his zenith as a tailor's dream.
Raiment became almost an obsession. A short, beetle-browed,

bestomached fellow, Jimmy did all that modern civilization made it possible to do to embellish his physical endowments. He bought fifty to sixty suits, scores of shirts, $2500 worth of the latter at one time; he insisted on bench-made shoes, specially made hats, imported French handkerchiefs and ties, and used nineteen pairs of spectacles, varicolored, vari-patterned, each to match a double-breasted suit. He did not bother about glasses for his singles, possibly because he had few singles. His sartorial advisers told him that the double was the thing for a man on the paunchy side.

Jimmy had a full-scale dressing room that was his temple. It was cedar-lined, with full-length mirrors at one end to permit Jimmy to inspect the final result of his thrice-daily experimentations; with shoe racks that extended in two directions, and tier on tier of clothes, ties, overcoats, suits.

Partly clothed, Jimmy was a more staggering sight than in full attire. His tailor had instructions to provide shorts to match suits, undershirts in the general color theme—plaid for a plaid, pale green for a pale green, blue dot for blue dot. Jimmy was determined never to be embarrassed if he had occasion to disrobe before a friend, or an enemy. Jimmy's suits were lined with a special Jimmy Moran silk. His shoes had special Jimmy Moran trees. No piece of investiture was ever lost to Jimmy because the finder did not know the owner. His full name was stitched into everything, shirts, shorts, trousers, coats. His car bore a plate of silver, declaring it a special job for James Moran. Diamonds spelled out his full name on his watches and belt buckles. In the year before the scandals came upon Jimmy's friends, he had participated in a contest sponsored by business groups to find the best-dressed man in New Orleans. Jimmy came second. Mr. New Orleans, by popular vote, was Seymour Weiss. Jimmy could not be blamed for feeling that greater political pull had been the only factor that permitted Seymour to edge him out.

According to the grapevine, Jimmy was disturbed only once when the grand jury questioned him about the slot machines and his source of income. An inquisitive lout, with no conception of the cost of maintaining oneself in all-matched splendor, wanted to know if it were true that Jimmy's raiment cost him almost $1000. Jimmy quivered: "What I have in my clothes closet is worth more than $28,-000, in case you're interested, mister!" This was the kind of low rating that hurt, as Alva Johnston related the incident.

Dixie Davis was called to New Orleans for the trial, and arrived with Hope Dare, but the intrigued under- and upper-worlds were not gratified by many glimpses of these personages. At the last minute, they were not summoned. James A. Noe, too, was listed as a prospective witness, and the state speculated about that; but he likewise was passed over at the end.

The trial was a jumble of lurid stories of non-existent individuals, created by joining the first name of a friend to the last name of another; unexplained "business allowances" of $110,000 or so; expansion of an original $15,000 by Costello and Kastel into a million and a quarter annual business; the tale of a widow of one of the partners who went to the safety deposit box after his death, only to find an empty compartment instead of large quantities of cash which she had reason to believe were there. (She had to content herself with a 35-foot yacht which no one had taken.) Jimmy Moran received heavy payments of cash, part of which went into bank accounts, part into safety deposit boxes. It was clear that Jimmy could have afforded even more suits and colored spectacles than he owned.

But the moment of maximum impact came when the

Government offered a sworn statement that it was Kingfish Huey P. Long who had brought the slot machines to New Orleans; that it was Huey's idea to make a deal with the Eastern elements to cover the city with the "one-armed bandits."

Costello, the czar of the slots, told a grand jury that Huey picked him to be "the lucky one" to install the machines and run them: "I was invited to come to New Orleans, Louisiana, in the early part of 1935, and got this proposition. . . . I was invited by a man called Huey Long . . . [He] asked me to put our machines there in Louisiana; he was going to pass some kind of ordinance for the poor, the blind—a certain kind of relief, to get a certain percentage—and we would have to pay so much per machine per year. Well, about six or seven weeks later, I got Philip Kastel, which is my associate, to go down there and work the thing out. He went down there and he incorporated, and from then on worked out the deal." Jimmy Moran took Phil around, while Phil surveyed New Orleans' trade opportunities "his own way." At the end, when the slots were driven out by the clubwomen, it was Jimmy who took the sad official word around.

The case had been an almost impossible one to develop and present, because of the carefully preserved element of secrecy. The judge declared that he recognized "certain practical difficulties," but that "the circumstances do not permit the court to relax the rigidity of the rules of a criminal trial." Thereupon, he ordered a directed verdict of not guilty. But the trial had its effect. It focused attention on arrangements that had been made between the Long men and their quieter associates. It established a situation and a series of relationships. And it offered another aspect of the life and deeds of Huey P. Long, the country-boy apostle

of wealth-sharing, who had achieved much of his early renown through his appeal to the rural Puritans against the
city sin.

In the meantime, former Governor Dick had again fallen
sadly afoul of the Federal law, thus completing a circuit of
indictments in all sections. In Southwest Louisiana, jurors
had named him for use of the mails in working a racket
with others to defraud the Highway Commission of $115,000.
With him were charged Abernathy, the former highway
commissioner, and a truck dealer. Through Dick's help,
trucks and other equipment had been purchased from the
dealer without open bidding, for sixty per cent higher than
they might have been obtained through the manufacturer—
an arrangement which the state could have utilized. The
contract involved a state sales tax of $5000, which the High-
way Commission paid out to the boys. Rogge had a description for this part of the project—"Tax paying in reverse!"
A go-between in the matter was a man who was agent in
Louisiana for twenty-five manufacturers of materials and
equipment. He had failed in business in New Orleans, but,
after going to Baton Rouge under Huey, he had moved
into the $100,000 class. Ninety-five per cent of his business,
he conceded, was with the state. He admitted that he shared
an apartment with the highway commissioner for two years.

Governor Dick, face to face with Rogge, admitted that he
had earned about $450,000 in his three years as Governor,
on a $7500-a-year salary. His income-tax returns showed an
increase from $14,000 in 1934 to $282,000 in 1938. Most of
his money came from gas and oil commissions, all honest, he
insisted. But Abernathy and the automobile dealer deserted
Dick, pleaded guilty and testified against him. In this case,
Rogge declared, "they not only stole big but they stole

little. They put cheaper bodies on some of the trucks, and they changed tires and rims to make it a better bargain." The jury was out twenty-three minutes, and Dick received the stiffest sentence of any of the scandal figures to date— ten years. He had made history again, as the first Louisiana Governor to be convicted by a Federal jury.

XVII

THE $500,000 IDEA

"THESE two boys are being pilloried on an arithmetic table!"

With this ringing pronouncement, E. E. Talbot, six-foot-four former Tulane football captain, broke down before twelve bemused Federal jurors at New Orleans. He struggled in his pocket, his eyes blinded by tears, and one of the dozen men handed him a mint. Sucking that, he revived, and went on to tell how Bobby and Norvin had been wronged by a fanatical Federal Government.

O. John Rogge had gone too far. A plebescite in the drawing rooms would have confirmed that statement. Everybody knew Bobby. Everybody knew Norvin. They were certainly, sir, not the type to be indicted. Rogge had reached into the upper classes—no Thelma Ford Smith *nouveaux riches,* but the authentic *haut monde* of New Orleans; and he had lost caste among some of the loudest of the genteel who had hailed him as the deliverer from the Long barbarians.

Bobby Newman and Norvin Trent Harris were the leading bond investment team of the city. They were young men about town; sportsmen, riders, party figures, the desirable type that combined the manners of gentlemen with a booming success in trade—not vulgar trade, but the respectable business of securities. Bobby, though the younger, was the brains of the firm, the senior partner. Norvin was the mixer, the gallant front man, the best bond salesman in Louisiana, and the handsomest, said the ladies. It was a combination that sometimes frightened the opposition. Bobby had a name that meant something in New Orleans; he was the son of a former city commissioner, a financier who had been connected with Huey's monopoly insurance organization, the Union Indemnity group. Norvin had a name that meant something in the South; he was one of the Kentucky Harrises, schoolmate of Randolph Scott of the cinema, a former member of the Royal Canadian Air Force. Randy Scott and Cary Grant were particular friends of Norvin's. They came to New Orleans. Norvin returned the calls and sometimes sold bonds to the better-grade movie investors.

But here were Bobby and Norvin, in December of 1939, with long prison terms threatening them. Rogge had chosen to link them with, of all conceivable individuals, the Abe Shushan person. Norvin, Bobby, Abe and two others (less glamorous respectables, merely prosperous) were charged with a gouge of about a half-million dollars into the funds of the commonwealth. It was high finance that had reached basement level, said the Government, and set out to prove it.

The Levee Board, which looks after the system of dikes that protects New Orleans from the Mississippi, was the beneficiary or the victim of Bobby, Norvin, Abe and the other two boys. The five had entered a quiet little contract with the board to refinance its bonds. They assured the world, now that the contract had come to light, that the board would be the better for the refinancing over a period of long years; that they had taken only a fair return for wise advice and assistance. Rogge called it, with perhaps a deplorable lack of vision, an act of piracy.

Here was one scandal case which had arisen not on the

initiative of official investigators, but through a citizens' movement that forced the matter to general attention, despite vigorous efforts to suppress it, and later resulted in governmental action.

The Bureau of Governmental Research of New Orleans was a private agency to which the machine's state and city officials had never taken a liking. It was primarily responsible for a series of unpleasant events that had culminated with Bobby's and Norvin's debut in their new rôles. The bureau had an evil-minded young executive, Sherman S. Sheppard, who, like Rogge, held the sometimes unpopular concept that public finances call for public honesty. For nearly a full year, in 1938 and 1939, he had annoyed Bobby and Norvin with hornetlike questioning, which a Newman and a Harris would ordinarily never have brooked. He suggested that Bobby and Norvin would want, of course, to clear up this inference, clarify that impression which the face of the record indicated. Bobby and Norvin looked down their noses, frowned, gave curt answers, which gave Mr. Sheppard the answers that he needed. But finally Bobby and Norvin reached the point at which they would talk no more. The bureau was satisfied that it had gone as far as it could, but that it had put its finger on the heart of the matter. It wrote the new chairman of the Levee Board that "There is every evidence that the contract was against the public interest, improperly interpreted as to the method of computing compensation to the company, and grossly wasteful of public funds." It urged the board to sue Bobby and Norvin, as "an inescapable moral and public obligation" to get back a large share of the money.

New Orleans and the state, their taste for scandal well whetted, pricked up their ears. It was the first time many had heard of this little item. The name "Levee Board" was enough to make some curious. The new chairman of the board, agitated, called an emergency meeting and invited Bobby and Norvin to attend. Bobby and Norvin accepted, and the chairman asked them bluntly if anyone else had shared in the payments. Bobby was seemingly as upset as he was hurt at this suspicion: "I will say that at no time has any state or public official received any benefit from this account." The chairman was not satisfied: "What the board is interested in, is if Newman and Harris company acted solely for itself, or as the head of a syndicate . . . Will you give us the names of others?" Bobby replied: "We will give you all pertinent information, and answer everything to the satisfaction of the board." The chairman persisted: "There's only one answer satisfactory to the board . . ." Bobby interrupted: "We would rather not answer verbally, because of the possibility of misinterpretation. But we will give your answer in writing . . ."

However, Bobby and Norvin never disclosed their other partners to the public, orally or in writing. They were ready, at first, to sit down and talk about the matter with the new Levee Board; and a session or two was called. But these broke up without result. Bobby and Norvin imported Eastern financial and legal experts for advice as it became clear that something was about to happen. The board retained a special attorney to file civil suit. Abe Shushan, because of general reports on the subject, was "earnestly" requested by the agency which had not long ago showered honors upon him as president, to attend a meeting and discuss the matter with it. Abe did not bother to answer. Then Rogge and the grand jury cracked down.

For days, the five boys now followed Rogge's presentation. First came the records of the Levee Board, telling of a meeting in July of 1936, two months after Dick became Governor. Bobby appeared with a proposal, "in the nature of a plan or an idea, of great benefit and value to the board." Because of its special aspect, Bobby's firm did not "want to leave it open for public inspection," and so Bobby asked that matters be kept confidential. It was a project "so important" that Bobby did not wish the board to act without approval of Governor Leche, and he had "taken the liberty of submitting it to the Governor." The usual public board might have felt resentment, or wonder, that an outsider—even a Bobby—should have gone first to the chief executive with a matter that involved it so vitally. But not the Levee Board.

The plan was this: Newman, Harris and Company would study all of the board's bonds, and would bring out substitute issues for whichever it thought advisable, seeking lower rates and shorter terms of years. The firm would get nothing unless the board got something. In that case, it would receive twenty-five per cent of "savings and gains." To fulfill legal requirements, Newman, Harris and Company would agree not to bid for the bonds. But this would not be known to the other bond houses; and the prospect of this extra competition from Bobby and Norvin would help the board get better prices.

At that first meeting, J. Andy Thomas, then the chairman pro tempore, observed that he had been called by Governor Dick about the proposition. Governor Dick thought well of it; it would be all right for the board to enter it. A few questions were raised. Had there ever been such a plan, to anybody's recollection, one member wanted to know? The answer was in the negative. The board's attorney considered the contract a proper one. Andy Thomas eventually expressed the view that the board had "everything to gain and nothing to lose."

Herbert W. Waguespack, chairman of the board's finance committee, was a quick advocate. The board, he noted, had been criticized for its high bond rates. It needed the advice of trained men; here was its chance. It was Mr. Waguespack who put the motion, and the idea was approved at the original meeting. No information was asked, none provided, as to the exact manner in which Bobby and Norvin were to compute their profits.

Three months later, Bobby and Norvin sent a letter as they prepared to float the first new bond issue. They let the board know that they expected to get their twenty-five per cent in cash as each issue appeared, and that they expected it on the basis of all future interest savings to the board, in whatever year those would occur. The board did not meet on this occasion; a secretary read or briefed the subject by telephone, and again no questions were brought up.

During the next year or so, millions in bonds were refinanced, in three issues. Bobby and Norvin estimated a saving of $2,000,000 to the board, of which Bobby and Norvin received a gross of about $500,000. Whenever the matter came up at board meetings, Finance Chairman Waguespack took a leading part in the discussions, usually presenting the motion to approve the successive steps. Bobby and Norvin went to each of the bond sales with bid blanks and their own checks in hand, waving them airily, looking on with the sharp interest of a prospective bidder. They did not, however, actually compete.

The contract had expired and two years had passed. Then, in the terrible fall and winter of 1939, the Bureau of Governmental Research had disclosed the results of its curiosity in the proceedings, and Rogge and the grand jury had dug back. First of all, Rogge was questioning the contract and the way Bobby and Norvin received their share of the money. As it turned out, the Rogge men claimed, the board obtained practically nothing, in fact may have lost money from Bobby's and Norvin's dealings with it. Critics estimated that the boys had taken just about every penny of the board's gains over the years.

The board's "true savings" were described as far less than the $2,000,000 set forth—actually somewhere between $550,-000 and $700,000. Bobby and Norvin might properly have claimed a percentage for reduction of the interest rates on the bonds, it was conceded. But they had also taken twenty-five per cent for everything that the board might receive by the process of shortening the maturities. As the Bureau of Governmental Research declared, the reduction in interest rates called for knowledge of the market and skill in investment. But the shortening of the terms of the bonds "required no special skill or even a favorable market. All that was necessary was an earlier use of public money for the retirement of the bonds." By the simple procedure of speeding up the rate at which the Levee Board was putting out its money, Bobby and Norvin had received the biggest part of their twenty-five per cent.

Furthermore, it was declared, the boys had worked a game on the state by the requirement that they take cash while the board received its returns over the life period of the bonds, forty years ahead. This arrangement, it was contended by the Government and by the bureau, failed to take into consideration the principle of "present worth." In the bureau's words: "A dollar on hand now is worth much more in 1939 than the promise of a dollar in 1950 or 1960. Conversely, a dollar to be received in later decades has a

411

present value of much less than one dollar." If a man were pledged a dollar in 1960, he should be prepared to take less than that today. He would have the use of the funds for the intervening years, and might with investment run the amount up to $2 in that time.

Thus, it was contended, when Bobby and Norvin received their $500,000 in cash and at once, they took all of the board's real profit.

The contract, declared the Bureau of Governmental Research, was "remarkable in its general terms and its vagueness on vital points." No definition was attempted of "the most vital point of all," the question of "savings and gains." Only three months later had that come forth. Bobby and Norvin were given powers to determine the dates for the issues, the terms, interest rates and other aspects of the matter, allowed to "write their own ticket . . . virtually to dictate the terms of the bonds." If the company recommended a refunding operation but the board did not agree to it, Bobby and Norvin would get twenty-five per cent of what might have been "saved" had the new bonds been floated!

As to the board's sprint-speed action in the matter, the bureau commented: "It is almost inconceivable that any public board could accept so important, far-reaching a contract with the slight group consideration noted in its minutes."

Also, Government witnesses declared that it would be 1962 before the board might find its finances improved, as a result of the firm's consumption of its cash on hand. The reduction in lifetime of the bonds had been achieved largely by providing much heavier retirement payments in the first few years. And that provision, as a matter of fact, was responsible for an immediate condition of near-havoc in the board's finances. Since the boys' operations, the board had faced deficits of $500,000 in one year and $375,000 in another, and had been forced to raise its tax rate to the legal limit. Even with this extra money, the board faced a major financial crisis in 1940-41.

Thrusting deeper, Rogge charged that the board could have received exactly the same assistance and advice, free of charge, from any bond house or bond houses in the city. Considering everything, what fee did he consider a fair one? Rogge asked his expert. "Two per cent."

Then Rogge leaped with joy to the heart of his subject—what had happened once the money reached Bobby and Norvin. About $100,000 went for expenses, forfeits and refunds, and the rest in this fashion: a full third, $132,000, to Abraham L. Shushan; $99,000 each, or twenty-five per cent each, to Bobby and Norvin; $46,000 to Herbert Waguespack, chairman of the finance committee of the Levee Board, and $19,000 to one Henry Miller, an accountant friend of Waguespack. An additional $12,000—and here the friends of Bobby and Norvin had their worst start—went from Bobby and Norvin to an employee of the Levee Board, to act as a "spy and informer" for the well-bred boys, to tip them off about the board's business. This man had since died, but, said Rogge, Bobby and Norvin had admitted employing him.

Mr. Waguespack came of a family distinguished in earlier Louisiana history. His grandfather had been a Supreme Court Justice, his father a United States Attorney. Herbert was an attorney who had been named to the Levee Board under the earlier phases of the dictatorship. Among his contributions to the board's affairs had been that of making the motion which christened the municipal airport with the lustrous name of Shushan. Miller was a minor pillar of New Orleans society, past president of the American Certified

413

Public Accountants' Society, past president of the state society, former president of the Young Men's Business Club, member of the Loyola University athletic council and member of the Loyola accounting faculty.

Mr. Waguespack, sworn to look after the board's interest and named by fellow members particularly to watch the finances, had been bribed to betray it and the state, said Rogge. Bobby and Norvin had entered a backstairs partnership with Shushan, under a "fraudulent, fictitious and false" scheme. Miller, like Emory Adams or Louie LeSage of the hotel double dip, was the "little cover-up man," used to hide the payments to Waguespack. Bobby and Norvin, though large men in their own right, had served partly to cover up Abe's part. (Had Abe's presence been sniffed at any point about the premises, everybody would have been sure something was wrong.) Bobby and Norvin had received all the money. Then they had split to Abe, who split to Miller, who split to Waguespack. As Rogge outlined it, it was an exercise in Art and in Craft.

To hide Abe's connections, and those of Waguespack and "Little" Miller, precautions had been elaboration itself. The New Orleans banks were to be used as little as possible. Eventual payments to the trio were generally by cashier's checks or by cash, often far outside the state. Sometimes the method was so roundabout as to arouse questions among the bankers, and had to be revised. Almost always Waguespack, the Levee Board member, received cash from Miller, whose payments by Newman, Harris were usually difficult to trace —and whose original source of payment, in turn (the Levee Board), was even more difficult to find. Most important, the checks were taken on a sightseeing trip around the country.

One example told the story. The Levee Board instructed

the successful bond firms to split their payments into two parts, one of which represented Bobby's and Norvin's twenty-five per cent of all future interest reductions, although, of course, outside companies could not have known for what purpose this check to the Levee Board's account was intended. Receiving the 25-per-cent check, the board then indorsed it to Newman, Harris and Company, and turned it over to Bobby and Norvin. Thus there was nothing readily available in the board's accounts to show that Bobby and Norvin had received the check. In this case the amount was for $235,000. Bobby and Norvin did not cash it in New Orleans; they mailed it to a New York bank and requested that institution to issue two checks against the larger one, $36,000 to Miller and $73,000 to Shushan. The bank declined, "for lack of identification and authority." Bobby and Norvin advised it to send the $235,000 check, instead, to a bank in Chicago. Chicago accepted what New York refused. Bobby and Norvin then advised the Chicago bank that they wished to withdraw $110,000 from the account—the total of the amounts that were now desired for Shushan and Miller. A check for $110,000 was accordingly sent from Chicago to New York—to yet another institution—and then to the institution that had first turned down the boys. Out of the $110,000, Bobby and Norvin now withdrew two checks, one for Shushan, the other for Miller.

To clinch his point, Rogge thrust several checks at a witness: "Is there anything to show that they came from Newman and Harris to Shushan?" "No."

Into the record Rogge introduced a telegram to Governor Dick Leche, from the records of Huey's "state bond and tax board." It declared: "PLEASE HAVE SENT RESOLUTION CONCERNING STATE BOND AND TAX BOARD AT ONCE. THANKS. ABE."

With a glance of scorn at the uncouth Middle-Westerner, the defense told its story, a story of the conception, birth, adolescence and maturity of an idea—a legitimate brain child but one with many fathers, product of a cross-fertilizing process to which Abe, Bobby, Norvin, Herbert Waguespack and Henry Miller contributed. Modestly, each gave the others credit for part parentage.

Miller the accountant explained that he was the first man on the scene. He received what might be termed the original mood from yet another. A fellow accountant of another city had suggested to him, back in 1935, that perhaps the Dock Board's bonds, or those of some other Louisiana agency, could be refinanced in an improved market. Nothing came of this, but the notion stuck in Miller's mind. At the Association of Commerce and other places about town, he heard that the Levee Board's interest rates were very high. Why not try out something there? He added two modifications of his own. The first was a guaranty of one per cent to the board, in the event that the new premium did not exceed the redemption premium. The second was the 25-per-cent contingent fee.

Miller had called on Herbert Waguespack, his "personal attorney," luncheon partner and former schoolmate. Yes, he knew that Herbert was on the board, but he did not approach him as a board member; he wanted to know if the project were legal. Waguespack mulled over the idea, then informed him that it was a "novel one" in several respects but would be legal if touched up here and there. Then came Waguespack's touchups. A firm hired on a contingent basis could not properly bid on refunded issues, but would have to content itself with profits obtained through the board's savings. Miller liked Waguespack's refinements, and a financial partnership was entered—Waguespack seventy per cent,

Miller thirty. Why did Waguespack take the larger share when the plan was Miller's? Oh, that was the "usual arrangement" when lawyers and accountants entered agreements. It was the basis on which the two friends usually worked; and Waguespack, being somewhat better off, was to take seventy per cent of the liabilities, if any. The collaboration had entered a broader phase than that of legal guidance from Waguespack.

Did Miller ask Waguespack if Waguespack had a right to take part? Yes. Waguespack took down a Louisiana law book and cited a provision prohibiting members from maintaining an interest in levee building; that was the only restriction. Miller had a pertinent observation: "In fact, it is common knowledge in Louisiana that members of public boards who serve without compensation usually expect and do usually receive a certain amount of business from their boards to compensate them for their loss of time." Rogge replied: "I suggest that the fact that a public servant serves without pay does not give him the right to loot the public purse."

Somewhere in these preliminary mullings, Miller gave up his thought of handling the matter himself. He decided that he needed a financial angel. Who more natural a prospect than Abe Shushan, a man of wealth, as who did not know; and, though retired from the board, "yet quite familiar with Levee Board financial transactions and bond issues"? So Miller called on Abe.

Despite his familiarity with such matters, Abe had never had an idea of this kind. He liked it thoroughly, so thoroughly that he took it from Miller, in toto. And now Abe made an addition of his own: It would be much better to bring an established bond house into the deal. Let Miller stand aside. Abe would handle everything with the bond

417

company, and share the expenses with it. What would Miller get? One-third of what Abe received, after Abe split with the bond house. Thus Miller, first father of the idea, was to take a sixth of what it produced, and then he was to give the larger part of his sixth to Waguespack, under his earlier, separate agreement. It seemed less than a real parent might expect, when his child was grown to manhood. But Miller had no regret at this treatment by fate and Shushan. He "simply sold his idea."

Eventually Abe had Bobby and Norvin in, and the chain was complete: Levee Board to Bobby and Norvin. Bobby and Norvin to Abe. Abe to Miller. Miller to Waguespack. But here was an important point or two: Miller at no time told Abe that Waguespack was Miller's partner. Yes, he knew that Abe knew Waguespack, had served with him on the board, had a mutual interest in its affairs. But somehow the matter had never come up. And Bobby and Norvin, though they dealt oftener with Waguespack than with anyone else in the matter, had no knowledge whatever that Waguespack was getting a piece of what they earned in the transaction with which all were associated.

Waguespack, the finance chairman and partner to Miller, took up the saga. At first, when Miller came to him, he thought the idea illegal; but then he recalled that bond attorneys had only recently ruled against a somewhat related proposal by another firm, declaring that if it bid on the bonds the firm would have an unfair margin. It was then that he proposed his little thought—that the firm refrain from bidding. Rogge pounded a question at him: As a matter of fact, hadn't he himself called Miller to suggest the whole thing, telling him about that previous proposal and suggesting a modification by which Miller might get a contract in this way? He had not, said Waguespack, although he might have mentioned the other matter, of course.

Waguespack was sure that he had a legal right not only to maintain an interest in the financing, but also to vote on the contract. If he was so clear about it, why did he keep his connection secret from Shushan? "No lawyer goes about disclosing his clients." Did he send Miller to Shushan? He did not; he left everything to Miller. Yes, he had known Shushan had an interest, through Miller. Yes, he may have seen Shushan from time to time, but he had not brought up the matter. Did Waguespack tell the other board members of his own interest in the deal? No. Why not? They were his friends, and he "wanted them to consider the proposition on its own merits." Otherwise, they might have been inclined to favor it unduly. Yes, he saw Bobby and Norvin often during the refinancing, called at their offices in fact. But he did not mention his financial interest in their contract.

Waguespack admitted having made a trip to New York with Miller, when one of the largest of the checks arrived. Miller cashed it there and paid Waguespack his part in cash. But no, that was not the reason for the trip. They had gone to Washington on income-tax matters, and had continued on to New York only because they had other work there. The cashing of the check was purely incidental, purely coincidental. Why payment in cash? That was his usual way; he had always liked to keep his money in safety deposit boxes. Also, he and Miller wanted to make sure that the bankers and other brokers did not learn of the Newman-Harris contract. Mr. Waguespack was ingratiating, plausible, all-reasonable.

Abe was a witness who talked back, who informed Attorney Viosca that he had been asked the same questions before, told him that some of them were not as important as

Viosca thought. Abe had "not the slightest reason to believe that Waguespack had any connection." He did not bring any influence on Waguespack; no, sir. Newman and Harris had asked that he "talk to" members of the board, but he had told them "definitely" that he would not. The picture of a Newman and a Harris asking a Shushan to do something unethical, and receiving a rejection from Abe, was an amusing one; and New Orleans grinned in appreciation.

As to that telegram to Leche, Abe admitted sending it. Bobby had mentioned a resolution that required approval by the State Bond and Tax Board, of which the Governor was a member, and had asked Abe to "see if he could get it." That was all. He did not urge Leche to bring pressure for the project; he did not even see Leche about it. Before Leche's election, he and Leche had been "very intimate friends," Abe admitted. "But afterward, I didn't see as much of him as you did here, Mr. Viosca." "Then you never talked with him about the deal?" "No, I never saw him then."

"Wasn't he surprised to get a telegram from you, when you hadn't seen him in so long, or discussed the matter with him?" "No, he never once mentioned the telegram."

"Oh, so you did see him since then?" "Yes, but it was afterward."

Abe, like so many others in these matters, was surprised at the size of his profit. "I had no idea it would be so large. . . ." Why was his name left out of everything, the contract with the board included? "I was a silent partner. There was nothing unusual in that." Now as to the payment of $12,000 to the spy . . . Abe's attitude here was not one of lofty moral values, as it had been in the case of the proposed pressure upon the board. Bobby and Norvin had asked him to "suggest someone" who could provide information about bond dealers who called at the board offices. Could not the secretary have given this information, if it were legitimate, to a firm which had a contract? The information, Abe replied, was used only to "protect the board's interests." But would the secretary not have been in a better position to provide it than an informer? Abe was annoyed. "You are making a tremendous thing out of this matter, when there was really nothing to it. I don't think Newman and Harris should have been ashamed of the employment." Abe, however, had to admit that he did not like the amount —not at all. It had cut down his share in the profits. It was too much to pay.

Last came Bobby. As with LeSage in the hotel double dip, the defense did not risk one of the defendants. The haggard Norvin Harris had difficulty in restraining himself as the case neared its climax. Abe cried quietly as Bobby told his tale. Bobby and Norvin had been at lunch at New Orleans' leading oyster bar when Abe went to their table. He could put them next to some good bond business, if they would give him his share. A few letters were exchanged, but only later did Abe tell of the unique part of the idea, which "made it legal"; i.e., that the two boys could not bid. Why was Abe taken in as a full partner? Would the firm not have preferred to assume the full financing, for a fuller share in the profits? And just what did Abe do in the scheme for his fifty per cent? Bobby informed the Government that it was the custom for bonding organizations to have others participate in profits and losses; even the Chase National did that. Shushan's part was the idea, which he passed on. Had the firm not thought it worth something, Abe would not have received a penny.

But Bobby gave Abe the lie as regarded one aspect of the subject. Bobby had not asked Abe to talk with the board

members. "I certainly don't recollect that." As to that telegram to Leche, Bobby "may have told Mr. Shushan about it,
complaining of the delay in getting a copy." But, like Abe,
Bobby wanted it known that this was one of those "unim-
portant details." The Government seemed disturbed over
routine practices among business men.

Differing again with Abe, he had to admit that he had "always been ashamed" of his employment of the spy. Originally no payment had been agreed upon, but the man had insisted that a large amount was due him. "It wasn't a particularly pleasant conversation," although Bobby did not re-
recall that the man made "threats of exposure." When Abe
heard of the payment, he "kicked like the bloody mischief,"
but finally agreed to it.

Bobby brought a towering chart into court, took a ruler
and lectured the jury. In kindly fashion, the rich man's son
who had made good explained to the clerks and petty merchants that he realized the matter was complicated, but
would do his best to make it clear for them. "There is no
magic here." He had had the board's best interest in mind
at all times. The firm, as a matter of fact, could have refunded all of the board's bonds at once and advanced the
maturity date of each and every one, under its contract, if
it wished. (Rogge had brought out this same fact as an
argument that the contract was an imposition which gave
Bobby and Norvin limitless powers.) The Government's
"present-worth theory" was a professor's concept; that was
all, Bobby insisted.

The final moments were earnest, stormy, impassioned. Talbot, Bobby's and Norvin's attorney, put his hands on the
jury rail and appealed: "These boys simply did a good job,
fairly, honestly, a legal, upright business proposition, obtained without misrepresentation and executed without

fraud. Young men in their enthusiasm make mistakes. All of us would like to do differently in almost every instance." The matter of the spy was "a mistake in judgment, not a subject of criminal intent . . . absolutely disjointed, disconnected with the case." Rogge had termed the one per cent guaranty "cheap window dressing." Mr. Talbot rose to his full height: "This may be cheap window dressing to Mr. Rogge, the New Deal representative sent down from Washington, where they throw millions away . . ." And he wanted "Hawkshaw Rogge, the Great Detective, to know that it is not a crime to be a former member of the Levee Board."

Waguespack's attorney termed his client's opinion as to the legality of his participation, "if a mistake, then one of judgment, not of heart." Waguespack was a "small-town lawyer; even the head of the legal department of the United States makes mistakes." Hugh Wilkinson of the tax racket inquiries appeared on behalf of Abe Shushan, as he had in Abe's previous trial in 1935. "This indictment was born of ulterior motives, conceived in hypocrisy—nothing but conjecture, innuendo and inference drawn upon inference." He asked: "Are you going to send these men to prison on the suspicions of Mr. Rogge?" He noted, in closing, that the Government had failed to call Leche.

Rogge, towering, frowning, gave the jury a theme to which he recurred repeatedly: "This was a raid, gentleman—a raid, put over as an inside job, made possible by bribery." He asked the jurors to go over their own business experiences: "Did you ever hear of so many 'silent partners'? Shushan was one. Waguespack was another. They say Shushan didn't know of Waguespack's part, and Newman and Harris didn't know of it either. The fact was that all five got together and concocted this scheme, with go-between and payoff men.

They didn't have the gall to put all of it in one document; they didn't dare to disclose until later the way the fee was to be computed. Newman and Harris should have given the advice free, and bid with others for the business. But they wanted a sharp contract, and they got it." Regarding Leche, "Somebody approached him and asked him to recommend the project. There's no question about that. It must have been either Shushan or Newman, either one. The Government didn't call Leche deliberately. I don't care what Leche said. He'd get up and say that . . ." The defense objections drowned this out. But Rogge managed to note that the defense had not called Leche either, when it might have used him in an attempt to refute the Government's claims. Viosca, closing, asked a question: "Gentlemen, how can you possibly believe them?"

The jury could not. Each was found guilty, and each received a sentence of two and a half years. Colonel Abe, who, like Colonel Seymour Weiss, "couldn't be caught," was added to the Government's list. The man who had escaped once was caught the second time. And Bobby and Norvin were to become the first social members of the parade of convicted.

The Louisiana art of bilking a public agency reached its full fruition with this case. There probably has never been a steal like it in American financial-political history. It was a theft against the future—forty years to come. The gougers had dredged up funds that had not been there, then quietly shoveled them away for their own. The incident is the technical guide par excellence for those who desire lessons in the combination of a dictatorship's protection with the purposes of business favoritism. Huey had made his contribution to the methodology of undermining democratic forms. Here

424

his followers demonstrated how to cash in most effectively.

The Levee Board gouge would have been impossible had not the dictatorship of Huey prepared the way, and the milder continuation of that dictatorship provided its co-operation. The State Bond and Tax Board, the agency which gave its approval, was created under Huey, its records kept secret on orders of Huey. And under the dictatorship, a measure was adopted to permit the Levee Board to refund its bonds "for economy purposes."

The case had repercussions. The Louisiana State University board disclosed that Abe, whose business was dry-goods, had received contracts with the college as a "supply agent" for firms that handled materials in much different classifications. It cancelled one which had been entered under Jingle Money Smith, on the grounds that full notice had not been given, that open bidding had not been followed, and that the university would have paid considerably less had Abe not been favored. In another trial it was brought out that Abe represented an equipment company which had done business with the university. Another firm sued the Charity Hospital board to prevent execution of a contract for sterilizer equipment. It declared that Abe was the agent in this instance, too; that his firm had submitted an illegal bid which did not meet requirements, and that at one point the board had excluded it but admitted Abe's organization to a conference that was followed by the award-ing of the work.

The municipal airport was de-named. Abe had often been quoted as boasting that it would cost $50,000 to $100,000 to take the Shushan tokens off the place. He had immortalized himself in steel, concrete, granite, chromium, tin, rubber and practically every other material available in the South. Where the space was too small for the name, Abe had used his initial. There were "S's" on all doors, including the lavatory, on lamp posts, in letters in the terrazzo floors, on the sides of buildings, in the pavement surrounding the structures, and in the floral patterns. From the air, passengers might appreciate that this was Shushan Airport before they realized they were in New Orleans.

One board member shook his head: "We haven't the kind of money it would take to get Abe off everything." As a result, Abe was removed only in part, as finances made possible. In late 1940, he was still being chipped off, ground, pried and pulled out. Some asserted that it might have been better to tear the airport down and start from scratch. A patriotic organization adopted a resolution suggesting that the simplest plan would be to leave the "S's" and retitle the place after some historical character whose name began with that letter. It was hardly likely that such a man would be indicted at this late date.

XVIII

CAMPAIGN À LA MARDI GRAS

Louisianians have learned to take their politics like their liquor; with a strong stomach for the raw stuff, and with infinite zest and curiosity for bizarre combinations. Since the first day on which Kingfish Huey splashed about, the state's campaigns have been things apart: rowdy, violent, holding to no rules of reticence, taste or regard for strict truth.

But the hostilities of 1939-40, as they approached their conclusion, were unparalleled even for Louisiana: an amalgam of deceit, garish abuse and helter-skelter comedy. It was not only the loudest and the funniest, but also the longest campaign in the state's history. It began when James Monroe Smith and Richard W. Leche left office simultaneously, and it continued a month longer than scheduled—or eight months over all.

The frolic started with masquerades, the tossing of tomatoes, the showering of candidates with handfuls of aluminum sales-tax tokens. (Louisianians called the tokens "monkey money" or "Leche money.") It reached a climax with gun threats and gun play, the raising of the race issue against the Federal Government, the beating of women as well as men at the polls. From start to end, the campaign was a procession of rough-and-tumble japes. Louisiana could laugh, though a significant era in American political history hung in the balance. An unexpected flesh wound in the

427

derrière of a savior is just as hilarious as the knifing of a villain, isn't it?

None of the candidates chose issues. These were settled for them, out of hand, by the rushing events of that sweating summer and harassed fall. The issues were, in more or less related combination, the witches' brew of corruptions, their depth and scope, with especial reference to the remaining figures of the Long machine, to Huey Long himself, to Bob Maestri and his rôle in the state's past, present and future; the relation of Earl Long to Former Governor Dick, to Huey and to Maestri; and the raging question as to whether any one or all of the candidates was, or had been, or might be expected to show himself to be, a thief. At one period, the essential qualification was an ability to demonstrate that the aspirant had not been indicted and seemed not likely to be. One or two of the major candidates took the rostrum on several occasions in a fret that the next courier might bring word that a grand jury had done what it threatened. The dictatorship, taking no chances, bridged over a dangerous phase by qualifying what amounted to a "second team," a full additional set of candidates. It would not let Rogge and Murphy catch it without reserve material.

For a time, it appeared that "every man a candidate" would be the order of the campaign. Sixteen or more announced. One of the aspirants was an automobile salesman who paraded inside a sandwich sign, and, to emphasize that he would clean up the state, carried a broom. Another leaped up on a platform to disclose his candidacy, then and there, as John P. (Huey P. Long) Short. Thus he wrote it; thus it must be written. He had a plan to keep governors honest: a fifty per cent pension for any chief executive who managed to finish his term without arrest or impeachment. Others proposed handsome annuities as inducements to keep

428

a governor on the right track. One suggested confiscation of the homes of Former Governor Dick, Big George Caldwell and Honest Abe Shushan, gold fixtures, Russian sheep and all, and their conversion into state parks with children's homes in the main residences and out-sized barns.

The number who would be Governor slowly dwindled to seven: Earl Long, Sam Jones, the attorney who had been proposed as a "Seabury investigator"; Jimmy Noe, the oil and gas man; James Morrison, attorney-organizer for the strawberry farmers; A. P. Tugwell, the state treasurer; Vincent Moseley, a Harvard graduate and World War aviator, who did not hope to win but ran because he liked to use pins to pop stuffed shirts; and, most exotic of all, "Couzain Dud" LeBlanc, South Louisiana mercurio-politico, once defeated by O. K. Allen for Governor, who competed again because he had "decided that the state needs an honest man and I must make the sacrifice." In later stages, "Couzain Dud" proposed that he be taken on as Jones' lieutenant-governor, so that he could "watch" Jones if elected. Otherwise, he threatened to defeat him. But he eventually went over to Jones. Tugwell, after some early yeoman's work against the machine, ran only for re-election as treasurer. That left five, who stuck to the unhappy final moments.

All of the other four were against Earl Long. But each, too, was against each of the others. It was a battle royal, no holds barred; the only rule, no hitting below the groin.

Earl's position was one of towering difficulties. He could not condone the boys about Former Governor Dick; but neither could he attack them too strongly, because he would be striking at some of his important backers. His definitive word on Leche came when he asked an audience how many had voted for Dick four years earlier. Nearly all hands went up. "You see," said Earl. "You're just as much to blame as I

am." Always, he insisted that he had had no part in the corruptions, that a lieutenant-governor was practically as important as the silver figure on a radiator cap. To which an
opponent replied: "Earl was either aware of what was going
on, and therefore part of it—or he was too stupid to know
about it, and too stupid to be Governor." At one point, Earl
declared that he was no fool, that he could have had his, were
he not made of finer stuff. The opposition had a field day
over that. So he had known, had he?

John Chase the cartoonist showed a fly-specked burlesque
hall. On the stage, singing close harmony, were eight or nine
mountainous knocked-about alley yeggs, dressed in angels'
garb, wearing patches—"double dips," "hot oil," "L.S.U.
chiseling," "dee ducts." At the piano sat Professor Earl.
Signs were plastered about: "Vote For Honest Earl; He Ain't
Like Us Burglars." And Earl, his hands busy at the keys,
told the reader: "I just work here. I eat out." In point of
fact, nothing of a criminal nature was ever discovered against
Earl Long during the scandal period. Grand juries investigated his affairs on many occasions; angrily, he cried that
"they'd of indicted me if I'd spit on the sidewalk." The
opposition sometimes granted that Earl had been kept to the
side by the boys when they thronged about the trough. "You
didn't have a chance to take anything," Noe once jibed at
Earl. "You were just a little fellow."

The issue of Huey and Earl, which had lost the machine
thousands of votes even in the Leche landslide, was an ever
more irksome one. Earl told with tears of his loving-though-
vitriolic relations with Brother. His spat with Huey was
something he would always regret. "I didn't agree with Huey
on everything," he told one audience. From the crowd, a
little weather-beaten wealth-sharer snapped: "Well, we did."
It spoiled the evening.

430

Nevertheless, said Earl, he was now ready to carry on for Huey, continuing the benefits, extending them here and there; and he made remarks that indicated an intention to revive share-the-wealth. This was not calculated to sit well with Washington, which did not like the name of Long in any event. To Earl's remarks on the subject Tugwell cried: "Earl Long posing as a leader of the Huey Long people! That's like Judas Iscariot running on the platform of Jesus Christ." Sam Jones declared: "Earl says he believes in the principles of Huey Long and O. K. Allen, but both of them said he wasn't fit even to be lieutenant-governor."

Noe could declare that he had told Louisiana so, years before, predicting everything that had happened. He had discerned the corruption at its head and had offered measures to prevent it, he said, by repealing many of the dictatorship laws. At the same time, he was still "one hundred per cent for Huey," and while he attacked Earl, Dick, Abe and Bob, he told his audiences: "I wish poor old Huey were here tonight to see this crowd." The Louisiana Association for Clean Government declared: "The people of Louisiana want to destroy the machine. Jimmy Noe wants to take it over and run it for himself. That's the difference."

Morrison was pictured by the *Progress* as "The Monkey Man, Bull Ape of the Jungle," who hung by his tail from a tree and gave interviews through an interpreter. LeBlanc was painted as a frantic fellow who operated an alleged "coffin club" for Negroes; who was, in the cartoons, forever the object of a chase by two hungry squirrels. Moseley, "a Harvard-bred socialite," was "a voice in the woods, whose actual existence has not yet been proved"; he was drawn as a little man the size of a half-used lead pencil. Tugwell, who had withdrawn for Governor, then announced again, then withdrawn, was a tousle-haired Louisiana version of an In-

431

dian fakir, in loin cloth, twisted like a rope, and telling his listeners that he "didn't know whether he's coming or going."

Noe needed, and received, special attention from the machine men. For two years, he had gone about the state, recognized by many as the leading oppositionist. About him he had gathered many of the boiling-point Huey advocates. To the *Progress* he was a brother who had turned on his family, a man without a political country. "Huey's ghost" pointed a finger of guilt at the quivering Noe in a cartoon that showed Jimmy hobnobbing with one of Huey's enemies. Earl declared that Noe carried an onion to help him cry about Huey; Noe, he insisted, had known Huey only a few years. He, Earl, had known Huey all his life.

Noe had the ill luck to figure in an indictment during the campaign, though he was not charged. Two conservation employees were accused of accepting bribes from two firms, in one of which Noe was a partner. The offense was approval of illegal "acidizing" of wells, to increase the flow—a practice which may be harmful to sound conservation, but unobjectionable if controlled. The two men charged that Noe had "squealed to save his own skin," had gone to the grand jury with the story to escape action, after having induced them to take bribes. Noe replied that the payments were not bribes, but shakedowns. Here was meat for the *Progress*, which chewed it for the rest of the campaign. Noe was pictured as a fat mother, carrying one baby, "Shakedown," showering attention on him, while a twin, "Bribe," sought vainly to rejoin the family after having been locked out. Noe was seen tossing "Bribe" out of a balloon or seeking to drown him, but always denying the relationship; yet "Bribe" always lived and pursued. An onlooker in one cartoon commented: "It seems sort of a miracle for a woman to have twins and be the mother of only one." A friend replied: "The grand jury has decided it is quite possible."

But for Jones the organization saved its best. Earl predicted the candidacy in advance, telling of a meeting of "the lords of the state, the great interests, getting behind a corporation lawyer, one of their kind, to break down what Huey has done." The *Progress* depicted a gathering of monocled, be-spatted nincompoops, "the fancy pants gang." Convening in an exclusive Vieux Carré restaurant, these sad creatures ate "nightingales' tongues, shrimp a la oulala and filet de truite a la Polish Corridor." It was a common-folks' cartoon, and a highly effective one.

Jones was a successful small city lawyer. Like Earl and Huey, he had left the rural areas as a younger man. Now, at forty-two, he was a partner in one of the best-known firms of Southwest Louisiana, a former state Legion president, a quiet, uncomplex fellow who was a moderate liberal. He did not have a third of Huey's color, but in the matter of simple character he was considerably above most of the state's recent governors. He had a good manner; he was an effective speaker; he had strong Legion support; he was not too prominently identified with past oppositionists; he had a record for honesty. The administration was properly disturbed.

A variety of forces united on Jones. Some were what Earl called them in his quieter moments: well-to-do men who did not want to face the problem of another Long, the continuation of a régime that had toned down in some ways, only to become worse in others. Other Jones supporters were business men, small and middlesized, who wanted to end a system of shakedowns, tax racketeering and other abuses. Still others were progressives, seeing in the Long machine a symbol of Fascist methods and aims which held only the prospect of further depredations for Louisiana, perhaps some day of another foray on the national scene. And to Jones' banner went others who were genuinely shocked and scornful of the scandals that had been revealed, who picked him as the man most likely to set up a system that would end these abuses. Some of this group included country elements which had once turned to Huey, but which were now sadly disillusioned by his successors. Three men led the backers who brought Jones into the campaign: a sugar planter, descendant of a former governor; a young attorney, son of a leading corporation lawyer of New Orleans, but a disciple of Thomas Corcoran of the New Deal; and an automobile agent who had ideas about administrative efficiency and a touch of Roosevelt in his philosophy.

At Jones, Earl tossed two deadly charges: he smelled sweet, and he slept in pajamas. "He's High Hat Sam, the High Society Kid, the High-Kicking, High and Mighty Snide Sam, the guy that pumps perfume under his arms," declared Earl and his *Progress,* and then went on to less elegant descriptions. The city slickers of the Boston Club were quoted: "If we can foist him on the people, we'll have twenty more floats for Mardi Gras." Jones' "annual personal budget" of $150,-000 was itemized, "a new suit every week, $100 each, $5200 every year; a new pair of silk B.V.D.s daily, $10 each, $3650 a year (never wears the same drawers twice); heliotrope cigarettes at $25 per carton; a watchman to turn his dogs over in their sleep, $1200 a year." He was "related to Queen Elizabeth and Louie the Fourteenth."

Earl used the same device that Huey had worked against Senator Robinson, when he read from an attorneys' list book of clients. He charged, with eight-column, red-ink banners in the *Progress,* that Jones represented forty-three corporations with three billion dollars in assets. "That makes him

434

more than a triple dipper; words don't go high enough for him." The machine quoted a circular of Huey's: "Be on guard for these corporation rascals, people! They are trying to keep you from having reduced licenses; they are trying to keep you from the right to vote without paying poll taxes. . . . Do not sell to hell. Stand up for right."

During most of the campaign, Jones stepped to the front of the platform with a well-worn felt hat on his head, to show that he was "not the high hat that the 'un-American *Progress*' pictured me." That publication, he said, ran his picture one week with a fake diamond painted into his tie. The next week it was gone. "That gang steals even from photographs." As to corporations, he declared that he had represented farmers and labor groups, corporations of all types and sizes, including one organized by farmers. He "read the record" on the machine in that regard, cited corporation ties of Harvey Peltier, the oil-speculator candidate for lieutenant-governor; highlighted the ever-close relations of railroad presidents and others with Huey and his followers, charged the machine with wholesale frauds in tax exemptions to corporations, assessment reductions and similar favors.

Jones made a distinction between Huey and the Leches, Earl Longs, Maestris and others. As a liberal, he said, he favored homestead exemption, better farm roads, free school books, better hospitals, income taxes, the greater services that Huey Long had given Louisiana. The clock could not be turned back; these were advances in which Louisiana had joined, sometimes led, other American states. But he attacked the dictatorship and its denials of rights, the removal of the checks and balances of the American system. He tilted at the demonstrated corruption of the machine, charged that $75,000,000 to $100,000,000 had been stolen from the state, and pledged his administration to recover every available

435

dollar and "throw every thief in jail." He pointed to closed records and secret audits such as that made into L.S.U.'s affairs under Leche a year before it was revealed; to the hobbling of home rule, the laws that forced acquiescence under the shadow of the lash. Then he offered "benefits" of his own: three-dollar license plates, removal of the sales tax, liberalization of welfare assistance, greater aid to the schools. It was an imposing list.

Earl Long charged that Jones was "fooling people by saying he'll give all those things when he knows he can't. He's nothing but a demagogue." Here was a curious charge from a Long. Here, too, was another sign of the times. A drop from the levels of public services established by Huey Long will be difficult for some time at least in Louisiana. No candidate can promise much less, with hope of election. No administration can provide much less, if it has hope of its own future.

Jones presented, too, a number of specific platforms which proved highly popular to Louisiana: a complete reorganization of the state governmental structure, something which Huey had promised twelve years earlier; a civil service system, a new financial accounting so that the public would have full information for the first time on state finances; reformed election laws; opening of the closed payrolls; an end to the dee ducts; reform of the state grand jury system; removal of the Governor's power over the militia.

Though Earl Long's energies were concerned largely with defense of his friends and former friends, he offered benefits of his own. Huey's homestead law called for tax exemption on individual homes up to a $2000 figure. The treasury had never been able to provide more than $1000 exemption. Earl looked into the state books and announced that he would raise it to $2000. ("The first Governor to make good a campaign pledge before the election," sighed the *Progress*.) The opposition declared that the exemption was governed by statutory regulations; that sufficient funds had accumulated to make possible the increase, no matter who was Governor. Earl then made a gift to the school children. Huey had provided free books; Dick, papers, pencils and erasers. Earl gave free hot lunches. He borrowed $250,000 and announced that the lunches would be permanent. Opponents, calling this vote-bait at a cheap figure, claimed that the money would last only through the election period in most parishes.

Over the campaign was the incubus of Huey and his methods. Most of the candidates used Huey's oratorical tactics, his jokes as well; retained his platforms, worked hard to be "second Hueys." Many have pondered the effect on Louisiana youth of the object lessons in demagogy which Huey held forth so vividly. A striking example was James Morrison, the strawberry organizer. He came of a distinguished family, of former wealth and present prestige. He was a nephew of Admiral Hobson of Spanish-American War fame, descendant of a revolutionary colonel and a United States chief justice. He had gone to Tulane University, the school Huey detested, and at fraternity parties he had amused his friends with a "Senator Jim" act, a slap-dash imitation of Huey, stamping, windmilling, talking about skunks and country preachers. Home again, he put to serious use the technique he had adopted first with a grin.

In this campaign, at the age of thirty-two, he developed into the most riproaring, greased-lightning candidate of them all. He published a journal, the *Farmers' Friend,* which for a time went further than even the *Progress* in uninhibited libel. He became the prime phrasemaker and name caller. Noe was James A. Affidavit Noe-Noe Nanette. Leche was Richard (Give Me a Yacht) Leche. Seymour was Seizemore

437

Weiss. Judge Platt of grand-jury renown became Melonhead
Platt or, more simply, Jughead. The most complimentary
name applied to Robert S. Maestri was Robert Sneaker
Maestri. Over the excess oil operations Morrison was particularly zestful: "Maestri-Hitler in 'Hot Oil' Combine" his
newspaper informed the world, and went on to describe a
"Russia-Berlin-Maestri Axis," asserting that Maestri had
"helped Hitler prepare for war by fueling the planes of his
killers." Earl Long wore a dunce cap in Morrison's publication; a dog collar was about his neck, and Maestri held the
chain. The Governor ("The Earl of Thievery") told the
readers: "Anything Bob says is what I mean."

Morrison called unindicted men outright racketeers, connected them with white slavery and the dope traffic. He hit
his height when he blazoned that one major official "will be
indicted," gave the day on which the jury would act, and
offered details. The indictment did not materialize. He circulated little "rhymes and riddles about the racketeers."

Epitaph to Louisiana Big Shots:

Wonders happen now and then.
They trapped themselves. That's all. Amen.

Who's four big thieves in Louisiana?
Tell me now, and please be quick—
Doctor Smith, Seymour Weiss,
Monte Hart and Walking Stick.

But Morrison's major contribution to Louisiana politics
to date has been his union of a campaign with a New Orleans Mardi Gras. He concocted a carnival of his own, Morrison's "Convict Parade," and sent it about the state. The
farmers built the floats and acted rôles upon them. It was a
hilarious, outrageous performance. By name, with huge pla-
cards on their backs, the machine men were pictured in

graphic action. Weiss, Smith, Shushan and others—among them men not charged officially with any crime—were seen in stripes, cutting cane on the prison farm. A man in convict garb, Leche (with a pillow at his front to denote girth), was seen climbing up toward a judge's bench. Just as he reached it, a man labeled Morrison would lasso him and drag him back. This was a continuous performance, enjoyed by all who had the desire to lasso Leche themselves. "King Maestri of the Underworld" sat tight on the top of the conservation books, on the next float. On another, the boys were portrayed in a huge barrel of "hot oil," screaming as they boiled. Thin men marched with fat ones; the former were the Louisiana politicos before they took office, the latter the same after eating at the trough. One float, titled "The Boat the Farmers Did not Give Leche," carried a broken canoe in which sat a striped figure, again Dick. Morrison went to New Orleans and beat Rex, King of Carnival, at his own game. He drew 100,000 persons to Canal, the main street, for what some called the biggest political meeting in the history of the state.

Morrison promised that he would build a special new structure at the prison farm for the Leche politicians, and "shove them in so deep they'll have to pipe sunlight to them." He carried a monkey and introduced it as "Earl Long," then made formal apology to the monkey. The real Earl replied by declaring that the animal was a relative of Morrison's; that one man had shaken hands with it, and given Morrison a peanut. The monkey went berserk. Morrison said that it had been called Earl too often. The *Progress* offered a message from monkey to public: "Regarding my late separation from Mr. Morrison, I wish to state it was purely a domestic affair. . . . After election, we are going away together on a long trip."

439

Because of the nationwide interest in the election, the American Institute of Public Opinion made a survey of the scene; and it expressed marked surprise at the result. Sixty per cent of the voters, the sampling indicated, thought that recent elections had been dishonest. Only twenty-five per cent believed them honest; fifteen had no opinion.

"In all its years of polling experience, the institute had never encountered such an amazing political situation. . . ." * The Gallup interviewers "ran into almost as much 'resistance' as they might face in a dictatorship. People were guarded in their replies for fear of reprisals and coercion. Time and again, both in New Orleans and in upstate Louisiana, investigators found doors narrowed to slits or slammed shut as soon as the interviewer disclosed his purpose. Fear of expressing an opinion on state politics was more common in the poorer districts, and men proved to be even more apprehensive than women. In the city of New Orleans, an average of one person in every five indicated that he was afraid to talk for fear of political reprisals or for other reasons, even though voters were given every assurance as to the confidential character of the interview."

Forty per cent of those interviewed said they thought the state's courts dishonest; only thirty-six per cent believed them honest; and twenty-four per cent expressed no opinion. But when investigators put the question: "Taking everything into consideration, do you think that Huey P. Long was a good or a bad influence in Louisiana?" fifty-five per cent thought him a good one, twenty-two a bad, fourteen per cent "both good and bad"; and 9 per cent—"no opinion."

The poll indicated that a great percentage of Louisiana's voters had lost faith in the administration; but they felt that they would not be allowed to vote it out. In a discussion, the

* Gallup and Rae: *The Pulse of Democracy* (Simon & Schuster; 1940.

440

Gallup organization headed the subject: "When Elections Fail."

In an honest count, the samplings indicated, Jones and Long would be almost tied; a runoff was indicated; and in such an event, it appeared that the reform candidate would win. The campaign speeded up from that point. Mid-January of 1940 approached. The anti-administration field was split; Gallup poll or no Gallup poll, things looked well for the machine. In a runoff, would Noe, the former machine man, throw his votes against his former colleagues, to a man whom the machine pictured as anathema to all who loved Huey? And would Noe's followers, many of them followers of Huey, go in that direction even if ordered? The machine pumped forth every resource for an all-out battle. Hundreds of thousands of dollars had been hoarded from dee ducts and other sources. Extra jobs were added, new deadheads given places. The rat problem in New Orleans unexpectedly became a subject of enlightened concern for the state, and hordes of new catchers were added to the Board of Health rolls. Every welfare client in the state received a "windfall" check of three dollars. Long addressed a mass meeting and casually let slip the word that the Dock Board superintendent had hundreds of new jobs available at once, because port business had been so good.

The Jones, Noe and other opposition forces were active and hopeful. But indications grew that the machine planned an election-day blitzkrieg, the use of every known ballot-thieving device, every subterfuge inside and outside the counting place. The old system was back, whereby the candidates and not the machine directly named the polling-booth commissioners. But most of the Jones and many of the Noe men were political amateurs. The machine maintained control of the election supervisors, final arbiters in disputes of

441

the day. In New Orleans, the ever-efficient Old Regular city organization remained allied with the state machine, and the polling-booth situation appeared well in hand.

The opposition went to Rogge with charges of intimidation and bribery of its men by the Long side, and Rogge came through in a way that many had dared not hope for. He gave out formal statements that, although the election was a state primary, the Federal Government had a legitimate concern in the many reports of pending frauds and thieveries, and would act if it learned of a single irregularity. He noted several ways in which the Government might take jurisdiction, among them his favorite, mail fraud. By state law, returns had to go by mail from the parishes to Baton Rouge. Let any fraud occur, and he would get the boys in that fashion. Also, the Government might claim authority under the civil-rights section of the Federal Criminal Code, dating back to Reconstruction times. The opposition adopted a slogan: "Not 'Remember the Maine,' but 'Remember the Mails.'" The machine men thought of sending the returns by automobile to forestall Rogge and his stamp tracing; but Eugene Stanley, the former district attorney in New Orleans, now supported by both Jones and Noe for attorney-general, observed that the law specifically required mailing. For the first time in years, it appeared that vote theft might be risky.

The antis prepared for election day as seldom before. "Schools" were held, with experienced lecturers to point out ways of averting the more obvious thefts. *Dirty Work at Dawn, or Tricks at the Polls* was a booklet to provide further guidance against some of the variegated devices and refinements. Instructors advised commissioners to take a friend or two on their trips to the polls, in order to avert sluggings on the way; to reject drinks, even of water; to take flashlights in case electric power failed by accident, and to study spe-

442

cially provided diagrams showing how particular finesse might be exercised against them.

Election day was violent and bloody, particularly in New Orleans. A new word gained currency, as "election goons" surrounded some of the polls and kept out those they disliked; ranged the city, beating up or threatening women as well as men, and performing general utility work. Special rackets were worked in some cases. In New Orleans, voting booths are open at the top. One was beneath a low-hanging gallery. Men and women sat above, watched how an individual ballot was marked, and pressed a buzzer to let the boys inside know when to spoil a wrong one. A Jones photographer tried to take a picture of the scene. Long men broke his jaw while, he said, a policeman held and kicked him.

As expected by most, Long came first in the counting, Jones second, Noe third. Morrison, despite the tremendous crowds for his parades, received only a small vote. Long did not have a majority; the combined anti-administration vote was larger than his. A second primary would be held if Jones wished to contest Long's lead. But that depended on Noe. If he threw his votes to Long, that would end the matter. If he threw them to Jones, it meant a fight, and perhaps a close one. Noe maintained silence. Would his long fight against the Leche element now be called off, for a union with his former friends? Or would he join Jones against those he accused of repudiating Huey? For a second time, Noe found himself edged out of what had seemed like the certainty of a gubernatorial term. First, the Leche-Maestri-Weiss group had stood in his way; now Jones had done the same thing.

Every influence was exerted to prevent a second primary. The state had not had one in sixteen years. Now everybody wanted peace, especially if "everyone" were on the machine side. Business men in the latter camp appealed for a surcease from "destructive politics." The Old Regulars wanted a new era of construction, not harmful dissension. Maestri appealed to Jones to step down, telling him he could not win. Noe was wooed in both directions. Earl Long charged that Noe spent three hours in a conference with Maestri, and that Noe asked $150,000 to come out for Long. Noe replied that this was a slight error; that he had been offered $300,000, but had turned it down. "We wouldn't give that guy three dollars. He ain't worth it," said the King-fish's brother. Mrs. Huey Long was reported pressed into service to plead with Noe. Finally Noe came out for Jones, declaring that they were fighting for the same things. The forces were combined, with promise of an equal job split.*

---

* In October of 1940, after the gubernatorial election, Senator Noe was indicted with Seymour Weiss, major figure of the machine faction which Noe opposed, for evasion of Federal income taxes in connection with the "Win or Lose Oil Corporation." Political opponents said that it "never lost." It was formed during the last year of Huey's life, and its profits came early and often. The indictment charged that the Kingfish himself, or his estate, was the direct beneficiary of a concealed split. Secret divisions were ascribed to Huey, Alice Lee Grosjean, O. K. Allen and others. The Shreveport *Times,* an opponent of Noe's, declared that the history of Win or Lose was "an extraordinary story of wealth building on a foundation of political influence and $200 cash." Noe received a favorable mineral lease without payment from Governor Allen, it was declared. He disposed of part of the holdings at once for "most favorable terms" to Texas firms, then formed Win or Lose and transferred twenty of the leased holdings to other corporations for $320,000 cash. The lease was so worded that Noe was not required to drill if he did not wish to do so, the newspaper noted. Win or Lose was an operating company only. In one year, the corporation showed receipts of $347,000.

In November of 1940, Seymour Weiss pleaded guilty to the Win or Lose charges, involving $32,000 in his case; the Leche-Burford-Weiss "hot oil" case, involving mail fraud of $67,500; a personal income-tax case involving $35,000, and a charge of conspiracy with LeSage, "little man" of the hotel double dip, to evade payment in income taxes. He received sentences to run concurrently, covering a maximum of four years.

Also late in 1940, Monte Hart, facing a staggering array of state and Federal charges, went to his cypress-paneled den, placed a gun in his mouth and fired a shot that blew off the top of his head. Before him was a printed Elbert Hubbard quotation: "Never explain. Your friends don't require it, and your enemies don't believe you, anyway."

Earl Long swung into action within hours of the combination. In true Huey style, he called a special session of the Legislature—the first since Huey's death. Benefits and concessions were its purposes: the first a $1,000,000 appropriation for hot lunches, since the fund had run dry; the second the long-sought repeal of the "sheriff's law," the step which the machine had refused to take for four years; the third the opening of records of the State Bond and Tax Board; and finally, a "compromise" on the sales-tax issue, to meet the promises of all other candidates for outright repeal. The machine would submit the sales tax to the electorate. At the same time, the Legislature refused Noe's demands to open all state records, provide full audits of financial records, require elected officials to state their incomes under oath, and abolish dee ducts and the fake "civil service" system. The boys still knew that there was a stopping place for everything.

The last weeks were at hand, the climax of the rampaging eight months. The Federal Government made good its promise of action in election-day irregularities. The grand jury handed down several indictments, under both the mail-fraud and civil-liberty statutes, in connection with the first primary. These cases, still pending, may establish important new jurisprudence in election matters. The charges were blows to the machine, clear warnings of more that might come. The machine men quickly took umbrage. In Washington, Senator Ellender launched a series of assertions that Rogge had invaded a primary to take sides, in violation of the principle of States' Rights. The Citizens' Voluntary Committee wired Attorney-General Murphy that Ellender "did not voice the sentiments of the decent, law-abiding citizens of Louisiana. Louisiana needs you and Mr. Rogge as it never needed any

445

man or men before. Your department and the courts of the United States are the last bulwarks standing between the people of Louisiana and their political enslavement."

Senator Claude Pepper of Florida, echoing Ellender, asked: "Do we admit to the world that democracy in America has so broken down that a sovereign state cannot conduct its own election? . . . If a people want their state government bad, then it is their privilege to have that kind of government." The Washington *Post* replied that genuine believers in States' Rights should welcome Federal authorities when their aid is needed to "restore the rights which corrupt state régimes deny them; the most certain way to destroy popular regard for the doctrine is to invoke it as a means of perpetuating intolerable conditions in communities where local government has ceased to function as a responsible agent of the people." Ironic was this appeal to States' Rights by a régime which had destroyed practically all local rights at home. Critics of Ellender and Pepper cited the Gallup findings and the belief that unless dishonesty were eliminated at the Louisiana polls, it would not matter what kind of officials the Sovereign State of Louisiana favored; the machine would count itself in.

The machine simultaneously introduced the race issue. A Negro newspaper appeared with a tribute to Rogge and his staff as liberators of the dark men of the state. Thousands of extra copies were circulated. Ellender displayed the publication when he returned to the state to take the stump, and he and others held forth a picture of pending race riots, attempts to vote the Negro and repetition of Reconstruction conditions. At one meeting, the attention of a crowd was called to a group of bedraggled Negroes on the fringe, with a question as to whether the audience wanted "them" to vote and run the state. Here was the lowest appeal of the Southern politician. Inquiry disclosed that the material had been inserted in the Negro journal for cash by outsiders, and that the machine had arranged for special reprints, with added comment.

Symptoms of worry developed on the administration's side. The last two weeks of the campaign saw, wonder of wonders, the revival of share-the-wealth's erstwhile orator, Gerald L. K. Smith. He was retrieved from the fields of anti-Communism in Detroit. Earl declared that Gerald had come back "because he thought we needed him." The *Progress,* which had once described Gerald as open to all takers at any price, was now cautious, calling him simply a "special attraction." With Gerald's first talk, it was clear that something was wrong. Before he opened his mouth, members of the crowd shouted: "How much are they paying you?" "Can you vote in Louisiana?" When quiet was restored, Gerald declared that he was "not on anybody's payroll; the only people I have to please are the poor and downtrodden." Gerald wanted it known that the press was connected with Dick Leche's fall from grace. "The first time Leche began to smell bad was when the newspapers began to play him up." He asserted that it was "we" who "hung the hides of Dick Leche and his thieves" on the fence. It was just what Gerald had promised to do if Dick went wrong. But now Gerald was back to help carry on for Huey. A woman called out: "Ain't poor Huey dead? You leave him out of this." The return engagement of Gerald was one of the major mistakes of the campaign.

In New Orleans, a district court had turned down the Citizens' Voluntary Committee in its attempt to see the mooted Conservation Department books, but the appeals court upheld it. The state appealed to the Supreme Court of Louisiana. By ordinary procedure, that body would have ruled be-

447

fore the second primary. But, by the customary political division of four to three, it granted writs for a further review; which meant, in clearer language, no decision until after election day, and the clamping down of the lid until that time. The Louisiana Association for Clean Government passed judgment on the state's highest court: "This is clearly a stall. The public has once more been cheated out of its rights by another branch of the machine."

The People's League sent pickets to City Hall: "Handbooks Open—Conservation Books Closed, Mr. Mayor"; "A Yacht in the Hand is Worth Two in the Books." Sam Jones told an audience: "Not even Maestri would support Earl Long if Maestri could get hold of those Conservation books." Orators asked what was happening to the books in the meantime. Were they being doctored or burned?

For months the Federal "hot oil" investigators had been at work, without striking results. Louisiana knew that Maestri was under questioning by various grand juries on oil operations. But little information came forth from any source. Now, with the election ten days or so off, strong reports spread that another fix had been maneuvered in Washington, a Third Louisiana Purchase. Ellender's visits to the White House were no secret. One day Rogge was called out of the Federal grand jury room to the telephone. Murphy "suggested" to him that it would not look well to indict additional political figures as an election approached. Opinions have differed as to the strength of the "suggestion." The jury was then considering evidence in a case involving Maestri and the Greek-American oil man, Helis. Its members did not receive enthusiastically the word that Rogge brought them. Indications were that Rogge himself did not like it. He went back to Washington, argued with Murphy, and appeared satisfied that he could go ahead "if he thought he had a good case." Further indictments came, but none against Maestri. A day or so later, Murphy telephoned to ask if he had "returned those indictments." Rogge's answer was that he had decided that the law would not back up an airtight case against Maestri and Helis. The Third Purchase stories grew in volume. Demands were exerted by citizens' and other groups; would Rogge deny the general impression, would he clarify the situation? Conferences followed, in New Orleans and Washington, and, on the eve of the second primary, Rogge and Viosca issued a joint statement which was one of the sensations of the scandals, one of the most controversial acts of the period.

The statement told why the Government had not indicted Maestri and his partner Helis. A flood of 3,111,000 barrels of "excess" oil had been permitted to flow from a single Louisiana field in less than two years by a group of firms including that of Maestri and Helis, it was asserted. Maestri had earned $1,157,000 from the oil business while conservation commissioner during part of this time, and later while mayor. The oil was produced over and above allowable orders for the field, orders which were "generally disregarded" by the company.

Under the Connally Act, as previously noted, any oil is contraband which is produced in excess of quotas set by state authorities. But, the statement declared, Maestri and Rankin as conservation commissioners had failed to follow the Louisiana law itself in issuing orders for the field. Their orders had two fundamental defects. They fixed amounts for the field but failed to set allowables for each well in the field; also, hearings had not been held, with notice to all interested parties in advance. Maestri and Rankin had "disregarded the mandatory provisions of the statutes of Louisiana. . . . The foregoing reasons are the only reasons for

449

the failure of the Federal grand jury to proceed with respect to the alleged violations of the Connally Act. . . ."

Eventually, a fuller story came to light of the oil operations of this period. Between 1934 and 1939, when the state's rich oil production reached new heights, an estimated 12,-000,000 to 13,000,000 barrels of excess or "hot" oil were produced, their value at least $12,000,000. About half the flow had taken place in a year and eight months of Maestri's régime as commissioner; the other half in the three years of Rankin's. A variety of methods was used to "straighten out" or "legalize" the flow. Sometimes allowables were set for companies as well as for fields, and both were exceeded. "Special orders" were utilized, as in the Burford-Leche-Seymour Weiss case, to permit favored producers to step up their flow, usually unknown to others whose property was drained. Such permits covered short periods, long periods, indefinite periods. Despite the fixing of a maximum monthly allowable for a field, a handful of additional orders might be handed down within a few days, to allow two or three companies in the field to produce, each, more than the allowable for the whole field.

Some particularly "special" monthly orders might be granted as late as the twenty-fifth of the month, giving subsequent approval to oil that had already been produced in large quantities. In one month, in one field, a number of firms produced more than four times the authorized amount. Blanket orders declared that all oil produced by a firm over a past period was legal, or that oil to be produced in future for an unlimited period would likewise be within the law, although exceeding the published figures.

The firm of Maestri and Helis was one among many which received special allowables or otherwise overproduced. B. L. Krebs of the *Times Picayune* declared that Maestri the conservation commissioner set limits for his company's production, then "looked the other way" when Maestri the oil man exceeded them. An illuminating memorandum from Dr. Shaw, the late proration director, indicated that these practices did not start only after the death of Huey Long, or go on as matters apart from the Kingfish's comprehension. This note, from Shaw to Maestri, declared that a firm had overproduced in two fields and underproduced in six, and added: "Senator Long authorized me to permit the Texas Company to produce these fields as a unit; in other words, if they overproduced in one and underproduced in another, it would be okay, provided they did not exceed their total allowable. Under these instructions, if their reports are correct, I find that they are not overproducing." However, one provision of the state law declared that each field must have its own allowable, and remain within that allowable. The potentialities of the lumping method are almost unlimited.

The statement on the Maestri-Helis operations had its effect throughout Louisiana. Some have felt that it was a final factor in tipping the delicately balanced scales in the direction in which they finally inclined. . . .

Election day came at last. The Noe-Jones forces formed a "Jackson Brigade" to "defend the polls the way Jackson's men defended New Orleans." Earl Long, in Huey's manner, ordered the National Guard mobilized, to remain on call "for anything that might arise." As in the great era of the Kingfish, the threat of martial law hung over an election. Louisiana was grim that Tuesday, February 20, 1940, when it went to the polls. An era unprecedented in the American story was reaching its climax. For the first time in twelve years, a statewide movement had gathered strong force against the dictatorship. A chapter in political violence was to be ended, or given a new start.

The voters had a last-minute prank of one of the dictatorship's pets over which they might ponder as they marked their ballots. Big George Caldwell, preparing to start for Atlanta and a prison term, gave a merry "going away" party in his mansion, and revealed that he had cast an "absentee ballot"—for Earl Long.

Louisiana's electorate stood up that day against vote theft, the weight of vote buying, the appeal of the benefits, and the force of habit. They did not know everything about Sam Jones, the man who was offering himself in place, not so much of another man, as of a régime and a system. They knew that régime and that system. They thought back over a decade and more that had seen bloodshed, a flaming crusade and its deflection; the bribing of other elected divisions of the state government by a central authority, the purchase, by and large, of the electorate itself; and a flashing, riproaring pageant withal.

Huey's poor whites in the hills, the small-town folk who had flocked to his side and the city followers who had arrived last, considered the factors, balanced them and made up their minds. On one hand, they could count the progress that had been achieved; but they could mark off, also, the losses that had gone with the period: the fitting of the lives of two million men, women and children into the pattern of totalitarianism, the extension of personal power during the life of the dictator, the continuation of group control and the same pattern after his death; and the inevitable abuses of power during both periods.

They chose the harder way. They had tried dictatorship, American style, and found it wanting. The decision was, by the records, a close one. Only 19,000 votes separated the candidates. Many are certain that the margin was much broader, that tens of thousands of ballots were stolen. Whatever the explanation, there is not much doubt that it represented the verdict of a majority of Louisianians, arrived at despite obstacles and hindrances. Sam Jones, the machine's opponent, won in the country parishes, the areas of Huey's hill men and the other original believers in his doctrine. Jones had taken the areas that were believed to be the dictatorship's base of power. But he did not win New Orleans. The amiable city, the final part of Louisiana to fall before the dictatorship, was the last to cling to it. And therein lay a convincing demonstration of the régime's transformation from the fervent ruralism of the dictator to the fully functioning bossdom, with strong surviving elements of dictatorship, of the Kingfish's heirs.

A wise editor had declared: "It will be well for American democracy if the complete collapse of the Long dictatorship occurs within the maturity of those who recall it in its heyday."

The Louisiana which recalled that heyday, which now saw that collapse, celebrated as the word spread of the victory. On election night, and the next night, and the next, thousands formed processions, joined parades of automobiles, wound in and out of towns and city streets; shook hands, knelt sometimes in prayer, made speeches of derision, of exaltation, of exultation, of bombast, of sobbing happiness. Louisianians who had been silent for twelve years as far as expression of their true thoughts were concerned, tossed handfuls of the sales-tax tokens in the air, carried mops to "clean up the state," wore mock high hats to throw back the charge against the victorious candidate, carried bedraggled bits of fur on sticks—"The Pelt of Peltier"—danced in the streets, as stores and theaters were closed for events that some towns termed "the biggest since Armistice Day." But the man who voiced the meaning of that victory was Sam

Jones, as he stood on a balcony above the men and women who had made him Governor:

"We're back in the Union now!"

Louisiana's experience has demonstrated, above some other things, the ease with which American democratic forms may be distorted to fit the purposes of totalitarianism. Louisiana's dictatorship kept the Constitution, but used it largely as a blind for the functioning of "government from above."

Dictatorship came to Louisiana because the democracy that the state knew appeared inadequate to the needs of large groups of its citizens. Huey Long's richly potent materials were not original to him. They were the same as those with which many another has aspired to power. But he alone was personally equipped, and rose at the moment—thus far—of maximum effectiveness, to reach close to his goal. The advantages held forth by the native totalitarianism were more inviting than the known services of the known régime.

In America as a whole, as in Louisiana, the old questions of human want and human security have not been fully answered. The wrench of a sudden further contraction in the nation's standard of living would be certain to cause new unrest, to thrust forward new figures to lead expression of that unrest. The end of the Second World War, the conclusion of the multi-billion defense program, inevitably will have sharp repercussions. Whatever the outcome of the war, America faces a process of readjustment in the next few years. Whatever America's rôle in that conflict, a persuasive voice may rise to offer its millions the "efficiency," the order, the burning appeal of the other way.

There are those in America who, impelled by temperament and circumstances, would follow such a man. And in the background there are others, the practical ones, who know good things when they see them; who would support him and take over when he left, as such men did in Louisiana; who would welcome a native Fascism in the name of Americanism. The answer is neither standpatism nor retreat. It must be a reaffirmation of faith in national unity, a rededication to democracy. To save democracy, have more of it, not less. Or there may be another Louisiana—or an Alabama, or a Mississippi, or California, or Missouri—hayride. And that one may bring the nation to a halt outside the borders of liberty.

ACKNOWLEDGMENTS

Gratefully, to Ralph S. O'Leary, Leonard Hinton, Dr. H. C. Nixon, Isaac S. Heller, Jo Thompson, Lyle Saxon, Edward Dreyer, C. P. Liter and Frances Bryson, all for their friendly and sympathetic assistance.

To the staffs of the New Orleans Public Library and the Howard Library, for their patience and their good advice.

To *The New Orleans Item-Tribune* for the use of illustrative matter in its possession; all photographs in this book being attributable to that source, except where otherwise noted.

For kind permissions to quote from published material:— To the Dodge Publishing Company (*Huey Long, A Candid Biography,* by Forrest Davis); to Marquis W. Childs and *The Saturday Evening Post* ("The Nemesis Nobody Knows," September 16, 1939); to Harcourt, Brace and Company (*Behind the Ballots,* by James A. Farley); to Harper & Brothers (*After Seven Years,* by Raymond Moley); to the Macmillan Company (*A Southerner Discovers the South,* by Jonathan Daniels); to James Rorty and *Current History and Forum* ("Callie Long's Boy Huey," August, 1935); to Simon and Schuster, Inc. ("Land of the Free," by F. Raymond Daniell, in *We Saw It Happen,* ed. H. W. Baldwin and S. Stone; and likewise *The Pulse of Democracy,* by George Gallup and S. F. Rae); and to United Feature Syndicate (*The Washington Merry-Go-Round,* conducted by Drew Pearson and Robert S. Allen).

457

Other published sources:—*Every Man a King*, by Huey P. Long, New Orleans, 1935; *My First Days in the White House*, by Huey P. Long, Harrisburg, Pa., 1935; *The Story of Huey P. Long*, by Carleton Beals, Philadelphia, 1935; *The Kingfish*, by T. O. Harris, New Orleans, 1938; *The Kingfish*, by Webster Smith, New York, 1933; *Machine Politics in New Orleans, 1897-1926*, by George Reynolds, New York, 1936; *Gang Rule in New York*, by Craig Thompson and Allen Raymond, New York, 1940; *The French Quarter*, by Herbert Asbury, New York, 1938; *Fabulous New Orleans*, by Lyle Saxon, New York, 1928; *Old Louisiana*, by Lyle Saxon, New York, 1929; *Forerunners of American Fascism*, by Raymond Gram Swing, New York, 1935; *American Messiahs*, by The Unofficial Observer, New York, 1935. Also Gayarre's *History of Louisiana;* Grace King's *New Orleans, the Place and the People;* Henry Castellanos' *New Orleans as It Was; Stories from Louisiana History*, by Grace King and John R. Ficklen; and *Historical Sketch Book and Guide to New Orleans*, New Orleans, 1885. Also a series of three articles by Alva Johnston in *The Saturday Evening Post* in May and June, 1940; a series of three articles by Hermann B. Deutsch in *The Saturday Evening Post* in September and October, 1935; "Huey Long and His Background," by Hamilton Basso, *Harper's Magazine*, May, 1935; "Gentleman from Louisiana," by F. Raymond Daniell, *Current History*, November, 1934; "Huey's Heirs," by F. Raymond Daniell, *The Saturday Evening Post*, February, 1938; "The School Huey Built," by Don Wharton, *Scribner's Magazine*, September, 1937; "You Can't Laugh Him Off," by Jerome Beatty, *American Magazine*, January, 1933.

Also, the files of *The New Orleans Item*, the *Tribune*, the *Times Picayune*, the *States;* and the *Louisiana and American Progress*.

INDEX

INDEX

INDEX

127; acceptance by Leche, 194, 200 ff.; requested by Maestri, 243 ff.

Federal Government. *See* Roosevelt Administration.

Federal Grand Jury investigations, 168-169, 181, 379-380

Federal inquiry into income tax reports, 163 ff.

Federal Revenue Department, Smith investigation undertaken by, 264 ff.

Fish, Hamilton, charges, against Hecht, 99

Fisher, Joe, income tax charges, 166-167; criminal case against, 174-175, 176, 183; vindication, 204-205

Fisher, Jules, 148; income tax charges, 166, 175 n.; free ferry "kickback," 173-174

Fleury, John E., 205

Fontenot, Rufus W., in Smith case, 264, 285, 336

Fournet, John B., in "Bloody Monday" fracas, 70, 71, 92; elected to State Supreme Court, 110; at Long assassination, 134; in machine politics, 148-149, 153; in Smith case, 274; in L.S.U. investigation, 382

Frazier, Senator, 189

"Free ferry" graft, 173-174

Frigerio, Placide, 395

Frost, Meigs, O., 268

Gallup poll, 1939-40 campaign, 440

Gambling, Long's crusade, 67-68; Federal inquiry, 170 ff.; in Byrne case, 363; effect on 1936 election, 393 ff.

Gasoline tax, 81, 143

Gas rates, 33, 65

Geology building mystery, 318 ff., 350

"Gift yacht," 332-334, 364, 371

Glass, Carter, 100

Glassell, A. C., in "hot oil" investigation, 323 ff.

Golf course investigation, 388

Graft discovery, Federal, 175 ff.

Grand jurors, indignation at Administration sell-out, 183; machine control, 256; rebellion among, 358 ff.

Gravel graft, 166, 178

Greek theater story, 33

Grosjean, Alice Lee, 266; in Irby-Terrell case, 83-85; off the payroll, 255; return to Louisiana, 390; in Win or Lose Oil Corporation, 444 n.

Gubernatorial campaigns, Long's, 50 ff.

Guidry, S. A., oil dealings, 391

Hammond, Hilda Phelps, 98

Handley, Mayor, quoted on Leche, 251

Harper, Senator, defended by Long, 44-45

Harris, Norvin Trent, 405 ff.

Harris, T. O., quoted on search for Long income, 128, 165

Hart, Monte, in candy racket, 245-246; in Smith case, 304; in L.S.U. investigation, 311; indictment, 313; in Rankin case, 319; in Bienville Hotel case, 338 ff.; in other Federal investigations, 348 ff.; suicide, 444 n.

Hartwig-Moss Company, 168

Heard, Coach "Red," 305

Hébert, Dr. Paul, in L.S.U. building scandal, 318

Hébert, F. Edward, 268

Hecht, Rudolf, 99

Helis, William, "hot oil" dealings, 392-393, 448, 449, 451

Henderson, W. K., anti-union operator, 50, 151

Hertz, Niels, 369; turns down law violations, 370-371

Hibernia Bank, 99

Highway Commission, gravel graft, 166, 178; bond issue graft, 167-168, 169, 170; "free ferry" graft, 173-174; shell reef graft, 174-175; in building racket, 221-222

Hill, Tom, in "hot oil" case, 328

Homestead exemption. *See* Tax exemption.

Honest Election League, 95

Hoover, Herbert, Long quoted on, 101

Hoover Administration, disregard of crop surplus, 86; Long investigated by, 164

INDEX

Rouge district, 102-103; Sands Point Bath Club incident, 103, 104; sagging prestige and recovery, 104 ff.; vice raid, 108-109; state control widened, 109 ff., 128 ff., 133; influence on Roosevelt Administration, 116 ff.; attack on Farley, 118; attack on Ickes, 118; Share-the-Wealth organization, 119-127; Administration's attack on, 120-121; answers Hugh Johnson, 121; 1936 plans, 125 ff.; dictator powers, 128-131; fear of plots against, 131 ff.; assassination, 134-137; appraisal of policies, 137-144; search for income, 165-166, 176-177; connection with stone quarry case, 169-170; graft attributed to, 175-176; estate accounting, 176-177; inquiry into death plot quashed, 195; development of L.S.U., 211-235; Porterie scandal, 248-250; corporation taxes graft, 255-256; controversy with Earl Long, 291; Stanley-Porterie case, 357-358; friend of Moran, 397, 399; linked with slot machines, 402; linked with Levee Board case, 424-425; cited in '39-'40 campaign, 427 ff.; in Win or Lose Oil Corporation, 444 n.; cited in "hot oil" case, 451

Long, Mrs. Huey P. (Rose McConnell), 42-43, 46, 195, 201; Share-the-Wealth membership lists to, 190; appointed Senator, 191-192; in WPA case, 310; in '39-'40 campaign, 444

Long, Huey P., Sr., quoted, 36-37, 39

Long, Julius, 46, 96, 170

Long, Rose. See McFarland.

Long, Russell, 232-234, 240

Long, Wade, charges against, 385 ff.

Lorio, Dr. Clarence, 310-312

Louisiana, acceptance of dictatorship, 4-10; historical sketch, 13-35; French rule, 13-18, 20; Spanish rule, 18-20; traded to United States, 20; physical and political divisions, 30 ff.; gains and losses under Long, 141-144

Louisiana Association for Clean Government, 431, 448

Louisiana Polytech, 351, 352

Louisiana purchases. See Second Louisiana purchase. See also Third Louisiana purchase rumors.

Louisiana Quarry Company, tax inquiry, 168, 169-170

"Louisiana Seabury Investigation," 294

Louisiana State Bar Association, urges Federal judgeship for Leche, 248; in Porterie-Stanley case, 249-250; in tax inquiry, 257

Louisiana State University, band playing in Texas, 185; commerce department disciplined, 200; Leche publicity, 205; promoted by Long as machine force, 211-235; stadium dormitories, 217; Long buys country club, 217; football team development, 218-219; Long develops band, 219-220; student football trips, 220-221; football-circus episode, 221; music school, 221-222; medical school, 222-223; student patronage, 223-225, 234-235; development under Leche, 227 ff.; agricultural center, 227; baseball stadium, 227; Leche Hall, 227; Mike the Tiger, 227; airplanes, 227-228; building racket under Caldwell, 230-232; Russell Long-Blondy Bennett episode, 232-235; Leche largesse, 236; in WPA investigation, 268 ff., 307 ff.; faces financial crisis, 303-304; geology hall scandal, 318 ff., 350; in Bienville Hotel case, 338 ff.; civil suits, 352 ff.; alumni criticism of Board, 381 ff.; Shushan contracts with, 425

Loyola University, 216, 338, 348

"Luxury tax." See Sales tax.

"Lyingnewspapers." See Newspapers.

McCarran Prevailing Wage Amendment, 117

McConnell, Mrs. Rose Long's brother, 319, 320

McFarland, Dr. Osymn, 240

McFarland, Mrs. Rose Long, 240

Machine politics, 7; Louisiana state, 157; in Shushan trial, 180; in Standard Oil tax case, 198-199

McIlhenny, Edward Avery, friend of

INDEX

ABOUT THE AUTHOR

HARNETT THOMAS KANE, born November 8, 1910, is a native Louisianian. A graduate of Tulane University (Class of '31), he has been in newspaper work since 1928, when *The New Orleans Item*, noticing a feature story written in his sophomore year, offered him a full-time job on the side, 3:00 P.M. to midnight. "The journalism professor and everybody else advised me to wait until I finished school," he says. "I didn't." Thereafter, and in addition to graduate study in sociology and psychology, he worked on the afternoon *Item*, the morning *Tribune* and the Sunday *Item-Tribune* as reporter, feature writer, political writer; as police reporter; and for a time on the copy desk, the city desk, and on the business run. "When the state scandals broke," says Mr. Kane, "on twenty minutes' notice I was sent to Baton Rouge to cover them; and I have stayed with them ever since." Among Mr. Kane's journalistic hobbies has been a five-year roving assignment to "bring back" the Crescent City's historic French Quarter, the Vieux Carré. Another assignment— "it took only a few months, this one"—was to rid New Orleans of an inefficient library head. "We unearthed his payroll and described his activities; the city now has its first trained Librarian." LOUISIANA HAYRIDE has grown out of the author's first-hand observations during the crucial and crowded years, 1928-1940, that saw the rise, dictatorship and death of Huey Long, the decline and overthrow of the Kingfish's Bayou State empire.